# TONY RUDD
*It was fun!*

Patrick Stephens Limited, an imprint of Haynes Publishing, has published authoritative, quality books for enthusiasts for more than a quarter of a century. During that time the company has established a reputation as one of the world's leading publishers of books on aviation, maritime, military, model-making, motor cycling, motoring, motor racing, railway and railway modelling subjects. Readers or authors with suggestions for books they would like to see published are invited to write to The Editorial Director, Patrick Stephens Limited, Sparkford, Nr Yeovil, Somerset BA22 7JJ.

# TONY RUDD
## *It was fun!*

## My fifty years of high performance

**Foreword by Jackie Stewart OBE**

**PSL**

Patrick Stephens Limited

First published in 1993

British Library Cataloguing in Publication Data:
A catalogue record for this book is
available from the British Library

ISBN 1 85260 413 1

Library of Congress catalog card no 93-78379

Patrick Stephens Limited is an imprint of Haynes Publishing
Sparkford, Nr Yeovil, Somerset BA22 7JJ

Typeset by G&M, Raunds, Northamptonshire
Printed in Great Britain by Butler & Tanner Ltd, Frome and London

# Contents

This book is dedicated to motor racing mechanics the world over. The ones I have worked with and know best are from the world of Formula 1. They give their all working to prepare some 36 cars (the spares are race-prepared too) knowing that there can only be one winner and that perhaps their car stands very little chance, but they will still give it their best effort. They will probably work a 20-hour day for at least 60 days a year. Remembering a remark I once made to the BRM mechanics nearly 40 years ago: 'Drivers win races — we only lose them.' One paddock garage, one international airport, one jet airliner is very like all the others, so there is not much glamour attached, but without them there would be no World Champions, I am proud to have been one of their number.

# Acknowledgements

PAM, MY WIFE, without whose love, support and encouragement there would have been far less fun, and probably not enough achievements to write about. Mrs Diana Stannard, my secretary, who having been released from durance when I retired, nevertheless produced the manuscript of this book. John Dixon, for his sense of humour and his photographs. The drivers' wives and girlfriends who made my life much easier, especially Bette Hill and Helen Stewart. Mrs Denis Austin and the late H.V. (Vic) Barlow of Dunlop for the use of photographs. David and John Owen, sons of Sir Alfred, for their permission to use the BRM material and their photographs, some of which appeared in *Motor Racing Research*, a booklet Peter Spear and I prepared for Rubery Owen. The late Maxwell Boyd, Peter Elinskas, T.C. March, Werner Eisile, *The Lincolnshire Free Press* and the British Racing and Sports Car Club for further use of their photographs already included in Rubery Owen publications.

GM's departments of Public Relations, especially Ralph Kramer and Ed Lechtzin, not only for the use of material, but for looking after me so well on public occasions, and Paul-Henri Cahier, photographer son of Bernard, who looked after me at Rodez. Ron Middleton of Focalpoint, Norwich, who not only took most of the Lotus era photographs but resurrected some of my own from years gone by, and took some especially for this book. It must be obvious that I took and processed over half the photographs myself — there are no prizes for guessing which. Thanks to Gilles Noghes and his wife, of Monte Carlo, for looking after me so well at AutoTechnologies.

I owe a special debt to all the people, machinists, welders, fitters, technicians and draughtsmen who turned my ideas into reality and made them work. Stan Hope of BRM used to say: 'If you can draw it, I can make it.' It was with difficulty sometimes.

I never managed to thank these people at Lotus, so I do so now. It was just as much pleasure to work with them as it was with my other friends at BRM and Rolls-Royce. I owe a debt to my fellow directors at Group Lotus who put up with me for so long and sometimes enjoyed the fun. Finally, I owe an enormous debt to all the great engineers, especially 'By' (Mr R.W. Harvey Bailey) and his colleagues at Rolls-Royce and elsewhere, who had the patience to try to pass on their experience to me.

# Foreword
## by Jackie Stewart OBE

IN THE LATTER part of 1964 I was 'romanced' by three factory Formula 1 teams. A very heady experience for a young, up-and-coming Formula 3 driver.

That year I had driven on many European tracks when Ken Tyrrell's Formula 3 BMC Cooper team, with one Jackie Stewart as a driver, was performing in the supporting events. As I was by then a good friend of Jim Clark, I spent a lot of time in the Formula 1 paddock and, as in that year I was amassing a great number of victories in the Ken Tyrrell managed F3 team, there was much speculation as to what the next step might be for the young Stewart.

By the time August and September came round, I had had approaches from Colin Chapman, whose Lotus team Jim Clark drove for; from John Cooper who had Phil Hill driving for him; and from BRM where Graham Hill and Richie Ginther were team mates.

A great racing name of the past — Raymond Mays — attended all the races. Louis Stanley and Mrs Jean Stanley, sister of Sir Alfred Owen, owner of the Rubery Owen Company, were deeply involved in the BRM team, which was managed by a gentleman bearing the name Tony Rudd.

After much deliberation, in 1965, which was to be my first year in Formula 1, I chose to drive for BRM. Tony Rudd had much to do with the decision that I made in favour of BRM. I thought that he would be a good man to drive for. He wouldn't push me too hard as a young driver, or expect too much of me too soon. I thought he would give me lots of testing, as Graham Hill by then was well known for pushing his teams to test and test and more test, and this is what I thought that I needed most — time in a Formula 1 car to learn the business.

Tony Rudd certainly knew the business, and the book he has now written records with amazing accuracy and evokes wonderful memories of bygone days when racing was very different from what we know today.

Tony Rudd has been one of those people who has in a way been ageless but — due to being an engineer first and foremost — has stayed with technology as it has accelerated so rapidly, particularly within motor sports. His time most recently spent with Lotus on advanced engineering certainly proves that point.

His reminiscences, as far as I am concerned, are hopelessly and colourfully accurate!

Tony is endowed with a very good sense of humour. He sees himself clearly as others see him, and has enjoyed considerable success, as well as the odd disappointment, which I fear we have all had to live with!

I am not sure that I will ever forgive him for having me drive round in circles with a very clumsy H-16 BRM for more miles than I care to think of; but I suppose I should put it down to character-building. My time with BRM and Tony Rudd was extremely educational on every front. I was able to understudy Graham Hill with his compulsion for minute adjustment and recording every roll bar setting, every tyre pressure, every roll centre in his wee black book. Aerodynamics had not arrived!

It was Tony Rudd who, unbeknown to me, suddenly had Stewart tartan material fitted around the body-hugging seat in my F1 BRM. So he had an eye for flair as well!

Colin Chapman saw the potential in Tony Rudd when BRM were no longer able to feed in rich pastures and took Tony into the fold, where he stayed until his retirement. A technical engineer with the knowledge and experience which Tony Rudd had, was a very valuable asset to any company or racing team.

Pam and Tony became great friends of the Stewart family. I enjoyed enormously my years with BRM and they were very significant in forming the skills I was later able to exercise to win more races for other people than I did for BRM. I am pleased that Tony Rudd has now taken a little time out of what has in the past been a fantastically busy life, to just sit down and write this book.

I know the readers will also be happy to know that 'it was fun'!

**Jackie Stewart OBE**

# Introduction

SOME 20 YEARS ago, soon after I joined Lotus, Colin Chapman and I were walking together to our cars after a late and intense session at a drawing board. He turned to me and said: 'I hope you are having fun. When it stops being fun for me I shall quit.'

I did not retire until I was 68, having been persuaded to stay on for three extra years, so it must have been fun.

There were some dark days, such as the death of Mike Spence on the threshold of what promised to be his best season ever, and when the H16 engine was being more than usually stubborn. Colin Chapman's and Graham Hill's deaths were different sorts of dark days; something I could not have prevented had I made a different decision. However, I cannot think of more than 20 days that have not been fun out of some 15,000 working days in the whole of my three engineering careers — with Rolls-Royce, BRM and Lotus.

I have tried to avoid a chronological history, but as certain events are a consequence of a preceding event there has to be some form of sequence in time. To me, looking back over the years — or reading through my old reports, notes and records, especially of the BRM era — is rather like turning the pages of an enormous photograph album, and despite the passage of many years some of the shots are in razor sharp focus. For instance, the prodigious wink Graham Hill used to give me as the National Anthem was being played, and the Union Flag hoisted, after we had won; the sight of a Lancaster in flight (the urgent crackle of its Merlins as it taxies out to take off still makes the hairs on the back of my neck tingle); the first sight of Monte Carlo harbour, Lake Geneva, and the entrance to the Autodromo di Monza, all through a Lotus windscreen, when you look at the clock and find you have done the trip half-an-hour quicker than the last time; a convoy of 15 Chevrolet Corvette ZR1s sweeping past Albi, viewed from the driving seat of number nine in the line, with Arv Mueller, a Vice President of General Motors and Director of Engineering, Chevrolet Pontiac Canada Group, in the navigator's seat feeding a recording of *Rule Britannia*, rock style, into the cassette player as we made our way to our night stop at Carcassonne.

I wish I could convey in this book some of the sound sensations that have been prominent in my life. On those occasions when moving paper from my 'In' tray to my 'Pending' tray began to bore me, I used to say to my long-suffering secretary: 'I am going to listen to the music', and I would take myself off to the test-beds. Unfortunately, even that pleasure is now nowhere near so enjoyable — about 25 cm of sound insulation and two sheets of armoured glass now mute the music!

This book is about my life and times as an engineer having fun in my chosen career. I have tried to avoid too much detail of what happened in the over 200 motor races in which I played an active part, confining myself to just enough background to explain the reasons for, and consequences of, engineering and policy decisions. There is an absolute treasury of books on past races — a few fantastically good (in my opinion), many good, some fatally flawed, but none really bad — which provide this information.

Talking of books on motor racing — and at least half of this book is about motor racing — leads me to one of the reasons why I have written it. I classify as fatally flawed some of the otherwise good books on racing and the motor industry because they either contain absolute rubbish — half truths and sometimes downright untruths — or, by omitting vital facts, they present a completely different version of events. For instance, there has been as much ill-considered rubbish written about the V16 BRM as true facts; some of it by people who could and should have known better. Some wild stories about DeLorean I know are untrue because I was present at the time. Many of the stories about 'Chunky' — Colin Chapman — are equally fictitious. I am not quite convinced he was a genius — within my definition — but he was most certainly one of the most brilliant engineers the racing and motor car industry has ever known.

This book, therefore, is my attempt to set the record straight, and I hope those who read it share in the fun I have had in living the life and career it attempts to relate and describe. I also hope some young hopefuls, on the threshold of choosing their vocation, will be persuaded after reading my book to have fun in the same way. I must, however, repeat the advice I gave to Peter Wright (my successor as Managing Director of Lotus Engineering and now Technical Director of Team Lotus) when some 25 years ago he applied for the job of being my personal assistant — 'It will be fun, but there is not much money in it'.

# CHAPTER ONE

# In the beginning — boyhood and apprenticeship

MY FIRST SNAPSHOT is from my fourth birthday when I was given a model of the Model T Ford. It had an exact replica of the four-eared screw radiator filler cap. My father had a full-sized Model T Ford, so I had a good idea of how to add water and the reasons why water was needed. We were having a ceremonial afternoon tea, and I was playing with my new toy on the hearth rug, when I suddenly seized the hot water jug from the tea service to top up its radiator. I still remember the consequences.

For my fifth birthday I was given a large Meccano set, and before even getting out of bed I proceeded to build the crane illustrated in the instructions.

Turning the pages of my album, I see the airship R100, designed by Barnes Wallis and built by Vickers, flying over my prep-school playing field. A few weeks later I was taken in our Essex Super-Six to see the state-built R101 at Cardington, a few hours before it left on its fateful flight to India. My own first flight soon followed — in Alan Cobham's DH61 biplane with a single Armstrong Siddeley Jaguar engine and ten wicker seats in its cabin. The flight took 15 minutes, and cost five shillings, (25p). I managed several more flights, usually in DH Fox Moths with four leather seats.

The Essex departed in disgrace. I well remember the incident which caused its demise on a beautiful sunny harvest evening, driving back from Wells on the North Norfolk coast towards my grandmother's home near Watton in Norfolk, when the engine stopped. There was a fault in the Autovac fuel feed system. The Essex was replaced by a Rover Meteor, with cycle-type front mudguards and a fabric body. Unfortunately I was too small to be able to see out of this car. I then fell in love with a car belonging to a friend of my father. A long wheelbase 1934 Aston Martin Mk II, the most magnificent car I had ever seen. It started my love affair with Aston Martins, and from this time on I had great difficulty in deciding whether I preferred cars or aeroplanes.

My mother's unmarried sister, Aunt Jess, spoilt me dreadfully. I have a number of vivid 'snapshots' of a Whitsun weekend I spent with her in London, aged 8¼. We started in Hamleys, the Regent Street toyshop, with a clockwork model Chrysler car, and then went on to all the usual places —

the Tower, the Science Museum, the Natural History Museum (which did nothing for me) and Victoria Palace in the evening to see Gracie Fields. To read on the way home, I was given Arthur Mee's *Encyclopaedia for Children*, which showed how the four-stroke petrol engine worked. I devoured it. In post-war years, Aunt Jess made vital financial contributions to my various Aston Martins. Unfortunately she was always car sick. I gave her a run in the DB2 when she must have been 70-years-old. She did not enjoy it all that much, but I had to try to share some of the pleasure with her.

Aunt Jess lived and worked in London with the Hunter family. One of their daughters, Lisba, married HRH Prince Chula Chakrabongse, cousin and patron of racing driver 'B. Bira'. I visited Chula's workshop, White Mouse Garage at 113a Dalling Road, Hammersmith, presided over by Raymond England, as he was known to Prince Chula. He is now better known as 'Lofty' or F.R.W. England of Jaguar Cars. Our paths have crossed many times since. 'Lofty', also retired, now lives in Austria and is still racing — me — to complete his autobiography first. I was looked after by Shura Rahm, one of the mechanics, a part Russian friend of Prince Chula's mother. Prince Chula's Siamese nickname was 'Nou' which means mouse. Bira painted a white mouse on the mirror fairing of each car, which is why the team was known as 'White Mouse Garage'. Team Members and supporters wore White Mouse badges in the same way that the Ferrari team wore the Prancing Horse, the Mercedes people wore the three pointed Mercedes star and Maserati the Trident.

By then I was completely hooked on racing cars and motor racing: The noise, the smell — everything. Prince Chula had promised to take me to a race, when disaster struck. In pre-war days before leaving school one sat for a School Leaving Certificate issued by either Oxford or Cambridge University. I was due to sit for mine in the summer of 1938, but my Christmas 1937 school report was endorsed by an irate headmaster: 'There is neither time nor opportunity in a large form to make a lazy but intelligent pupil work.'

It was a complete bombshell. No racing cars nor cars of any sort, no aeroplanes, no pocket money. To make matters worse, my younger brother contracted chicken pox which I also caught while home for half-term, so my preparations for the mock examinations held in March were interrupted. But all was not lost. Prince Chula had written a book about Bira's 1936 season, entitled *Road Racing 1936*. He sent me a suitably inscribed copy, and the various bans were relaxed to allow me to read it. I really had got the motor racing bug badly.

While they were in Siam, Lisba, Chula and Bira used to write to me, so I sold the stamps from their letters to buy motoring magazines, *Autocar*, *Motor*, *Speed* (now defunct) and *Motor Sport*. With pocket money banned this revenue was important. Fortunately I obtained good results in the actual examination in the summer and all the bans were lifted. I stayed with my indulgent aunt, to spend the rest of the summer holidays in the White Mouse Garage. By then Lofty had gone to Alvis and Stan Holgate had been promoted; but Shura was still my mentor. I cleaned the Delages, counted and packed their spares and generally avoided making a nuisance of myself.

I started back at school a lofty sixth-former, with a series of blind eyes turned to enable me to go to Brooklands on 17 September 1938 for the

BRDC Road Race which had replaced the former 500 mile race. It was run as a capacity class handicap. Prince Chula entered their older 1500 cc ERA 'Romulus', reasoning that at Brooklands it would not be much slower than their other ERA 'Hanuman' with its Porsche suspension and 36 psi (2.45 bar) boost Zoller supercharger. 'Romulus' was virtually totally reliable while 'Hanuman' was, at best, only a 50 per cent certain finisher. Chula patiently explained to me all this and his planned tactics of bringing Bira in to refuel and change rear tyres on the same lap as Raymond Mays in his 2 litre ERA R4D, which was in the unlimited class and thus had to give Bira a lap. He reasoned that the works ERA team might panic and make a mistake. With others, I had to watch for when the ERA works team gave their 'come in' pit signal, so that the same could then be done for Bira. His tactics did not work immediately. Bira's stop, with only two mechanics permitted — for fuel and rear tyres — took 57.6 seconds, while Raymond Mays's stop took 58 seconds. However, R4D developed engine trouble, and Bira took the lead on the last lap. My first motor race, and what a race!

September 1938 saw the Munich crisis and the threat of war with Germany. Fortunately it subsided in time for me to go to Crystal Palace on 8 October for a five lap match race between Bira and Arthur Dobson driving virtually identical ERAs, with Dick Seaman as the starter. This was the highlight of the meeting. I was put in the care of Pridhi, Prince Chula's secretary, to watch from Stadium Dip. Bira took the lead and was drawing away by 0.4 or 0.6 seconds per lap when he picked up a nail in his left rear tyre, and that was the end of the match race. In the main race, George Abecassis driving an Alta, stole a march on everyone and fitted twin rear wheels. It was raining, so no-one even saw which way he went. On the way back into London in Prince Chula's Rolls-Royce I grumbled because we had not won. I got a 30-minute wigging from Chula. One cannot expect to win every race, he told me. Though thinking back on why he was so cross, I'm sure that he really did expect just that!

Bira, Chula and their wives went to Siam for the winter of 1938, and belated honeymoons, taking 'Romulus' and Freda with them. Freda was a large Himalayan tree bear kept in the garage as a pet and night watchman. She was very tame and quite friendly, but she could open her cage and wander about the garage. Standing up, she was 5 ft (1.52 m) tall, and quite a deterrent to intruders. Freda was sent to the docks with the heavy luggage. On the way she opened her cage and wandered around the furniture van, and when the dockers opened up they were confronted by a large and confused bear, not in the best of humours. Shura had to rush down to the docks to get her back into her cage.

My use of the stamps from their letters to fund the purchase of motoring magazines so amused Prince Chula that he arranged for a letter to be sent to me with one of every denomination Siamese stamp on it. I still have it, and will never know how many magazines I could have bought if I had ever sold it.

During the winter I decided that my best choice of career would be to become the Chief Engineer of Aston Martin, rather than an RAF pilot. It was accepted by my family that I would not be able to bear another two years at school and thereafter go to University. They mildly suggested that I might need some training and experience before Aston Martin would let me loose on their cars. So, after a series of family conferences, with contributions from my godfather — a very senior RAF officer — and Prince Chula, the unanimous conclusion was that I should be sent to Rolls-Royce at Derby as an engineering apprentice. This also involved taking an external University degree in my 'spare time'.

I went for an interview with Mr H.A. Ward, the Apprentice Supervisor. I knew from the book *The Magic of a Name* (Foulis, 1938) that 'Tubby' Ward had been riding mechanic to James Radley's private Alpine Eagle Rolls-Royce in the 1913 Alpine trial and Radley's 26-hour trip with Billy Rhodes-Morehouse from London to Monte Carlo, also in 1913. I was completely overawed by 'Tubby'. What he thought of a diminutive 16-year-old surmounted by an enormous Bogart-style trilby, I never knew. He must have seen them all, I suppose. I was duly told to present myself at No. 1 gate, Nightingale Road, with my overalls, and after the formalities I reported to the Apprentice Training School just inside No. 1 gate.

Pre-war there were three grades of trainees among the 10,000 Rolls-Royce employees at Derby. Included were 300 trade apprentices, who as their name suggested were being taught a skill — fitting, machining, the forge, etc. — and 50 engineering apprentices, of whom I was one. The many applicants were weeded out by a Selection Board and replaced the former premium apprentices. They normally spent three months at a time in various departments. After two to three years they had a second interview with the Selection Board to determine their aptitude and aspirations, and were then given appropriate training until they were 21. They also spent one day and four nights a week at Derby Technical College, and if they worked hard enough and were lucky, they obtained a London University external degree. Finally, there were graduates (older) who already had a degree, who also went through the Selection Board procedure. In their first year they also spent three months in appropriate departments before being sent to a specialist department for their second year's training.

For my first exercise I was given the drawing of the Merlin camshaft bearing casting to copy. Thus the invisible omnipotent process of training for an unspecified goal had begun. I never knew at the time the career training the Selection Board had chosen for me, but looking back I can see they intended I should go into car design.

The next step was to make a scraper, and then I started on the ubiquitous scribing block. Suddenly I was presented to George Hodnutt, Foreman of Department 142 — 'Boys Burring' — and told to go and 'help him'. He took me to the far end of No. 1 shop where there were about 30 boys of my age working either side of a long gangway. I looked around: on my right there were long bays of machine tools; close to me were Herbert No. 9 centre lathes making, as I later found out, propeller hubs for Rotol and motor car drive shafts; and several rows of Ward No. 7 capstans working on a mixture of aero-engine and car components. To my left were steel- and glass-walled offices the length of the shop. No. 1 shop, built in 1908, is still working today. When I took some Senior GM Engineers to see the Rolls-Royce Advanced Integrated Manufacturing System (AIMS) in action in 1988, the computer control room was located just about where my vice was when I started work. On the far side of these offices was the Motor Car Erecting Bay.

My rapt interest in all this was interrupted by the simultaneous arrival of three large tins of round-headed bolts, about 1600 of them, and a short red-haired gum-chewing individual, wearing a brown cow gown or coat, who introduced himself as Ron the chargehand. He presented me with a small half-round file and showed me how to file the machining burr from the bolt head. He also showed me how to decipher the drawing and the process and routing card, from which I learned that they were bolts used to hold the flywheel to the crankshaft of Silver Ghost armoured cars.

On Saturday morning I was initiated into the intricacies and mysteries of the bonus system. So many minutes were allocated to my operation, and if I completed it in less time, the time I saved was multiplied by my hourly rate of pay. This gave a value which should have been added to my salary. However, as an engineering apprentice I was not entitled to a bonus, and in any case my weekly salary was only 4s 8½d — that is about 23 pence today — for 48 hours work, so my bonus was not a significant sum. However, the bonus I did earn was put in the pool system and shared amongst the other members of the department who may, for some reason have had a misfortune. It also ensured that the engineering apprentice, or 'Dook', as I was known, was a welcome member of the department.

I lodged at the Toc H hostel (Mark 21) at 228 Osmaston Road, just over a mile (2 km) from the factory (known universally in Derby as 'Royce's' — never Rolls-Royce or Rolls, always Royce's.) There were 30 people living in Toc H Mark 21, nearly all of them Rolls-Royce engineering apprentices. I shared a room with a fellow apprentice, some two minutes senior to me as his name was Robeson. We made several abortive attempts to teach him to drive. One day he escaped and joined the RAF, as a pilot, finishing up with BEA as a TriStar captain. We still exchange Christmas cards.

There was not much in the way of social life. We rose at 7 a.m., had breakfast — most of us walked to work — and clocked-in by 7.55 a.m. Smoking was only permitted from 10 to 10.30 a.m. The 'bull' (hooter) went at 12.25 p.m. when you divested yourself of your overalls and bolted home for lunch, clocking back in again at 1.25 p.m. Thirty minutes smoking was 3.30 to 4.00 p.m., with the 'bull' at 5.30 p.m. and then home. On the evenings you were due at the Technical College, it was leave at 5 p.m., signed out by your foreman — clean up — something to eat — college from 6.30 until 9.30 p.m. One day a week — college from 9 a.m. until 5 p.m., generally back again that evening. Work on Saturday morning until 12 noon, with eight to ten hours of prep in Mark 21's quiet room.

At the end of my first fortnight I went home for the weekend. My mother spent about two hours picking metal splinters out of my very soft hands, and it took much willpower to return to Derby on Sunday evening. I could not admit, after all the fuss I had made, that I was not enjoying my apprenticeship.

I had begun to learn Rolls-Royce speak. For example, 'stretching' meant straightening, and 'early' meant advanced ignition. I finished the Silver Ghost flywheel bolts and was given 1200 cotter pins — spares for Kestrel aero-engines. I must have convinced Ron that I was not likely to scrap expensive parts, as I started to get small batches of components from the Experimental Department (which was not in the bonus system, neither did it have a deburring department) — such things as a 12 in (30 cm) diameter aero-engine reduction gearwheel, on which I had to chisel and file a radius around the ends of the teeth. I was also given jobs that had very generous bonus times, to avoid squabbles. One example was the aluminium plugs used to seal the hollow Merlin crankshaft. The bonus time was 24 minutes, but I could do one in five minutes. Of course, you needed the drawing to make sure you were performing your operation correctly. Sometimes it arrived with the parts, but if not you had to go to the Print Stores underneath the main Drawing Office, where you handed over your chit. Sometimes, instead of the drawing, you would be given the chit of the person in possession, probably the man who had performed the previous operation. This might mean a trip to the Experimental Department. During these visits I saw the 24-cylinder air-cooled engine, the Exe, as well as Griffons and Vultures, but you had to keep moving otherwise Roy Speed, the Shop Manager, or Jack Warwick, the Fitting Shop Foreman would have you. The errand boy was supposed to fetch drawings but, for obvious reasons, I never tried very hard to find him!

There was a very strict hierarchy concerning toilets, with a different one for each of eight different staff grades. The engineering apprentices would wander around the works on Saturday mornings for a chat with one another, and the trick was to see how many different toilets you could visit en route and not get caught by 'Piggy' Davis, the deputy Apprentice Supervisor. Your own chargehand was generally pretty tolerant.

Eventually the music stopped and all the engineering apprentices moved round after I had served less than three months in Dept 142. You saw your foreman's report after you had moved and I was surprised to see that the rather remote George Hodnutt noted that I had 'adapted quickly and well to factory life and discipline'. I then moved to the Motor Car Erecting Bay, generally a six-month move, and started right at the beginning in what was known as 'frame stretching'. Cars were built in batches of 100, at the rate of 16 or 17 per week. When I arrived, a batch of six-cylinder Wraiths was in progress, with an occasional 12-cylinder Phantom III outside the batch system.

I then progressed through the rear axle bay to front suspensions, built on a massive sub-frame, and thereafter into gearboxes. My arrival in the engine bay coincided with the first small batch of 25 Mark V Bentley engines. Here engines were built, run on town gas, stripped, any faults rectified, then rebuilt and retested on petrol. Engineering apprentices also showed visitors around the factory — generally customers whose cars were in the Service Department, and who were offered a trip round while they waited. It was good training. If you did not know the answer to a question you had to find out. The standby, when you were caught out, was: 'I am sorry, but I am not allowed to tell you that, it's still secret.'

Social life improved a little during the college summer holiday. We cycled to the municipal baths on Sunday mornings, getting there by opening time at 8 a.m., and returning for breakfast. There were also evening trips to swim in the River Trent at Swarkestone and Shardlow. For the Hospital Rag Day, the Apprentices Association, armed with collecting boxes, and wearing white overalls with a big RR badge on their backs, escorted a show engine on a works lorry through Derby's streets.

On Sunday 3 September 1939 we were all spread around the lounge of Mark 21, after our swim and breakfast, reading newspapers, when we heard Prime Minister Chamberlain's doleful broadcast to tell us we were at war. That night there was an air-raid warning, so we trooped down into the cellars, full of such things as dismantled Scott Flying Squirrel two-stroke motor cycles undergoing overhaul. It was, of course, a false alarm.

Next day, work was in chaos. The Motor Car Erecting Bay was to be cleared and filled with machine tools, and car build staff were to go to No. 6 shop, on the other side of Nightingale Road, to join the Aero-Engine Repair Department. A few experienced staff were left behind, plus the apprentices, to finish off the Mark V Bentleys. When they were finished, they were sent to the coachbuilders and issued to various senior British officers. We learned much more, building a new engine, under first-class supervision, than we otherwise would have done. Overtime began, working four nights a week until 7.30 p.m. but, because of our four nights a week at Technical College, it had no significant effect upon us.

The outbreak of war coincided with a change in apprentices' status, and our pay increased to 15s 9d (78p) a week. The coal shed at Toc H Mark 21 was commandeered as an ARP (Air Raid Precautions) post. Black-out was enforced; Peter Davis and R.W.P. (Mac) MacKenzie went into the RAFVR as potential pilots, soon to be followed by Ron Butterfield, whose father had been the Manager of the Vickers plant at Howden where the R100 was built.

We were soon at loggerheads with the ARP post, who complained we were so noisy they could not hear their telephone. We were also careless with the black-out, we didn't carry our gas-masks and we generally behaved in a very irresponsible manner towards the very serious war that was raging around us. Shortly afterwards the ARP people lost all their tin helmets, only to find them again two or three days later with handles welded onto them!

In October I was moved into the Grinding Shop, but before I moved I was interviewed by 'Tubby' Ward who told me that there was a war on and things were now all very different. I would be making history as the first engineering apprentice in the Grinding Shop and he did not want any trouble, such as the Shop Superintendent telling him he would not have another engineering apprentice in his shop. The term 'grinding shop' was perhaps somewhat misleading since its main products were crankshafts and camshafts which, of course, involved much grinding amongst other things. Sir Henry Royce had designed and developed his own camshaft grinding machines way back in 1914, and they were built by Rolls-Royce. The shop was rather archaic, with many of the machines driven by belts from overhead shafting. I was allocated one of the oldest, a small Churchill external grinder. Not only was it belt-driven but its clutches did not disengage too well. I had to drop a wooden wedge between the belt and the safety guard to stop the centres rotating. My first job was 2000 throttle control ball ends which had to be spherically ground — a very tricky operation. You had to line the ball up accurately with the groove in the grinding wheel, otherwise you scrapped the component. It took me about 15 days to complete the ball ends. I graduated to a bigger, more modern Landis for grinding aluminium pistons, oval and tapered.

My next machine was an enormous Snow horizontal grinder, bigger than the average room, grinding the faces on Merlin cylinder blocks for the inlet and exhaust manifolds. The blocks were mounted in a massive fixture, but as a skilled tradesman I had a labourer to lift the block and fixture onto the machine with a crane. His name was Sam — he was about 50-years-old with a massive beer belly secured by a three-inch deep leather belt. We became good friends. He could have run the machine himself better than I

could, but demarcation rules would not permit that. He saved me from
disaster more than once. I did not realize it at the time, but I and my fellow
apprentices were very well treated. With the need for increased production
we could have been used as cheap labour, but our training never suffered.
The apprentices all agreed that time was always spent making sure we were
properly and thoroughly trained.

The most skilled man of all was the 'setter' who set up the machines. Alf,
who looked after two bays, took me under his wing. He showed me how to
change the grinding wheel — how to dress it with a diamond to true it up,
and generally how to set the machine. I graduated to trueing the 24 grinding
wheels for the Rolls-Royce cam grinders. After they had been trued
everything had to be reset so that all the cams were the same size. This had
to be done after every 80 camshafts, and since every Merlin engine had two,
and every Vulture had four, with Merlin production moving up to 70
engines per week and Vultures to four, I was kept busy.

The shutdown of the car assembly line had put my moves out of step with
those of my fellow apprentices, so I spent four months in the Grinding Shop
before moving to Aero Fitting, another first for an engineering apprentice.
The department to which I moved was known as 'the dump' — producing
small sub-assemblies. I found myself working on water pumps for the
Vulture. There were two per engine mounted one each side of the
supercharger. Our foreman was a dyspeptic old campaigner called Joe
Storer who viewed me with great suspicion.

I did not work much overtime, because of college attendance, but
sometimes it was necessary on Saturday afternoons for 'rush' jobs.
Homework increased, because I had moved up a year. Social life was
minimal because of the black-out and petrol rationing. There was a new
intake of apprentices, bringing with them some exotic cars.

We managed to liven our dull existence now and again. One day we
found a collection of stage props, used for some Toc H event, that included
a policeman's uniform. Colin Hewson, known as 'Split Pin' as he was over
six feet tall and very thin, tried on the uniform, and pursued some of the
party on to the roof. People living on the other side of the road thought they
saw a policeman having a hard time, and phoned the real police, who sent
reinforcements. The results were inevitable. The bogus policeman and
others descended, locked the access skylight, removed the ladder and other
evidence and wandered across the road to the local pub known as 'Ma
White's'. It was not very salubrious but, on this occasion, proved to be a
very good vantage point. It took several weeks for the furore to die down.

Then the Germans invaded France, Holland and Belgium, and Rolls-
Royce went over to a real war programme — 8 a.m. until 8 p.m., six days a
week; 8 a.m. until 5 p.m. on Sundays, for the day shift. The night shift
worked 8.30 p.m. until 7.30 a.m. seven days a week, with shifts changing
every fortnight on Sundays. There was no dodging; if you did not turn up at
work, a works security man came to see why.

I was due to leave the 'dump'. I was told the only chance of a good report
from Joe Storer, was to take him out for a boozy evening, but at that time I
had not acquired a taste for beer. Two pints of cider was my limit. The
venue was set at Joe's local pub, The Lord Nelson in Normanton, a Derby
suburb, where Joe had a fearsome reputation. I talked a fellow apprentice,
John Addison-Rudd into joining me. (We caused much confusion, because

in the works records he was A-Rudd, and I was A. Rudd.) Cunningly we arrived at 9.30 p.m.; as with closing time at 10.30 p.m. we could not get into much trouble. But Joe was ahead of us. After several pints of bitter, we retired to the landlord's sitting room with a bottle of whisky, for which I paid. To this day I cannot stand whisky, even the smell makes me ill and quarrelsome. Although I had a monumental hangover, Joe's was even worse. By the time I clocked-in on Sunday morning, Joe had not arrived, and when he did he could barely see the clock, let alone clock-in. It was the custom, on special occasions, for everyone to hammer the metal covered benches, and Joe got the full treatment, but he played fair and gave me a good report.

My next posting was to the Millwrights, the group responsible for maintaining the factory and everything within it. I was attached to Jimmy (I never knew his surname) who was also the departmental shop steward, another redhead, and an inveterate pipe smoker. I was delighted to find Jimmy was responsible for the whole of the Experimental Department, machine tools and test beds — including a department known as the 'Tomb', run by Alf Towle. The Tomb was a rig shop, the prototype for Dante's Inferno — deafening noise, the floor awash with a mixture of oil and glycol and half-submerged enormous power cables everywhere. The most incredible rigs, some crude, some ultra-sophisticated, doing the most terrible things to various components. Alf, clad in rubber boots, a long leather coat and an even longer woollen scarf, could solve any problem — results within hours. Alf and his team improvized. I also learned the hard way that not only did Jimmy and I work 8 a.m. to 8 p.m., we worked through meal breaks and the night if need be. If anything went wrong — machine or test bed — we had it back in action as soon as humanly possible. I devised odd tools to save time. I had what looked like a burglar's kit for clearing a clogged suds pump on a Ward 7 lathe. Normally, you removed the pump, carted it some 400 yards to the millwrights, stripped and cleaned it, reassembled it, took it back and refitted it on the machine, all of which took two hours. With my kit I had the pump back in service in ten minutes. Here I made the acquaintance of the fearful 550 hp V twin research engine — two cylinders of the V12 sleeve valve, direct injected, two-stroke, two-stage supercharged (one a turbo) — known as the Crecy. The cynics said it should have been called the Waterloo.

This was the summer of 1940, France had fallen — the Battle of Britain was about to begin. We were told by the works public address system that every Rolls-Royce engine, every horsepower, every foot of height counts. 'Work until it hurts.' A number of American machine tools destined for France, with French instruction plates, were intercepted and diverted to Rolls-Royce. They were installed by the 'Heavy Gang', a villainous-looking bunch of labourers, armed with crowbars, rollers and wedges. They could manoeuvre a 40-ton Cincinatti HydroTel down 100-yard-long gangways into impossible spaces with no cranes or power assistance whatever. Because I could read French, I was put in charge of the installation of these machines. The heavy gang never spoke more than five words at a time to me but I used to tag along with them at all sorts of weird hours. They shared their tea with me, a fearsome brew which was beyond the old 'stand a spoon upright in it' joke — in this stuff the spoon would have dissolved instantly! I learned a tremendous amount, enjoyed every minute, and somehow managed to take and pass my exams. Social life, strangely, also improved. It must have been the frenetic times through which we were living. The war was brought home to us — Colin Hewson's brother in the army was killed. Mac, fatally wounded, landed his Spitfire at Biggin Hill and died in his cockpit.

I never saw Jimmy take time away from his job for trade union matters, but he served on the Joint Production Committee, a 1940 version of the Japanese car industry's 'Quality Circles', where people from all parts of the factory met to solve problems and increase production.

All too soon my time as a millwright was over and I moved to the other end of the spectrum — the Tool Room. This was on the third floor of No. 6 Shop, the opposite side of Nightingale Road. I joined the fitters under Bill Teague, making gauges and assembling jigs and fixtures. I worked at a long bench against a glass partition, forming one side of an air-conditioned shop containing eight Société Genevoise Jig Boring machines, each weighing 30 tons. One bomb would bring the lot down on the Aero-Engine Repair Department below. It was very interesting, very precise, but nothing like as much fun as the Millwrights.

It was at the height of the Battle of Britain. The day's score would be given on the works public address system, just like a cricket match. On Sunday 15 September when we were told 183 for 36, there was a terrific cheer.

The Tool Room was a very clean place to work, so I saved time in getting to the college, but cleanliness went out of the window with my next move, to Aero Fitting, this time to the team building Vulture auxiliary gearboxes located in the former rear axle bay of the Motor Car Erecting Shop. Previously all the accessories — such as air-compressors, pumps for gun turrets, undercarriage and instrument vacuum — were driven from any convenient shaft on the engine. They looked like Christmas trees. The Vulture system was a big step forward. One shaft from the engine drove an auxiliary gearbox, like a large brief-case, mounted on the aircraft bulkhead, driving all the accessories. The installation was simplified, so was engine changing. The gearbox included an oil pump assembly to circulate oil through the box, and a tiny pump to provide high pressure oil for the Heywood compressor. My prime job was to build and rig-test these pumps. Provided nothing went wrong I could keep up with the gearbox build team — mainly pre-war car gearbox fitters — led by Arthur, a veteran of the Henry Royce days, but two oil leaks in a week destroyed me. Every bath I took left an oily scum on the water.

The Padre at the Toc H hostel persuaded the younger inmates to act as auxiliary stretcher bearers at the Derby Royal Infirmary, as we were on bad terms with the local ARP and too young for the Home Guard. Although the Blitz had struck London, Coventry and Birmingham, Derby had only occasional alerts. On these occasions we took our gas-masks, walked just over a mile (2 km) to the hospital and dozed on the out-patient's benches until the all-clear. Derby was protected by a smoke screen created by a collection of foul-smelling, diesel-burning, dustbin-like canisters along the main roads, continually smoking away and obscuring Derby from the air. They were tended by unfortunate, equally foul-smelling Pioneer Corps soldiers. Sometimes a can would blow or be knocked over; there would be an enormous sheet of flame and a flurry of Pioneers.

However, towards the end of the winter Derby was bombed and about 20 people were killed. Following the warning we set out as usual. When we were about 200 yards (185 m) from the hospital we heard bombs falling. The only cover was the gutter, against the curb, fortunately deep and dry. I vividly recall seeing, by the light of one of the first bomb flashes, the window display of an antique shop in the road, but when we moved on and passed the shop the antiques were back in the shop and there was a crater in front of the chapel on the other side of the road. That bomb must have blown the antiques back again!

At the hospital we were told that casualties were coming in from the Sunny Hill district. We went to unload the first ambulance, there seemed to be little sense of urgency. Then we found that they were all dead, and we were asked to unload them at the morgue, so the ambulances could return for the lightly injured. The next batch of ambulances brought the serious casualties who had been dug out of collapsed houses. More bombs fell on the railway station, and we became really busy — many seriously injured people, blood and brick dust everywhere. I began to lose interest in the stretcher bearing business. What with this, and more homework, social life flagged. It began to be a cold miserable winter.

I found college work very interesting as we had just started on two-stage compressors. I had seen Merlin engines with enormous two-stage superchargers and biscuit-tin sized intercoolers. Fascinating — now I was seeing theory being put into practice.

Then 'Tubby' Ward sent for me. I searched my conscience for the crime he had discovered. He told me that 'Hs' had asked to see the three best apprentices, with the intention of sending them to the new Glasgow factory to form the nucleus of an apprentice training scheme. 'Hs' — E.W. Hives, Director and Works Manager, as he was then — was the second most important man in Rolls-Royce history, after Sir Henry Royce. He eventually became Lord Hives, a Companion of Honour and Chairman of Rolls-Royce. My old boss, Alec Harvey Bailey, christened him the 'Quiet Tiger'. We appeared before the great man, who showed us photographs of the factory nearing completion, and told us what a wonderful place it would be. When he asked me if I would go, I said: 'No, I am still learning. There will not be as many people there to teach me.' I waited for the explosion, but all he said was: 'You are turning down the chance of a lifetime.' It was back to Vulture gearboxes for me: I am sure it was the right decision.

By the time I completed my three months in Aero Fitting, I had also completed the first two years of my apprenticeship, and I thought I might be due for my pre-specialization Selection Board interview. But instead I was sent to the Aero Test Department which, although it involved shift work, was a practical way of helping you through the vital exams for your degree. There were three eight-hour shifts, starting at 6 a.m., 2 p.m. and 10 p.m. After a brief spell in the shop, stripping engines from the test beds, rectifying any faults and reassembling them, I moved to the test beds proper. They were far from the clean, quiet, clinical operating theatres of today. A row of corrugated iron sheds, each 30 ft (9.1 m) long, 15 ft (4.6 m) wide, and high, roller shutters each end. Down the centre line was, first, a large electric motor, a 4 ft (1.2 m) diameter cut-down four-bladed propeller, known as 'a club', which blew cooling air over the engine. There was also a big Heanan and Froude water brake, controlled by a handwheel mounted on the brake. At the business end a 27 litre 1730 hp Merlin which, when running-in (which took two hours), had two water-cooled exhaust manifolds connected to two 20 ft (6.1 m) vertical silencers outside the bed. In bad weather you could pull down the shutters, but not for a power check, when twelve exhaust stubs were fitted. Then the club would produce a howling gale, driving rain, oil and everything else moveable from the cell. On the occasion when the King and Queen made a morale-boosting visit, testers were briefed not to lose any more time than was absolutely necessary. The engine was shut down to idle as the King and Queen passed, then opened up again. The remainder of the Royal entourage looked like a cross between scarecrows and chimney sweeps. With the exhaust stubs glowing bright red, a Merlin on full song, running 30 per cent rich, would use 180 gallons (800 litres) per hour and fling 15 to 18 gallons (70 litres) of oil from its breathers. When I hear motor racing people speak of the sound and the fury, I always think of a Merlin at full power on the test bed. There would be between 15 and 18 engines running at full power at the same time. The noise was known as the Derby 'hum'. I loved every minute of my time on the test beds.

The morning shift was tough — leaving only just enough time to eat, do some homework and get to college at 6.30 p.m. — with more homework in the evening, then work at 6 a.m. next morning. The afternoon shift was fine: work at 2 p.m., home at 5 p.m. for college; all next morning for homework. The one week in three on the night shift was not so good. After an evening at college, it was work at 11 p.m., home to bed at the end of the shift at 6 a.m. the next morning, with 1730 hp ringing in your ears, and up for lunch then homework in the afternoon. Social life was impaired by extreme deafness, and a unique form of BO from a mixture of 100 octane petrol and oil.

We socialized with other apprentices lodging elsewhere in the town. Two more of our friends were lost flying Hurricanes in the Western Desert. We added John Cope-Lewis, a draughtsman, to our circle. 'Cope' was a Warrant Officer in the local ATC Squadron, so had petrol for his Standard Nine. The 'nine' indicated its people-carrying capacity — in, on and around! When we visited the Palais de Dance at Nottingham it was my duty, since I preferred beer to dancing, to ensure 'Cope' did not get too paralytic to drive us home. (In the 1960s he became Works Manager for Lotus at Cheshunt.)

Eventually I had an interview to advise me of the Selection Board's decision. It was Motor Car Design — and so I joined the staff of the legendary 'By', in peacetime Chief Engineer of the Motor Car Division. 'By', Mr R.W. Harvey Bailey, was now known as the Chief Technical and Development Engineer. He was, within the Rolls-Royce system, the Quality Director, but unlike in most companies, he had the authority and the organization to redesign the engine if he deemed it necessary to cure a service problem. 'By' joined Rolls-Royce in 1908, designing the 190 hp Falcon aero-engine in World War I. He was the engineer in charge of the factory, while Sir Henry Royce, because of failing health, lived first at St Margaret's Bay, near Dover, then Le Lavandou in France, and finally West Wittering in Sussex. Mr A.G. Elliot, 'E', who was in charge of Sir Henry's design office in France and Sussex, became Chief Engineer, Aero-Engines.

I was walking on air even though I did not start to design immediately. As an extremely junior draughtsman I drew repair schemes, known as 'RScs' on special aluminium sheets for printing and inclusion in repair manuals. I also drew wear reclamation schemes known as 'WRs'. I quickly learned a tremendous amount, dealing with battle damage, wear and just old-fashioned mistakes. I also had to do the leg work, making sure the scheme really fixed the problem. Some had to be tested; all had to be signed off by the AID, (Aeronautical Inspection Directorate), the RTO (Resident Technical Officer) of MAP (Ministry of Aircraft Production), and finally 'By' himself. My lettering (printing) left something to be desired. It still does. I was given an American spring catalogue to copy in print to try to make an improvement. One day, some of the senior staff came to my board to look at a scheme I had produced. As they departed, Stanley Bull, 'By's' right-hand man, and later Service Director, looked sorrowfully at me and said: 'My boy you will never make a draughtsman.'

A few months later Alec, 'By's' son and one of my friends, proposed that I join him in his embryo Defect Investigation Department. Defective (failed) engines were routed through this department on their way for repair. Here the failure was investigated, a reason found and recommendations made for action to eliminate further failures. 'By' was of course heavily involved. In the early days the relevant broken parts were always put in front of him. 'By' ruled that I was too young and inexperienced for this, and he chose George Hancock's assistant, Dick Green, whilst I should take Dick's place, which would be good training for me.

Dick took me to meet George and show me what I had to do. George had been riding mechanic to 'Hs' in the Alpine Trial and was the 'fiery little Yorkshireman' referred to in the book *Magic of a Name*. Before the war George ran the Continental car test department at Chateauroux in France. Prototypes and cars with new features were sent to George for test and to have 10,000 miles put on them as quickly as possible.

George's job was to keep 'Hs' and senior management briefed on service problems and remedial action. 'Hs' was fond of George and trusted him completely, but George was getting on in years and finding it hard to learn new tricks. He was a fund of tales about 'R', Sir Henry Royce. He was also not lacking in vitriolic criticism of some of his contemporaries. George came under 'By's' control, but really worked for 'Hs'. He could get in to see him without an appointment, or get straight through on the telephone.

# CHAPTER TWO

# Learning to be a Rolls-Royce engineer

WORKING FOR GEORGE, my job was to review all the failure reports, correlate them, from first intimation to investigation report, and analyse by factory and modification standard. I had to quickly learn failure diagnosis. For instance, a blued, broken connecting rod hanging through a hole in the crankcase was obviously a connecting rod bearing failure. But what was oil on the windscreen accompanied by loss of boost pressure? I soon found it was a supercharger bearing failure. The Derby and Crewe factories between them were building at this time 860 engines per month. More than 240 engines failed every month, and 220 reached their specified overhaul life — which was 240 hours in a fighter, 360 in a bomber. Another 180 were damaged in crashes, and the rest lost through enemy action.

Full of youthful zeal, I talked George into the installation of Kardex slotted metal wall charts, with celluloid tabs showing failures, colour-coded by factory and the remedy (fix), grouped by problem and showing how quickly the fixes were coming into service. 'Hs' would come up at all sorts of odd hours to look at the charts. He described me as 'that clever bugger upstairs, who makes figures stand on end'. One Thursday he arrived, saying with some heat: 'Stanley Bull (the Repair Supremo) says repaired engines are more reliable than new ones. It is so much rubbish, give me the facts.' It was a stupid argument: older engines, retrospectively modified, with at least 150 hours of their life already used, could never be as good as factory fresh ones. After he established the rules, to compare like with like, and agreeing that the previous six months would be an adequate period for analysis, he asked 'how long?' 'A week,' I replied. 'On my desk noon Monday' was his instruction as he swept out. You had to deliver. Failure and excuses were not part of his regime. You got a nod or a grunt if you performed; and were packed off — maybe with a terrible blast — if you did not.

'By' gave me assignments, generally information gathering, in the factory. I did not know if he was finding out what I could do, or grooming me for a different job. He was more formal, but more generous with his praise than 'Hs'. Alec's Defect Investigation Department had moved from a corner of No. 6 shop, to Longden's Mill in Agard Street, one block north of Ashbourne Road and conveniently close to the Friary Hotel. In peacetime Longden's Mill was a corset factory, but was now making webbing equipment for the Forces, especially paratroops. His business was booming. The Glasgow factory had come on stream, there were now 300 defective engines per month out of 1900 engines produced, excluding Packard in the USA.

I started a card index system, recording the details of every engine that came to our notice — engine number; factory of origin; modification standard — cross-referenced to the aircraft in which it was installed, plus squadron, airfield and so on. Today it would be computerized. To handle it in 1942 I used a team of young ladies, ranging from a former chorus girl to ex-WAAFs. I provided a service, primarily to Agard Street. People would ring up and ask: 'Engine number so and so, anything known?' We generally had some information. When I was transferred to Agard Street I took the records and the chorus line with me.

Squadron Leader Starkey, responsible for factory defence (meaning air raids), occupied the next office. One of his concerns was loss of production due to genuine, or suspected, unexploded bombs. This was a national problem, and the Home Guard had started to form auxiliary bomb disposal units. Starkey persuaded me to give up stretcher bearing and join 69 ABDU — the Rolls-Royce unit. Several other units had already been formed. Some idiot told 'Hs' that the regulations provided for an ABDU to do the whole job: removing the fuses and disposing of the bomb, after training on real enemy bombs. As usual, Rolls-Royce had to be first and best. A group of us were trained in fuse disablement. Mine were Type 17 and 50. Type 17 was a clockwork device — at first we unscrewed it and threw it away. The enemy's counter-move was to include a simple device to trigger the bomb if anyone did this. So we then used a large electro-magnet. You listened to the bomb ticking; at first with a doctor's stethoscope, and later with a remote microphone. Then you stuck the magnet gently on the bomb, switched on and, if you were lucky, the ticking stopped. You then either steamed the explosive out or put the bomb on a lorry and took it away to blow it up.

The enemy took serious offence at this, and fitted a second fuse (a Type 50) with a chemical delay, and a magnetic anti-handling device. If you went near it with anything magnetic, the device closed a circuit and up you went. The answer was to pump it full of a liquid which dissolved the insulation. You then hoped it was disabled so that the magnet could be applied safely.

We had the theory; now for the practical experience. The Royal Engineers took us to a field near Immingham Docks where there was a stick of genuine unexploded bombs, and all we had to do was dig and find the bombs, disable them, then take them away and blow them up. During the proceedings there was another air raid, and the district was stitched up with 2 kg anti-personnel bombs, known as the butterfly bomb. We gained additional experience helping to clear these. Finally we completed our training and were entitled to wear the Home Guard version of the red and gold bomb badge on our sleeves, to indicate we were qualified disposers of bombs. Fortunately for the factory, we never had to perform.

All this association with explosives and pyrotechnics had an unfortunate effect upon me. As a schoolboy I had firmly secured the lids on tins filled with acetylene, and dropped them from a bridge into the river below, producing a violent upheaval. In Toc H Mark 21 I applied potassium iodide to the lavatory seats; on contact with something, there was a satisfactory crack. It took a while to get the proportions right, by which time most people had been alerted. The climax was reached when we fired an RAF signal rocket on a nearly horizontal trajectory along one of Derby's main streets. We fired it just as a group of policemen were dispersing to their various beats. Not surprisingly, the sight of the rocket on its way towards them caused consternation.

Our anti-social activities brought us under suspicion for complicity in an incident following the bombing of the factory. Unknown to anyone, the bombing caused one of the underground test bed fuel pipes to leak, and petrol vapour got into the sewers. There was a habit of avoiding the 'no smoking' ban by visiting the toilets for a quick cigarette. One day there was an almighty explosion in No. 2 Shop toilets. No one was seriously hurt, although a number gave up smoking permanently. It was some time before we emerged from the cloud of suspicion. When my children hear me reminiscing with my friends, they always accuse me of double standards.

Once installed at Agard Street my comfortable existence, contrived to help me through my college exams, came to a sudden and abrupt end. 'By' impressed on us that every day lost in an investigation meant another 42 potentially defective engines would have been built, increasing the dangers to pilots and crews. Although he was carrying an immense load of responsibility with intense demands on his time, during an investigation he always made sure we understood every step of his reasoning. I am still convinced that the ability to read a failure is one of the most valuable attributes of an engineer. He would take me through the mechanism of a failure with immense patience and no little courtesy. This courtesy towards the young was a characteristic of all the senior Rolls-Royce engineers. Rowledge (who, when at Napier, had designed the 12-cylinder broad arrow Lion engines), Cyril Lovesey (Head of Engine Development), A.G. Elliott (Chief Engineer Aero Engines, later joint Managing Director) and Frank Stark (designer of the air-cooled sleeve-valve engines) were all courteous and considerate to the young hopefuls, such as myself. It might have been the generation, I suppose, because I found Wally Hassan, Chief Engineer of Coventry Climax, just the same. I think it came from an inner confidence. They knew they were the best in the world and did not have to throw their weight about to prove it. I vowed that if ever I reached their position of eminence, I would treat the younger generation with the same tact and courtesy, to avoid bruising their egos. I have tried but not succeeded.

Another of my tasks was to produce 'The Rolls-Royce Repaired Engines Monthly Review', a 50-page report for the Directorate of Repair and Maintenance (DRM) of the Ministry of Aircraft Production. Being Rolls-Royce it had to be the best, and was published first each month to beat the other engine manufacturers. It was the biggest as there were more Rolls-Royce engines in service than all the others put together. By 1943 the Glasgow factory had reached its planned output, and the Ford factory was on stream and catching up fast — British production was nearly 3000 engines a month. Page one of the Review was a statistical summary, showing that out of more than 1100 engines passing through the repair organization each month, 300 or more were defective, 250 had been damaged by crashes or enemy action and 250 or more had reached their specified life. The remaining category was 'Other Causes'. Three or four pages were devoted to explanations of failures and action taken to eliminate them, plus a list of every failed engine with a one-line description of the

failure and action. 'Other Causes' embraced such things as the Bomber
Command Engine Changing Programme. It also included the controversial
list of 'Unsubstantiated Defects'. If a pilot took a dislike to a particular
engine, on rare occasions the RAF Engineer Officer concerned might get rid
of it by claiming it was difficult to start, ran roughly, cut out, or misfired.
We would have to put the engine on the test bed to investigate, wasting our
time and valuable test bed time. Fighter Command exacerbated the situation
by 'snipping out' the section concerning a particular engine and sending it
to the Engineer Officer concerned, demanding an explanation. He never
saw the pages where Rolls-Royce admitted the engine had failed, with an
explanation of the remedial action. A certain amount of anti-Rolls-Royce
feeling developed within Fighter Command as a result, which culminated in
an incident later named after the Wing Commander concerned, who was a
very tough and capable Engineer Officer. He had been 'snipped' and was
still smarting when one of his Spitfires crashed following an engine cut as it
took off on a test flight. The Wing Commander was determined to make this
one stick. The RAF Form 1022 reporting the defect was accompanied by
many photographs, including the cockpit, showing the position of the
controls, exact details of fuel, oil and coolant. When we stripped the engine,
we found it had seized through overheating. However the Form 1022 was
explicit, the cooling system was still full after the crash — and we found the
coolant pump and its drive still worked. Eventually we had to let the engine
go for repair, even though we had no explanation for the failure. I kept the
Form 1022, with the photographs, on my desk to remind me we had not
completed our job, and suddenly I saw the answer in one of the
photographs. The side water pipe from the pump to the cylinder block was
missing, but the pump outlet and the block water rail were securely blanked
off. This explained the overheating — no coolant circulation — although
the system was full, but not why the vital pipe was missing. The Form 1022
supplied the answer. The previous day there had been an investigation into a
complaint of rough running — the engine-mounting rubbers had been
changed. The side water pipe had to be removed to facilitate this — if you
were quick you could blank off the pump and block before much coolant
was lost, avoiding a drain and refill. You had to make sure the blanks were
tight. In this case they were even tight enough to pass a pressure test. We
had the story, but how to tell the Wing Commander, who stood as high in
our esteem as he did with Fighter Command. Ronnie Harker's Service
Liaison Team came to our rescue.

We learned a lesson from this. One of us would spend an afternoon with
the pilots on the Fighter Command Engine Handling Course. This
culminated in an enamel bucket of Pimms being lowered to them from Alec
Harvey Bailey's top floor flat, opposite the Friary Hotel where the end of
course party was winding down. I suspect Alec's wife would not let them
into the flat for fear she would never get them out. The engineer officers
from the other commands, when on their courses, used to visit us at Agard
Street, when we would answer questions and look up engine details in our
records.

We often dealt with Alex Henshaw, author of *Sigh for a Merlin* (John
Murray, 1979), who was Chief Test Pilot at the Castle Bromwich factory
where most of the Spitfires and latterly some Lancasters were built. He had
three magneto skew gear failures in one week, thus effectively switching off

the ignition. After he put the third Spitfire down by the expedient of going between two houses (taking the wings off in the process) he made a reverse-charge phone call to 'Hs' demanding action; which he got.

Our turn came when the Merlin 66 was introduced. The 66 with two-piece block, two-speed two-stage blower with a bigger first stage impeller (and its Packard equivalents the 266 and V1650-7) was probably the best and most reliable engine in the wartime Merlin family. Another of its features was a Bendix Stromberg injection carburettor. Henshaw discovered that the engine would now run upside down. After some even more hair-raising inverted passes than usual he discovered that although the carburettor worked upside down — the oil system did not, and the engine seized. But as usual he was equal to the situation.

'Hs' dropped another of his bombshells on me. He had an argument with Air Marshal Harris C-in-C Bomber Command. Harris said he could not prosecute the war because of the unreliability of the Merlin. 'Hs' replied that Harris only heard of the ones that went wrong; he never heard of the hundreds that gave no trouble. I was ordered to refute 'Bomber' Harris's claim. Aided by the ladies, I did 15 days work in three and found 'Bomber' was more nearly right than 'Hs'. I found several Lancasters that had nine engine failures in six months, during 1943. Nine months later, when I dared make another survey, we were down to ones and twos.

During the summer of 1944 it was clear we were on the way to winning the war. Production was now 3200 engines per month, excluding Packards, and defects were dropping fast to below 200 a month — nearly all older unmodified engines. The Defect Investigation Department was on its way to becoming redundant. Stanley Bull, who had been running the Repair Technical Office was sent to London to reopen the Car Service Department at Hythe Road. Alec took his job, Dick Green escaped into the RAF as a pilot. I was left more or less running Agard Street, but not for long, for in the autumn we merged with Alec's Repair Technical Office. There just were not enough defects to investigate, and those we had were old known problems.

It was suggested I might like to join 'Tiger Force': Bomber Command's impending contribution to the war in the Far East, where there would be two major differences from the way they fought in Europe. First, much longer distances to the target would be involved. Second, 'Tiger Force' would operate from primitive airfields some 6000 miles from the manufacturer's engineering centres, instead of less than 100 miles from Derby or Manchester to their Lincolnshire bases. There was, therefore, a need for an even stronger support team than the highly efficient organization already functioning. I agreed to go, but was told I needed training and practical experience in the field first. Off I went. It took me a long time to get used to seeing the temperature gauges on the stops for ten minutes at a time. I found it even harder to practise what I had been preaching for years — high boost and low revs to save fuel. The Merlin in the Lancaster seemed to me to run much more smoothly and happily at 2250 rpm and negative boost than at the prescribed 1850–1900 rpm and full throttle — the speed was the same, but fuel consumption was ten per cent less. It was mostly long periods of boredom, punctuated by a few seconds of terror caused largely by inexperience. Tiger Force planned to use the Lincoln — a bigger, more powerful, longer range version of the

Lancaster, able to carry an even bigger bomb load. So when the war in Europe ended I got down to sorting out the Lincoln's engines. It now had Packard Merlin 68As in place of the Derby-built 85s, of which we had some experience as they had been used in the Pathfinder Master Bombers' Lancaster VIs. There was trouble with misfiring and rough running which was traced to the 4.8cc of lead per gallon of fuel not being fully burnt, mainly due to the intercoolers reducing the charge temperature so much. We specified opening up the engines for a few minutes to burn off the lead. It was not a very good solution, but we were being pressed to be ready to leave for the Far East in September and it was the best we could manage in the time available. It meant many hours in the air all through the summer of 1945 — then the war ended suddenly and I was soon back at Rolls-Royce Hucknall, doing nearly the same job.

Rolls-Royce always attached great importance to 'customer' service, typified by the phrase from the Silver Ghost owner's handbook: '. . . gentlemen of engineering training, whose sole duty it is, to call, by appointment, on the owners or chauffeurs of Rolls-Royce cars . . .' During the war Rolls-Royce had more and closer contacts with the services than other manufacturers, and many more flight development staff. There were the test pilots who were pilots with engineering knowledge — Ronnie Harker's Service Liaison Pilots who were equally good pilots and engineers — then there were some people such as I who were engineers first and pilots as a convenience.

Cars were my first love, but you could relax and look around in the air (after the war), and admire the magnificent cloudscapes, sunrises, sunsets and clear-day views. Twenty years later I used to take the Auster up on a summer's evening just to relax. In a car you have to concentrate every second.

# CHAPTER THREE

# Having fun at Hucknall

WHEN I LEFT home I had promised my father that I would neither buy nor ride a motor cycle. In return he undertook to buy me a car when I was old enough to drive one. Keeping my side of the bargain had been no problem, with petrol being severely rationed, and non-existent for private use.

As Alec Harvey Bailey wanted to sell his 1930 International Aston Martin — in good condition with its appearance improved by small wheels and larger section tyres — I put it to my father that as I had kept my promise, it was now his turn. I do not think he had an Aston Martin in mind when he made his offer.

After negotiation, and with help from Aunt Jess, the Aston was mine, delivered to the only garage I could find — in the grounds of Highfield maternity hospital — by a pushing party in return for free beer. Strangely enough I cannot remember learning to drive. I drove an Austin Heavy 12 used to tow the mowers for the school playing fields and, during school holidays, a paraffin-fuelled Fordson tractor. I graduated to wartime Hillman Utilities, to Humbers, to Cope Lewis's Wolseley Hornet, and eventually to Rolls-Royce Wraiths, converted to nine-seat shooting brakes. I rode with George Hancock on the rare occasions he drove prototypes, Phantom IIIs, Mark V and 8-cylinder Bentleys. There was, therefore, an assumption — which I did nothing to dispel — that I had been cleared to drive company products. By the time someone checked up, I had enough experience to be cleared.

After some wheeling and dealing I had the Aston Martin added to the works driving list so I could use it on company business. It had suffered from having been laid up for several years, so the journeys became sagas. Its first was to Oxford, and on the way home the water pump gland started to leak. It gradually got worse, with stops for water every 20 miles. A fortnight later, on my way to Portsmouth, the electric fuel pumps stopped working — no electricity (a flat battery). The dynamo had ceased charging. I borrowed a fully charged battery from a garage near Daventry, and pressed on. With magneto ignition and hand starting, I hoped to get to Portsmouth and back. During the night some exuberant sailors stole, among other things, the starting handle. A Fleet Air Arm party push-started me, and I drove home in fear of stalling or boiling in traffic; but luck was with me. It broke a piston ring on the way back from a visit to Vokes at Guildford. In the course of the rebuild I learned the hard way about air leaks on the suction side of oil pumps. The Aston then behaved itself for a few months.

Mechanical devices have a way of teaching you not to be complacent. Another run in the Aston was punctuated by a pool of Castrol R beneath the rear axle. The locking ring on the worm had unscrewed, and the worm had burst out through the casting. Fortunately Aston Martin at Feltham had the spares I required in stock for £7 0s 10d (£7.05). It was a body off, major rebuild. This made me decide on a complete winter overhaul, down to the last nut and bolt. It cost more than I paid for the car. Ginger Wood, an ex-racing motorcyclist and now the SU representative, provided two new carburettors, and the BTH man a new magneto. I raised the compression, bringing the engine up to Mark II specification. It would do 100 mph and between 25 and 30 mpg It became a very nice car, but despite its 14-inch (35.5cm) brake drums, did not possess much in the way of stopping power.

At Hucknall I worked in the newly formed Power Plant Quality Department. During 1936 Rolls-Royce (probably 'Hs') realized that many of the performance and reliability problems arose from the way the engine was installed in the aircraft. Radiators and cooling systems are just a nuisance to the aircraft manufacturer, whereas they are life and death for the engine. The Flight Development Division was formed, based at Hucknall airfield, near Nottingham and shared with the RAF. They had a strange collection of aircraft, ranging from a Merlin-engined Horsley to a Heinkel He 70 with a Kestrel engine. Hucknall made a major contribution to the Hurricane and Spitfire. But it was one step down a long hard road. The next giant step was the interchangeable power plant, designed and built by Rolls-Royce. This included cooling systems, water and oil, engine mountings, cowlings, exhaust systems, hot and cold air intakes, all the services such as undercarriage and gun turret pumps. The first such power plant was designed for the twin-engined Bristol Beaufighter II, but was also adapted for the Lancaster. The Halifax, which used the same engines, just did not have the performance or the reliability of the Lancaster.

Hucknall was staffed by a mixture of people — some from Derby, steeped in Rolls-Royce methods and traditions, some from the aircraft industry and a large proportion of hostilities-only personnel. The Rolls-Royce spirit was so heavily diluted as to be nearly non-existent. The head of the newly-formed Quality Department, Frank Nixon, had been imported from Bristol Engines where he had earned a reputation for applying American quality methods to oil coolers. He seemed, therefore, to be a good choice, radiators being top of the list of power plant defects. Every manager at Derby was the best in the business; if not, 'Hs' immediately replaced him. There was a wealth of talent, experience and tradition to draw upon.

The Derby managers were described, with some justification, as a bunch of turbulent robber barons, but they shared a determination to make the very best aero-engines in the world, and when assailed from without they instantly closed ranks. 'By' was a single-minded engineer of absolute integrity. He was also a lay preacher and enthusiastic rose grower. His blistering denunciations of his peers, who did not appear to him to share his dedication to total reliability, did not always endear him to them. He would say that it does not matter what lies you tell or deceptions you practise, the engine will always tell the truth. Cyril Lovesey, who ran Merlin

Development, was another great character — small, always cheerful, with a Punch-like nose and chin. He matched 'By' in his determination, this time to wring the last ounce of performance from the Merlin. In the course of its life its power doubled, yet its capacity remained unchanged at 27 litres, and maximum rpm remained at 3000. The doubled power all came from increasing the boost pressure. At the same time its overhaul life doubled from 240 hours in 1941 to 480 in 1945. The engineers were matched by Swift (Sft), General Manager Aero Production, who took Derby from producing 100,000 hp per week to 200,000. Not many people will believe that a Rolls-Royce wartime horsepower cost the British government £1 sterling, while a Bristol horse power cost nearly £2 and that from Napier almost £3. This is confirmed by Rod Banks, wartime director of Engine Research and Development, in his book *I Kept No Diary* (Airlife Publications, 1978). A 1710 hp Merlin 61 cost £1643 in 1942.

After the war a number of Derby personnel, including me, became available and were drafted to Hucknall to reinforce the assault on the civil air transport market. Rolls-Royce realized that their image suffered, unfairly, from the Avro Manchester debacle, they determined not to let it happen again. Wartime aviation history books tell future generations that the Manchester was nearly a good aircraft, ruined by the dreadful Rolls-Royce Vulture. It is just not true. The Vulture was not a world beater like the Merlin; it lacked the elegant simplicity of the Merlin, which had Sir Henry Royce written all over it, and not an ounce of surplus metal anywhere. The Vulture (42 litres of it) was two Peregrines on a common crankcase — workmanlike but not inspired. However, it did give its designed 1780 hp, but it had to work much harder than anticipated to propel an aeroplane 30 per cent overweight and 22 per cent up on aerodynamic drag. It suffered from cooling problems, mainly because of the aircraft installation, and the propellers were prone to run away. The unfortunate pilot saw all these just as Vulture engine failures. Rolls-Royce, with lofty disdain for publicity, never bothered to tell him that the engines were working some 45 per cent harder than they were designed to do. If the Vulture had been given two-piece blocks and its power increased by a central entry blower, as was the Merlin, it could have coped. 'Hs' and his advisers realized this was a waste, finding more power to bring an inefficient aircraft back to specification. The same factories and labour could produce many more engines and specific horsepower by concentrating on Merlins to the exclusion of all else. This was taken by some aircrews and sloppy historians as an admission by Rolls-Royce that the Vulture was a failure.

Avros — certainly their Chief Designer, Roy Chadwick — were fully aware of the Manchester's shortcomings, and the reasons why. They made sure that when the Lancaster went into service, that it was down to the design weight and surpassed its aerodynamic performance targets, with a contribution from Witold Challier, the Rolls-Royce aerodynamicist. It was all kept very quiet. Most people in the Air Ministry, MAP, and the RAF did not realize what had been done. The thickness of the skin was reduced, the pitch of ribs increased by 15 per cent, and so on. However, Rolls-Royce learned the lesson, they realized image was very important in the airline business, of which they were determined to take a large slice.

There was, spearheaded by Frank Nixon, an intensive programme to make every single Merlin power plant component — nearly all designed and supplied by sub-contractors — completely reliable, especially to eliminate coolant leaks and take the sting out of the taunts of 'wet engines'. Nixon made me responsible for all the rubber components from hoses to vibration insulators. 'Make it an engineer's material, not a black art' was his instruction. Another of my problems was the coolant loss warning transmitter. We had learned by bitter experience that the temperature gauge gave no warning of coolant loss. A leak caused first an imperceptible rise in temperature, as the reduced volume of coolant had to work harder followed by a drop, because of insufficient coolant to activate the temperature sender. The warning transmitter sensed a reduced rate of flow and lit a warning light in the cockpit. The pilot shut down the engine, diverted to the nearest airfield, often to find it was a false warning, due to transmitter malfunction. False warnings enraged the airlines more than real ones. In conjunction with Smiths, the makers, we developed a reliable unit.

The post-war world brought the five day week — no work on Saturday morning. With two friends I spent the weekends sailing on the Norfolk Broads. We used the two-seat Aston Martin to get there as it made the best use of our combined petrol ration. The 145 miles from Derby took 200 minutes traversing six large towns. This was before the existence of motorways and by-passes. In 1990 I drove my 140 mph Lotus Excel from Derby to Thurne (our 1946 haunt) in 200 minutes, all the towns by-passed plus some motorway. Even the fuel consumption was the same: 26.6 mpg!

In 1947, travelling south down the A5 from Derby to Luton, I hit a 5-ton truck, heading north, which had crossed in front of me to reach a café on my side of the road. The Aston was a write-off, and so was the lorry. I did not do too well either. The lorry driver was prosecuted, I received £650 compensation, sold the engine (which survived) for £150 and bought a beautiful 105 mph Ulster model Aston Martin. As its 9.7:1 compression engine did not like pool petrol, I ran on a mixture of two gallons of methanol and one gallon of benzol to 13 of pool. I obtained the vital ingredients from Reg Parnell's garage, about 100 yards away from my lock-up in the maternity home in Derby. I suppose I had a subconscious feeling that if I still lived in Derby I might get moved back to the main factory one day.

I never felt the same affection for the Ulster as I did for the troublesome International, but it was dead reliable and fun to drive. I converted it to hydraulic brakes which proved so good that they wound up the leaf springs, necessitating radius arms. I sold it for £850. With the money I bought 'Jock' Horsfall's spare 2-litre engine and, inspired by Cameron Earle's Intelligence Objectives report on the pre-war German Mercedes W165 (published around 1946 by HMSO), set about building a car. Accles and Pollock made the special oval tube for me, but the minimum batch they would make was enough for four cars. It had independent suspension front and rear, with swing-axles at the rear, I am ashamed to admit. I made a sheet steel trans-axle with Aston gears. I learned about heat treatment the hard way. I left machining allowances in the bearing housings to take care of welding distortion, but the residual stresses were so high there was even more distortion. My friends rescued me.

I was assisted by an ex-merchant navy engineer, who now worked in the Rolls-Royce film negative library. After surviving three sinkings, two from torpedoes, one from a mine, Willy Southcott had 'swallowed the anchor' at his wife's insistence. He was a wonderful craftsman with infinite patience. His conversation was larded with nautical expressions delivered in a rich Devonshire accent. Bulkheads and decks were walls and floors, 'going ashore gear' was your best suit. One weekend he just did not turn up; no explanation. I found he had left Rolls-Royce. At Goodwood in September 1950, with Bira, I met Willy again. He was at that time a member of the BRM team.

The motor sports enthusiasts at Rolls-Royce usually had decrepit Austin Sevens as their daily transport: the more decrepit the better. Mine, bought from the breakers, was a 1926 fabric-bodied saloon with seven spokes remaining in each wheel. Your super sports car was kept for special occasions. A Saturday morning line-up would include three Astons — mine; that of Harry Grylls, then personal assistant to 'Hs' and later Director in charge of the car factory at Crewe; and Roger Craster's, who also went to Crewe. Gahagan (cousin of 'Bugatti' Gahagan) in charge of exhaust development, had a 2.3 blown Alfa Romeo and Geoffrey (Oscar) Wilde, the compressor genius, had a Lancia Lambda. There were Bugattis, chain-drive Frazer-Nashes, even a boat-tailed 1926 Delage. My room-mate at Mark 21, John Craig, nearly broke ranks. He had a Tickford-bodied 2.6 litre MG drophead coupé. John took over the car Service Department after Stanley Bull retired. Because of his dignified demeanour and the geographical location of the service department, he was known as the 'Bishop of Willesden Green'. John, in his turn, retired to Vancouver.

When I moved from Derby to Hucknall, I struck up a lasting friendship with John Dixon, who made the same move at the same time. John was a rabid photographer and some of his work adorns this book. He terrified us with his enthusiasm for close-up in-flight photography. Being able to count the hairs in the eyebrows of the pilot of a formating Spitfire was not good for the nerves of any of those involved.

It will be clear that fun took precedence over work. One of my friends, whom I met when he was running the Service Department reporting team, was W.E. (Bill) Harker. Bill, and his elder brother Ronnie, who told his own story in *Rolls-Royce from the Wings* (Oxford Illustrated Press, 1976) were former premium apprentices. Bill had a sabbatical with the Gas Turbine team at Barnoldswick, but reappeared post-war, and I became involved in the rebuild of his 1100cc 8-cylinder Harker Special. It had two crankshafts geared together on a common crankcase, and it derived most of its running gear from an 'R' type MG. A roller chain drove the camshafts and it sported a Zoller blower, the same size as those used on the works 2 litre ERA. The immediate job was to fit Derwent V turbine oil pumps. This car contributed to my near fatal fascination for geared crankshafts, it was extremely quick, and would give a 1500cc ERA a good run. The chassis was from a French 1930s sports car, a Lombard; suspension was by flexible chassis! Bill moved the Harker into my new garage where my new car was taking shape. Bill was wonderful company, a vivid raconteur, disorganized and a considerable distraction. One of our colleagues, 'Knocker' West, who looked after electrical systems, including sparking plugs, talked Bill into using aircraft platinum pointed plugs in the racing car. We could warm up and race on the same plugs, Bill told me. I told him he was living in cloud cuckoo land, the Merlin sparked its plugs 1500 times a minute, yet although his engine might put less heat into the plug per cycle, it did so 4000 times a minute. Sure enough he burned a hole in a piston. In a spirit of 'I told you so', I disdained to assist in the repairs. Bill did not entirely clean out the piston debris from the oil system, and the camshafts soon seized through the oil feed becoming blocked by aluminium particles. Eventually Bill's second love, Falconry, claimed him and I saw very little of him until he came to Bourne in 1955 to see Raymond Mays, who was an old friend and rival. Bill is no longer with us, although the car is being rebuilt by its new owner.

Frank Nixon was an inveterate empire builder. He gradually moved the frontier between engines and power plants, exerting more and more influence on the development of Merlins for airline use. Derby was changing to gas turbines, with a big influx of non-traditional newcomers from Barnoldswick, and the retirement of such stalwarts as 'By' and Lovesey. Eventually Nixon took over all engineering at Hucknall, and his deputy, Les Wood, took over the Quality Department from Nixon. I found myself with the Merlin flight development team. I started, unwittingly, my habit of unorthodox assistants, with J.R. (Jumbo) Pope. This upheaval was brought about by over-runs in the Avon and Dart turbine engine programmes. I recall a group of us looking at a Meteor aircraft having its Derwent Vs replaced by Avons. We noted the engine thrust exceeded the all-up weight of the aircraft, so we reasoned it should be able to go straight up; that is, climb vertically. It did.

The Merlin Programme had two Lancasters, one for single stage engines for Yorks and Lancastrians, the other plus a Lincoln for the two-stage engines for the Tudor and Canadair IV. We had frequent visits from the latter aircraft. I had to go to BOAC's York maintenance base at Hurn near Bournemouth with a colleague who lived in Hucknall. We used the Ulster, the return trip on a beautiful summer evening in 1947 took 210 minutes for 201 miles.

But Hucknall did not enthral me in the same way Derby had; maybe there were more external distractions. Prince Chula decided he did not care for the post-war racing scene. Most of his money was tied up in Thailand, which had been marginally on the wrong side in the war. He gave Bira their new 4CLT 48 San Remo Maserati and retired from motor racing, while Bira gave 'Romulus' to Chula. I went to the first British GP at Silverstone with Bira, where he finished fifth, troubled by failing brakes, having ignored advice to modify the linings. In 1949 he teamed up with de Graffenried and Enrico Plate. It looked to me, and perhaps others, like a 'starting money operation'. Race organizers would pay £350 for Bira to start in their race and £300 for de Graffenried. Their two Maseratis were carried one above the other in an open Fiat truck, attended by Plate and two mechanics, one of them a tiny silver-haired Italian called 'Titch'. The more races in which they started, the more money they earned, sometimes a race every weekend.

The 4CLT Maserati, with two-stage supercharging, was a very fragile machine at its best. There was precious little time to give them a thorough overhaul, and fix last weekend's failures, generally a piston. In 1950 I wangled a business trip to the south coast, and then on the overnight ferry to Jersey where there was a race along the sea front. Bira's engine blew up early on, with the usual piston detonation failure, and de Graffenried had piston ring trouble. The oil tank on the 4CLT was under the seat, with the filler in the cockpit. With adding oil in a race legal then, Plate just up-ended a 20 litre can of oil into the cockpit. Some went in the tank! He finished third, but it took a series of baths to make him sanitary.

Bira was flying one of the first post-war twin-engined light aeroplanes, a Miles Gemini, which he eventually flew to Bangkok. It was a much under-rated aircraft — the twin Comanche of its day.

Bira had a serious talk with me after the race, telling me of his plans for the coming season. My distaste for the starting money operation must have showed. He had done a deal with the Maserati brothers, who, having been bought out by Count Orsi, were now running a small company called OSCA, making very quick small sports cars. They were making him an unblown 4.5 litre V12 that would fit into the 4CLT chassis. It would develop 300 hp, enough to get in between the Ferraris and the Alfa Romeos. There would be no need for fuel stops, and it should be reliable. The existance of the unblown Ferrari was rumoured, but it had not yet appeared. Bira wanted me to join his new operation as manager. I expressed polite interest and asked for time to think it over. I was slightly disillusioned with my career at Rolls-Royce, and the future did not look good. The airlines were not buying Merlins and the British Tudor had been withdrawn. The Canadair IV, a licence-built cross between a DC4 and DC6 with two stage Merlin 626s, was the only hope. The York, with Merlin 500s, was only a stop gap — slow, noisy but reliable and a good load carrier reprieved by the Berlin Air Lift. Airline passengers preferred the Lockheed Constellation, 25 mph faster than the Canadairs and much quieter. After a fairly meteoric career during the war, I now felt myself in the doldrums.

I had heard about the BRM and the start line fiasco at Silverstone. Rolls-Royce gossip had it that the top BRM people did not have what it took to win races. They cited the 'E' type ERA, which never looked like even starting in a race until Humphrey Cook took it away from Bourne.

I had sold the 2 litre special to a Melton Mowbray enthusiast. It was good, but was outclassed by Gillie Tyrer's BMW and the new generation of 2 litre sports cars from Frazer Nash. I was negotiating for an Aston Martin DB2, which was really beyond my means, and I was making dissatisfied noises at work. Bira, who had spent the winter in Thailand, had arranged to meet me at the Ship Hotel in Chichester on Friday evening ready for the debut of the OSCA at the 1951 Easter Monday Meeting at Goodwood. There was no sign of him, but on Saturday morning a message arrived saying: 'The car has just left Modena, and will arrive on Sunday. Please arrange oil, fuel, tyres and plugs.' No indication of brand, type or size. Fortunately Bira arrived in the afternoon with most of the required information, accompanied by his new wife Chelita and a blonde English girlfriend.

When the lorry with the OSCA arrived at Dover, in the care of Reg Williams, son of Prince Chula's gardener in Cornwall and ex-Plate 'Titch', Customs took a dislike to the whole enterprise. Prince Chula was persuaded to put up a bond to cover the duty, the car arriving at Goodwood very late on Sunday ready for an untimed special practice early Monday morning. The engine started easily enough, although at 7 a.m. it was extremely cold, then the oil pressure faded away. Wilkie Wilkinson, of Ecurie Ecosse, an interested spectator, suggested that the Castrol R oil was too cold to flow from the tail oil tank to the engine along some 8 ft (2.4 m) of small bore pipe. We hung a 25-litre drum of oil from a tree and heated it with a borrowed oxy-acetylene welding torch, and warm oil found the pressure.

Then we found the threads on the Lodge racing plugs did not match the Marelli terminals, so we had to butcher the terminals on the Marelli warm-up plugs. Bira went out on his untimed practice; the first time he had driven the car and, as I found later, the first time anyone had. The circuit was wet, but he put up some credible times. He coasted in and said: 'It's all over, the incredible power of the engine has burst the gearbox, I knew it would.' The gearbox was the only part of the 4CLT Maserati that had not given trouble. I put the car into each gear and rocked it to and fro. All the gears seemed to be present, but the poor mechanics were too tired to care. I persuaded Bira to try one more lap, and he confirmed what I suspected — it had just jumped out of gear. Some fiddling with the selector springs solved the problem.

The first race, the five lap Chichester Cup, was run in heavy rain. Reg Parnell in a 4CLT Maserati won, Shawe Taylor in an old ERA was second, and Bira third, still learning the car and complaining bitterly about lack of grip from the Dunlop tyres. After he convinced me, I had to persuade 'Dunlop Mac' to remove the Dunlop tyres and refit the half-worn Pirellis on which the car was delivered. It was still wet for the main race, the 12-lap Richmond Trophy. Parnell led away but Bira, who was exceptional in the wet, passed him before the end of the first lap. Reg had a slide on the second lap, caught up again, but his engine blew on lap six leaving Bira an easy winner. The first race of the day was won by S. Moss in a 2 litre HWM, the first win for that combination.

Next morning Bira reopened the idea of my joining him permanently as his manager, but I was not very enthusiastic. I retained memories of Chula's calm efficiency and the Rolls-Royce relentless drive for reliability; they did not go well with Bira's happy-go-lucky approach. I had also just had a brush with the manageress of the Ship Hotel who objected to Bira taking his early morning tea with his lady guests one each side of him in bed! Bira told me that Raymond Mays was talking to him about a possible drive for BRM, but Bira did not seem very enthusiastic.

I related the Rolls-Royce gossip, some of my friends involved with the supercharger said they were worried by the failures, which they could not reproduce on their test rigs. Peter Walker's Barcelona failure had the characteristics of lack of lubricant, yet eight hours on the rig, on dry air, producing higher temperatures than with alcohol fuel, had not reproduced the failures, at speeds equivalent to 13,000 crankshaft rpm. (The BRM engine peaked at 12,000 rpm.) Rolls-Royce specified Fischer bearings with ribbon steel cages, but the BRM project had support from Hoffmann, so they used a Hoffmann bearing with a heavier pocketed cage. This enclosed the balls and shrouded them from the cooling oil/air mist. Again Rolls-Royce specified BS 369 for the piston ring type oil seals. BRM's suppliers could not handle this and provided DTD 459 which permitted a much higher leak rate.

These factors lead the gossiping junior Rolls-Royce engineers to suspect BRM would not be above tampering with the oil supply. The senior engineers responsible for the blower, Prof. Allen and 'Oscar' Wilde kept their own counsel, but they had never been allowed to see an engine run. I had worked with 'Oscar' during the war and had a tremendous regard for his ability. I also told Bira that Rolls-Royce were planning to post a junior engineer with BRM in an effort to find out what was really happening. Bira immediately suggested that I become this junior engineer and look after his affairs as well. I declined, pointing out I was no longer a junior engineer, and shared allegiance was something they would never permit. I also declined to go to Bordeaux with him, because I had begun to suspect and dislike the OSCA. However, we agreed to meet again at the BRDC Daily Express race at Silverstone in a few weeks. When we did, I was the Rolls-Royce man at BRM, and Bira was about to drive one. I never knew what part, if any, Bira played in my joining BRM.

My disillusionment with my job at Hucknall was increasing, and a cut-back was imminent. The Canadair IV, now in service with BOAC under the class name 'Argonaut', was just recovering from a major cooling system problem, the worst thing to happen to a 'wet' engine. This had caused a crisis, which may have been magnified by BOAC since Canadian Pacific, who also used the same aircraft, had very little trouble, which is just as well as their Trans-Pacific routes involved really long hauls (no diversions possible). There were no new piston engine projects. All the plum jobs were going to the ex-Rover or Whittle turbine people, who met the comment: 'Sir Henry would not have this' with a blank stare. I even went for a job interview with BEA and was rejected — not enough experience. I was told a bright future awaited me in the Dart Project team. However, the man who eventually got the job lost it in the 1971 crash.

Unfortunately the Dart was in the centre of a political crisis. The post-war committee on the future of civil aircraft, named after its chairman Lord Brabazon, identified the need for a 50-seat turbo-prop airliner for European routes. Two different prototypes had been built. From Vickers came the Viscount with four Darts. The Viscount was a typical Vickers aircraft, a delight to fly, strong, efficient and with the Vickers organization behind it. Armstrong Whitworth had the Apollo with Armstrong Siddeley Mambas. The Mamba had axial flow compressors, but axials were very expensive, and more difficult to make than the Dart's double-sided centrifugal compressor. But, when right, they were more efficient, and the complete engine had less frontal area. The Apollo was an orphan and had stability problems. The airlines, led by BEA, resented government committees telling them what aircraft they had to operate to make a profit, and asked for Mamba-powered Viscounts. This was a foul, and it caused an enormous furore. The Apollo group retired hurt, while Vickers got on with their Viscount, realizing they were on a winner whatever happened. The fight was between the Dart and the Mamba, or rather Rolls-Royce and Armstrong Siddeley. There was a general election in the offing, so the politicians were more than usually confused. I canvassed my knowledgeable friends for advice, which added to my confusion. I had bought the Aston Martin DB2 by hire purchase and had moved into a larger and more comfortable flat. I could now worry about my future, and financial commitments, in comfort and style.

About two weeks after my Easter conversations with Bira, I attended a meeting in Derby chaired by A.G. Elliott ('E'), then joint Managing Director with Lord Hives. The subject was the service life and reliability of a number of troublesome accessories. 'E' was a benign, silver-haired, courteous, typical senior Rolls-Royce engineer. He caught 'Knocker' West unawares with a barbed question, and while Knocker was spluttering and stuttering, one of his colleagues tried to rescue him saying 'What E means . . .,' which is as far as he got. 'E' sailed in and said: 'When I cannot express myself clearly, I shall retire. Until then hold your tongue.' I was still chuckling over this exchange, as I left the meeting, when I was waylaid by one of 'E's' personal staff, who said he would like to talk to me for a few minutes about motor racing. He asked if I did not think there was something peculiar about the BRM supercharger failures. I replied very cautiously that I had heard rumours. He told me that it had been agreed, in response to a request from BRM for more technical support, that Rolls-Royce would lend them an engineer for three or four months to help in any way possible, looking after Rolls-Royce interests at the same time. He would remain on the Rolls-Royce payroll, but BRM would pay for accommodation and out-of-pocket expenses. He went on to say my name had been mentioned as a possible candidate. I told him I would like to look at the BRM set-up before committing myself, which produced a frown, but was agreed. At Bourne I met Peter Berthon (who I liked), Raymond Mays (charming as ever) and, to my surprise, Bira. I was not shown the cars or workshops and was told they would consider whether I was suitable and so advise Mr Elliott, implying that they had profound influence with 'E'. Next day, back at Rolls-Royce, I was told I *was* suitable, and should start next week. I sold the DB2, emerging sadder, poorer and much wiser. I requested from 'E's' man a briefing on what to look for, how to behave and to whom to report. I was given a folder of reports and told they were strictly confidential. The answer to the last question was that I was to report to 'E's' man.

The contents of the folder shook me to the core. My first surprise was how long the project had been running, the second was the tremendous effort Rolls-Royce had put into it. The first report was dated 17 November 1945. The next, dated 2 September 1946, dealt with obtaining sufficient boost at low rpm for good acceleration, recognizing that, although a centrifugal was not ideal in this respect, it offered the best all-round possibilities. There was no established displacement supercharger that had anything like the efficiency at high pressures, or mechanical balance, freedom from wear and all round reliability. Various solutions were advanced and discussed in the report. It should be borne in mind that there was not as much experience of axial compressors then, as there is now. If a mechanically blown high-boost engine were designed today, it would probably have an axial.

A later report examined the various design cases. One was to apply vortex throttling at crankshaft speeds above 10,000 rpm, allowing the engine to go on to 12,000 rpm. Another was variable vortex vanes in the first stage entry, along the lines used by the German Junkers 213 aero-engine, which was rejected because, with the BRM design proportions, there would have been a slight loss of power proceeding from 10,000 to 12,000 rpm. The final recommendation was to use inter-stage vortex throttling, controlled by a boost regulator. This pushed the boost curve downwards by 2000 rpm, so that the boost at 7000 rpm would be what you would see at 9000 rpm with a simple blower. A supercharger along these lines was built and tested, performance data obtained and initial settings for the boost regulator determined, all by mid-1949.

I was greatly encouraged. All the gossip and pronouncements of the beer-mat engineers had been confounded. The centrifugal blower, properly thought out and planned, Rolls-Royce fashion, would be an advantage not a handicap. There was even a report dated 30 November 1950 on the Barcelona supercharger bearing failure, concluding that although the bearing used by BRM was of an unsuitable design, failure was because of an interruption of the oil supply. I have gone into some detail as I have always been intensely irritated by the condemnation of the use of a centrifugal blower by the so-called experts, particularly when all the data was published by Rolls-Royce in the form of Institution of Mechanical Engineers papers in the late 1950s.

So I set out for Bourne in the Austin Seven — after checking the number of spokes in its wheels — with high hopes, and feeling a little like Dick Whittington; not realizing that it was the end of my Rolls-Royce career.

# CHAPTER FOUR

# BRM beginnings — the V16

THE EARLY BRM 'snapshots' are a bit hazy and out of focus because of the combined effects of lack of sleep and excitement. The Austin Seven expired eight miles from Bourne and I eventually arrived in the local undertaker's 1920s taxi, to be received by Jim Sandercombe (Sandy), the Company Secretary. Sandy was an ex-captain in the Royal Signals and retained as much of army procedures and vocabulary as Willy Southcott did of the Merchant Marine. Sandy, on loan from Rubery Owen, was absolutely incorruptible, and ran a pre-war 2 litre AC. I was handed over to the Works Manager, Pete Brothers, who took me for lunch. He gave me a precis of the organization, followed by a fishing trip as to why Rolls-Royce had sent me. It was quite a shock when he told me there was already a Rolls-Royce fitter in residence updating superchargers. No-one had told me about him. Later, when I met him, I found no-one had told him about me either.

Bourne was a sleepy little market town of about 2400 inhabitants (in 1951), located on the edge of the fens and the southern edge of the Lincolnshire wolds. I was booked into the Nags Head pub, run by the Holcroft family, where I lived well for my first three months. There were some other BRM people staying at the pub, and some transient Rubery Owen people. The BRM works were in an old maltings on the Spalding road, half a mile from the town centre. Just before the maltings was a derelict gas works dominated by two gasometers, and an equally derelict coke house. Through the yard between the maltings and the gas works was the garage of Raymond Mays and Partners, who included the Prideaux Brunes (of Winter Garden Garage in London and the actual owners of ERA R4D driven by Raymond Mays), Anthony Crook (Flight Lieutenant T.A.D. Crook, later of Bristol Cars fame) and J.W.E. (Billy) Banks, a local farming JP, a great motoring enthusiast and later importer of Koni shock absorbers. Further through this yard on the left was the BRM test bed, and on the right was a single-storey workshop which housed ERA R4D and the Raymond Mays Special being built for hill climbs. This yard was the back way to Eastgate House, home of Raymond Mays and his mother.

Peter Berthon duly arrived. He lived in a caravan on the airfield at Folkingham, the home of the rare running cars and where they were tested. PB as he was known (Raymond Mays was RM) explained my duties — to help wherever needed. I was officially assigned to Birmingham-based Peter Haynes, the Lucas Competition Manager, who doubled up as BRM Team Manager when they actually went to races. He spent most of his time looking after Lucas racing interests. Peter Haynes had left me a 33-item list of problems encountered during the 1950 season, particularly during the trip to Barcelona. I was expected to have dealt with these before the first race of the season.

I was allocated a desk in a narrow hardboard hutch that traversed the upper floor of the maltings, which I shared with Pete Brothers and the Supply Manager, Clarence Brinkley, an old ERA mechanic with a fund of stories concerning the old days. 'Brink' as he was known, had a vocabulary all of his own. One of his expressions was 'letting his lal out', which meant talking too much and all of it rubbish. So he was also known as the 'lalograph'. He looked at my job list and snorted: 'You'll be lucky if you manage a quarter of that.' Pete Brothers then took me on a tour of the factory.

After a few days working from 8.30 a.m. to 5.30 p.m., I began to wonder when I was going to see some action. I sought an interview with PB to get something to do and some means to execute Peter Haynes' job list. Most of it concerned the racing equipment at Folkingham, which was out of bounds. Finding PB was not easy. He used to arrive just before lunch which he generally took with RM at Eastgate house. He reached his office at about 2.30 p.m. His secretary (nicknamed Katrina by Brink) sent for you when he was ready to see you. He agreed that I could go to Folkingham using the Austin Seven, with a mileage allowance. He said to make my visits useful by contacting Ken Richardson, in charge at Folkingham, before starting out. The ten-mile journey, which I came to know well, was up the A15 to Aslackby village; up a one-car wide lane for three miles, past Klingoe's Farm, through the old bomb dump and petrol depot, on to the airfield perimeter, part of BRM's test circuit, and round to the BRM compound surrounding the old control tower. This involved driving the wrong way round the circuit, so you needed to know when testing was in progress. In 1951 you were fairly safe! The runways were in good condition. The airfield, completed in 1944, was briefly occupied by 313 Troop Carrier Group of the 9th Division of the USAAF. Its finest hour was when elements of 2 Para emplaned for Arnhem on 17 September 1944. Soon after, the 313th moved to Europe, and the airfield fell into disuse.

I found Ken Richardson and one or two live mechanics ostentatiously doing nothing, but no racing cars. I crossed the perimeter track to a large nissen hut housing the Commer Q7 Avenger workshop lorry and two Austin Lodestar transporters, one for each racing car. My job list included conversion to cross-over fuel filling for each vehicle. 'Hammy' (Arthur Ambrose — Brink's gopher) explained that on the trip to Barcelona refuelling the three vehicle convoy every 350 miles (572 km) took 30 minutes. The vehicles had fuel tanks with separate fillers each side, and the manoeuvring to fill both tanks at a simple roadside filling station, in 1951, was quite incredible. It made much more sense to fill both tanks through one filler. The job list also included a shut-off valve, to cope with a leaking tank. Also on my list was the refuelling gear. F1 races were then 500 km (308 miles) in length. The Alfas did about 1.5 mpg (1.8 litres/km); the BRM, on a more exotic fuel, 2.5 mpg (1 litre/km). A BRM could carry 80 gallons, (350 litres) weighing 600 lb (275 kg) so pit stops to refuel plus tyre changes were inevitable. Most teams used two 50-gallon (225-litre) barrels joined together and pressurized with nitrogen for refuelling — but not BRM. There were snags with pressure refuelling. The most serious problem was anticipating when the tank was exactly full, because of the decreasing rate of flow as the barrels emptied and the nitrogen expanded. BRM had a Thompson aircraft-type refuelling pump, with a 180 gallons (800 litres) per minute rate of flow, powered by a 500cc side-valve Norton motor cycle engine. The Norton could not be started for the Barcelona pit stop, and both cars nearly ran out of fuel. Other jobs included making the winches work that were already installed in the transporters, so that two men could winch one ton of BRM up the ramp into the truck, instead of about ten pushing. The steel loading ramps also buckled very badly under load.

I asked Ken Richardson for help from some of his mechanics to get the work underway. He explained, first that he could not spare them and secondly, that I must not immobilize the transport in case it was suddenly required for a test session. I retired, baffled. No sympathy from Brink, and I could not find PB, so I put the problem to RM who saw things the same way as Ken. He told me to hire a transport mechanic, to look after the vehicles and then said: 'But what about Ambrose? He is doing nothing.' Brinkley went out through the roof and said Hammy was most definitely not available and, more sensibly, although Hammy was very willing, he was not a fitter. I then went to Sandy, who said we could not afford any more staff, and in any case additional staff must be authorized by PB. I cheated and serviced the refuelling gear Norton myself, getting it to start first time, every time. I did a gopher deal with Brink for a van and took the outfit to Thompsons the makers, who serviced the pump and fitted it with a clever centrifugal clutch so we could warm the Norton up without pumping any fuel. They also showed me how the balanced nozzle worked. There was quite some energy locked in a flow of 22.5 lb (10 kg) per second in terms of reaction at the nozzle, and there was a distinct possibility of blowing the bottom out of the fuel tank.

I then went to see what a fuel tank looked like, where the sheet metal workers had their own little shed in the compound. They were all from a Rubery Owen subsidiary, Motor Panels at Coventry, controlled by a 16 stone (100 kg) ex-actor called Stan Hope. They only made fuel tanks, as the body panels were made by the Gray Brothers of Emsworth, who had made all the ERA bodies. Stan assured me that his fuel tanks could stand anything I could do to them, which was at least a new approach. I had a good look at them, and promptly fell foul of Stan by describing them as a stack of biscuit tins. They were made of tinned 0.02 inch (0.5 mm) steel sheet with many baffles soldered together. I debated whether a 25-second refill was necessary as 1951 race regulations generally restricted the number of people working on the car at a pit stop to three. The tyre change would take much longer. I had no chance of measuring how long it took us to change tyres — no car! I looked up race reports for times of other teams' pit stops, none of them helped. I decided finally I could get away with a slower rate.

I planned to put a predetermined amount into the tank by timing the refuelling, but when I described my plan to PB, he said I was stupid. If we cut off the fuel one second too soon we would be four gallons short — so we should fill to the brim every time. I argued we would need Mercedes-style windows in the tank so that the refueller could see when it was getting nearly full, otherwise we would have four or five gallons all over the hot exhaust pipes (Seaman and the 1938 German GP all over again). So, deadlock. I did not worry too much over this. We were a long way from a running car, far less a pit stop in anger!

I was able to get some of the smaller jobs done, including preventing en-route tyre damage. Tyres were carried six a side in racks down the sides of the transporters, but on the road the tyres shuffled about, chafing their side walls. Three were lost during the 2000 miles (3225 km) to and from Barcelona. I collected old inner tubes, slit them around their inner circumference and slipped them over the tyre assemblies.

I renewed my acquaintance of 'Tres'. Stewart Stuart Tresilian was a brilliant engineer, and had been a young but vital member of the 1931 Rolls-Royce Schneider Trophy team. He had led a car engine design team in the period of anarchy following Sir Henry Royce's death in 1933 and before 'Hs' took control in 1936. He had joined us on some of the Harker special outings. Then he vanished, apparently following a row with 'Hs'. Tres became a consultant and came into the BRM orbit. He had a very uneasy relationship with PB, who recognized both Tres's considerable ability and the shortness of his temper. Tres was supposed to be helping with design issues, but there was not much designing going on. Everyone was trying to make what we already had work.

Tres did not believe the explanation for the recent massive engine failures — that the spark jumped from one plug lead to another, firing the cylinder at the wrong point in the cycle and causing total destruction. The high cylinder pressures, because of the high boost pressure, did indeed call for high voltages to spark the plug. However, it did not make sense to Tres, who reasoned that if the cylinder liner was strong enough to stand the peak working pressure, it was more than strong enough to stand firing at some other point in the cycle where the pressure was bound to be lower. Calculation and stressing was Tres's forte. He recalled my defect investigation experience and asked me what I thought. I told him I had not seen an engine run, neither had I seen a failed engine, so I could not challenge the argument.

Eventually I managed to get sight of the Race Programme. Our first race was the Swiss GP, unusually early in 1951 as there was no race at Monaco. The French GP at Reims on 1 July came next, followed by the British GP on 14 July. Then a big gap before the Italian GP at Monza early in September, and finally the Spanish GP at Barcelona in October. We were already into May and had not even completed our first car. It was clear to me that our first race might be the French GP, but more likely the British. We had a seconded Rubery Owen production man, Cliff Mander, who kept complaining about lack of planning, production schedules and priority lists. Whenever he asked what was needed first, he was always told 'everything'. It was too much for Pete Brothers, who resigned, so Cliff Mander became Works Manager, working from Monday to Friday.

The first car was sent to Folkingham for Ken Richardson's racing mechanics to complete. The second car took its place in the Bourne workshop. Jack North's build team were working until 10 p.m. from

Monday to Saturday, and to 5 p.m. on Sunday. This was an 83-hour working week. With premium overtime, double-time on Sunday, time-and-a-half on Saturday etc. BRM were paying for 107 hours per week. The staff were so tired they were walking zombies, and it is very doubtful if they actually did more than 50 hours of useful work per week. This is absolutely no reflection on the work people; they were very willing, and most of them extremely competent, but they had reached their physical limits. They were so exhausted it is small wonder they made mistakes.

Nothing could be done without PB's sanction. Any problem had to wait until he appeared and approved the solution. If this was first thing in the morning everyone had to wait until he appeared at noon, if we were lucky. If not, then it was 2.30 p.m. There were 10 or 12 people milling around the car waiting their turn to get to attach their particular piece. I mildly suggested a night shift to Jack North, who said he had already suggested it to PB who had ruled there were not enough staff to make it effective. I also suggested some of the decision making should be delegated to Tres and possibly to me, to save time. I got a right ear bashing from PB, plus a lengthy review of my lack of real racing experience and how any simple mistake could kill someone.

Ken Richardson and Brink had a special relationship dating back to their ERA days. Ken was known to Brink as 'Tinker'. He was busy at Folkingham pulling the first car to pieces to put right all the stupidities of the Bourne build team. I was kept busy ferrying parts to and from Folkingham; all urgently needed to complete the car and to replace those Ken rejected as unsuitable. I noticed that he had an even more special relationship with RM and that PB rarely interfered with him. Tinker was a real artist at welding. I had learned at Rolls-Royce that the most elegant looking welds were often not the strongest, but Ken's welds were both elegant and effective. The effects of Ken's rejection or modifications on his production disciplines drove Cliff Mander absolutely hairless. His schedules were in total ruin. Parts planned for the third engine and second car were being used on the first. He confronted PB who said: 'Motor racing is always like this, you must build more contingency into your plans.'

I had been at BRM two months and had yet to see an engine run. I, too, was like a zombie, spending 120 hours a week either at Bourne, Folkingham or on the road. A typical day for me started at 6 a.m. to drive R4D's old Dodge truck for overhaul by Parr's of Leicester, Bob Gerard's firm. Then by train to Birmingham to collect from Austin, at Longbridge, the third transporter which, unlike the other two, had an electric shift for its two-speed rear axle. Then to Standard at Coventry for a machined crankcase. It was 2 a.m. next day when I arrived back in Bourne.

The sheet metal teams were now working a night shift at Folkingham, as the fitters could not get at the car while the 'tin bashers' were wrapping it in aluminium.

Eventually we started testing the first car, driven alternately by Tinker and RM. The glorious sound of the 16-cylinder engine acted like a tonic on all of us. When Bira tried it the front gearbox mounting failed, causing a minor oil fire. Bira decided that the V16 was not for him and resigned, telling me to do likewise while I was still sane. It was too late, however, I had the bug. I admired the quick and effective fix PB produced. The car was running again within 36 hours. Familiar as I was with Cameron Earle's

report, I observed that the gearbox was a 'Chinese' copy of the 1.5 litre
Mercedes. On the rare occasions the V16 performed it produced more than
double the Mercedes torque, which had to be transmitted by the gearbox,
and which was only preserved by the dreadfully inadequate traction.

A test session was planned at Silverstone, with Tinker and Peter Walker
to drive. Lorna Berthon, PB's wife, had me victualing the mobile workshop.
The shopping list was incredible: whisky, Bovril, soup, bread, ham, pork
pies, etc. Sandy nearly fainted when he saw the bill. At Silverstone I was
given a massive Heuer stop watch and appointed official team timekeeper.
Alfa's best time in 1950, on the pre-chicane circuit was 1 min 48 sec.
Tinker got down to 1 min 50 sec, when the engine gave up — nothing
major. Walker never had a run. We returned a few days later with Reg
Parnell, but it did not take him long to put a rod through the side.

The second car was sent to Folkingham to be built alongside the first one.
The racing mechanics and the build team were divided into two shifts,
which made sense and life a little easier for everyone except me. I now had
two shifts to cover. The French GP passed, unremarked.

One afternoon Tres invited me into PB's office to view Parnell's
Silverstone failure. There was little evidence of seizure, but one of the
broken connecting rods had the characteristic twist of hydraulicing,
generally a consequence of water in the cylinder. Tres offered me the
cylinder-head joint ring. There it was, the characteristic signs of a blowing
Merlin top joint ring. The engine had four separate cylinder heads, each
head pulled down on four soft aluminium joint rings. Tolerances were wide,
and it was possible for one ring not to be adequately compressed, and in any
case the material was unsuitable. We changed to Merlin mod 155 high
copper content material, tightened up tolerances, lapped all the rings against
plate glass, to exactly the same thickness and rebuilt all three serviceable
engines to this standard.

We were testing the first rebuilt engine at Folkingham on the Sunday
before the British GP, when a visit from Mr Elliott of Rolls-Royce and a
cam and rocker failure coincided. The pressure reducing valve, which
controlled oil flow to the camshafts and supercharger, had been incorrectly
adjusted. I volunteered, with Tinker, to remove the supercharger for
examination in case it had also suffered from lack of oil, while the long-
suffering mechanics got some rest. While removing the blower I discovered
the evidence I had been sent to find — it shone out like a neon sign. Tucked
away in a recess was a small needle oil flow control valve, with a 'clicker'
control mechanism. This explained the whispered 'five-eights' instruction
PB would sometimes give to the engine fitters. It meant the setting of this
valve, which made a serious reduction in the flow of oil to the supercharger
bearings. This also explained all the supercharger problems, and confirmed
'Oscar' Wilde's failure analysis. RM had taken Mr Elliott to dinner. Livid, I
confronted PB with the evidence. He tried to brazen it out, but to no avail.
Finally we agreed that next time the engine ran the clicker valve would be
set wide open, and we would both check the plugs and the induction system
for oil leaking from the blower seals. No. 2 car ran first. There was no trace
of oil on the plugs or in the induction system, although the flame traps were
slightly oily. Willy and I calibrated one of the clicker valves and found that
the flow at 1.25 turns open was equal to the flow through all the jets in the
blower. I agreed with PB to retain the clicker valve, but set to 1.5 turns open

until the racing crisis was past or a new system devised. I did not tell the 'voice' at Rolls-Royce that I had done the job I had been sent to do.

The spare engine holed a piston on the test bed, so even the British GP began to look doubtful, and certainly practice was out of the question. I managed a practice pit stop on the Friday evening before the race — refuelling and a tyre change. The front tank air-locked during the refill. The two tanks were joined low down by two 3 inch (76.2 mm) diameter pipes. When we filled the 25-gallon (111.25-litre) rear tank, fuel flowed into the front 52-gallon (231-litre) front tank. Air trapped in the top of the front tank was supposed to escape through two smaller pipes which ran in a 'U' bend round the side of the cockpit and up to the rear tank filler. These pipes had gradually filled with fuel under acceleration and deceleration and air-locked the front tank. All we could do in the time available was to fit a tap to drain the 'U' pipes into the main balance pipes. The driver was told that when he got the 'come in for fuel' signal he was to open the tap, draining the 'U' pipe into the bottom pipe. The system then would be nearly empty, so this should solve the problem. There was no time to prove this by testing.

Lorna Berthon kept up a steady flow of bacon and eggs; sleep was snatched on camp beds in the control tower; and by midnight on Friday 13th, with the race 14 hours away, it began to look as if we might just make it. Then the workshop lights failed. The circuits were so overloaded that the main fuse in the village had blown! Two rabid BRM Supporters' Club members, Evans and Cutler from Totnes, drove all the cars they could find into the workshop, and ran the transporters up to the windows, so we could finish the cars by the light of their headlamps. At dawn we set off for Silverstone, with only the drivers of the transporters — who I suspect were Evans and Cutler — being awake. At Silverstone we did our race preparation — 70 gallons (311 litres) of fuel, with plans to stop on lap 43, when we would add 60 gallons (267 litres). PB told the drivers, Reg Parnell and Peter Walker, not to exceed 10,500 rpm instead of the usual limit of 12,000 rpm.

We all changed into clean white overalls and somehow managed to get the cars to the back of the starting grid. They got away satisfactorily. First time around both drivers gave us a cheery wave. Only 89 more laps to go. I pushed the thought to the back of my mind that we had never ever managed more than 100 miles without a failure; neither had we ever run on full tanks. Despite the limited rpm, they gradually picked off the old ERAs and Maseratis, so by lap 30 they were 8th and 10th with Tony Vandervell's Thinwall Ferrari sandwiched between them. Alfa Romeo started their pit stops, both our cars sounded and looked good, although I was worried because the drivers' heads seemed to be nodding, and they were slow to acknowledge pit signals. PB suggested an earlier pit stop to see what was the matter. The Norton started first time. Dunlop Mac and Don Badger of Dunlops stood by to check the tyres to see if we needed to change. I showed Parnell our green flag with a white St Andrew's cross. He came in, and got out (which was not planned) complaining: 'It is burning me.' 'Never mind,' said PB, 'get back in and get on with it.' Tinker refuelled. Dunlop Mac waved the tyre crew away. The stop took 25 seconds which made me think that we could not have completely filled the tanks. We had Peter Walker in two laps later, and his stop was even quicker. We did not let him get out. He, too, said his legs were burning. We found we had only added 25 gallons (111 litres) to each car. The drivers must have forgotten to open the drain valves, and so we would have to stop again. The Thinwall had had a three minute pit stop because of brake trouble; Sanesi had a rear wheel jam on his Alfa causing a very long stop. This moved Parnell up one place, and Peter Walker two.

We prepared large pads of cotton wool saturated in aquaflavene burn dressing and brought them in again. I opened the fuel drain valve and wrapped the drivers' legs with the cotton wool. We managed a 35-gallon fill (156 litres) in 18 seconds for both cars. Further down the pit road Ascari was getting out of his car (having blown up) amid speculation that he would take over from Gonzales, but this was prohibited by the local race regulations. Farina went missing with only 15 laps to go. We urged Parnell to speed up, but he was in too much pain to do anything but finish, although he managed to stay ahead of Sanesi. We eventually finished 5th and 7th.

Our pit was mobbed after the race. It was one which made history, because it was the first time Ferrari had broken Alfa Romeo's stranglehold. Gonzales had beaten Fangio in a straight fight. Denis Jenkinson pointed out in *Motor Sport* that Parnell's average speed of 90.5 mph (146 kph) would have very nearly won the 1950 GP, when the winner's average speed was 90.95 mph (146.7 kph). PB and RM took the drivers for medical attention whilst I went through the post-race check routine, fuel, oil, coolant, tyres, and so on. We drained and cleaned the magnesium alloy carburettors which would otherwise corrode from the action of the alcohol fuel. We went to our hotel in Brackley where we had two or three drinks — paid for by Stirling Moss.

After 12 hours blissful sleep we drove slowly back to Folkingham, unloaded and dispersed to the Bourne pubs. It could not have felt better if we had won. We had nearly got amongst the Italians. But it was only seven weeks to Monza and the euphoria soon evaporated. PB tore a terrible strip off me for cleaning the carburettors. Apparently both drivers had reported that as the race progressed their engines began to hesitate out of corners and would not accelerate cleanly. He suspected that road and tyre dust was getting into the low-mounted carburettors, and now I had destroyed the evidence. Willy and Dave Turner, who stripped the carburettors said they were quite clean. This did not help, and it was over a year before I found the real reason.

# CHAPTER FIVE

# The struggle continues

I HAD THEN been with BRM three months, so I checked with the 'voice' at Rolls-Royce, who said: 'With both cars finished we assume you have sorted out the blower problems.' I gave a guarded reply, and was told to check again in a month. 'That will be right in the middle of preparations for Monza,' I replied. The 'voice' said: 'Wait two months, nothing has been decided yet.'

We did not get much done during the remainder of July — we were too busy shaking hands with ourselves. When we did start running we had misfires at over 10,500 rpm on the test bed, and in the car, which could neither be explained nor cured. I began to get some idea of the various BRM political problems. I knew we were always short of money, and inflation was taking its toll of the various support agreements. £1000 pledged in 1949 was only buying £750 worth of work in 1951. Budgets were not PB's or RM's strong point. No one else in the BRM Trust had any idea of the sort of expenses that could crop up, although Sandy was learning fast. I do not think the top management at Rolls-Royce had many illusions. I had heard comments, attributed to 'Hs', such as 'It's our name on the blower' and 'gilded popinjays'. I moved from The Nags Head to the greater comfort of The Angel, run by a young ex-naval couple — Eric Oatts had been a minesweeper commander and his wife Jean a formidable WREN officer. It was their first Trust House posting as manager and manageress. Tres and I had a very comfortable lifestyle when I had the time to enjoy it.

We came to our next crisis. Peter Haynes, the official Team Manager, advised he could not go to Monza. One of his twin children was dreadfully ill and eventually died of meningitis. PB said I was not suitable to take his place as I was too soft with the men. I had always subconsciously adopted the Rolls-Royce style of leading rather than driving, assuming everyone else in the team was the best in the business and wanted to win as much as I did. There were some who did become the best in the business, and I have never quite understood how a sleepy little market town like Bourne managed to produce such an array of talent. However, PB said he was not happy and would not give me the job. To make matters worse, the mechanics complained that at Barcelona they had no Spanish money and had to ask even for a stamp for a postcard home. The official counter-argument was that there were strict currency regulations which could not be broken. But the private version was that they could not be trusted with money as they might waste it on strong drink and women. I negotiated with Sandy a 10s- (50p) a-day laundry allowance, to be deducted from their pay on their return home. It later turned out that Sandy had not confirmed this with PB or RM or, if he had they had denied it, which is more likely. Just before we were due to leave, PB decided that I would be in charge on the way to Monza. On arrival, control of the mechanics would revert to Tinker, who was to drive at Monza in place of Peter Walker. Once the flag fell I would be Pit Manager as at Silverstone. Tinker would travel out with RM in his new Ford Zephyr Six.

Sandy produced a very military movement order, setting out the timetable. It all worked until our Dover-Dunkirk train ferry had to return. The lock gates had jammed and we could not get into our berth. We disembarked in Dover at 8.30 a.m., at which time we should have been about 100 miles (160 km) into France. The mechanics went to a hotel to sleep, while arrangements were made for us to travel on the 5 p.m. Townsend ferry to Calais. This was a converted World War II frigate onto which vehicles were lifted by crane, so I had to take the workshop lorry to find out whether the crane could manage its ten tons. I was to pick up French money left for us by RM at the Lion d'Or hotel in Reims. After some heart-stopping moments with the crane overload indicator twittering with the weight of the workshop we got aboard. We had bacon and egg on the ferry. The Townsend people looked after us incredibly well and forged a lasting relationship with BRM. RM had alerted the French Customs who waved us through without looking at the paperwork, which was a mistake.

There were no autoroutes in those days, and the road was not very good. The 172 miles (270 km) to Reims (where I duly collected the money) took five hours. We had the next bacon-and-egg stop at Gray near Besançon and reached the Franco-Swiss frontier at Vallorbe by 5 p.m., where trouble awaited us. As none of the carnets had been actioned by the French Customs at Calais, we were told to go back and get it done before we could leave France. I argued that as we were not legally there they could not stop us leaving! After some more argument they decided we were too much trouble and let us go. The Swiss were not even interested: they just sealed the vehicles. We reached Lausanne about 7 p.m. — a day late.

Next morning we had a very pleasant drive up the Rhône valley to the Simplon pass. The Austins began to boil, dragging along behind the slower workshop, so I sent them on ahead. But the real trouble began on the descent when there was a strange smell of burning brown paper in the workshop's cab, and we soon found we had run out of brakes. The workshop did not have enough lock to get round some corners in one swing. The Italian Customs were very friendly, but said we were wasting our time trying to beat the Alfa Romeo and Ferrari, and stamped everything about ten times.

Late in the evening we reached Monza where we got lost. Finally we saw a sign marked Autodromo di Monza. I asked a yokel in my best Italian for the Albergo Marchesi, and got a real Brummy mouthful. I had accosted Ray Woods of Lucas! We unpacked in the garage at the back of the hotel, little realizing we were going to be there for three months. We also had two lock-ups in the paddock.

All went well at first in practice. It was stinking hot. The Alfas were down to 1 min 52 sec, Ken had just broken 2 min and Reg was down to 1 min 57 sec. Not for the last time at Monza we had the wrong axle ratio. Everyone assumes Monza is very fast, but it just is not as fast as it looks. Changing gear ratios was an overnight job. Then Ken Richardson went off at the second of the Lesmo corners damaging the front of the car. We had a spare radiator and front suspension assembly, but no spare steering arm, a beautiful cast steel 'H-section' piece, with lightening holes everywhere. Count 'Johnny' Lurani arranged for Alfa Romeo at Portello to straighten and, more important, crack test it. Guided by an Alfa mechanic, I went in one of the transporters, where they did a very quick and efficient job. There was also concern as Reg's engine had developed a high-speed misfire. Peter Knight from SU, who eventually became their Chief Engineer, diagnosed carburettor flooding due to vibration. We rubber-mounted the float chambers on the chassis, which meant making pieces on the workshop's lathe. Cyril Bryden our machinist was also the gearbox fitter, and was busy changing ratios, so I worked the lathe. In second practice both cars were about two seconds a lap quicker, mainly due to the drivers learning the circuit.

I have never believed that fine-tuning gear ratios makes much difference to lap times, although correct gear ratios do make the driver's job much easier. The misfire was now affecting both cars and getting worse. PB blamed the Italian-brewed Esso fuel. Parnell's engine then blew up in a big way. It looked like a bearing seizure, not the old liner problem. We would have to fit the untested spare. I never found out why the engine failed. It was rebuilt while PB, Tres and I were all out at Monza. RM took Ken Richardson for a proper night's sleep before his race, while PB stayed with us preparing the cars. I became embroiled in a discussion with Peter Knight and Ray Woods as to whether it would not have been better to keep the higher axle ratio. The engine gave over 500 hp at 10,500 rpm where the misfire set in, and using a higher ratio might have kept us out of trouble. RM arrived looking very worried, as apparently the RAC had refused to confirm Ken's permit to drive. Ken was not on the FIA list of approved drivers, but had temporary clearance subject to observation and a favourable report. I never knew all the details, and I was more concerned with the cars than with drivers. In the middle of the night, Hans von Stuck, a pre-war Auto Union driver also staying at the Marchesi, appeared and was fitted into Ken's nearly complete car. The race organizers had agreed to him driving, provided he did five observed laps before 8 a.m. We had both cars out at first light, Ken running in the new engine for Reg and Stuck in Ken's car. Within a few laps, both had stopped. Reg's car with a seized engine and Stuck's with transmission failure. In the Monza paddock lock-up we started to take the good gearbox from Reg's car to put into Stuck's car for Reg to drive. PB and RM disappeared to talk to Bacciagaluppi, the Clerk of the Course. PB reappeared at 11 a.m., when the change was nearly complete, and announced: 'You can stop work, both cars have been withdrawn.' We all ignored him. He then took me to one side and said he suspected the gearbox had seized because of the prolonged high speed running, as Monza was much faster than any circuit we had run on before. He feared the second box would do the same thing, locking the wheels, and possibly leading to a high speed spin. Not only might the driver get hurt, but the car might go off the road into the crowd. It made a little sense, so I persuaded the exhausted mechanics to stop work. They went off to the Ferodo van, where they could be sure of a decent cup of English tea.

An announcement was made over the PA system that the BRMs had withdrawn. There were boos and cat calls, and the Tifosi on the other side of the wire fence jeered and started to throw stones. I told the mechanics to take off their overalls, but they could stop to watch the race if they wished or go back to the pub and bed.

I was then ambushed by Mr Vandervell who wanted to know what had really happened. He had obviously had Ken Richardson's version, which was different from the Press release. Ken, understandably, was very bitter and upset. Mr Vandervell was in a flaming temper. As a member of the BRM Trust he was entitled to know what was happening and to have been consulted by PB or RM before decisions and Press releases were made — so he told me. He was all the more enraged because RM had told journalists that Parnell's withdrawal was due to bearing failure, and they were Vandervell bearings. I told him the gearbox story, the risk to the driver and spectators. He was no fool, and he accused me of covering something up. He said: 'I thought you were the Rolls-Royce whiz kid and dead straight.' I assured him that I had only told him the truth. I was glad to escape and watch the very exciting race.

Afterwards we went back to the pub — in 1951 it took an hour, now it takes five — and sat in gloomy silence at our long table at the end of the dining room. Our party included Ray Woods, Peter Knight, and the Dunlop tyre fitters. Reg Parnell appeared and said to cheer up. As far as he was concerned we had done everything humanly possible to get him to the starting line. He would have taken his chances with the gearbox. He knew there was a risk and would have been watching for it. He then placed two enormous bottles of Chianti on the table and said to have a good night. There was a terrific row when RM found out Reg had put them on the BRM bill!

In the morning we opened up Stuck's gearbox and found the plain bronze bearing in second gear had seized on the shaft. The gears ran freely on the input shaft in bronze bushes; the selector mechanism moved a face dog into engagement with the gear and locked it to the shaft, all the others were still running freely. If one of the free-running gears seized you had two gears at once, the box locked solid, the back wheels stopped turning and you would spin. PB was right. When we looked at Parnell's engine the filters were full of lead bronze and there was a nasty bulge on the side of the crankcase indicating big end or connecting rod failure. The gauze inlet filter in the oil tank was completely blocked with a mixture of jointing compound, sludge and bearing debris. It could not have been cleaned out following several previous engine failures. It was, as RM said, a bearing failure; but any bearing that does not get enough oil will fail. This one was down to us, the mechanics; we did not have a routine engine change drill. Someone just removed the oil tank and wiped the outside; another person might pick it up to replace it and if he saw that the outside of the tank was clean, he assumed that the internal filter had also been removed and cleaned.

After lunch PB and RM appeared, we were to keep all serviceable material and build all the unserviceable material into Ken's car and send it, with some of the mechanics, back to England. Ken would resume his duties as Chief Mechanic, and the rest of us were to stay at Monza to try to resolve some of our problems. The Lucas and SU people were asked to stay as the priority one problem was the misfire above 10,500 rpm. The Lucas representative in Italy, an English resistance hero from Modena known as the Mad Major, also appeared and was very helpful throughout our stay.

Before we settled into the routine the mechanics told me they were not satisfied. They recognized it was their job to work all hours to get the cars to the starting line for a race, but they were not going to work these hours on a testing trip. And, where was the allowance negotiated with Sandy? Ken kept out of it all. I took the problems to PB, and once again we went all through the business of my being too soft with the mechanics. However, he agreed the working day would be 8 a.m. to 7 p.m. with an hour for lunch, unless at the circuit. We would work Saturdays and Sundays if needed. We would also get a bottle of beer or 0.25 litre of wine with meals, and 10s (50p) per day in local currency, not to be deducted from our pay.

Peter Knight of SU did not believe that an engine running on 70 per cent methanol could be as sensitive to mixture strength as this one appeared to be. PB would not tell him what the actual fuel mix was, but he did admit to it being 70 per cent methanol. Peter Knight believed that the carburettors were flooding, and he was bothered that the float chambers were so far off the centre line and therefore affected by cornering loads. He argued that as they were 4 inches (102 mm) offset, this was highly probable. We managed to rearrange them with their offtakes on the centre line to minimize this. Peter also insisted that we set the float levels under fuel pressure. We were running at 4 psi (0.3 bar). As the story unfolds it will be seen that it was all a waste of time, but just at that particular moment passions were running high, with several different theories as to why we were dogged by this apparently incurable misfire which had been with us for months.

One morning we had just reached the pressurized float level setting stage when both Peter Knight and I were called away. PB, still in Milan, wanted to know when we would be ready to run. Taruffi and Chiron were coming to drive the car. When I returned to the workshop I found that Ken, who had not been privy to all these discussions on float levels, had instructed the mechanics to revert to the old system of setting with a depth gauge and not to mess about with pressure bottles and Peter Knight's stupid ideas. I asked him to come and talk to me outside as I did not want to have an argument with him in front of the mechanics. He then went back into the hotel and sat drinking coffee where PB found him when he arrived. PB asked why I had thrown Ken out. I explained that I had not, and merely wanted to avoid having a row in the workshop. We were in enough trouble without the mechanics realizing we did not know what on earth we were doing. PB made no comment, and just asked if we would still be ready to run in the afternoon. I said that we would be. Ken drove for five laps, still misfiring. Taruffi arrived, and he showed me how to break the track up into sections. I have included among the illustrations my original chart from that afternoon of 19 September 1951 to show how it was done. These days this timing service is provided for every car, every lap during a race, practice or test session — life is so much easier now.

After his run Taruffi said we lost out badly at Lesmo, and Vedano, even more through the fast curves. We picked up a little, not much, in speed on the straights. I suggested to PB that we should go back to the higher axle ratio so we could tackle some of our other problems, and he agreed. We saw nothing of PB and Ken the next day, and Peter Knight and Ray Woods had gone back to England. We spent the day on carburettor levels and changing gear ratios.

The following morning, at the circuit, we had followed the usual practice of hitching the car up to the transporter on a tow rope, to start from cold. When PB arrived he was alone. He looked straight at me and said: 'Ready?' I said: 'Yes'. He said: 'Get in and warm it up, wait until it shows oil pressure before you switch on.' I had no problems, and was particularly struck by the complete absence of vibration.

After it was warm PB put a cap on back to front, in best Etancelin style and did five laps. Taruffi arrived and did about 20 laps. PB said: 'Pack up and ride back to the pub with me.' He told me Ken had gone back to England. We had to cut down on the number of people, hotels were costing a fortune. He was going to move in with us and wanted me to select the people I could spare and send them back to England by train. The following morning an incredibly tall Italian, Inginere Bei, from the Ruggeri organization arrived. Ruggeri was a consultant specializing in supercharging. He was involved with a highly-boosted San Remo Maserati alleged to give 300 hp. Knowing how fragile they were at 240 hp, I could not see any value in this. The Alfas were reputed to be giving 430 hp and Ferrari 380. At least it established the Ruggeri outfit as fuel specialists and Bei, who spoke a little broken English, told me he was going to show me the way to an Italian fuel brewing company called Martelli and Zampatori who would provide a special fuel which would cure the misfire. I took some barrels, Willy and a transporter. Guided by Bei, we sortied into Milan. Because of the language problem we got lost three times in south-west Milan. Bei suddenly pointed to a tram and said follow the 'treno'. We nearly lost it as its tracks took it down a central tree-lined strip with the main road on either side. Having absolutely no intention of getting lost again, we followed the tram down its tracks. It was all very bumpy, the extremely tall Bei banging his head on the roof many times. While he was muttering and holding his head, we stuck to the tram like glue. Eventually we came to a major intersection controlled by several whistle-blowing policemen. After the initial shocked silence as the tram rattled by closely followed by the black and silver transporter, they went berserk blowing themselves inside out with their whistles and throwing their hats on the road. Eventually we reached Martelli and Zampatori. Our barrels were taken away, and after about two hours they were brought back with all sorts of chalked hieroglyphics on them. We prepared to return to the Marchesi. Bei, clutching his head, muttered taxi and disappeared. Surprisingly no one asked us for money. After a short excursion on the Turin autostrada — in the wrong direction — we found our way back to the hotel.

PB was not pleased when he found I had no idea what was in the barrels, saying he sent me because he thought I would keep my wits about me. However, I got the hotel owner to telephone Mr Zampatori to ask what was in the fuel. After deciphering the Italian phonetic spelling of the exotic ingredients, there was half a per cent of this, half a per cent of that, and 85 per cent methanol. I asked PB whether we would have to reset the carburettors as we now had more methanol. He just rolled his eyes and said 'yes'. He finally told me the fuel mix so that I could work out by how much we should richen the mixture. 70 per cent methanol, 18 per cent alkylate iso-pentane, 8 per cent acetone, 0.3 per cent halewax oil, 0.7 per cent water and 3 per cent benzol. Next day PB took the car out, and if anything the misfiring was reduced. Misfire was really misleading terminology. Some people called it 'woofling' others 'burbling'. We went back to the Marchesi to scratch our heads.

Most of us had planned to be away for ten days, we were now into our fourth week. Cyril Bryden had worn great holes in his only pair of shoes, Gordon Newman had split his best shirt and the laundry had lost another, so Lorna hosted a shopping expedition into Monza.

The next event was the arrival of Hammy with an engine and a host of spares in the Standard Vanguard van plus many English newspapers and magazines. We learned that there had been an upheaval within the BRM Trust. Mr Vandervell had resigned and there had been some pretty savage attacks on BRM generally, particularly on Mays and Berthon. I rang the 'voice' at Rolls-Royce, who said: 'You are doing a good job. Call me when you get back to England. There have been no major changes here.' Stirling Moss then arrived, he was in his first year with HWM and was much better known and respected in Italy than in England. He soon got used to the car and drove it very quickly in damp foggy conditions, getting within two seconds of Farina's pole position time. It was some years before I saw his famous 93-item job list, although he told me of most of the problems. He also complained of a cramped driving position. He liked to lean well back with arms straight out, as did Farina. It is now the universal driving position, but was unusual then. He said the engine had plenty of power, but you just could not use it. Stirling had to go to a race somewhere, and PB went back to England for a BRM Trust meeting, leaving me with instructions to remove the engine and gearbox in the car and replace them with the engine and new gearbox, with needle roller bearings in the driving gears, that Hammy had brought from England.

After we had done this I remembered that during the war *The Autocar* ran a series of articles by Freddie Dixon on how he got such incredible performance from his unblown Rileys. One of his tests stuck in my mind. He jammed two blocks of wood between the front wheel rims and the chassis and then turned the steering wheel to see just how much the front axle moved sideways on the leaf springs. I did the same thing on the V16 and was astonished — I could turn the steering wheel a quarter of a turn: 90 degrees! Everything flexed — the maligned worm and nut steering box mounted on a beautiful aluminium tower on the front cross member, weaved and twisted about 0.25 in (6 mm). We made some steel tube stabilizing struts which reduced the deflection to 0.025 in (0.6 mm). The steering arms flexed; the beautiful universal joints, machined all over, that threaded the steering column over the engine and around the blower — all of them had far too much clearance and made the steering feel lumpy.

After two days hard work we had reduced the 90 degrees to 10 degrees; still far too much, but all we could do with the facilities at Monza. We practised refuelling, with a float-operated air vent in the top of the front tank. It worked well, and we managed 65 gallons (290 litres) in 25 seconds. However, we had spilt several gallons of fuel over the garage floor. When Cyril Bryden walked through it in his beautiful new shoes, the fuel glued the soles to the concrete and dissolved the joint to the uppers, so we had barefoot Cyril again.

PB and Stirling returned at the same time, but Stirling did not think much of the steering improvements. The new engine overheated, which was cured by changing the radiator. The roller bearing gearbox did not seem to make any difference. There was no significant gain in lap times. We still had the burble, so it was back to Martelli and Zampatori for two different Ruggeri brews, one containing ethanol, but the engine did not like this at all, and we went through a piston in zero time.

Willy rose to the occasion, took the blower off, opening up the front of the engine, and replaced the piston without removing the engine. He saved the valve timing by marking matching gear teeth with blue. This cost us two days and more of Stirling's enthusiasm. He told me the main and biggest big problem was that the front end was completely unpredictable. Going through a corner such as Lesmo the car would gradually develop understeer which he could live with, then suddenly lose all front grip. The front of the car would step sideways and the whole process of building up a gradually increasing amount of understeer would start again. The car could be in balance, then something, not always a bump, would unbalance it, and the whole cycle of building up grip had to start all over again. The trouble with this was that you could not hold a line and, of course, you could not race close to other cars. Stirling believed the cure was rack and pinion steering, but I could not understand this. He said that any racing car worthy of the name had rack and pinion steering. 'What about Ferrari and Alfa Romeo?' I asked. I thought about his straight-arm driving position, but there was nothing we could do at Monza. It meant cutting into the fuel tank — a major operation involving steaming out the fuel residue.

Ten years later, with all the resources of Rubery Owen, I carried out some tests. I found that with a near vertical steering column, and the driver sitting over it, he could exert the maximum amount of torque to turn the steering wheel. With a near horizontal column, and arms straight out, you could produce the maximum speed of rotation, but least torque. Stirling's ideas thus made sense; you could correct a slide far more quickly with straight arms. The cockpit and driving position of the V16 were a relic of Raymond Mays, who, when the car was designed, was one of Britain's best drivers and, of course, he had his own way. Also, you were unable to heel and toe, which did not matter to RM, who had been brought up on ERAs with preselector gearboxes, where you moved the lever to the gear you wanted and kicked the change pedal when you wanted to change. Even when he drove an F1 Talbot it had a Cotal electric gearbox. I managed to make some changes to the pedals and I tried to reduce the incredible amount of friction in the front suspension ball joints which made the steering heavy and lifeless. I lapped them all in, and adjusted clearances, but it did not make much difference — only a 15 per cent reduction in torque at the steering wheel. Stirling used to have long talks with PB, and then PB would give me a job list which would consist nearly all of measures to combat the misfire or burbling, and to find more horsepower, never measures to improve the handling.

One of his anti-burbling measures was for Ken Richardson and Hammy to bring from England 500 gallons (2225 litres) of fuel, in ten barrels, in a transporter. We received phone calls on their progress, and one evening PB came away from the phone laughing his head off. 'Guess what,' he said, 'they are in jail at Domodossola!'. (Automobile fuel, of course, is subject to heavy taxes in most countries.) They had crossed France and Switzerland with no difficulty, by having the vehicle sealed, but they could not do this when entering Italy and they did not have enough money to pay the duty. However, after much argument they were allowed to go to Central Customs in Domodossola to resolve the matter. Ken's story was that they missed the turn to the Customs, but they were stopped by the police, having passed through the town, accused of trying to evade Customs and put in jail. Eventually the Mad Major got them out, but the fuel was confiscated.

After a week the money was raised and, armed with the necessary paperwork, Hammy and I went to Domodossola to fetch it. After several hours and much stamping of forms we were taken to a warehouse where the fuel was stored. As we started to roll the barrels into the transporter, one of the Customs officials said: 'Wait, you have paid duty on the fuel, but not on the barrels.' I recognized what he was after, but it was too much for me. I opened one barrel and started to pour the fuel down the drain. They got very excited. I said: 'It's our fuel, you have just given me the paperwork to prove it, so I can do what I like with it. I will give you the barrels, we do not want them.' A senior Customs official appeared, and we were allowed to go — with the fuel. To add to my fury, it made absolutely no difference to the burbling.

'Oily', one of the circuit employees, so called for his habit of scrounging 'oily' from us, appeared one morning to tell us Alfa would be testing their Barcelona cars that day. He said they were set up for Barcelona, so we knew not to expect comparable lap times. Sanesi would be driving the Muletto (the development car) set up for Monza.

Willy and I went to the circuit to time them, but Guidotti, Alfa's Team Manager suspected what we were up to. So I sat in the cab of the transporter with my back to the track, apparently writing up log books, but watching Willy in the mirror who was sitting on the pit counter smoking and watching Alfa's tests. Guidotti pointed out smoking in the pits was not allowed, so Willy touched his ear, and every time he did, I pressed the button on the watch. There was no difference between our times and theirs, Vedano to the start line. We were one or two tenths quicker to the Grande but lost two seconds through Lesmo. We had about the same time along the back straight but lost another second round Vedano. I tried to solve the blower lubrication problem, while waiting for PB and Stirling. Essentially it consisted of a separate boost-pressurized oil tank to feed the blower bearings. The idea was that while the engine was boosting, the blower was fed with oil at boost pressure (rather more oil than it would get with the original system). When the driver took his foot off — no boost pressure — no oil to the blower. It worked perfectly at Monza. I gave one to the Rolls-Royce fitter, who said 'very interesting'. Six months later he told me it was not necessary, the seals were now so good, there was absolutely no risk of leaks into the induction.

Tres arrived, although I never knew why. He was very interested in all that we had done, and asked many questions, including when was I going back to Rolls-Royce. He told me that Ken Richardson was going to work for Vandervell who was sueing RM over the bearing story. We had several wet days. Stirling eventually persuaded PB to let him try the softer front roll bar. We only had two and usually ran the stiff one. He was running with the bar removed altogether when he came in saying the engine felt very funny — no loss of performance, just a very strange vibration. We could find nothing wrong, but Stirling was adamant. Eventually we removed the blower to look inside the crankcase, and we found one of the molybdenum crankshaft balance weights had come adrift. Stirling must have had incredible senses to have felt this happen. Had we ignored him and continued running we would have destroyed the engine completely.

The weather was getting worse and Stirling was getting restive. PB argued that we must wring every last day, every last minute out of this very expensive expedition. Then it rained heavily, flooding the entrance tunnel to a depth of six feet (1.83 metres). The only way we could get into the track was by 'Oily' opening all sorts of gates and driving along the circuit proper. We all realized it was time to give up and go home; so we started to pack, but there was one small snag. In the course of the misfire problems Lodge, our plug supplier, had pointed out that the BRM engine's special 9/16 inch threads (unlike everyone else who had 14 mm) meant there was not the same range of plugs available for us to try. A set of cylinder heads with 14 mm sparking plug threads had just been flown out to enable us to try surface discharge plugs which were available in 14 mm, but as usual they were stuck in Customs who demanded the most inordinate amount of duty. Looking back on the Monza tests makes one appreciate the Common Market.

The Mad Major arranged that we would pay the duty, but if we took the heads out of Italy within 24 hours via a predesignated Customs post, the duty would be refunded. The packages had to be sealed to prove they had not been used during the 24 hours.

We set off with me driving the mobile workshop, with Cyril Bryden, a non-driver, as navigator, and Gordon Newman and Geoff Aldridge sharing the driving of the transporter. All the direct Alpine passes were closed by winter snow — it was long before the tunnels — and there were disturbing reports of heavy rain and floods in southern France, particularly in the Durance valley. I hoped we could manage the journey via Genoa and along the coast in three days. At Milan central Customs, early Thursday morning, the first problem arose when they could not find the cylinder heads. It took until 4 p.m. All the paperwork had been stamped, at 10 a.m., Customs would not change anything. This meant that we had to get to San Remo Customs before 10 a.m. the next day, Friday. We made good time to Genoa. In rain and darkness between Savona and Finale Ligure the road had been washed into the sea. The whole return trip was like this — we just made San Remo Customs in time. I do not know if the duty was ever refunded. We fell foul of the Italian Customs as we had been in Italy too long for our tourist papers, we had trouble with the French (while we had been away a new law concerning prior authorization of the route for lorries had come into force), as well as the more straightforward problems — shortage of money, bad weather, diversions. We were glad to reach Bourne late on Monday evening.

Next day PB offered me a permanent job at BRM for more money than I was getting from Rolls-Royce; telling me that RM had already cleared it with Mr Elliott. I rang the 'voice', who was very vague but made an appointment for me to see him. He said stay at BRM a little longer, as he still had no visibility as to what my future would be. Somewhat exasperated, I told him to stop looking at my future, collected four months back pay and went to London for the weekend, which included the British Racing Mechanics Annual Dinner and looking for another Aston Martin. I closed down my flat in Derby, and put the furniture into store.

PB was very vague about what my job was to be. He said: 'You decided you could manage without Ken so you had better run Folkingham.' I accepted his offer and pressed him for a winter job list. Engines and gearboxes would be updated at Bourne. I was to prepare an improvement programme for his approval which I would then execute. I later learned that the BRM Trust had forced the departure of Ken Richardson and my recruitment. Years later Sir Bernard Scott, Oliver Lucas's former assistant and representative on the BRM Board, told me that PB had supported the changes. By then Sandy had gone back to Rubery Owen at Darlaston. We saw a little more of Alfred Owen, the Chairman of the BRM Board and Trust, and Chairman of Rubery Owen, then the largest family-owned business in Britain. A.G.B. Owen ('AGB' as he was known) seemed an odd mixture; generally vaguely benign, occasionally very sharp, decisive and to the point.

I sent PB my job list and received a very cryptic document in return — a list of numbers with either B, F, N or SM against them. They were my job numbers — B meant Bourne would do it; F meant my group at Folkingham; N meant No, no one does it, and SM meant see me.

A collection of modified parts began arriving from Bourne. The reasons for some of these we understood, such as new mountings for the steering box, new steering arms machined from solid, a new front suspension set up deloading the front suspension balls to reduce the friction. Others we could not understand, like new front and rear hub carriers machined from solid lumps of forged duralumin. Martin Redmayne, Chief Engineer of Girling Brakes, arrived and explained they were going to convert our three-trailing shoe system to Girling disc brakes. I had been vaguely aware that aircraft used disc rather than drum brakes. A new gearbox also arrived incorporating a mounting for the brake servo pump, which had previously been engine driven, which meant if the engine stopped you had no servo-assistance and thus very little braking.

I spent a comfortable winter at The Angel with Tres and mine hosts Jean and Eric Oatts. After I returned from work, cleaned up and changed, I used to go into the bar for a drink with the locals: Mr Bedford, the Manager of the Bourne Lloyds Bank, who urged me to marry my girlfriend (a piece of advice for which I shall be eternally grateful), Horace Stanton, a local solicitor, Arthur Stubley, the local 'Mr Fix It' (I never really knew what he did), and Jack Rickard, a partner in a local firm of agricultural engineers. We dined about 8 p.m., then Tres and I would sit over coffee and put the world to rights.

I learned much from Tres, who was running the engine development programme and the test bed. Much to my surprise he told me that PB had just said we have never had cars built as well as these, meaning the two I was putting together at Folkingham. PB used to walk round the racing shop between 11.30 a.m. and 12 noon before departing for Bourne and was generally highly critical.

The disc brakes arrived. Girling fitters fitted them to the cars and piped them up. Stirling appeared in a new Jaguar XK 150 Coupé, and we spent a long time making him a bucket seat exactly to his requirements. We retained the drawing and patterns, and later in 1959 when Stirling drove the Type 25 we made a seat from these dimensions which still fitted him perfectly, and I think surprised him not a little. He drove the car with the new brakes, reporting that the stopping power was remarkable but the pedal position was inconsistent. 'Redders' (Redmayne) was ready for this and fitted small non-return valves, so that when the discs moved sideways within the caliper (a phenomenon we learnt to call 'knock-off') the pressure trapped by the non-return valves pushed the pads in on one side and out on the other, without moving the pedal.

We prepared to return to Monza with two cars, one with discs, the other with the old three-trailing shoes. By this time I had graduated to driving the V16 for such purposes as bedding brakes, and I had also bought a 1937 2 litre Aston Martin saloon. Ken Wharton, who was then British Hill Climb Champion, came to do some testing, as he was to join the party at Monza.

We had a pleasant trip out; the long way round again up through Genoa as it was early March. There was drama at the Franco-Italian frontier. We tore the cross-over fuel pipe off the workshop and a car broke loose in the transporter.

Stirling soon got down to some good times, but there was still a trace of burbling. We had new Lodge surface discharge plugs (405s) which seemed to be a big step in the right direction. Back on 53s burbling was as bad as ever. Raymond Mays arrived in a new blue 4.5 litre R-series Bentley. He was delighted with it and fussed over it every minute. He could not understand a peculiar sandy rash developing on the scuttle just below the windscreen. I could, someone had put battery acid in his screen washer instead of distilled water! Within a few days the aluminium panel had nearly disappeared.

RM was an odd character — extremely superstitious and a 'Stage Door Johnny'. He would never get into a racing car from its right hand side. We would put all sorts of obstructions in his way but he would not get in the car until we had moved it. If he saw a white horse in a field he would always mutter a little verse. He always spent Tuesday evening in London, staying at the old Berkeley Hotel, going to a theatre, then dinner at either the Mirabelle or the Ecu de France. He always dramatized motor racing crises, especially those concerning BRM. Tres coined a phrase for him: 'What's wrong, here's a night and nobody working'. He seemed to think that working through the night was an essential part of preparing for a race. He was very suspicious when, as Chief Engineer I cut the working day and looked upon an all-night session as a disaster. When we managed to do this and win races he was completely mystified. He was never quite sure what to make of me. Incidents which drove him round the bend, just made me laugh.

After a few more inconclusive days of testing, Stirling left for the Lyons-Charbonnières Rally in his new Jaguar with Gregor Grant, editor of *Autosport*. We all liked Gregor, or 'Grogger' as Graham Hill called him.

Gregor was intensely pro-British and would always find something good to say about any serious British effort, even though he was violently and intensely critical of any of our stupidities. While Stirling was away Ken Wharton took over. He was very precise and pedantic: not as quick as Stirling, of course, but he gave us useful information. We had improved the handling a little but not enough; throttle response was better, brakes were extremely good, but it was wasted by the dreadful lack of traction. It was becoming clear that we had out-Ferraried Ferrari. We had put a wheel at each corner of a very powerful engine, but the snag was that our engine was nothing like as reliable as a Ferrari. One day when Redmayne was in bed with a stomach upset, Stirling hit a stag, smashing the nose and radiator, and Stan took the pieces back to the Marchesi to straighten them out. Redmayne feeling pale and interesting went to investigate, saw the wreckage and the blood and promptly returned to his bed.

With a race having been organized at Valentino Park, Turin, with a big Ferrari entry we started preparation of the disc-braked car for Stirling to race. Then on the Thursday before the race PB appeared, obviously very cross and upset, and told me to 'pack up the disc-braked car, pick your two best mechanics, and take it back to England as quickly as you can. RM has signed Fangio, and we will not be running at Turin.' I argued that surely Fangio will wait a few days, while we race the car and find out how much we have improved it, but PB said: 'No, RM says it is vital to get the car back.' It was obvious that PB agreed with me, and was just carrying out RM's instructions. Stirling was furious, understandably so. Gregor Grant ran an *Autosport* editorial attacking the decision. Just before we left — PB was already on his way — I was called to the phone to speak to RM in England who gave me an ear bashing because we were not well on our way. He asked when we would arrive, and I said: 'Noon on Sunday, ready to run on Monday.'

We had a very good run back, the long way round, through Genoa with Gordon Newman and I sharing the driving of the transporter. We put 100 km into the hour several times. They had the same Austin Princess 6-cylinder engine that was used in the Austin Healey and were remarkable vehicles for their day. I dropped off in Bourne to pick up the Aston. When RM saw me in the yard he flew off the handle because 'they' were not back yet, completely oblivious of the fact that if I was there, so was the car. To add to our mortification, Fangio went to Turin to watch the race, assuming that we would not be so stupid as to pass up a chance of proving to the world the BRM was raceworthy and there was a chance of good racing between BRM and Ferrari.

We had to wait a week before Fangio arrived. He went round Folkingham three seconds faster than anybody had done before, then went off the road, taking off an exhaust pipe in the process. We took the car to Silverstone where Gonzales joined in the fun. It rained but neither of them seemed to notice. They went round Silverstone with the car at 45 degrees to the line of travel. Neither of them spoke English, but we had Eric Forrest Green, the Rolls-Royce importer into Argentine as go-between and interpreter. When he returned to Argentina he left his son to carry on.

We asked Fangio what he thought of the car. He said: 'It is very good, but why — was he not going fast enough?' His philosophy was that he would drive the car as hard as he could, but he would not criticize it. If the times were not as fast as we wanted, it was for us to decide whether the driver or the car was at fault. If it was the driver, get another; if it was the car, fix it. It was not for him to intrude.

Gonzales was a little more helpful. He told me that the big problem was you could not drift the car in the dry. I did not know how to drift a car anyway, so Gonzo took me out to give me some tuition using a Standard Vanguard — the vehicle that invented oversteer. He then stood me in the middle of the track at Folkingham and tried to drift the BRM six inches from me. I did not like that one bit. I could understand what he was saying but could not see why it happened.

One day Gonzales was driving up the lane to Folkingham in the Vanguard when he ran into a large pig taking its customary stroll from the farm into the woods. The impact was violent and the pig fell into the ditch and lay still. The Vanguard was somewhat deformed. The Farmer appeared from nowhere and Gonzales handed over a large wad of fivers — about £50. When Gonzales told us about it, we convinced the farmer that £25 was reasonable. Just before Christmas, one of the habitués of The Angel bar, 'Boney' Wells the local pig killer, gave me a large piece of pork, with a wink. I enquired as to the provenance of the pork. 'Boney' said: 'It's a piece of Gonzo's pig. He did not kill it, I just did.'

Our first race of the season was Albi, near Toulouse in France on 1 June with Fangio and Gonzales, followed six days later by a race at Dundrod outside Belfast in Northern Ireland with Fangio and Stirling Moss. I thought and said, we are mad. Two races within six days; 1000 miles (1600 km) and two channel crossings apart. In 1952 the lorries had to cross Dunkirk-Dover taking seven hours, then an overnight crossing from Liverpool to Belfast. I took RM and PB through the logistics of leaving Albi early on Monday — Dover Wednesday morning, with luck, and Belfast just in time for practice, but certainly no time to do any work on the cars at all. Bear in mind that it took ten hours to change an engine, and we only had three. No one took much notice, although it was decided to organize a Silver City Bristol Freighter to fly the cars from Toulouse to Nutts Corner in Ireland, with a stop at Hurn near Bournemouth to refuel. The flight was scheduled for Tuesday. We would spend Monday sorting out the cars post race. The mobile workshop would then leave Albi on Monday night, travelling non-stop via Bourne to restock, and hopefully it would arrive in Belfast on Friday morning. But then, as we prepared for Albi we ran into problems and panic; porous castings, and main studs either pulling out or breaking. We then committed the classic first-year student's blunder — using higher strength heat-treated super-alloy steel studs. This put us back into cylinder-head joint troubles. The higher tensile studs stretched less, and any relaxation left the studs without sufficient tension to compress the seals. Leaking head joints returned and, even worse, thermal expansion overstressed the studs which just fractured.

We had an uneventful journey to Albi, but when we unloaded the cars we found a water leak indicating a broken stud. So it was engine out, and we had not even started to run. PB stopped me applying a 10 per cent overload to all the studs to see if we had any more that would break. However, we managed to get to first practice, and found there was little opposition — old Ferraris, Talbots and 4 CLT Maseratis.

It soon turned into bedlam. A spare engine intended for Dundrod, but untested, was flown out to Toulouse. Our garage the night before the race was a rare scene — Fangio operating an electric power saw cutting slots all over the bodywork, Gonzales holding panels while Stan knocked louvres into them. None of it worked, but it probably made them feel better. We got both cars to the line — just. Gonzales was out after five laps in second place, while Fangio lasted until lap 16 in the lead, then he too was out, both with severe overheating. Back at the garage we tried to get ready for Dundrod. It was intensely hot. Sanitary facilities in the garage ranged from appalling to non-existent. We tried to dissolve the broken studs out with acid, and loaded potentially salvageable heads into RM's Bentley for him to take back to England. The flight to Belfast was a nightmare. The aircraft was so noisy that it was impossible to sleep, although we snatched half an hour on the grass by the aircraft while it was refuelling at Hurn. Dundrod was even worse. The snapshot album is not very helpful — I have a sensation that there was no film in the camera. Fangio managed three laps in practice, but Stirling none at all.

In the race, as Stirling had not been allowed to practise a start, he nearly stalled and half burned the clutch out. On the second lap Fangio spun, providing the famous photograph of Fangio and Stirling in BRMs travelling in opposite directions. Stirling was soon out with clutch and overheating problems. Fangio came in on lap 15 with a blocked fuel filter. We cleaned it out, but he was in again within another ten. Fangio had planned to fly with Bira in his Gemini to Monza, but as Bira had dropped out even earlier, he left without waiting for Fangio. As a result Fangio arrived at Monza at the last minute after a hectic drive, and then in the race had the disastrous crash which put him out of racing for nearly a year. We found that the deposit that had blocked the fuel filter was a fuel problem; ironic after Esso had been unfairly pilloried for last year's Monza troubles. This time it really was in their court but no one would believe us. Stirling, quite understandably, resigned and Fangio was out of action for a year.

Our next race was a Formula Libre event preceding the British Grand Prix at Silverstone — Gonzales and Wharton driving. Panic really set in. We painted the cars dark green — it was luckier than light green. I consoled myself that dirty fingermarks did not show as much on dark green paint. The panic included fitting (without any testing) enormous radiators and enlarged waterpumps.

Taruffi had Vandervell's Dundrod-winning Thin Wall Ferrari. Gonzales was fastest in practice, but early in the race he ran wide at Stowe. He drove back to the pits in a vast cloud of steam with a piece of fence post still sticking out of the radiator. I gave him the 'come in' flag to show to Wharton, then in fifth place, so Ken would know why he was being called in. As he stopped, Gonzales seized him by the scruff of the neck and threw him over the pit counter, gibbering away in Spanish, as he climbed into the car. He drove like a maniac taking two seconds a lap off Taruffi who was not hanging about. After 22 laps of this the gearbox input gears gave up. How the engine survived we will never know.

A fortnight later we had another Formula Libre race at Boreham airfield, now home of Ford's Advanced Vehicle Establishment. It rained throughout. Gonzales spun off again, while Wharton plugged on a long way behind Mike Hawthorn in a Cooper Bristol, until the BRM's gearbox input gears failed, certainly not through overloading. By this time the BRM Trust were becoming very restive, with shareholders of their supporting firms asking why their money was being publicly wasted. The writing was on the wall.

In late August there was a Formula Libre race on a disused airfield at Turnberry; near the golf course. We ran two cars for Reg and Ken, now with enormous fuel filters. On the start line we found that the pipe from the filter to the carburettors on Reg's car had cracked. With less than two minutes to go we were frantically fitting rubber hose over the cracked pipe. Hawthorn — alongside on the front row — seeing the panic, got out of the Thin Wall and strolled over to watch us. 'Take your time chaps,' he said, 'they will not start without us.' When we had finished, and started replacing the bonnet he walked back to the Thin Wall and nodded to the starter as if to say let battle commence. Unfortunately, the Thin Wall's transmission broke on the line. Reg won after a battle with Ron Flockart driving the ex-Raymond Mays ERA R4D. Wharton retired with a broken steering joint.

After the race Tony Vandervell politely asked my permission to buy all the BRM mechanics a drink — they were all served with a pint of Pimms. Later Hawthorn enlivened the evening by dropping potted plants from the hotel balcony onto the golfers relaxing below, with warning shouts of 'Timber'. After someone went through the glass doors into the swimming pool without first opening them, and taking most of the glass with him into the pool, the hotel management called a halt. About 5 a.m. someone told me we had left a transporter's engine running. I found Gordon Newman asleep on the grass alongside the transporter. The noise was Gordon snoring.

During the pre-Goodwood testing I was presented with an enormous clue to the burbling problem. The cars were low-geared for Goodwood, and RM reported after his test run that the car was going extremely well and he had 'reached an honest 12,000 rpm before the first runway intersection.' During routine carburettor cleaning before loading, Jack North showed me one of the carburettor needles from this engine — it was an unmachined blank and would have only flowed a minimal amount of fuel. I could not believe it, but the pressure of other problems pushed it from my mind.

Our drivers were Gonzales, Parnell and Wharton, the latter distinguishing himself by discovering that if he turned the fuel off on the main straight, there was still sufficient fuel in the enormous filter to get him to the starting line. Fuel was always turned off when the engine was not running, because with full tanks and low-mounted carburettors, there was a risk of flooding and hydraulicing. Shortly afterwards we found that even if we pushed the car a quarter of a mile, half way round Madgwick corner, we still could not raise enough fuel to refill the filter, far less start the engine. Wharton's stupidity kept him out of the first race, which was won by Gonzales, with Farina driving the Thin Wall in second and Parnell third. The Thin Wall gave trouble in the main race, so Gonzales, Parnell and Wharton finished an unopposed 1, 2, 3.

Our next race was in Jim Clark country at Charterhall. We were based in Jock McBain's garage, home of the Border Reivers. Parnell's gearbox input gears failed early on, and surprisingly enough so did Farina's in the Thin Wall. Bob Gerard, with an old ERA converted to 2 litres managed to out-fumble Wharton, who spun, and Bob won.

It was a very eventful autumn. The BRM Trust decided that it was time to put BRM up for sale. The only sensible offer came from Alfred Owen, who resigned as Trust Chairman to make his bid. On 23 October, at an Extraordinary Meeting of the Trust, his offer was accepted and we had a new boss.

# CHAPTER SIX

# Alfred Owen's V16s

TRES HAD BEEN busy designing the new 2.5 litre four-valve, four main-bearing engine and car, but a few days after the takeover he told me that he had resigned. He had told Alfred Owen there was no way he could continue to work under Berthon's direction. Once Tres got into his stride he was quite a performer, and he advised AGB that to continue with the present set-up would just be a big waste of time and money. Not surprisingly AGB, having just bought BRM, did not intend to make any changes, so this left Tres with no choice but to resign.

I was very sorry to see him go. Not only was he a very nice chap, and very good company, but he was an absolutely brilliant design engineer. His only problem was his very short fuse. A few days later PB sent for me. Knowing that Tres and I were good friends, he asked me which side I was on. Very diplomatically I replied: 'The car's.' He then said he was taking over design of the new car and engine, and he wanted me to take over V16 engine development. My immediate programme was to clear up the misfire problem.

My comfortable existence at the village pub was further disrupted. Not only was I losing Tres, but my landlord and landlady, having completed their training and making a good job of running the pub — nearly doubling the takings, perhaps with some help from me — were promoted to take over The Crown at Woodbridge.

Fortunately there was a silver lining. There had been a very convivial party in the pub on Good Friday lunchtime, during which I was introduced to a very attractive young lady, the daughter of a local dentist, who worked as head lad in a local horse racing stable. During the summer I was rectifying blowing exhaust valves in my Aston Martin in a lock-up at the back of the pub. The young lady, passing by on her way from tennis, occasionally stopped for a chat on her rare days off. In September, during pre-Charterhall testing, I experienced a burst scavenge pump followed by an oil fire ignited by the hot exhaust. This led to my removing my oil soaked overalls at the trackside and, later that evening, much hilarity at my expense. The catch phrase was 'Repeat after me, I am a ball of fire.' That evening I asked the young lady for a date, the first of many. The departure of Tres and the Oatts was not so hard to bear, after all.

Eventually, there was a V16 engine for me to run on the test bed. It was a good installation, if a little on the small side, with a Dynamatic electric brake donated by Heanan and Froude. The drive shaft that emerged from the engine, rotated at 0.518 of crankshaft speed, power being taken from the centre of the crankshaft by a pair of reduction gears. The data plate showing the dynamometer constant, necessary to calculate the engine's power output, had been removed. I was told it was in PB's office. When I asked him for the constant I was told: 'Just give me the loads, I will work out the power.' It was very stupid. Perkins Diesel at Peterborough had similar dynamometers. We had a good relationship, and often called upon them for spares, particularly the electronic valves controlling the load application mechanism. (Transistors had not yet been applied to dynamometers.) I found from Perkins that the constant was 400.

Soon after we started running the engine the dynamometer electronics gave trouble, so we ran with all the covers removed so we could watch the electronic valves light up to see which one was defective. When working properly they glowed bright blue. I held the engine at 10,000 rpm as we watched the illuminations, and while doing this we also saw the cause of the burble. The SU carburettor pistons reached full lift at 10,000 rpm, and at that speed the needles came right out of the jet. It did not matter, therefore, what needle you were using, blank or otherwise; it was not controlling the jet area as it was right out of the jet. No one had ever bothered to do a few simple sums. One of the SU tuning methods was to move the needle in or out of the carburettor piston. PB refused to believe me and I got into a fearful row for trying to wreck the dynamometer by running it without protective covers on the control gear; another for running without the cold air supply, and a third one for talking about it in the engine shop. Cruellest of all, a fourth for not spotting it sooner. Who was the development engineer? When we next ran a car, with longer needles so part was always within the jet, the engine went up to 12,500 rpm as clean as a whistle.

The next few months were disjointed. They were bursting with interest, but the hours I worked nearly wrecked my budding romance. I had rig tests running in parallel with the test bed work. Although, with only three engines, each taking a week to rebuild, there were many days when there was not an engine to run. It was clear that we had major distribution problems, both air/fuel and water. I found the post-Albi water pumps were far too big and cavitated with the slightest trace of steam. There was an individual outlet for each cylinder head, and we found water only flowed over the middle cylinders at 8,000 rpm, none over the end ones and just a faint trickle over the intermediates. Even at 11,000 rpm there was only a faint dribble over the end cylinders.

After I had sorted the water flow out by new pumps and adjusting the size of water passages I took all my data to one of my old friends at Rolls-Royce Hucknall, who helped me design a centrifugal steam separator. I spent most of December soaked to the skin and half scalded at the same time. The system which finally evolved had an aluminium condenser tank mounted high up on the bulkhead, exposed to the air flow. The steam condensed back into water and was piped into the eye of the water pump, the point of lowest pressure. Condensation was provoked by the combination of the large pressure difference and temperature drop from the cooling airflow. This got water distribution under control. (For more information see IME Paper D04190 1990).

With everyone wearing respirators we ran an engine on stub exhausts to check fuel distribution. A copy of the results is reproduced in the illustration section. The middle cylinders on one bank and both ends of the opposite bank were too rich. Correspondingly some of the opposite cylinders were too weak. We made a stepped diameter inlet manifold. This improved mixture distribution, although it was still not perfect.

I turned my attention to the oil system. The engine was never very good at holding oil pressure when hot. I suspected the sleeve-type oil relief valves, located in vertical drillings in the sump, were sticking. We made a disc-type relief valve which screwed into the end of the main oil gallery and piped the spill back to the oil tank. This gave us plenty of oil pressure at all times and showed, as expected, that there was far too much oil in circulation. The engine also threw vast quantities of oil from its breathers. The engine was a 135°V; this meant that oil could not drain from the exhaust cam boxes by gravity and had to be pumped out by small camshaft-driven pumps. We measured the amount of oil coming out of these oil pumps and found to our surprise it was virtually nil. The gear driving the pump churned the oil away from the pump inlet. We jettisoned the pumps and fitted pipes to drain into the sump. We fitted chimney-type crankcase breathers with angled baffles, and joined the two inlet cam covers together with a large baffled chimneystack breather. This enabled us to dump 27 lb (12.3 kg) weight of breather pipes, including 34 hose clips.

The inlet valve seats from a used engine looked dreadful. By calculation the valve seat loading from the spring, with every part at an adverse tolerance, permitted the valve to blow off its seat at 94 psi (6.4 bar). We were running at 72 psi boost. (A bigger first stage impeller and a slightly increased drive ratio had been introduced during the winter of 1950/51). An outrageous theory occurred to me. What happened if the boost pressure blew the inlet valves open? It seemed very far fetched, but deserved investigation. Sure enough, when we tested heads in current use, we found inlet valves that would blow open at 60 psi, they would be well open at 11,000 rpm. Valve seats had been recut two or three times, the hairpin springs had lost poundage, and both the steel seating platforms in the head and the hooks under the valve caps had worn. When we restored the spring loadings it cured the original problem but brought back our rocker wear troubles. Shell, now our fuel and oil suppliers, came up with an oil additive which solved this problem.

When we ran the first full 1953 specification engine 20/3 on 22 February 1953 it produced 430 hp at 9000 rpm, 518 hp at 10,000 rpm, 585 hp at 11,000 rpm and a thunderous backfire at 11,500 rpm when we had just seen 612 hp. The blower was literally blown up like a balloon. The backfire was attributed to the very high exhaust back-pressures imposed by the water-cooled silencers. We dare not run on open exhausts again, we were already subjected to regular visits from the local police inspector who lived just across the road. We nearly always started running about 6.30 or 7.0 p.m., when he was watching his favourite TV programme. The electronic interference from the electric dynamometer meant that, when we started up, the picture promptly fell off his screen. There were still plenty of unsolved problems, but Goodwood Easter Monday was getting dangerously near. The main problem remaining was a very high rate of wear of the piston ring grooves. After four or five hours the vertical clearance had increased to an unusable amount. I also found the exhaust valve guides filled with carbon, causing the valve to lag behind the cam. We tried to taper the valve stems, but Bill Scott, an old Rolls-Royce friend, now Chief Engineer of our valve suppliers said it was not a practical proposition. Tapering the guides was not practical either, as we could not achieve a good enough finish. The solution was a double diameter guide, with a special tool, which we fitted over the sharp-edged top of the guide and dealt it a violent blow with a hammer. This closed in the top of the guide to give zero clearance. It was not a complete cure, and we still had guides occasionally carbon-up after 180 miles (290 km). The symptoms of carboned-up guides, which caused the valves to lag behind the cam, was a burnt patch in the carbon at the end of the exhaust pipe and a change in the exhaust howl. Fangio could mimic this change of note precisely. When his engine developed the problem he would take my arm and hiss into my ear!

For Goodwood we had Wharton and Parnell against Taruffi in Tony Vandervell's disc-braked and much improved Thin Wall Special (he had stopped calling it a Ferrari). Despite the rows, Alfred Owen and Tony Vandervell got on very well together. Vandervell had a very large hospitality caravan which dispensed champagne to his friends, and tea for Alfred Owen. It was quite incongruous to see the two of them, side by side in their grubby raincoats, watching their cars perform. Either one of them could have bought a battleship had he so wished.

It rained for the first race, when we were confounded by de Graffenried in one of last year's unblown 2 litre Maseratis, who led from start to finish. Wharton was second, Taruffi third and Parnell fourth. I watched the race with AGB who had been given a colossal build-up as to how much the cars had been improved over the winter. He was not amused, and gave me his version of a good going over: 'What had we done wrong?' I explained that in the wet you could only use as much of the vast horsepower available as your tyres could put on the wet road. If it was less than 200 hp, then de Graffenried was no worse off than we were. In fact, he was better off as his Maserati only weighed 1550 lb (710 kg) while the V16 weighed 2600 lb (1220 kg). 'What can you do about that?' he asked. I told him that with what we now know we could build a much smaller and lighter car. 'How much lighter?' he asked. 'About 600 lb (275 kg).' 'How long would it take?' 'About four months.' 'How much would it cost?' 'Not much, because we could make most of it ourselves, using the existing engine and gearbox, brakes and hubs.' He said nothing else; just stared into the distance.

He was a remarkable man with a computer-like memory; very mild-mannered, worked very long hours, driving himself all over the country in his Bentley, often arriving home at 2 a.m. having stopped for beans-on-toast at a lorry drivers' pull-in. He was Chairman of the Staffordshire County Council, and a Methodist lay preacher giving two or three sermons every Sunday. He richly deserved his eventual knighthood for public services. This particular afternoon he surprised me by his ability to read a race. He did not have a stop watch or a lap chart, but he knew exactly what was happening at the back of the field.

The main event was for 15 laps. It had nearly dried out. Parnell led until the blower drive quill-shaft sheared. Ken Wharton had an easy win from Taruffi and de Graffenried. As AGB departed, he said to me: 'Thank you for all you have told me this afternoon, I shall think about it very carefully.'

We started to get ready for Albi. Fangio was now fit, and we also had Gonzales and Wharton. The race was to be run as two heats and a final. One heat would be for the old blown F1, the other heat F2 (that is unblown two litres) and the final would be for the fastest from each of the two heats. Albi was fast, with long narrow tree-lined steeply-cambered bumpy straights. I thought we stood a good chance, even when I saw Farina down to drive the Thin Wall, and Ascari the six-carburettor Indianapolis 4.5 litre Ferrari.

As usual, we tried to shoot ourselves in the foot. I was absolutely furious to find that Wharton was due to take his car to Charterhall on the Saturday before we were due to leave for Albi. In this race Wharton spun, fortunately without damaging the car, and finished third behind two old ERAs. The mechanics drove through the night, arriving at Folkingham by 2 a.m. We had the heads off, valve guides reamed and back together again, for me to test on Sunday afternoon. It was no way to prepare for the most important race of the Owen BRM era, and typical of the stupid decisions that got BRM into such trouble in the past.

We were running an engine one Saturday evening, when routine inspection of the valve gear before a power check showed one of the camshafts had scuffed. Raymond Mays, ever alert to the lack of noise from the test house at the end of his garden, came to see what was wrong. I said: 'We have found a scuffed cam and we will have to change it.' He came out with a remark that has passed into BRM history: 'Never mind the camshafts, get the engine running.' I told him why we could not; we needed spares from the stores, always locked and barred against such as us on Saturday evenings. I told him: 'We will remove the camshaft tonight, and Brinkley will meet us at 6 a.m. tomorrow' (Sunday). Everyone, including myself, was looking forward to an evening off. After a day in the test house with a V16 you certainly needed it. But RM sent Dave Turner to find Brinkley and get a new camshaft there and then. RM said there is not a minute to be lost, you must work all night. I do not know what Dave said to the 'lalograph' when he found him in The Golden Lion at about 9 p.m. He returned with a very coarse and vulgar message and some completely impractical advice for RM.

There was a violent thunderstorm. It was raining heavily, and RM was waiting for Dave in his shirtsleeves with a large pale blue umbrella. When Dave — empty handed — delivered the message, with relish and possibly slight embellishment, RM threw the umbrella to the ground and jumped on it. We thought he was about to do the witch and broomstick act. He vanished, and so did we. Brinkley was eventually suspended for a month, just when we needed him most.

I had a pleasant social interlude before we left for Albi, when Peter and Lorna Berthon's only daughter, Jacqueline (Jackie), had her 21st birthday party at the old Berkeley Hotel, in London. Jackie was a tall stunningly attractive blonde whom I had dated a few times during her rare visits to Bourne. Normally she lived in her parents' flat in Mortimer Mews at the back of the BBC. Her visits were infrequent, possibly because PB noticed she distracted the mechanics, who as a tribe are probably even more licentious than the soldiery; one thing that has not changed over the years.

There were about 100 guests. It was a terrific evening. Jackie was good company, but my relationship with the dentist's daughter, as Reg Parnell persisted in calling her, was progressing most favourably.

After a good trip to Albi we installed ourselves in the same garage as the previous year. The mechanics were armed to the teeth with disinfectant (Jeyes fluid and so on), and they worked on the toilet facilities to such effect that the French workmen would not go near them. We had new overalls: heavyweight, blue-grey striped, scratchy denim. The idea was they would not show the dirt as badly as our white ones — they looked dirty to start with. The first practice showed the way ahead — two fearsome needle matches, one between Fangio and Ascari, the other between Gonzales and Farina. The BRMs were half-a-second ahead in both. Next day it was even more intense. With five minutes to go Ascari took 0.2 of a second from Fangio's time. 'Not to worry,' I said, 'you are in the middle of the front row; it is probably the best place to be, and there is not enough time to do anything about it anyway.' He gave me a very faint smile and got into his car. As he approached the line, after his warm up lap, Charles Faroux, Clerk of the Course, was waiting with the flag to terminate practice. The start-finish line was just after a 90 mph corner. Fangio held a very tight line in a really lurid drift; the flag man jumped for cover. Fangio took 3.5 seconds off Ascari's time and qualified at 2 min 55.2 sec — Ascari 2 min 58.7 sec and Gonzales 2 min 58.9 sec. When Fangio came in, to a jubilant welcome from the mechanics, he took my arm and whispered his burbling noise in my ear, sure enough there was the tell-tale bald patch in the exhaust pipe. We were well organized to deal with this by now, even if we still did not have a permanent fix.

There had been an ominous incident in practice. Gonzales had completely stripped all the tread from his left rear tyre when flat out on the main straight, leaving all the white cord exposed. The flying pieces of tread had ripped off the exhaust and a piece of windscreen. Dunlop's Vic Barlow was obviously very worried. Fortunately we had brought 18 inch rear wheels with us, as well as plenty of standard 17 inch. I gave Fangio's rebuilt engine a quick run at first light on Sunday morning. It seemed good, and we were ready for the battle.

The start was the stuff that 'Jenks' drools about. Charles Faroux just dropped the flag and ran. He said he could see that everyone had their engines running, he felt that someone would jump the start or otherwise cause an accident, so he let them go early. The front row was Fangio, Ascari, Gonzales, and the second Wharton and Farina. They all left black lines to the first corner and some way down the straight beyond.

You could hear them all the way round the circuit. The order, first time round, was Fangio, Ascari, Gonzales, Farina, Wharton. They stayed like this, with Gonzales and Farina dropping back, until Ascari came in with an obviously blown engine. Two or three laps later, Farina came in in the same state; not so much smoke but a bonnet-off job nevertheless. We were one, two and three. Then Gonzales came in with his left rear tyre minus its tread. We did a quick pit stop but the permitted two mechanics could hardly move the car. The pits were on a slight up hill and there was probably some rubber trapped in the brake caliper. Gonzales hopped out, chuntering away in Spanish and gave it an extra push, crumpling the sides of the cockpit, then he was back in and away. We finished the heat with

Fangio first, Wharton second and Gonzales fifth.

When we arrived at the circuit and the mechanics unloaded 22 spare rear wheels, PB suggested that I was out of my mind. Now, for the final, we stood amongst them debating which ones to use, at what pressure, and with how much tread. Should we ease off down the straights or take it quietly around the corners? Gonzales, who had a wicked sense of humour was trying to do a financial deal with Wharton to let Ken have second place. Finally Gonzales started on 18 inch wheels, and the others on 17 inch. They just cruised round, but by the eighth lap Gonzales was in with the left rear tread missing. Two laps later Fangio came in with the same trouble, and unfortunately he had slid into a wall and cracked the hub, so he was out.

This left Wharton in the lead all on his own, but he had been so busy following the other two he had not established his own line or cut off points. Within two laps the inevitable happened; he went off the road, the car rolled over a ditch, conveniently placed for Ken to fall out into, before it went on to demolish a house. We were debating whether to call Gonzales in, before we had another accident, when he arrived with another stripped tread. He insisted in carrying on, saying he knew what the trouble was, so he could anticipate it and would not take risks. He finally finished second to Rosier's 4.5 litre Ferrari. Ken just sustained cuts and bruises. His tyres were intact, and it was as we thought. The car was a write-off, although the engine and gearbox survived.

In the evening we set off to drown our sorrows. We tried to take Vic Barlow with us, but thinking we had come to lynch him, he locked himself in his room! We felt that as it was the first time we had the car running properly, and trying to put 600 hp on the road, Dunlop could, perhaps, be forgiven. Traction, or rather the lack of it, was the car's worst problem. With 600 hp, no traction worth speaking about, and skinny tyres, colossal tyre-wrecking wheel spin was inevitable. On the way home we stopped in Paris for lunch, and watched the Coronation of HM Queen Elizabeth on a television in a shop window. A large crowd gathered around the convoy, thinking we were part of the BBC Television Service.

A 50 lap formula libre race again preceded the British GP at Silverstone. Fangio and Wharton against Farina in the Thinwall. Fangio's valve guides carboned up again during practice, which saw the first 100 mph lap at Silverstone by Farina. As part of our quick head-reconditioning kit, we had 17 pre-lapped cylinder joint rings for each engine, with the 17th lapped to the greatest thickness in the set, in case one got damaged. For some reason the spare thick ring had been fitted in place of the correct one. When we filled the system with water it came out everywhere, so we had to take that head off again. I left the garage at Brackley when it was clear that we would just get the car to the line in time, and set up a 'mini' pit at the corner of the start line marshalling area at Woodcote. I was pursued by AGB, who wanted to know where his car was, and Wharton, who assumed his car would be given to Fangio, as well as the race organizers and the Press.

Raymond Mays drove the car through the traffic from Brackley, loving every minute. He was quite a showman and revelled in every bit of drama. We changed wheels, plugs, fuelled up and got Fangio to the line just in time. But the engine was not right and he did well to finish second to Farina with Wharton third.

After the race AGB decreed that Wharton's Albi wreck should be rebuilt

on the lines of his talk with me at Goodwood. PB — extremely diplomatic
— suggested it might diminish efforts on the new 2.5 litre car for 1954.
AGB said I had told him we could build the new V16 within our resources
at Folkingham. So it was agreed that the new car would be built at
Folkingham by the chalk on the garage floor method. I could have such
help as PB could spare from Bourne.

Desmond Scannell, the BRDC secretary, had made a generous offer for a
BRM demonstration between the heats of the BRDC Empire Trophy race
for sports cars in the Isle of Man. I took Maurice Dove, Dick Salmon, a few
spares and Fangio's car. When I reported to Scannell he asked who was
going to drive, Parnell or Wharton? I said I had no idea. We rang RM who
said: 'You are on the spot,' (he was dead right) 'you decide.' Reg was
driving the first Aston Martin DBR1, and we were sharing a garage with
Astons. Ken was driving a very quick 2 litre Fraser Nash. I decided that Reg
should drive the BRM. I estimated he would win the Empire Trophy race,
which he did — after his three laps in the BRM. Afterwards, at Ken's hotel
to collect the money from Desmond Scannell, we had a demonstration of
Reg's considerable financial acumen and technique, when he said to Ken: 'I
am surprised at you, sleeping in ———'s room', naming a motor cyclist
who had recently been killed. Ken replied: 'No I'm not, I'm in room
number so and so.' Reg waited until Ken went to change and ordered
champagne all round charging it to Ken's room number!

On the way back to Bourne we stopped at Reg's farm, near Derby, and he
gave us a baby pig, with a sack tied round its middle to preserve some
hygiene during the journey. When we were caught in a traffic hold up in the
middle of Derby, the traffic policeman was surprised to be greeted by the
pig, poking its head out of the window. It was installed on the airfield and
duly fattened up for Christmas. It was extremely tame, and wandered about
the airfield. When Maurice Dove whistled, it would look up. He would
shout: 'Don't go too far away', and the pig would return to its sty.

We had a quiet spell until the Autumn Goodwood meeting when
Hawthorn was down to drive the Thin Wall against Fangio and Wharton.
For once we had a trouble-free practice and Fangio was on pole. Mike had a
piston failure with the Thin Wall. Vandervell's mechanics whipped it back
to Acton for repairs. While we were warming up, Mr Vandervell wandered
across and told us his transporter was stuck in holiday traffic, and he did not
think it would get back to Goodwood in time. He said he would like to give
the BRM mechanics a drink. He always addressed me as Monsieur. I
politely replied: 'Not until after the race please Mr Vandervell.'

We were on the starting line with engines running and the flag up, when
Hawthorn appeared. He had quite a job to get lined up on the grid as he
could not find reverse, so he was about a wheel over the line at a slight
angle. John Morgan, the BARC starter looked at me and pointed at the Thin
Wall. I pointed down the road and waved to him to get on with it, and
Fangio did the same. Mike won. We were invited to protest but Fangio and I
both declined. He had won by more than the wheel advantage he had at the
start. While we were loading up, Mr Vandervell and his staff filled the
cockpits of both cars with bottles of champagne, saying that racing against
true sportsmen was what he enjoyed most in the world.

The season ended with Ken Wharton in a minor race at Castle Coombe.
We had another trouble-free practice, and we went to the cinema to see

*Genevieve*, which seemed highly appropriate. Ken was again out-fumbled by Bob Gerard in a 2 litre Cooper Bristol, and Bob won our last race of 1953.

Hammy having collected the remainder of my Aston Martin special oval tube, we began to build the new car, to be known as the Mark II, or BRM Type 30. One of the problems with the old cars, now known as Mark Is was the flexibility of the cast aluminium pillars for the trailing Porsche arms of the front suspension. I designed a steel front cross-member (which Stan Hope, who made it, described as lightening holes welded together) having two hefty tubes, bracing it back to the oval main frame tubes. There was an oval tube cross-member at the back of the engine and a round tube cross-member at the back of the gearbox. It had a single large tubular propeller shaft in place of the Mark I's two-piece shaft. The wheelbase was 6 inches (15 cm) shorter, all taken out of the fuel tank — cockpit section. The front of the car was just an aluminium shell — a 42-gallon (170-litre) body-profile tank, with a single central baffle, being installed at the rear of the car. The driver shared the cockpit with, on one side, a large honeycomb circular oil cooler from a Westland helicopter, and on the other a fat cushion-shaped oil tank. Air was ducted down the sides of the car from alongside the radiator to the oil tank and oil cooler, and escaped through the cut outs for the twin parallel tube de Dion radius arms. A single piece welded de Dion tube replaced the very expensive and complicated Mercedes copy used on the Mark I.

We converted a Morris Minor rack and pinion, using a housing turned from a solid lump of duralumin, with only one of the original very expensive universal joints in the steering column, plus another made from spring steel strip. I was somewhat confused, having watched Stan Hope carefully line up the hole in the centre cross-member for the propeller shaft, to find that when the car was standing on its wheels, the shaft was no longer in the centre of the hole. It was some 3 mm out. The chassis had bowed to that extent under the weight of all the components. I did the bending moment sum for a simply supported beam with a uniformly distributed load and found that it was about right. Never was Sir Henry Royce's first law more appropriate — 'every material an engineer uses is rubber-like, and if you approach it with a lighted match it will expand.' I could also see the logic of space frames.

The car, finished early in 1954, weighed 1960 lb (890 kg). With the steam-separating cooling system I was able to dispense with the enormous radiators, so I resurrected the original aluminium radiators. Lucas came up with four motor cycle magnetos to save the weight of the battery, needed by the Mark I's coil ignition system. When we started testing, admittedly in the depth of the winter, we had to blank off over 40 per cent of the small radiator. When Raymond Mays saw the car he said to PB: 'Peter, the radiator is too small.' I produced all my data, and prepared to fight to the death. PB compromised: 'You are probably right,' he said. We made, at some expense, another radiator about 10 per cent larger. This blew our budget and was just not necessary. As soon as I had a chance I put the small one back.

Ron Flockhart came to do some of the testing. RM had been impressed by Ron's handling of RM's old ERA R4D, and Ken Wharton was in New Zealand with a Mark I, supported by Willy Southcott and Gordon Newman, where they had an absolutely chaotic time. The main race was won by Stan Jones, father of Alan Jones, driving his very efficient Maybach Special. Ken had trouble in the race: a stone broke a brake pipe, which they hammered flat. We never knew where Ken finished as the official time keepers got in such a mess with Ken's long pit stop. Some people said second, others third. In the next race he ran out of fuel in sight of the line, and was pushed over in third place.

Our first race with the new car was the 1954 Goodwood Easter meeting — Ken with the Mark II and Ron Flockhart a Mark I. Roy Salvadori was there with Sid Greene's new 250F Maserati. During practice the Mark II's engine lost compression on No. 2 cylinder. A big piece had broken from the ring land of a piston, which was made from a new material. Our piston suppliers were still trying to combat the ring groove wear problem. We managed to change the piston through the blower aperture, and RM arranged for me to run in the new piston using the runways at Ford airfield late on Sunday evening. Ford was still operational, and had not yet become an open prison. I followed the runway lights, and was able to drive down one side of the runway and back up the other. I ran too close to the lights and the Mark II's stub exhausts put quite a few of them out.

Ken won the first race, but the magnetos did not like the heat of the V16 and developed a misfire. He took the Mark I for the final and won again after a serious coming together with Salvadori, putting Roy out and irrevocably bending the Mark I's chassis. Ron was fourth in both his races, but he lost 25 seconds with a spin in the first race and more due to the Mark II's misfire in the second.

The new-construction fuel tank gave much trouble in the early days, as did the motor cycle magnetos, but as the tank saved 84 lb (38 kg) and the magnetos eliminated a 36 lb (16 kg) battery, we had to persevere. PB decided to increase the blower speed again by changing the gears. Rolls-Royce had lost interest in us, as we were no longer competing in international races, although they still serviced the superchargers which by now were completely reliable.

PB was concerned that although the car was over 600 lb (272 kg) lighter, it still had a job defeating a well driven 240 hp Maserati. His solution was even more power. Unfortunately, as part of the 2.5 litre programme, the V16 engine test bed had been dismantled ready for the new installation at Folkingham, so we had no facilities to test the engine with the speeded up blower. I was sent out one wet day to obtain a boost curve. The car was fitted with a big boost gauge in the middle of the windscreen with one needle knocked on by the other. All I had to do was to accelerate at full throttle to a predetermined rpm, lift off, read the boost from the tell-tale, then write it down on a test pilot's knee pad. At lower rpm, with luck, I could get two readings a lap. Above 9000 rpm it was only one reading a lap. Above 10,500 it got really hairy. Even though the rain had stopped, the track was still wet. We had over 85 psi (5.8 bar) boost, which meant 625 hp. I plotted a very nice boost curve.

Nearly all the readings fell on the curve I extrapolated up to 12,000. I took it to PB, who spotted that my little crosses stopped at 10,500 rpm. 'This is no good,' he said. 'It is the readings over 11,000 I want. Go and do it again and do not chicken out.' I managed a reading at 10,750 rpm, but at 11,000 rpm — about 190 mph — the car aquaplaned into a huge, lurid spin, finishing up about 400 yards from the runway. Luckily I had a reading at 11,000 rpm, and both readings were on the line. I refused to do any more.

Ron took the car with the speeded-up blower to Snetterton and won easily against no opposition other than a split fuel tank. A fortnight later we went to Ibsley on the edge of the New Forest. Ron spun in practice buckling wheels and the tail, but still won against no real opposition. We did some testing on improved magnetos, trying to run for 100 miles non-stop. It took four attempts and two different designs of magnetos. Eventually we managed it at an average speed of 98.4 mph. A 100 mph lap at Folkingham was 1 min 44.6 sec for the 2.905 miles.

The second car was completed on 18 May. I did a 100-mile shake down, then we took them both to Aintree. The race, two heats and a final — in the opposite direction to the more usual clockwise — was run in the rain. Ken finished fourth in the first heat, behind Parnell in a 2.5 litre Ferrari, Collins in a sick Thin Wall and Stirling Moss in his new Maserati. Wharton said he did not want to risk the car in the rain. In his heat, Flockhart beat Salvadori to win. In the final Ken spun off, and Ron finished third behind Stirling Moss and Peter Collins after losing 90 seconds with a spin. At the Goodwood Whitsun meeting Ron led for three of the 15 laps. He was then passed by Peter Collins in the Thin Wall and finished a worthy second. Ron was not up to Peter Collins. Ken Wharton complained that a rear suspension strut had failed, but we could find nothing wrong. Ken took his car to a very wet Shelsley Walsh hill climb where he managed 37.8.

Ron and I carried out some tests at Folkingham to try to help the traction problem; Mark II No. 4 had the 180 mph top gear with a high second, and Mark II No. 5 the 208 mph ratio with a low second. No. 4 reached 12,000 rpm by the 800 yard (727.3 m) mark in 15 seconds, changing up at 11,000 rpm. After some experimentation we got the other, higher-geared, car to the 800 yard marker in 12.8 seconds by changing from second to third at 9500 rpm, third to fourth at 10,500 rpm and fourth to fifth at 11,000 rpm. Ron was lifting off at 12,000 rpm, 208 mph, well before the 800-yard mark, proving conclusively that the driving technique we had developed improved acceleration by 15 per cent. If you remember that a margin of 0.1 per cent is enough to win a race by 10 seconds, it gives some idea of the value of the technique. We explained it all to PB, who half believed us. Ken Wharton, though, would have none of it; neither would RM.

Our cause was not helped when we went to Castle Coombe in August and Ron was beaten by Bob Gerard in a 2 litre Cooper Bristol. Ron complained of locking brakes and a misfire, but his best lap of 1 min 16 sec did not compare well with Ken's 1 min 13.8 sec in a Mark I. We hoped for better things at Charterhall, but on the first lap a stone got into the carburettor, jammed it, and that was the end of the race.

Fangio paid us a social visit, using the new gear-change technique he took a Mark II round Folkingham in 1 min 39.6 sec compared with 1 min 43.8 sec in a Mark I two years earlier. During the Goodwood September meeting Ken exercised his right as number one driver, and took car No. 4 which was usually Ron's — finishing second to Peter Collins in the Thin Wall, complaining of a misfire which we traced to defective plugs. Ron spun into a turnip heap on his first lap. My notes read: 'Engine stripped for removal of turnips.'

We ended the season at Aintree. Ken was second fastest in practice to

Stirling, 1 min 3.8 sec to 1 min 3.4 sec. Peter Collins in the Thinwall 1 min 4.2 sec, Ron 1 min 4.6 sec. We noticed Ken was changing up early; he had got the message, even though he denied it at debrief. In the race Ken had a coming together and retired, sharing fastest lap with Stirling of 1 min 3 sec. Ron was third plagued by plug trouble.

During the season Gordon Newman and I had tried to improve our understanding of the air struts. Originally Automotive Products supplied and serviced them, but like most people they lost interest in us. We learned the details of the system, and with the benefit of hindsight I realized that had the spring medium — air — been enclosed in a rubber bag like the Citroen, to eliminate the appalling friction, and if we had, as we did later, increased the volume of air, they would have worked extremely well. The damper system was very effective and could easily have been made infinitely adjustable under driver control, if only we had known what the car needed. There were no plans to run the Mark IIs in 1955. We gave then a paraffin overhaul, inhibited them, and put them into indefinite storage. The Mark Is had ceased to exist with Ken's Albi and Goodwood crashes and the need for spares.

In 1955, following Ken Wharton's defection and Peter Berthon's accident, we very fortunately acquired the services of Peter Collins, and to keep him interested we entered a Mark II for Easter Monday Goodwood. Peter came to Folkingham to try the car, and he told me it had much more power than the Thin Wall, but he just could not use it — the back broke away so suddenly. Two times out of three round the same corner it would be fine, but the third time it would catch him out. He just dare not put all the power down. It sounded to me like a consequence of the rapidly rising spring rate that came with the air struts. We made some new lever arms for the rear suspension which changed the strut-to-wheel movement ratio and moved us down the rate curve. It was as much as we could physically get in without the strut fouling. Peter said it was a significant improvement; about half of what was needed. We made a few other minor changes. He won both races very easily, admittedly against little opposition.

It was obvious that we had considerably improved the car. We now had a driver who could really drive it and, even more valuable, could tell us what was needed to make it go faster. To me he was worth more than Fangio. Obviously he was not as quick, but as Peter could tell me what was needed to make it faster (something Fangio also knew, but for some reason would not tell us) Peter was more valuable to the Team. However, signing autographs in Goodwood paddock after the race he kept the engine running and cooked it, distorting one of the heads. The only immediately available spares, were for 14 mm sparking plugs, the engine was rebuilt with 9/16 inch plugs one side and 14 mm the other. We went to Snetterton at the end of May, and within six laps Peter had a 15 second lead over Salvadori, and had carved a big chunk off the lap record, when he touched a back marker, burst a front tyre and was out. The 1.5 litre sports car race was won by a C. Chapman, ahead of T. Sopwith in a Cooper. We put the V16 away until Aintree on 3 September when Peter drove it again and had a very easy win from Salvadori and Tony Brooks. The car was inhibited, and put away. It was now a museum exhibit. However, it made some demonstration runs under the guidance of Wilkie.

The V16's last run for me was at Kyalami in 1968. The race organizers offered astronomical amounts of money for Graham Hill to open the circuit in a V16 BRM. I was up to my neck in problems, but Willy found time to get the car ready. Shell sent us a barrel of fuel, and another out to Johannesburg. Willy kept bleating that we needed to recarburate it for Kyalami, which was 5600 feet (1697 m) above sea level. I told him to stop worrying, the engine was supercharged and could take care of itself. Eventually, without giving the matter enough thought, I told him to take out the 4.5 in (114 mm) diameter carburettor mounting plate, which is a restrictor; to fit the Rolls-Royce iris diaphragm throttle and the variable geometry system. This would give it a 6 in (152 mm) diameter air intake, and at full throttle it would get nearly 50 per cent more air. Willy ran the car, reported all was well, and we shipped it to Kyalami. Graham was allowed a few laps to get to know the car. I warned him that although the tyres were new rubber they were still the old construction and grip was virtually non-existent. I took him through the gear-change drill. He asked what it would pull in top, and I told him somewhere between 'ten five' and 'eleven'. He tried a gentle start and commented: 'It's got absolutely no grip, but colossal power.' Willy and I were stunned by the amount of fuel it had used — something like two thirds of a barrel for about 30 miles (48 km).

On race day I warned Graham that he could only do three laps, otherwise he would have to walk, as the fuel consumption, for some reason, had gone crazy. With a big display for the crowd he disappeared in an enormous cloud of tyre smoke. He performed three very spectacular laps, but when he came in the engine appeared to be perspiring oil; there was a faint film all over it. Graham said: 'What's all this rubbish about 10,500 rpm? Before I got to the pits I looked at the clock and the needle was out of sight.' It was a strip-type rev counter and the needle disappeared at 12,500 rpm. When I had time to work it out, I calculated we must have been pulling 780 hp, which ties up with Rolls-Royce predictions made when Peter Collins was interested in trying for the world 1.5 litre speed record. They said it would pull 800 hp with all the goodies, and 1000 with a sprint fuel. Tom Wheatcroft now drives it as if it were an ordinary touring car. It seems incredibly docile. Willy put the old carburettor set-up back after Kyalami.

The V16 never came anywhere near its objective of winning the World Championship. It was a classic case of too little too late. Nevertheless, it provoked Tony Vandervell to his efforts with the Vanwalls, and a number of the lessons we learned from the V16 helped us towards the 1962 championship with the V8. It is said you learn from your mistakes. If so, I must be an absolute genius!

There are so many myths and half-truths surrounding the V16. Several times I have seen 610 hp on the test bed, with the intermediate 75 psi blower set up. The centrifugal blower was not a mistake. In some respects the engine was ahead of its time and the car was just not up to it. Handling and road holding was nowhere near as good as its contemporaries, such as the Thin Wall, and its traction was absolutely appalling. It was, though, the first car to race with disc brakes.

It is worth noting that the 1939 W165, 1.5 litre Mercedes gave 330 hp, while 12 years later the Alfa 159s were giving over 400 hp and the BRM over 600 hp. PB estimated that with the highest speed blower, used from 1954 onwards, it must have been giving 646 hp. In 1981, the turbo

Renault's were using 750 hp for qualifying. The BRM V16 engine was massive, weighing 505 lb (230 kg); the Alfa weighed 450 lb (204 kg).

There is no doubt the project was a classic case of mismanagement. It typified management by a committee. Raymond Mays wanted to win, but not badly enough to change his lifestyle. Peter Berthon wanted to win, too, but he was often distracted by the other pleasures in life. The V16 was a foundation stone, albeit a rickety one, on which Britain's dominance of F1 was built some seven or eight years later.

One of my sons-in-law gave me a recording of the V16 exhaust noise, and I drove out of the Lotus factory one day in my Excel with the cassette player at full bore and the windows open. The security men at the gate dived for cover. Maybe this gave Malcolm McDonald some of his ideas for the development of Anti-Noise with a pleasant sound superimposed on an unpleasant one.

# CHAPTER SEVEN

# The Maserati

IN 1954 FORMULA 1 became 2.5 litres unsupercharged, so Ken Wharton persuaded A.G.B. Owen that BRM should buy one of the new 250F 6-cylinder Maseratis. The new 2.5 litre BRM would not be ready until late in 1955. Ken convinced AGB that racing the Maserati would be good experience for him and the mechanics, and the designers and engineers might learn something from it as well. PB did not see it in the same way. He told me it was an appalling waste of time and money, and he was going to have absolutely nothing whatever to do with it. 'It's yours', he told me. 'See it does not interfere with our programmes, in any way.'

Ron Flockhart and Arthur Hill were sent to Modena to collect our car, No. 2509. Several other private owners, notably Stirling Moss, and Sid Greene of Gilbey Engineering, also bought cars and had their mechanics working at the Maserati factory building them. I had the impression that Stirling's mechanic, Alf Francis, made sure Stirling's car received the best components. After him, the other mechanics did the same, including Reg Williams looking after Bira's car. It followed that we had what was left.

The handover was completed with a test session at the Autodromo with the customer's driver. After this run someone from Maserati rushed up and said congratulations, you have just broken the lap record! To the best of my knowledge No. 2509 was the only private owner's car that never held the Modena lap record.

When it arrived I tried it around Folkingham. The drum brakes were dreadfully heavy after our feather-light servo discs, but the road holding was a whole new world, and the engine seemed to have plenty of torque. PB reminded me of the plan. Arthur Hill in charge of the car, with a different 'guest' mechanic for each race.

No. 2509's first outing was the French GP at Reims, marked by the reappearance of Mercedes Benz and the W196. Maserati had produced new, stronger ratio change gears to overcome failures, and they were bringing some for us to Reims. As usual they missed first practice. Our car developed propshaft vibration, and we found the shaft was bent.

I had plenty of time to goggle at the new Mercedes; warming up engines and transmissions on jacks at a constant 2500 rpm. I had to tear myself away and return to worn camshafts and rockers. Wharton retired about half-distance with the replacement propshaft also out of true. We were all mesmerized by the W196s. If this was what they did in their first race, what would they be like when they were sorted?

Back at Folkingham we found all the rockers were worn — using the wrong oil we were told. Maserati sent us an American-speaking mechanic — Dan. When Willy and I put the engine on the Dynamatic, we found 208 hp against the claimed 240. After a rework, with help from Dan and several phone calls to the Maserati works, we saw 222 hp. With its propshaft realigned and balanced, we took it to Silverstone for a wet British GP, where we again found Dunlop tyres were not as good in the wet as Pirellis. We were still waiting for a full set of gear ratios from Maserati, who again missed first practice. When they eventually arrived we found they were much bigger, and we spent most of the night chipping and filing off the casing to get them in.

The car went well in the race, until a misfire developed. Ken tried to help us by switching off each magneto in turn, 'so we would know which plugs to change', he said. We knew the answer anyway — all of them! This cost 105 seconds, dropped him to eighth place instead of fifth and earned him a lecture from me on sticking to driving and leaving the brainwork to me. After two all-night sessions, the mechanics were in no state to drive back to Bourne, so I sent them home with people from the factory who had come to watch, and I drove the transporter, although I was not in a much better state than they were.

RM was anxious to increase Flockhart's experience, and Bira had a tummy bug, so a deal was done for Ron to share the driving in the British GP with Bira. Not in the plan was that Ron would roll Bira's car and severely damage it. Bira said to RM: 'I have a race next weekend at Caen in Normandy, for very good money. What are you going to do? Pay me the money I will lose or lend me your Maserati?' Although PB, RM and I approached the problem from different perspectives, we all reached the same conclusion — neither. Reg Williams, Bira's mechanic, brought the wreck to Folkingham on the Sunday morning after the race where we helped him strip it for assessment. They compromized, put Bira's engine and gearbox in our chassis and body; painted it Bira blue and sent it to Caen. We would repair Bira's chassis and body, and install 2509's engine and gearbox. We had already planned to convert to disc brakes before the next race — the Swiss GP at Berne, five weeks away.

While Stan Hope and his team did their stuff with the chassis, Willy and I squeezed 238 hp from the engine. The gearbox was overhauled and converted to drive the servo pump. PB, despite his aversion to the Maserati had commissioned a beautiful tapered propshaft; the sort of thing only BRM could or would make. We already had the engine and gearbox in the chassis, but when Dan tried to fit the new propshaft, he found it was much too long. After a fearful witch hunt in the Bourne Drawing Office, and several phone calls to Modena, we found Bira's car was the prototype. This had a 220 cm (86.6 inch) wheelbase and did not handle very well. The standard cars had 228 cm (89.8 inch) wheelbase, and the Monza specials 235 cm (92.5 inch). I was all for getting 2509's chassis and body back, but PB said that by the time we had finished arguing, the season would be over. We moved the engine forward 7 cm (2.8 inch) and used the plunge in the splines to cope with the rest. We managed a run on the Sunday evening before leaving for Berne, and in the dusk the discs glowed bright red. Dunlop said it was only a minor adjustment; which it was.

We took Dick Salmon as guest mechanic to Berne. It rained most of the time and Ken kept whingeing about the Dunlops' lack of grip in the wet, even though he had split the works Maseratis and was on the third row. It rained even harder on race day, so I produced the set of Pirellis I had saved for a 'rainy' day. Ken, with his usual stupidity, on the fourth lap behind Mieres and ahead of Mantovani (both in works Maseratis), gave Mantovani a brake test, which the drum-braked Maserati failed, pushing Ken off and losing him 31 seconds in the process. It was incredibly stupid as Mieres's Maserati in front was also drum-braked. He finally finished sixth, 22 seconds behind Mantovani and 26 behind Mieres. But for his stupidity he could have been fourth. His best lap was 1 min 44.8 sec, compared with the winner Fangio's 1 min 42.2 sec.

PB, with his daughter Jackie, came to watch, as did Flockhart with RM, but none of them came near us. I went to see RM for money on Monday morning, and I sensed some sort of crisis, but was anxious to start on the journey home. The Maserati travelled 'Under Treasury Direction' as it was registered as a Rubery Owen development vehicle, and no tax or duty had been paid on it. That meant a Rubery Owen man had to meet us at Dover with all the paperwork. He would not wait if we were late. We had a hard, wet drive back. The Rubery Owen man was not there, and we had to wait eight hours for him. Then we were stopped for speeding on the way to Bourne, only escaping by showing the police the car. Next morning I found an irate AGB, who had interrupted his traditional Norfolk family holiday, waiting for me. Fired up by Ken, who had given him a glowing account of his performance at Berne, he had agreed we should race the Maserati in the Italian GP at Monza. The plan was we should have gone to Monza direct from Berne, and overhauled the car there, drawing on Maserati for spares. Why had I ignored the plan? No one had bothered to tell me, and now we did not stand much chance, having to overhaul the car and get to Monza. Fortunately Flockhart telephoned AGB at the vital moment with an explanation. I never knew what it was.

The car went to Goodwood for the September Meeting, but threw a rod in practice because of a valve spring tip passing through the pump drive gears, and did not race. We rebuilt it in time for the Spanish GP — on the Pedralbes circuit, just outside Barcelona. Willy was guest mechanic. It was a long drive — no autoroutes, no costas and surly Spanish Customs, but fortunately we had some BRM as well as Maserati pens and badges.

At Barcelona we shared a garage with the works cars. I was on good terms with chief mechanic and tester Guerino Bertocchi, who hinted he would like to try our disc brakes. Before practice the BP man suggested we all contributed 25 litres of fuel to last-minute entry Bira to enable him to practise. There had not been time to ship fuel for him with ours, but it would arrive in time for the race. At this moment, to my surprise, PB appeared. He said most certainly not. Obviously the Caen business still rankled. He said he would not interfere with us, as he had come to see the new Lancia D50 V8s — Barcelona was to be their first race.

Bira soon drew blood. He asked Wharton how the short chassis handled. He had found our longer one a dream. Ken, as intended, took umbrage. No one had told him about the exchange. It was possibly too wet at Berne for him to detect the difference. We had all been sworn to secrecy by RM and PB, although I was assured that AGB knew of the exchange. It was all I could do to get Ken in to the car for practice. He whinged as he had never whinged before, and he was something of an expert. He said the car was not directionally stable; it had no power; the disc brakes were no better than the works cars' drums. I suggested we should get Stirling or Bertocchi to try it. We settled on Guerino, who said the car was as powerful as theirs. Handling was normal, but the brakes were fantastic. Afterwards, in the garage, he told me there was too much front braking, and the car pulled to the right a little, but the brakes were out of this world. We changed the front to rear ratio from 70:30 to 65:35 and, as we were having a little trouble with the pads not retracting, we also reduced the pad diameter to reduce the risk of sticking. When I ran it round the circuit for a few laps early on Sunday morning it seemed fine.

Ken started and finished eighth, after coming in for a chat and a rest. The race, won by Hawthorn, was in the morning, so afterwards everyone could go to the bullfight. The British, led by Mike, cheered the bull; not the last time Mike got us into trouble. After collecting some money via PB, we set off for the Customs hassle, where we were the last. Fortunately they had become bored with tormenting foreigners, so we passed straight through.

Back at Folkingham I gave the car a check run. The brakes worked well, although they might not have been quite as sharp as before the race: it pulled 7300 against 7200 rpm. There was a very strong cross-wind while I was running, and at over 100 mph it weaved slightly either side of the centre line. I could not correct this, neither could we find a reason. It had never done it before — but I had never driven it in such a strong wind either. During the race the car used 46 gallons of BPK for 304 miles, and it leaked over one gallon of oil from the exhaust cam cover and most of the timing gear cover plates.

There was then an interval for me to marry Pam, the dentist's daughter, and for the honeymoon which concluded with the Mechanics' Dinner at the Park Lane Hotel. We found Ken Wharton in the Steering Wheel (club) with a new girlfriend. He was an odd chap. He used to fly in to Folkingham for a test session in a chartered DH Rapide. His girlfriend would wear a very smart suit; and on one occasion a hat made of multi-coloured feathers. Inevitably it was mislaid. It reappeared some time later when for a long time it was standard protective headgear when working under a car.

When I returned from honeymoon we put the engine on the bed. It gave 248 hp just as it did before the race. PB returned from holiday and told me to get the Maserati on top line as it was to be used as a stalking horse for our new car. Find the best fuel, and PB would talk to SU with a view to fuel injection. I did all the usual things; compression ratios; ports; lined everything up, and it then gave 255 hp. We tried different cam forms — no improvement; varied the fuel, which was 50 per cent methanol, 35 per cent avgas, 10 per cent acetone and 5 per cent benzole — nothing significant. But, with all the running, it had improved to 260.8 hp.

I turned my attention to the chassis. The torsional stiffness, measured over the wheelbase, with an applied torque of 1800 lb ft, was 240 lb ft per degree. Most of the deflection took place either in the driver's or fuel tank bays. Some diagonal tubes brought it up to 440 lbs ft and increased the weight by 6 lb (2.7 kg) but a tidying up campaign saved 30 lb (13.6 kg). We pushed and pulled the suspension and failed, in our innocence, to find anything to excite us. A year later Peter Collins told me it was much quicker than other Maseratis through slow corners, especially out of them, and as quick in the faster corners. We knew it was 8 per cent lighter, had a little more power, and much better brakes than the works cars. I noted that the works cars for Monza 1956 had their frame stiffened in exactly the same way as 2509, which had been to the factory for Brabham's engine rebuild in June '56!

In February 1955 PB sent me to the Maserati Factory to buy any performance up-dates going. Alfieri and Guerino Bertocchi were very friendly and helpful, but there was nothing available. Bertocchi gave me a run in the new 2 litre sports car, and a grappa hangover. I found myself with a very bad cold. This was two days before PB's accident, which pitchforked me into the Chief Engineer's responsibilities.

I cancelled the injection programme, as Moss's car — already with SU injection, was only giving 235 hp. I told Dunlop we could not spare the car for tyre tests, as we were too busy with our new car. This may have been a mistake as the new Dunlop R4 was at last better than anything Pirelli had to offer. We finally turned out for a test day, after Wharton had done his deal with Vanwall but before he told us he was leaving. We confirmed the Moss test results, the R4 was good, but we were told that there would only be one set available for us in time for the Daily Express Trophy.

Wharton's defection opened the way for us to have Peter Collins. We could not give him as much time to familiarize himself with the Maserati as he or I would have liked. For some reason Wharton still drove Raymond Mays and Partners' Ford Zephyr at Silverstone. This had a Rubery Owen manufactured Raymond Mays cylinder head with twin SUs. The preparation of the special racing version was another of my problems and distractions. He finished first in his class and fourth in the race, behind Hawthorn, Jimmy Stewart and Desmond Titterington, all in Jaguars.

Peter, learning the car, minus R4s, was on the second row of the Silverstone Daily Express Trophy grid, with 1 min 51 sec to Salvadori's pole of 1 min 48 sec on R4's. Moss also had them, but Hawthorn and Wharton's Vanwalls were on Pirellis. After a terrific battle with Dunlop, I eventually obtained the promised set for Peter, but not until race morning, so he had to 'scrub' them during the race. John Wyer kept my lap chart. Salvadori made the most of it and led away, but after six laps Peter had sorted his handling on the new tyres and was looking up Roy's exhaust pipe. On lap 25 he got in front, but Roy regained the lead on lap 27; Peter then overtook him for good on lap 34. The 1 hour 49 minutes and 50 seconds he took for 60 laps left me quite limp. Peter made a tremendous fuss of his mechanics, pointing to his clean overalls — no oil leaks — unique for a Maserati. I drove Pam home in the racing Zephyr, at peace with the world.

We had another race at the end of the month — the London Trophy at Crystal Palace. Pam and I travelled there and back with RM in his new S-type Bentley; all very luxurious. It was very hot; the surface was breaking up and Peter slid off in practice, damaging the tail. Peter just won the first heat from Roy Salvadori, but Roy's engine blew on the third lap of the second heat. All Peter had to do was keep ahead of Bob Gerard in his very quick and nimble Cooper Bristol, which he did.

The heat was now on. The new 2.5 litre BRM ran for the first time on 5 June, but it was clear we would have to use the Maserati for the British GP at Aintree on 6 July. The test bed was now set up for BRM engines, but the Maserati felt good when I tried it at Folkingham. During practice the engine blew up, the tip of a valve spring having somehow eluded our post-Goodwood gauze screens and passed between the oil pump drive gears, wrecking the drive, and causing the engine to seize through lack of oil circulation. We had to use Maserati spares for an all-night rebuild, running-in on jacks, as much as we could in the wash bay of Prout's of Liverpool, with water hoses on the radiator and sump.

Peter had to start well back — alongside a newcomer, J. Brabham — but by one third distance he was leading all the Maseratis. Alfieri came to our pit and said to keep him after the Mercedes, and they would overhaul the engine free of charge. A promise he had to keep, as one of the Maserati-supplied overnight spare connecting rods failed from a forging seam, which we had neither the time nor facilities to give our usual metallurgical inspection. He had climbed up to fifth place, behind the four Mercedes, when the rod opened up from the forging lap just like a split pin, cutting the engine nearly in half. Ron Flockhart, who had his own Auster light aircraft (Cal-air he called himself) flew the damaged parts to Modena by way of the Rhône valley and round the coast. Maserati kept their word and replaced the parts, even though they did not get to see the cylinder head, which survived. There were now no plans to race the car again, and I was told to rebuild it ready for sale.

After the debut of the new BRM at Oulton Park at the end of September it was decided to run the Maserati in a minor race at Castle Coombe the following weekend, while we recovered from the carnage caused by Oulton. However, it did not work out as planned, for while I was giving it a shakedown on Friday morning there were signs of a blowing head joint. This meant I had to drive the transporter from Bourne to Castle Coombe at 4 a.m. on Saturday with Willy and Arthur Hill asleep alongside me. In the race, during a tussle with Harry Schell in a Vanwall, the de Dion broke. This was a common Maserati problem we thought we could avoid by regular alignment and crack tests. It was repaired by welding a new tube to the Maserati hubs.

As I left Castle Coombe, Peter said his goodbyes. He said he could not stand working with RM any longer; he did not tell him the truth. He said he had nothing against me or the mechanics, but please keep it to myself. He was going to try for a drive with Ferrari, but he did not know what his chances were.

I managed to run the rebuilt Maserati engine on the test bed, it gave 256 hp on its first run. The Aintree damage to the combustion chambers must have cost us some power. We had by now signed Mike Hawthorn to lead the Team with Tony Brooks, but were not happy to send the new four-cylinder BRMs all the way to Argentina, so instead we sent the Maserati in the care of Bira's ex-mechanic Reg Williams. Mike finished third to Fangio (Ferrari) and Jean Behra (works Maserati), complaining of extreme discomfort in the small cockpit. In the following non-championship race, the temporary bracket to keep the steering wheel clear of his knees broke, but he still finished tenth.

We never touched the car again. It was sold at the dockside to Jack

Brabham, with two hard races behind it, so it was well overdue for an overhaul. Jack took a chance and ran it at Aintree, where it finished third behind Tony Brooks who was in brake trouble with his BRM. Instead of the very much overdue overhaul, it ran in the Daily Express Trophy at Silverstone, where the inevitable happened, the engine blew and was destroyed. We had always limited the engine to 500 miles between overhauls, yet it must have had over 1100 on it when it failed. We were sad to see the engine on which we had lavished so much care, literally go up in smoke.

The next time I saw the Maserati was in 1961, in New Zealand, driven by its new owner, Lenny Gilbert. Willy went to have a look at it. Only the gearbox remained of the original 2509. The chassis came from Bira's 2501, most of the body was new following Flockhart's crash or during my weight-reduction campaign. Much of 2509's engine was wrecked in the British GP, and what was left, at Silverstone nearly a year later. I found you could become fond of anything if you spent enough nights with it, and the Maserati had at least 20 all-nighters from me. It helped make the BRM handle better. For years the 250F was the car to beat on handling. It was a pleasure to drive and certainly the best car Maserati made.

# CHAPTER EIGHT

# The 2.5 litre
# 4-cylinder BRM

THIS ALBUM BEGINS in 1954, and is about the 2.5 litre BRM; a car which was to have been the complete opposite of the V16 — light and simple. It may have been, but it had just as many problems; probably because the cast of characters was unchanged.

The new 2.5 litre Formula was noteworthy for the return of Mercedes. Although quite a few teams missed the first race, including Mercedes (and it was two races before they were ready), it was nearly two years before BRM were ready!

Early in 1954 the BRM test house at Bourne was dismantled and re-erected in the old airfield fire station at Folkingham. The Dynamatic brake was sent back to Heanan and Froude for major overhaul. It would now have to deal with 9000 rpm instead of 6000 rpm (the V16 output shaft turned at 0.518 crankshaft speed). A smaller DPX2 water brake of 100 hp capacity, to handle the single cylinder research engine, was added. The engine build shop moved into a new building, east of the control tower at Folkingham. A new workshop was erected behind the existing racing shop for new car build. Raymond Mays's garage business was also expanding and he wanted more space.

The Control Tower at Folkingham was converted into a flat for the Berthons. PB told Jock, the Geordie caretaker, that he could not stand an Elsan chemical toilet any longer, so please install a proper flush system. With help from the racing mechanics, who poured water down various drains while Jock lurked by the brook 500 yards away, a flush toilet was indeed installed. It worked satisfactorily for about a year, then we ran into trouble with the telephone. When the telephone engineers investigated, it became clear that Jock (or the mechanics) had got the conduits mixed, so the Elsan was brought back into use for a few months.

The BRM pig was fully grown and sold to Marsh and Baxter, at a profit of £21.25. We were sorry to see him go. With appropriate BRM transfers, he was taken to market in one of the transporters. His memory lingered on in that particular transporter for months, even though it stood with the doors open and a water hose permanently running.

PB began the programme by running Tres's original design concept single cylinder research engine, which had a 4-valve aluminium-bronze cylinder head. The engine was enormously over square, 102.8 mm bore and 75.0 mm stroke. The single cylinder immediately ran into terrible head gasket trouble, so PB decided to change to a two-valve layout, using the Ferrari technique of screwing the cylinder liner into the head, and making the gas seal with a Wills gas-filled ring. This caused a major delay while the new parts were designed and made.

Just before I took the Maserati to Barcelona, PB introduced me to an aircraft engineer called Killeen, who brought his sports car with MG engine and running gear. It was a beautifully made full monocoque (in October 1954). The engine dropped through an aperture at the front. There were three massive bulkheads, the front carried the front suspension, one separating the engine and driver, and one in the tail carrying the rear suspension and fuel tank. Driver and passenger gained access through another aperture. Any loss of stiffness was made good by a very carefully shaped deep propeller shaft tunnel rather like a Lotus Elan; but remember this was in 1954, some eight years before the Elan. The whole car was very carefully designed and beautifully made. I spent an afternoon testing it and was absolutely entranced. It was completely rigid, with extremely soft suspension, and handled like a dream. The aerodynamics were very good, with a blown perspex windscreen. I was required to write a full and detailed assessment of the car, copied to AGB. It had a profound effect on me, and launched me on my stiffness crusade. PB gave his usual impersonation of the sphinx but I think it got to him.

Before we left for Barcelona, PB laid down the rules for making the new car. The light-hearted piracy by which I built cars at Folkingham had to stop. The Type 27 would be designed in the drawing office and built to their drawings. No more chalk on the garage floor. Development was my responsibility; but until the car was built and there were engines to test, concentrate on the Maserati and do not interfere.

When PB and I returned from holiday and honeymoon, respectively, he told me to torsion test the nearly complete new chassis. It was virtually a monocoque but, unlike the Killeen, had four parallel steel tubes joined together by welded steel cross members. The front was a very complex structure carrying double wishbones and the air struts — lightening holes welded together again, like the Mark II V16. The engine/driver bulkhead was two elektron sheets framed with 0.75 inch (2 cm) square steel tube bent to the body profile. The rear bulkhead, carrying the rear fuel tank, gearbox and rear suspension was again lightening holes welded together. The aluminium skin was rivetted to the steel structure, so that it was in effect a monocoque, but with high stress-point loads carried on the steel structure.

After an argument as to whether my applied load of 1800 lb ft (250 m/kg) was excessive, PB told me to use my judgement and stiffen it up as I thought fit. I also checked the front suspension and found it had the most appalling bump steer. The geometry was awful, but we did not know much better on Christmas Eve 1954. In January 1955 I was put in charge of building the new car, with authority to change it as necessary. PB continued single cylinder testing in total secrecy, and there were horror stories of a major disaster every week.

PB's contribution to chassis stiffness arrived, and this was bolster-type side fuel tanks made from 0.2 inch (0.5 mm) sheet steel welded around a well-perforated 4 inch (101.6 mm) diameter tube, running the length of the bolster with end plugs secured to the middle and rear cross-member by a multitude of small screws. Amidships the tank carried the front end of the de Dion radius arms. The tanks increased chassis stiffness from 480 lb ft (66 m/kg) per degree to 740 lb ft (102 m/kg). We had to cut enormous holes in the side of the car to fit the tanks; otherwise the stiffening effect would have been greater.

It was clear that what is now called the critical path ran through the single-cylinder test programme, which was making absolutely no progress. Without information from this we had no main engine and no car.

In mid-February 1955, after a trip to Maserati had sent me to bed with a fearful cold, Pam told me PB had been seriously injured and was in Peterborough Hospital following a 3 a.m. crash on the A1 at Stilton. He had apparently fallen asleep at the wheel returning from London. It was clear that he would be out of action for at least three months.

It was no time for colds; I had a meeting with RM. Ken Wharton had decided — telling us at the last minute — to join Vandervell, which gave us Peter Collins. I thought we had by far the best of the exchange. We agreed on a minimum number of races with the V16 and Maserati to keep Peter happy until the new car was ready. I went through the main engine programme with John Botterel, the Chief Draughtsman, to set priorities. We decided to build the first main engine without waiting for the answers from the single-cylinder tests. I suspected, and was not disappointed, that we would find plenty of time-wasting silly mistakes. We would modify it later in the light of single-cylinder information, and hoped we might have it running by the end of March.

I found PB's notes on the single testing. The best he had seen was 52 hp at 5000 rpm. As it was a research unit and did not drive its water and oil pumps, this meant — times four cylinders — the main engine would give less than 200 hp driving its pumps. We ran it to 3000 rpm and then stripped it, in an attempt to avoid the disastrous blow-ups which had been stopping any progress. We found both valves had touched the sides of their cut-outs in the piston, and there was no carbon on the inlet face, indicating the valve was nearly touching and certainly would at higher rpm. We increased the clearances, sacrificing compression ratio in the process from 11.8:1 to 10.3:1. We gradually worked up to 7500 rpm, stripping the engine after every 500 rpm increase, to see what troubles we were about to encounter before a destructive failure occurred. We saw 62.2 hp at 7500 rpm, and a greatly daring 61.5 hp at 8000 rpm.

We were running with a single conventional SU carburettor at the end of a long ram pipe. The main engine was intended to run on SU port injection with a mechanical pump. We needed the data on ram pipe and exhaust lengths to make the systems for the main engine, which by now was installed alongside on the Dynamatic. The single was in dreadful valve spring trouble, and there was no reason to believe that the same spring in the main engine would not be in the same trouble. They were traditional BRM hairpin springs. True to tradition, they deformed, broke, and lost poundage — every defect a valve spring could possibly suffer. We ran the main engine confirming, if we needed to, that it was in valve spring trouble, but we managed to learn how to make the SU single-point injection work. The key to it all was the air bleed hole.

The single showed we needed 22 inch- (56 cm) long ram pipes from the large aluminium plenum chamber to the inlet valve, with a single throttle butterfly at one end. To Willy's intense disgust, the sheet metal workers called the plenum the 'Queen Mary'. Willy protested loud and long: 'The "Mary" has only three funnels.' 'Call it the "Titanic" then', was their riposte. We worked the main engine up to 255 hp at 7000 rpm.

Water flow was too low, so there was a delay while a bigger water pump was made. The car had an aluminium honeycomb water-oil heat exchanger in the oil tank, cooled by water on the way from the pump to the cylinder block. Adequate water flow was therefore vital.

I began to feel I had the situation under control. The racing programme was going well. We had so far won every race we entered with the V16 and Maserati. I went to see PB in the Mount Vernon Hospital, Northwood, where he was having plastic surgery to rebuild his shattered jaw. I told him that we had got the first car as far as we could without an engine, which was held up by the valve spring problems and I was proposing to put the first engine into the car, so that we could at least complete the pipework, even if we had to remove the engine later to fit improved valve springs. PB hoped to pay us a visit, which he subsequently did far too soon and, as a result, contracted pneumonia. While he was with us I asked him what shape he had in mind for the tail, as no one at Bourne knew. He vaguely described a shape to me, so I made a sketch of an extension to the basic body profile, surmounted by a large 'D' type Jaguar combined head fairing and fin. 'That's it,' he said.

On Sunday 5 June 1955 the car was completed. It weighed 1094 lb (497 kg) dry. PB arrived for my first run. I ran for 19 laps, limited to 6000 rpm. There were no problems, although after the Maserati I felt the vibration levels were very high. Next day I drove it harder, and the propshaft centre bearing — housed in a concentric rubber bush under the front edge of the seat — failed. The rubber bush went up in smoke, causing me some concern.

By the time the car was a week old I had run over 150 miles, and it now had a two-piece propeller shaft. Using an aircraft air speed indicator taped to the body, I had found the best location for the single rear brake disc cooling duct — high up by the driver's shoulder. I did not bother to test to find the best exit location, and just cut a hole, to match the radiator intake, in the extreme end of the tail. Imagine my chagrin when after a run in the rain we found air also entered through this hole. We had a new injection pump, and fuel was boiling in the pump, making hot restarts difficult. First impressions were terrible vibration and the absolute lack of any form of throttle response out of a corner.

Peter Collins came up on 18 June, and a valve spring failed after he had done 19 laps. Willy and I did some tests to measure the lack of throttle response. Using a Girling brake testing device which fired a chalk pellet at the road, we discovered that after I opened the throttle the car travelled six lengths before the engine responded. We fitted 54 DCOE Weber carburettors. With these the engine gave 244 hp against 258 hp on SU injection, but the car was transformed.

We had an appalling job fitting them. The heads had been designed for injection with ports at 80 degrees to the centre line, and a threaded adaptor screwed into the head. The carburettors had to be mounted at an angle, so even if one induction port length was correct the other was either too long or too short. It was also extremely difficult to support the weight of the carburettors as they hung outside the stressed skin structure. The injection system drew air from a gap between two halves of the radiator matrix. This was not possible with the carburettors, and we had to make a Dzus-fastened external air intake which further weakened the over-stressed skin.

We screwed an additional steel air bottle into the air struts, doubling the air volume and moving us a long way down the rate curve. As a result I thought the cars handling had improved, and felt about half way to the Maserati. Flockhart was coming to try it, but before he arrived the engine dissolved in a shower of sparks — No. 1 timing gear had failed, the first of many such failures. We tried to reduce the vibration by clutch changes. Finally we arrived at a diaphragm spring (Belleville) clutch instead of balance weights and springs but, if anything, this made the vibration worse, which should have given us a clue — the diaphragm spring clutch was much lighter. In 20 days of testing I covered 430 miles, had two brake pipe failures, three seized gearboxes, two broken valve springs, a propshaft bearing and a timing gear failure. I had tried all the roll bars and 17 suspension settings. It always seemed dawn or dusk, yet they were a long way apart in August.

We went hopefully to Aintree, with Peter Collins and the newly completed second car 27/2 plus the V16. The new car weighed 1068 lb (485 kg) and had been built for carburettors rather than cut about to accept them. Weight distribution empty and dry was 50.6 per cent on the front wheels. The high finned tail on 27/1 weighed 5 lb more than the new tail on 27/2.

We did not last long at Aintree. On his second practice lap Peter spun off on his own oil from the breathers, hit a concrete post and the car was too badly damaged to race. PB embarked on the design of a series of scavenge pump non-return valves. In the middle of it all my father died suddenly, so I had to abandon them. While I was away they took the car and Ron Flockhart to Oulton Park where they wasted three days, exhausting the possibilities of non-return valves. Finally we cured it with an extra scavenge pump on the unused third magneto drive, this lead to a much more sanitary solution; a Ferrari-style three-gear pump with two inlets and the two outlets combined into one — twice the flow for just for one extra gear. Les Bryden made this pump in 30 hours of non-stop machining. He was a tower of strength and could always rise to this sort of occasion.

When Peter Collins then tested the car at Oulton Park, with the triple gear pump, he managed 32 laps, and there were no problems from the oil system, although he grumbled non-stop about the handling. For the Oulton Park Gold Cup race we used the third engine, No. 253. We were dogged by propshaft failure throughout practice. In the race we managed ten laps, starting well back on the grid, and in the course of those glorious ten laps Peter had passed everyone except Stirling in his Maserati. He overtook the two Vanwalls, Salvadori, and Castellotti and Hawthorn in Lancia Ferraris. Then he came in with low oil pressure. We subsequently found the fearful vibration had shaken the needle off the oil pressure gauge, and the engine had plenty of oil pressure. To overcome this we went to a rubber-mounted instrument panel.

Ken Wharton won his class in a new Mark II racing Ford Zephyr. We went back to Bourne very tired but in rather better spirits than we had been for some weeks. Gregor Grant treated *Autosport* to a green cover with a photograph of Peter in the BRM, something he normally reserved for a major British international success. We returned to Oulton Park with Ron Flockhart while Peter Collins was partnering Stirling Moss in the Targa Florio in a 300 SLR Mercedes, but we were rained off before we got very far. I was taking a holiday with a pregnant Pam when Peter Collins's move to Ferrari was announced.

We had another test session at Oulton Park in mid-November with Stirling Moss, who was already committed to Maserati. We spent most of the time sweeping the leaves off the corners! Stirling's best was 1 min 52.2 sec — just a whisker better than his Maserati time — then the oil pressure dropped. If we filled the tank full, the engine threw it out; if we reduced the level to keep the oil in the tank, we lost pressure because of surge in the corners. If you improve one aspect of the car, and go a little faster, you uncover a whole nest of new problems. We went back yet again to Oulton with three cars. The Maserati as a reference, a Lockheed-braked type 27, and a Dunlop-braked 27. Hawthorn, Jack Fairman and Ivor Bueb were the drivers. Mike managed 1 min 55.6 sec in the Maserati, 1 min 55 sec dead in the Dunlop-braked BRM, and 1 min 57.2 sec in the Lockheed-braked car. Both BRMs had failed — Lockheed brakes and valve springs — before Fairman and Bueb had a chance to drive.

As usual, we went into winter hibernation. PB was far from well, having returned to work several months too soon, and I was very tired indeed. I had started the season on a high note with everything going well, believing all the BRM problems had been designed out of the 2.5 litre, only to find they had multiplied. Pam and I had moved into a new flat in Bourne for which we paid the princely sum of 30s (£1.50) per week. A settled home life was the only thing that kept me sane.

We converted to gearbox-driven servos but could not choose between Lockheed and Dunlop brakes. We made lighter fuel tanks, and there was much experimentation with air struts. The winter of 1955/56 was terrible. We lost a week in February with heavy snow blocking the roads into the airfield. I rolled one of the Standard Vanguards on an icy road on my way to work, and was sent for X-ray to Peterborough Hospital where I met Pam. Her doctor had sent her there, too, as our first child was some 15 days overdue. Next day it snowed very heavily. We had an old London Transport 26-seater bus to ferry the staff to and from Folkingham, now that engine and car build staff worked there too. We left for home on Tuesday at 7.30 p.m., me somewhat apprehensive as the doctor said the baby would appear within 24 hours from Monday afternoon. We got stuck, two miles out of Folkingham village, despite Jock having conducted a reconnaissance on the Ferguson tractor. It took three hours to walk home through the snow, and when I arrived I found PB installed in the room set aside as the maternity ward, having got two cars stuck in his efforts to reach the airfield. The baby finally arrived the next evening. There was never a dull moment that winter.

Notwithstanding the serious handling problems, PB launched me on a major engine performance improvement programme. He had commissioned four new engines for 1956 — numbers 256/1 to 4 — to supplement the five we had at the end of the 1955 season. The '56 engines had right-angled ports to make carburettor installation easier. I had to try fuel-injection again, but with four individual throttle butterflies close to the valve — 44, 46 and 47 mm chokes — BPK and BPL fuel (BPL had more alcohol), three different inlet camshaft profiles and tulip-shaped inlet valves. Frank Walsh, Joe Craig's draughtsman at Norton Motorcyles had joined us. He was the driving force behind the different valves and camshafts, and the tulip-shaped inlet valves were known as Norton valves. The engine was designed for three sparking plugs. Cylinder heads were tapped for three and there were drives for three magnetos, but the engine seemed to prefer the two outer ones, so we blanked the centre hole off and saved the weight and power to drive a third magneto.

The best set-up using BPK fuel gave 132.5 hp at 4000 rpm, 190 at 5000, 232 at 6000, 252 at 7000, and 261 at 8000. This was about the same maximum power as the Maserati, but a much fatter torque curve.

Easter Goodwood was upon us — too soon as usual. We only got one car to first practice, Tony Brooks having to wait for his. Stirling was competing with a Bosch fuel-injected works Maserati. Mike was about two seconds off the pace in practice. In the race, Tony Brooks lost oil pressure, then Mike had a most spectacular crash at Fordwater. The pot-type universal joint on one of the half-shafts seized, the car went end over end, fortunately throwing Mike out onto soft earth. The rubber gaiter retaining the lubricant had split. After two months investigation, involving a high speed cine camera, we found that the heavy oil we used in the joint collected on one side and rotated in a lump under centrifugal load. The high-speed cine photograph which confirmed it all is reproduced in this book. We were given an early clue from bright marks on a frame tube some 5 inches (12.7 cm) away from the rubber, which told us that the rubber had been whirling.

Our next race at Aintree was hectic. Mike had a clevis pin drop out of the Lockheed brake master cylinder assembly. Tony Brooks, in the Dunlop-braked car, ran completely out of rear brake lining but managed to nurse the car home to finish second. I had a hilarious breakfast with Mike and Peter Ustinov next morning; which showed me who was the inspiration for Peter Ustinov's famous recording of the 'Grand Prix du Roc'.

We sent one car to the Daily Express Trophy at Silverstone, as it was the week before the first GP of the season at Monaco. Mike went straight into the lead in front of the new Vanwall, but after 14 laps No. 1 timing gear broke and wrecked a badly needed engine.

I was in a pretty poor state of health, with a large crop of boils, and tubes to drain them, so I travelled to Monaco in the back of RM's Bentley via Grenoble and Digne. First practice showed us what we were in for. The hollow Norton valves were sealed with a disc welded into the crown. Discs fell out on both engines. There was also trouble with spark plugs, and the Dunlop brakes on Tony's car. We managed to repair one engine and we fitted the spare, but we repeated the performance on Friday. Another engine was flown out and the least damaged engine rebuilt, but Mike had another failure on Saturday. Both cars were withdrawn, and as many useless mouths as possible, including mine, were sent home on Saturday afternoon in the DH Dove that had brought out the spare engine. It was too noisy for any of us to sleep.

Our only way out of the Norton valve trouble was a much heavier valve, which cost 750 rpm, we tried to get some of the lost power back with nitro methane. Unfortunately the law of diminishing returns sets in, but with 15 per cent nitro we had much more torque and a little more power, despite the lost rpm. The power was now 212 hp at 5000 rpm, 260 at 6000, 277 at 7000 and 276 at 7500 — our new limit.

For the British GP at Silverstone, although we had to pull a higher gear because of the reduced rpm, there was still a risk we might have to stop for fuel, but we need not have worried. To accommodate the lanky Mike we had lengthened his car, 27/1, by 3 inches (7.6 cm). The car handled better, but we were back with propeller shaft vibration troubles. Mike, who was very tense because of external pressures at this time, became very concerned by the possibility of a shaft failure, and insisted on a massive steel guard. The Press criticism over his exemption from National Service was getting to him. He was not the happy-go-lucky Mike of a few years ago. (Mike invented the champagne spraying custom, only he used Guinness.)

In the race, Mike and Tony Brooks went into the lead and pulled away. Ron, in the third car, was soon out with a timing gear failure. Tony Brooks's car's handling deteriorated, developing more and more oversteer, and he was caught by the Fangio-Moss battle. Mike led until lap 23 when he saw the tell-tale oil stains on the side of the cockpit, indicating that a pot-joint rubber had split again. Tony Brooks then came in with a broken throttle rod. We taped it up and sent him out again, but the throttle stuck open at Abbey causing him to spin, and he was tipped out as the car rolled over. He was taken to hospital with a suspected fractured jaw, and the car was totally destroyed by fire. We derived a little comfort from the speeds down Hangar Straight. Mike was timed at 137.4 mph, Harry Schell's Vanwall at 136.8, Tony Brooks 136.3, Fangio's Ferrari 134.8, Collins in another Ferrari 134.3 and Stirling's Maserati 133.8. Mr Owen was not in the least bit impressed by our performance and sent his man Spear with a posse to sort us out. I managed to get the broken pieces of the throttle rod to Rolls-Royce for investigation as they were all Rolls-Royce parts. They found that we had not brazed the end fittings into the tube correctly. They had survived the fire.

During this crisis the brake lining suppliers came up with a mass of information on the problems with the single rear brake. The theory of a single rear brake was that as the front to rear braking ratio was 70:30, each front brake would perform 35 per cent of the work and the rear 30 per cent, so we only needed one. The logic was unassailable. Dunlop specified Mintex, so it was their linings on Tony Brooks's car at Aintree. Mintex said that our rubbing speed was too high. The single rear disc driven off the transmission ran at 3.5 times road wheel speed. The Lockheed car used Ferodo pads, and Ferodo were also adamant that we had to bring the speed down, and moreover bring the disc temperature down by at least 100°C (212°F). We managed to fit a reduction gear unit in the back of the gearbox, but even so the rear disc was rotating at the equivalent of 200 mph (323 kph) when the car was doing 150 mph.

Late one night at Folkingham, waiting for an engine to be ready to run on the test bed, I was reading the *Engineer* magazine when I came across a patent application for disc brakes for use on the Berlin 'U' Bahn (the equivalent of the London tube system). It referred to a ventilated disc; in effect two discs sandwiching a series of curved vanes so that air was drawn through the disc and after cooling the surfaces was expelled around the periphery. I grabbed Freddie Bothamley, the Lockheed man, who was fortunately visiting, and he put it to Fred Ellis, Lockheed's engineer in charge of disc brakes (and also a fellow Aston Martin enthusiast). They agreed that a ventilated disc might help. They made a drawing double quick, Peter Spear got one of the Owen organization companies, Conegre, to cast 24 in a cast-iron alloy which I used to describe irreverently as old gas stoves.

After the disasters at Silverstone A.G.B. Owen ruled that BRM would withdraw from racing until we had solved all our problems and demonstrated the fact by running a race distance at racing speed. PB proposed tests at Monza, but Peter Spear wanted justification as to why it should be Monza. He visited us once a week with his posse, comprising his personal assistant and two or three members of his staff. There were five pages of minutes covering everything: air struts, pot-joint rubbers, valve springs, vehicle dynamics, valves, brake pipes, drivers, press relations, a possible skid pan, vibration testing, car test schedules and so on. It was clear that PB's intentions were not to let Peter Spear interfere or find out anything. Spear's intentions stopped just short of proving to AGB how he, Spear, could do a better job of running BRM. He was at least intent on highlighting PB's shortcomings as a manager. Making a better racing car was well down everyone's priority list.

We converted 27/3 to independent rear suspension. It had a massive triangulated bottom link, still with an air strut. The top link was a fixed length universally-jointed drive shaft. It was very like the suspension used by the E-type Jaguar and Lotus Europa but pre-dated them by five years. It worked quite well, but unfortunately we did not understand 'jacking' loads (where the vertical component in the cornering reaction greatly exceeds the weight on that wheel). As the car went round a corner it looked quite horrific; the back had jacked up two or three inches and the outer wheel had positive camber. Tony Brooks did most of the driving. Surprisingly he was not as critical as I would have expected him to be, after watching him round a few corners, with about five degrees of positive camber.

The next move was to convert the rear suspension of 27/1, Mike's long-chassis car, to Maserati-style transverse leaf spring, mounted on rollers so it had some anti-roll effect. We fitted Armstrong-type lever dampers, and the de Dion was located by what was known as a Connaught link. We copied it from Connaught, a car that seemed to handle well. The Connaught link also appealed to me as it reduced some of the considerable friction in the suspension. (See the photograph, taken at Monza in October 1956, reproduced in this book from Denis Jenkinson's 'Motor Sport' Racing Car Review.) I had found the friction in our rear suspension under cornering loads was about three times that of the Maserati. Most of this was because of the air struts, but the friction in the pot-joint universals and the de Dion slide was also double that of the Maserati.

We took this car to Silverstone on the 18 September. Tony Brooks got down to 1 min 44.1 sec. His comment was: 'It's better than any BRM I have ever driven, but the back end still slides out on the bumps.' Roy Salvadori, first time in a BRM, managed 1 min 45.8 sec. Roy was fresh from a successful season in his Maserati and his comments were illuminating — 'terrific oversteer, terrific vibration, heavy brakes but impressed by the engine's performance.' Tony Brooks tried again, 1 min 42.6 sec, and said: 'The car is half way from the previous one to perfection. The engine does not feel as powerful as the one I had for the GP.' This was both perceptive and correct — it was not on nitro methane. Tony said he could nearly drift the car. We saw him at 15 degrees to the line of travel through Abbey. His accident had not left him with many ill effects. A broken exhaust valve spring brought testing to an end.

The fourth car, 27/4, was completed in mid-September. This had a raised cockpit enclosure and tail. I reasoned its better aerodynamics would make it faster, but more important to me, the new cockpit structure increased the torsional stiffness considerably — by over 50 per cent. This car also had the leaf spring rear suspension, but we could convert back to struts in about 60 minutes. The Silverstone tests added up to 270 miles, (435 km) in ten-lap bursts, but at least the speed was respectable.

PB won a fortnight's testing at Monza. Taking two cars, 27/1 and 27/4 (both with leaf spring suspension), and five engines (all with lighter valves) we were now back to 8000 true rpm. The best engine, old 254, gave 272 hp. All the others were a shade under 270 hp, and without nitro there was less torque. PB never really recovered from his accident. He could not drive long distances, so I shared the driving with him in his Ford Zephyr with Raymond Mays conversion, and we took Pam with us.

We stopped overnight at Lausanne and picked up Dick Dawson, the plastic surgeon who had put PB's face back together. After lunch at Martigny, we crossed the St Bernard pass in the afternoon with PB driving and Pam and I in the back. Dick remarked that he was very surprised at Pam sleeping through all this beautiful scenery. Pam told me she had her eyes firmly shut because she was so frightened!

At the Marchesi Hotel we found Peter Spear, Tony Brooks and Ron Flockhart. Ron had just finished fifth in a Connaught in the Italian GP, run on the new combined road and banked circuit. The new circuit, which chopped a bit off Vedano — the south turn now renamed the Parabolica — rendered all our previous data irrelevant. We started testing on 2 October using the road circuit only; in a drizzle, certainly not the reason why we came to sunny Monza. Our first problem — both cars dumped 0.5 gallons (2.2 litres) of water. This was cured by resetting the header tank pressure relief valves to 15 psi (1 bar) instead of 10 psi. Then a new (slightly welcome) problem. Tony Brooks, driving 27/4, complained of understeer at Lesmo. It was nearly always oversteer the driver complained about. He gave 27/1 a quick check, then we were rained off. The rain did not clear until 6 October, when Tony Brooks started the 300 mile run. With ten laps completed he hit a pheasant, severely damaging the nose and radiator.

After repairs, we managed 25 laps, controlled at Stirling's recent Maserati average of 1 min 45 sec, then the clutch failed. Tony complained he still could not drift it, and the car was jumping off bumps. He believed 1 min 43 sec was possible, and Tony was not a driver who failed to deliver. We lost a day rebuilding the clutch, then Ron Flockhart took over, as Tony had to return to England. Ron only managed 50 miles before the engine blew up badly. He said the car was handling much better than at Silverstone, and better than the Connaught he drove in the Italian GP. While we were changing the engine in 27/4, Ron tried for 300 miles in 27/1. He stopped after 101 miles (162 km) with a blown oil-cooler water-joint, a broken inlet valve spring and a cracked sparking plug. On the 11 October we tried yet again, Flockhart in 27/4 using engine 254 fitted with 256's head. On lap 51 he stopped for tyres and eight gallons (36 litres) of fuel. Poor old 254 blew up on the 83rd lap. No. 2 inlet valve spring had broken and the engine was badly damaged. He had covered 297 miles (479 km) and his average speed was 118 mph (190.3 kph) so we had nearly met AGB's directive.

Ron said the car felt very stable; superior to 27/1 on handling, it was two thirds of the way to an ideal car. It used 44 gallons (196 litres) of fuel, no water, and two pints (1.1 litres) of oil.

The whole circuit was closed for a few days for a minor race meeting, then the road circuit was not available, but we tried on the banking alone. 27/1 broke a valve spring after 30 miles, and both this car and 27/4 were dreadful on the banking. When the road circuit re-opened, Salvadori drove 27/1, but it was really too dangerous; wet leaves were everywhere. Roy went off at Lesmo without doing any damage. We tried again with 27/1 on the banking. Ron said it was so bad over the bumps he was nearly thrown out of the car. We packed up, ready to return home.

Just before we left, Castellotti tested Firestone tyres on a Lancia Ferrari. (Ferrari had used Pirelli for the 1956 season.) We timed him — using Pirellis to set a base line for comparison — at 2 min 44 sec on the whole circuit, 1 min 0.2 sec on the banking and 1 min 43.6 sec on the road. The experts, Bacciagaluppi and Denis Jenkinson told us that the run-in, from the banking onto the road circuit, was worth 1.5 seconds, so Castellotti's 1 min 43.6 sec would be 1 min 45.1 sec on the road circuit alone. Ferrari spotted us timing, so stopped running on Pirellis and did their testing on Firestone. We saw the car weighed, 661 kg dry, 27/4 weighed 508 kg dry on the same scales. Our old friend 'Oily' told us the engine gave about 260 hp, which made us think. We had more power in a lighter, smaller car. Tony Brooks was faster than Castellotti, so where were we going wrong?

Back at Folkingham I tried 27/3 again, still with independent rear suspension. It was an answer to our traction problems, and I was sorry it was abandoned, but as I could not solve the jacking problem, I could not argue. Tony Brooks politely declined to drive for us in 1957 and wisely joined Vanwall. Roy Salvadori said: 'Maybe, but you will have to make it handle better before I will sign.' We were getting very confused. RM invited Alec Issigonis and Major Alex Moulton to advise us. They recommended rearranging the front struts and rear springs to eliminate their influence on roll stiffness, so that all roll resistance came from the roll bars.

While these changes were being made, Flockhart and I ran a car at Silverstone to try the effect of lowering the front end of the rear radius arms to give us some anti-squat, and hopefully increased traction. Ron found lowering them 1 inch (2.5 cm) produced a dramatic improvement in feel, but no gain in lap time. Lowering them 1.5 inches (3.8 cm) produced no further improvement, so we settled for one inch. Silverstone had no slow corners, neither had Folkingham.

PB was enraptured with his desmodromic valve gear; on rig test, when it was not seizing rockers, it was breaking them! So we did not have much contribution from him towards resolution of the handling problems.

We went to Silverstone on a wet 4 January 1957 with 27/1 and 27/4 — Flockhart and Salvadori driving — which added to the confusion. Flockhart said number 27/1 was easily the best handling car, Roy said 27/4 was the best, but it twitched. After getting them together, they agreed 27/1 was better on fast corners and would accept more throttle sooner. This car still had the radius arms lowered 1.5 inches.

We then repeated the tests at a slightly wet Goodwood, when we succeeded in totally confusing Roy as well. One of his front roll-bar links broke so that the car had no front roll stiffness at all. It should have oversteered off the road but Roy never even noticed, yet he was a very sensitive and observant driver.

For Easter Goodwood we had Orteva valve springs, 7.5 per cent nitro, and 280 hp. So we thought we stood a chance, but on the warm up lap Roy's front brakes applied themselves. We released the pressure by opening the bleed screws but it happened again on the first lap, putting Roy out of the race. Ron complained of a seized left rear damper and spun twice at St Mary's, finishing third behind a Cooper and a Connaught.

After changing dampers we ran Ron's car on Tuesday after the race with a new driver — Colin Chapman. He was very polite, very non-committal, and asked for a set of drawings saying he would try to come up with some ideas. After a fortnight he came to Folkingham, tried the car again and asked many questions, but by then Monte Carlo was upon us.

We took the cars with the Goodwood set-up. All cars had to qualify, and the fastest 16 started. Ron was 11th but Roy was still in terrible trouble with his brakes and was 17th — a non starter. He had a major row with RM and resigned. By half distance there were only five cars left — most of the English contingent (Stirling, Mike, Peter Collins and Tony Brooks) collided at the chicane on the first lap. Ron was plugging on, last and fifth, keeping out of trouble, but on lap 60 No. 1 timing gear failed yet again and that was the end. I really began to hate Monte Carlo.

Colin Chapman came to our rescue, including finding a new driver, Herbert MacKay-Fraser. Colin brought him to Folkingham when he delivered the drawings of his conversion schemes. He said he was not very happy with the front-suspension geometry, but it was too much of a tear up to realize his ideal layout. He specified coil springs and Armstrong telescopic dampers which were interchangeable with the air struts. This called for much ingenuity and compromise by Armstrongs as well as by Colin to get their length down to fit in place of the struts. He called for the de Dion tube to be bent to give half a degree of negative camber and 0.25 inch (0.65 cm) toe-in on a Dunlop gauge. The de Dion was now located by a Watts link, set to one side of the propeller shaft, lowering the rear roll-centre by 5 in (12.7 cm) — not enough, but all that he could get in. Working non-stop, we converted the first car in about 100 hours, while MacKay-Fraser sat on top of one of Jock's step-ladders watching everything. I gave the car a shakedown, then Colin tried it. He suggested more front camber, then MacKay-Fraser and Flockhart tried it. It felt totally different, just like a touring car, yet there was very little wheel movement visible.

To eliminate the pot-joint problems and as a major step in my anti-friction campaign, we had designed new half-shafts with ball-loaded splines and needle-roller universal joints, rather like those used by Ferrari. They were taking a long time to make because the grooves in which the balls operated had to be very hard. As the balls could not be more than 0.25 inch (6 mm) in diameter, the grooves in the female element were very difficult to grind. Eventually we had to lap them. We hoped to have the first set for Rouen, as Colin Chapman had warned that his new suspension would significantly increase wheel movement and probably land us back in pot-joint troubles, but there was no chance. They cost the earth but when we did get them they were literally worth their weight in gold.

Colin was very interested in the independent rear suspension layout on 27/3, which stood in the workshop minus an engine. He asked to try it but we did not have an engine to spare at the time.

After a mad scramble we got two cars to the next race. This was the French GP at Rouen, where everyone had new transporters except us. The garage accommodation allocated by the organizers was quite impossible. However, BP rescued us by letting us use the transport shed in their oil refinery complex at Petit Couronne, close to the circuit.

A series of needle matches developed at Rouen: Fangio, Behra, Menditeguy and Harry Schell on Maseratis; Musso, Collins, Hawthorn and Trintignant in Lancia-Ferraris and Salvadori and Lewis-Evans in Vanwalls. Stirling had given himself severe sinusitis water skiing, and Tony Brooks had not recovered from a crash at Le Mans.

The start was unusual; no pushing and everyone had to use remote starters. There was the sort of chaos that only the French can organize. Everyone boiled on the grid, but fortunately we were well back and clear of the real trouble. After a spectacular start we were completely stunned when MacKay-Fraser came round on the first lap in sixth place! Salvadori's Vanwall oil filler cap came undone, and most of the oil spilt out. Ron, close behind, went off on the oil on a nearly flat out curve. His car hit a concrete bridge and was a total write off, and Ron sustained a broken leg. At quarter distance, MacKay-Fraser had fought off challenges from Hawthorn and Lewis-Evans. Not only was he holding his sixth place, but he was gaining slightly on the fight between Maserati team-mates Carlos Menditeguy and Harry Schell for fourth place. We feared they were a bit rough for a new boy. On lap 26 he came in with the dreaded oil spots on the cockpit side; a pot-joint rubber had split.

We returned to Bourne with mixed feelings. There was only a fortnight to the British GP at Aintree, and we were a driver and a car short, but at least we seemed to be on the right track. Archie Scott-Brown tried a car at Folkingham, where he went quite well, but rang up next day and said: 'No thank you.' We managed to complete 27/5 in the nick of time, but then we were devastated to hear that MacKay-Fraser had been killed driving a sports car at Reims. RM then did deals with Les Leston and Jack Fairman.

The new half-shafts were still not ready, and it was a miserable race. The drivers were still getting used to their cars, and by half distance they were both out; Les Leston with a broken camshaft and Fairman with a cooked engine — new troubles.

We were drowning our sorrows back at the hotel when I was summoned by RM. I was then introduced to Jean Behra and asked if we could get a car to Caen — who paid exceptional starting money — for Jean to drive the following Sunday. I said we could, although it would be touch and go whether the new half-shafts were ready. We could rebuild a car to the Aintree specification and send it in a transporter and wait until the last minute for the half-shafts and send a second car by Silver City Air Ferries from Southampton to Deauville. I persuaded the mechanics to make a dawn start to Bourne where RM literally had everyone waiting for us. So, as planned, we sent 27/1 in a transporter loaded with spares. We built a second engine with so much backlash in the timing gears you could walk between the gear teeth. To get the second car the 42 km (22½ miles) from Deauville to Caen, we planned to tow it behind RM's Rover. It would be dark and the gearbox would not be circulating oil, the pump was driven from the input shaft. Risky, but not impossible. Another transporter with more spares would arrive in Caen after first practice.

The precious half-shafts finally arrived the night before we were due to leave. I managed a quick five laps in the failing light, and within 200 yards I could feel the difference. I had another run at dawn the next morning, putting as much load on them as I could, and they seemed fine. We sent the car to Southampton airport in the third transporter while I took a quick bath and then rode down to Southampton with RM in his Rover. He hated flying, so I regaled him with stories of disaster from my days as an accident investigation engineer! RM towed me faster than I liked, but I remembered to dip the clutch and slip into gear now and again to get some oil round the gearbox, and no one ran into me in the dark. We arrived safely in Caen around midnight.

The next morning Jean Behra descended on me like a hawk. He tried both cars, setting first- and second-fastest practice times by about two seconds. He recognized the benefits of the new half-shafts at once. He doubled the front caster and had dampers, pedals, front camber, toe in, and jets changed. Next day he was even quicker, but the engine in the chosen car, 27/5, became rough at the end of practice. We changed the precious half-shafts onto the older car, crossing our fingers for engine reliability.

RM, always sensitive to starting money situations, turned up with Harry Schell, whose private Maserati had just blown up, to ask if we could fix the other car for Harry to drive? I said we couldn't, and even if we could Behra would drive it. After considerable persuasion, we tried turning the propshaft a quarter of a turn, checking the bearings and their clearances. I gave it a quick run on Sunday morning, and it seemed all right, but I did not think much of its chances. I told Harry and RM that it was a starting money special!

Harry drove it out to the circuit — his only chance to get to know the car. He had to take his Maserati time of 1 min 28.4 sec compared with Behra's 1 min 21.1 sec and Tony Brooks's 1 min 23.6 sec in a Cooper. On the first lap Jean was the length of the straight in front, and he just drove off into the distance. Harry passed Tony Brooks for second place, and by lap 27 he had Behra in sight, who was taking it very easily having set a new lap record of 1 min 20.7 sec. On the 59th lap Harry's engine threw a rod, the only failure on the massive four-bolt rod we ever had. Jean lost eight seconds on one lap and frightened us all out of our wits, but he then continued on his winning way; his average speed faster than the old lap record. He gave me some of his champagne, and said: 'You drive it back to the garage', putting the laurel wreath in the cockpit with me.

Pushed by jubilant mechanics, I tried to put it into gear. I found the gear-change mechanism had broken, the rocking lever at the universal joint where the gear-change tube passed under the de Dion had broken away from the chassis. Jean had just pushed it into top, which explained the lost eight seconds, and finished the race in top gear! I wedged it into second and drove it to the garage.

The transporters left early next day, but RM stayed talking about the future with Jean and Harry. We had Tripes à la Mode de Caen for lunch and set off home in much better spirits. RM told me he hoped to run three cars in the postponed Daily Express Trophy meeting in early September. (The race had been postponed because of fuel shortage following the Suez crisis). He also planned to run two cars at Modena when Ron would be available, and he hoped for two at Casablanca at the end of the season. He could not see any point in going to Championship races at Monza or Pescara as we would not have any worthwhile drivers. I was relieved to hear him talking sense. Pam and I were having a house built in Bourne. I had also been promoted to the Rubery Owen company car scheme and now boasted an Austin A35.

We had prepared carefully for Silverstone — ball half-shafts all round. Panic — for once not car-related — set in the week before. Ron Flockhart's doctors said his Silverstone programme was too ambitious; a Lotus in the sports car race, a Jaguar in the production saloon race and a BRM for the Daily Express Trophy; two heats and final. The doctor recommended missing out the F1 race. Harry Schell shunted his Ferrari during the Tour de France and had hurt his hands and wrists, while Behra had a very bad cold. However, they all turned up for practice. Jean was extremely confident and his message was: 'Just go fast enough to get on the front row. Don't wear the cars out, we will win easily.'

Tony Brooks threw RM into a panic with a practice time of 1 min 43 sec in Rob Walker's 2 litre Cooper Climax. Jean was unperturbed: 'We are all on the front row. I can do 1-41 if I have to, for as long as the car will stand it.' Jean and Ron got away well in their heat, and poor Tony's Cooper broke its gearbox on the line. Jean finished 45 seconds ahead of Ron who let Masten Gregory in a 250F Maserati get too close. Harry Schell had a very easy time in his heat, the only opposition being Jack Brabham in another 2 litre Cooper and Jo Bonnier in a 250F Maserati.

Jean was exuding confidence for the final, but Ron's leg was hurting him badly. Harry was hypeing himself up and I was getting nervous about a 105 mile (170 km) final — a long way for us. Harry made a bad start but they soon got into formation. Jean put in a quick one on his third lap. Harry ran to team orders, while Ron — driving in top gear to rest his leg — was nearly caught by Bonnier. There was a lot of speculation in the Press as to whether the BRMs could have beaten the Vanwalls had they entered, but it was clear to me that we could not. The Vanwalls were as quick; much more reliable; much better organized; and both Stirling Moss and Tony Brooks were quicker than Jean. Tony Vandervell had the last word, saying: 'We are out to beat the bloody foreigners, not our fellow Britons!'

When the engines were stripped I was very disturbed to find that a gudgeon-pin circlip had disappeared on Harry's engine, and he would not have lasted another 25 miles. Behra's engine had the same symptoms, although not as advanced, and there were oil leaks everywhere. We only had a fortnight to get ready for Modena where Jo Bonnier was to drive for us, with Ron. I drove PB and Lorna out in his Ford Zephyr, now fitted with a special high-lift camshaft. The regrind had gone through the case and the cams wore badly. I spent the night stop in Lausanne resetting tappets, and again during the lunch stop at Brig!

The most significant feature of the race at Modena was the first appearance of the new Ferrari Dino V6's, running on petrol instead of alcohol in anticipation of the 1958 regulations. Peter Collins had the 2.2

litre, and Mike Hawthorn the 2.4. They were very nice neat little cars. In the race Ron had a fuel pump mounting break, and his leg was still giving trouble. Bonnier had a broken wheel-end universal joint. Fortunately it was not part of the precious half-shaft.

It was a long way to Casablanca, a completely new circuit, and therefore a non-championship race. Everyone chose different routes. We sent three cars in their transporters to Bordeaux, thence by sea to Casablanca. Our drivers were Flockhart and Trintignant. Ron and I flew by Air France Constellation with an overnight stop in Paris. Hawthorn, on the same flight, caused mayhem by readdressing our luggage.

Although Morocco was an Arab country there was still a strong French influence. The organizers laid on plenty of entertainment; the cars gave very little trouble and the sun and sea did wonders for Ron's leg. 'Trint' was an ideal driver. He knew exactly what he wanted; very polite, very fair and got on with it. Peter Collins and Mike Hawthorn had swapped engines in their Ferraris, so Peter had the bigger 2.4 and Mike the 2.2. Maserati were out in force with the 12-cylinder as well. Brabham had a 2.2 litre engine in Rob Walker's Cooper.

Most of the drivers suffered from a peculiar flu virus, and Stirling felt so ill he went home before the race. Peter Collins, Hawthorn and Fangio were the worst sufferers, but this did not stop Mike causing more trouble when the British contingent visited the Casbah. No alcohol, but coffee kept warm by a spirit lamp. The guests showed their appreciation of the dancer's act by tucking coins in her scanty garments. Mike heated his with the spirit lamp first! We had to form a traditional British square to escape.

There was no practice on Saturday so that everyone could go to a reception given by the King of Morocco. I also visited the hotel where Churchill and Roosevelt met in 1943; while others visited the Sphinx at Fedala, supposed to be the most luxurious 'house of ill repute' in the world. On race day the first Sud Aviation Caravelle made a low fly pass, and when the King arrived all the drivers were presented to him.

Peter Collins led from the start, to unjustified amazement. Using petrol he was only carrying half the weight of fuel compared with other cars. Another surprise: Trintignant was fifth, and Ron was sixth, ahead of Fangio in a standard Maserati. Ron collected the only bird in Morocco, as big as a crow. It went into his carburettor air intake and eventually black feathers jammed the throttles. Fangio lost more time, because of a pit stop for a new wheel, and was then caught in the Brabham black flag incident. Trint eventually finished third, 50 seconds ahead of Fangio, and Behra won. The whole BRM team was entertained by Trintignant who said the car had run trouble free. He had not pressed it, as he did not think he had could catch second-placed Lewis-Evans. None of the Maseratis he encountered, including Fangio's, could catch him. At last we had finished a full GP in the money. We also discovered that the money was considerable when the traditional 10 per cent share out was made at the end of the year. I flew back direct to London where Customs at Heathrow were relieved to see me. I was the first person off the flight who did not have a souvenir camel saddle. This was many years before the Green Channels.

Jean Behra had given me a long and severe lecture on how important it was to improve the front suspension for next season, and what was wrong with what we had. PB had given me a massive engine job list, including conversion to Avgas. The oil companies had rebelled against the outbreak of chemical warfare; nitro methane and so on. The fuel we were using bore absolutely no relationship to the petrol used by the average motorist yet, as the fuel company's contribution represented a major part of most teams' budgets, they were entitled to call the tune.

The plan was to use pump petrol, but no one could define it. 'Freely available at wayside pumps in the country where the race is held or the country of origin of the car', was the wording in the rules, but it was still too difficult to enforce. 'Avgas', aviation gasolene, was the standard commercial aviation fuel for piston aero-engines all over the world. It was agreed that this would be acceptable.

We had acquired a Sunbury battery-powered indicator to measure instantaneous cylinder pressures. PB had commissioned five-main-bearing engines as he was sure that crankshaft weaving was causing all our timing gear problems. By now the timing gears were nearly as big as the gearbox gears. He then told me he was going to take a few days holiday in Morocco and that I had plenty to get on with, which was undoubtedly true.

I schemed a new tubular front end with much longer bottom wishbones to hold the front roll-centre a constant distance from the centre of gravity of the front mass. Stan Hope and his crew produced it very quickly, ready to join onto the engine bulkhead of an existing car. We converted 27/3 back to de Dion rear suspension in place of its independent system and left it in the jig ready for the new front end.

In parallel with this I ran old 254 on Avgas, and I was pleasantly surprised to find that advancing the ignition and recarburating were all that was necessary to get it to run happily on petrol, producing 272 hp compared with 287 hp on 10 per cent nitro methane in 50 per cent methanol base fuel.

PB had still not returned from his holiday, so I took my courage and a saw in both hands; cut the front off 27/3, and welded on the new one. Jean and Harry came over to try the car at Folkingham. Jean pronounced the improvement as 'nuit et jour'. They spent some time in financial negotiations for next season with A.G.B. Owen himself — more playing bar-billiards in The Angel at Bourne.

Then PB returned. He built up an enormous head of steam when he saw the new front end, but before he blew his top and fired me, he asked whether it worked. When he found it was two seconds a lap quicker he subsided. He tore a monumental strip from me for not asking RM to contact him so it could have been discussed. Having been asked by RM two or three times a week if I had had any word from PB or knew where he was, I was rather mystified.

Having got away with it, I then pushed my luck and tried to sell PB the idea that with Avgas instead of alcohol we would do 9 or 10 mpg instead of 6 or 7 on BPK, our 50 per cent methanol fuel, and 5 mpg on nitro. Instead of 45 to 50 gallons (200 to 222 litres) we could get away with 33 to 35 gallons (147 to 156 litres), which meant a smaller and lighter car.

We had developed a technique of threading aluminium rear fuel tanks onto rubber hose wrapped around detachable frame tubes, so why not make a proper space frame using the Chapman inspired rear-suspension and our new front end? We could give this spaceframe a detachable skin, as we wasted much time working on the old car through lack of accessibility.

PB asked for numbers to back up my arguments. I calculated a spaceframe would weigh 75 lb (34 kg); a detachable elektron skin, 50 lb (22.7 kg), and 36 gallon (160 litre) fuel tanks 35 lb (16 kg). A total of 160 lb (72.7 kg) against 186 lb (84.5 kg) of the much modified over-stressed skin cars with 48 gallon (214 litre) tanks.

After a week's thought he asked: 'What Drawing Office support would you need?' 'None.' 'Are you sure it will work?' 'Yes.' 'Very well, build two side by side, and save time.' I was thunderstruck. I mildly suggested that this meant two jigs with the cost and space that went with them, but I took his point. The five cars we eventually built followed each other at monthly intervals.

# CHAPTER NINE

# The spaceframe 2.5 litre BRM

FOR 1958 WE had to decide our brake supplier, Lockheed or Dunlop. It was not as clean cut as it seemed, because we also used Lockheed clutches and filters, and Dunlop tyres. We had experienced a fair amount of trouble with Lockheed's swinging caliper brake, but PB inclined towards the simplicity of their set up with one piston and seal. Dunlop had twice as many and were adamant that hard Mintex linings were used. However, over the years we had built up good relations with Ferodo whose soft linings Lockheed preferred. All parties concerned flexed their muscles a little. I believe A.G.B. Owen had the casting vote — stay with Lockheed.

We heard rumours that the Vanwall engine was not taking kindly to Avgas. I could not understand this; the cylinder head was supposed to be based on the Norton motorcycle which had used petrol.

Jean Behra was a frequent visitor to our new house; our young children loved to see him. He would take off his plastic ear and hold it out to them saying: 'Made in England.' When he crashed at Dundrod, his spare goggles that he wore around his neck, like most drivers, had sliced his ear off. We torsion tested the first chassis. It came out better than I anticipated at 2586 lb ft (356 kg/m) per degree, but it was a pound overweight at 76 lb (34.5 kg). We converted four of the 1957 engines to Avgas as well as old 254 from 1955. The first two 1958 five-bearing engines were waiting for their crankshafts when it was time for the Goodwood Easter meeting; where it snowed.

The main opposition at Goodwood was Mike Hawthorn in a full 2.5 litre Dino Ferrari and Brabham in a Cooper. Jean went into the lead but lost his brakes after three laps and hit the chicane, catching his foot in the steering wheel which stopped him being flung out. The servo side of the master cylinder had failed. Soon after this Harry Schell came in with his rear disc incandescent. He had the same problem, but his servo piston had seized at the other end of its travel. Jean could not put his brakes on, while Harry could not get his off!

Jean was bruised and shaken. This did not stop him getting to work on me. 'We were the lightest of the grand marques, yet we were the only ones with servo brakes — why?' He thought we would gain more time with instant brake response than by waiting for servo-power. Lockheeds sat on the fence and said we could try it if we wished. The new spaceframe car, known as 256 as it was a type 25 and not a project 27, was not ready, so we converted 27/1 and 27/5 to simple twin master cylinder brakes with a balance bar.

We took these cars to Aintree, where Jean was running second when he came in with another brake failure. The intense vibration of the 2.5 litre had cracked the production soldered brake fluid reservoir, so we pulled Harry in before he suffered the same trouble. With servo brakes the car had a BRM-manufactured rubber mounted reservoir. When we went to standard brakes we used a standard reservoir. Jean said that the non-servo system was much better. He was much quicker than he would have been with a servo, but I noticed that some of his confidence had gone. If this was not enough of a problem, when we ran the first 1958 five-bearing engine it only gave 245 hp on test, yet the old 1957 four-bearing engines were giving 265 to 270 hp. However, the first run of 256 cheered us up. Ron managed to get it round Folkingham in 1 min 35.4 sec, whereas Jean's best in the hybrid 27/3 was 1 min 36.5 sec.

Next day saw first practice at Silverstone for the Daily Express Trophy, with Behra in 256 and Flockhart in 27/1. We could not get the new car to run properly — vibration was causing the carburettors to flood. We whipped the car back to Folkingham and rubber-mounted the carburettors. We just got back to Silverstone in time for practice but, although the engine sounded better, lap times were awful. We found Jean's seat was moving about, wedged it in place with rubber hose, and at last we got a decent time.

The front row was nearly all Coopers — Salvadori, Brabham and Stirling — plus Peter Collins with the new Ferrari Dino. Collins made a good start but was chased by Jean. Stirling stalled on the grid. On the fourth lap Jean got into the lead and started to pull away. Ron was fourth, having a tangle with Brabham. As Jean passed a back marker a stone smashed his goggles. Following his Dundrod accident he refused to wear spare goggles. He came in with much glass in and around his eye. I removed as much as I could. He said the pain was bearable, put on his spare goggles from his helmet bag and was away in 11th place. Collins was leading, Flockhart second. Then Bruce Halford and George Wickens had a coming together, and Ron ran into the result, writing off his car. Jean finished fourth, after which he was taken to hospital where they got some more glass out of his eye. Despite it all, he cheered up considerably and told me he would make fastest time on the first day of Monaco practice and, if the car held together, he would win. I was rather doubtful, so he bet me £10 for fastest time and £5 on the win. We were not getting any more power out of the new five-bearing engines so PB sent one of the heads to Harry Weslake to see what Harry could suggest.

New 256, and old 27/5 went with the workshop lorry to Monte Carlo. The second new car, 257, followed one day later in an open truck, borrowed from Rubery Owen and known as the coal cart. Jean did his stuff in first practice and produced fastest time. Finally Tony Brooks in the Vanwall just pipped us for pole position. Jean said not to worry, the middle of the front row is the best place. He led for 27 laps and then a brake pressure pipe from the master cylinder to the front brakes cracked and he was out. Harry came in at half distance on two cylinders — a float needle had stuck. We changed it and he finally finished fifth, but well down. Jean and Harry introduced us to the Hotel Metropole at Beaulieu and took us to dinner at various restaurants in Nice and Villefranche. They were in top form throughout the weekend. Harry's technique was to ask for the proprietor and insist on inspecting the kitchen everywhere we went before he allowed us to sit down. We were all going straight on to Zandvoort the following weekend. PB was not up to driving, so I had to drive all the way.

In first practice for the Dutch GP, Behra went off at the corner behind the pits which he said was his fault — no damage. The front row was all Vanwall. Lewis-Evans was fastest using the old wire wheels. The others were on the cast ones. It was typical Zandvoort weather: cold, a very strong wind, and heavy rain race morning which depressed Jean. There was some pushing and shoving in the first corner, and after ten laps Stirling was leading Lewis-Evans by eight seconds who had Harry Schell up his exhaust pipe, and on both sides of him at the same time, with Jean just behind. Eventually Lewis-Evans dropped out — his turn for a broken valve spring. Harry was now second and Jean third.

I was cross with Harry. Right at the end of the race he was second, 45 seconds behind Stirling and 50 ahead of Jean, when he decided to have a real good scrap with Mike Hawthorn to lap him for a second time. Harry eventually took to the grass in a totally uneccessary effort to get by Mike. Jean said his car would not go any faster, and it cut out on right hand corners and misfired, although we never heard it. Actually there was a reason for the cars to misfire on right hand corners, the carburettors were mounted at ten degrees to the horizontal. After Zandvoort we reduced the angle to five degrees. This was the first sign of Jean's Latin temperament. When things went well he was on top of the world, but if things were not quite right he was dreadfully depressed and just did not try.

The next race was the Belgian GP at Spa on the original long circuit. PB insisted we ran the five-bearing engines, still only giving 245 hp, which both drivers instantly detected. In first practice oil blew out of Jean's oil tank breather onto his rear tyres when he was doing 160 mph (258 kph) through the Masta kink. The car spun twice, then Jean spun it deliberately again to miss the houses and barns, but the fence inflicted plenty of damage. The cars were not handling as well as at Silverstone and Zandvoort. Stiffening springs helped a little, but Jean, not surprisingly, was well down on the grid, while Ferrari's power brought them to the front. Eventually Harry finished fifth, with not much oil pressure, Jean having given up early, claiming no oil pressure. We cured the breather problem overnight with a bulkhead mounted oil collector tank to catch the oil from the breathers, and a small pipe and non-return valve to drain the oil back into the sump.

Things were even worse at Reims. In spite of — or because of — everything we did the five bearing engines' power had dropped even more — the best gave 235 hp. We took three cars, another new one, 258, for Trintignant as it was the French GP and Toto Roche paid big money.

We used a mechanical tachometer with a 'tell-tale' finger and magnetic reset. Harry carried a magnet which he used to reset the tell-tale if he over-revved, so we had sealed the reset button. We noticed that as the oil temperature climbed higher, not only did the oil pressure drop but so did the power. The engine was obviously an oil boiler. We had fitted an additional five-row oil cooler behind the radiator which helped a little. Our confusion was complete when Harry managed second fastest time to Hawthorn in first practice in the very powerful Ferrari. Harry was cock-a-hoop, but Jean was in the blackest of moods and demanded Harry's car. Harry, not to be outdone, demanded Trint's, who, ever the gentleman, said he was happy because he now had Behra's car and, knowing us, it would be the team's best-prepared car with the best engine.

Harry Schell had driven from Paris to Reims with his girlfriend Monique, in a four-wheeled Vespa, the ultimate mini car. He went back to the hotel after the first practice and car swap drama, full of himself, saying he was going to have a steak, a bottle of Beaujolais and spend the afternoon in bed with Monique. When he got to his room it was absolutely bare, and by the time he had realized that even the telephone had gone, someone had locked them in. Harry was very vocal in his complaints, so the next stage was the Vespa was moved into his bedroom. The management started to show signs of running out of patience, so a large party of drivers, including Fangio whose last race it was before retiring, carried the Vespa down the main staircase and into the road.

Harry made a good start and led for most of the first lap. Luigi Musso went off on the long corner after the pits and was killed. For a time Fangio, driving the lightweight Maserati had a tussle with Moss, Schell and Behra for second place. Behra gave up with boredom; Trint had a fuel pump failure; and the water pipe to the oil-cooler in the oil tank broke on Harry's car. It was a very dismal race, only enlivened afterwards by Hawthorn's antics in Bridget's. Alleged to have a rather doubtful reputation, it was favoured by the English contingent as it served good draught beer. I was using the black demonstration Raymond Mays Ford Zephyr and had to leave very early Monday morning to make the journey back to England in search of the missing horsepower. I had left the Zephyr outside the hotel the night before, but there was no sign of it in the morning. Eventually my suspicions were aroused by an enormous pile of dustbins. After moving most of them, there was the Ford!

Silverstone, for the British GP was even worse, despite Harry Weslake's ministrations, which included sleeving the inlet ports reducing their area by 20 percent and giving us five more hp, plus a seven-row oil cooler. We did not even get Harry's car to first practice, Jean was extremely miserable and threatened not to drive, but he eventually managed 1 min 41.4 sec compared with his Daily Express Trophy time of 1 min 40 sec. When Harry's car arrived for second practice he quickly got down to being second fastest to Moss with 1 min 39.8 sec. In the race Harry finished fifth, again with second fastest lap time 1 min 41.1 sec, to Hawthorn's 1 min 40.8 sec. Jean was in eighth place when he came in complaining of poor handling. This was the famous hare incident — he had run over a hare, and one of the unfortunate animal's bones had punctured the left rear tyre.

As if we were not in enough trouble, we were committed to race at Caen next day, necessitating a dawn take-off by Silver City from Blackbushe to Deauville. We already had a spare car there for Jean, but Harry had to use his Silverstone race car fitted overnight with a new engine. After a battle with Stirling in Rob Walker's Cooper, Jean retired with a broken timing gear, the first for some time and the first with a five-bearing crank which, after all, had been introduced to overcome timing gear failures. Harry finished well back. We found the gearbox scavenge pump had failed, and he had been running with a gearbox full of oil.

Gordon Newman, our Chief Mechanic, who had not been well for some time, had a furious row with PB and resigned over the waste of human resources. I made the explosive situation worse by putting a 1958 cylinder head on to a 1957 four-bearing crank case and getting 270 hp! PB would have none of this and demanded I found the power that I claimed we had at the beginning of the season. Tempers were really getting frayed. Harry Weslake then suggested some more port changes. We managed to get 240 hp out of a five bearing engine and consoled ourselves that good road holding was the short-term answer to all our problems.

I went to the Nürburgring with PB and Lorna in a Ford Consul with a prototype Raymond Mays conversion. We had conveniently forgotten the lessons from last year when the Vanwall, also Chapman inspired and a good handling car, ran into trouble at the Ring. We were in desperate handling trouble. We wrecked the spare car. We tried every spring and roll bar that we had, but the problem was clear to me — not enough wheel movement. Either the unsprung mass had to travel further to absorb the kinetic energy or we had to make it lighter.

There was nothing we could do at the Nürburgring. It was a very wet and miserable weekend, made much worse for us by the tragic death of Peter Collins, who had been extremely popular with the workers. Harry led for the first few miles and then had a front brake failure. Not the sort of thing to have at the Ring. Jean had a fit of the sulks and gave up with low oil pressure, described by Denis Jenkinson as driver boredom. It was made even worse when we all realized that had he not given up he might well have been second to Tony Brooks. The Vanwall mechanics told us at Nürburgring that they too were in high temperature and low oil pressure problems and would be fitting very big oil coolers on top of the nose for the next races. We were all good friends, even though Tony Vandervell could not stand RM.

The Portuguese GP used a new circuit through the streets of Oporto; cobbles, tram tracks and a Rouen-like downhill series of sweeping curves, described as Fangio country. We also had bigger oil coolers. Jean liked the circuit and for some time had fastest practice time. There was a dangerously stupid scene on the starting grid. Officials chased all the mechanics away, unfastened, then refastened, all the engine covers to make sure they had been securely fastened. As some of them did not know how to do it correctly, several cars had to come in after their first lap either with their bonnets off or about to come off — including Harry's.

Jean was running second when the internal gas seal of a spark plug failed and the whole ceramic electrode blew out. He finally finished fourth on three cylinders. Harry was sixth, his rear shock absorbers having given up. The needle match between Stirling and Mike for the World Championship was at its height. On the last lap Mike spun, stalled, then pushed his car down hill, the wrong way of the circuit but on the pavement; jumped in; restarted and rejoined the race. There was protest and counter protest, although none from Vanwall or BRM. The results were finally given at 11 p.m. — Moss first, Hawthorn second. At our post mortem it became clear that our dampers were overheating badly. Colin Chapman had warned us that the measures taken to shorten them so they were interchangeable with the air struts might get us into this problem. When I laid out the new front suspension I made room for longer front dampers, but as we never had any trouble at the back, I did not bother to do the same for the rears, which now proved to be a serious blunder.

Willy and I flew home on a TAP Constellation laden with rear shock absorbers for modification. The cars went direct to Monza, the engines were flown home for overhaul and sent out to Monza in the coal cart, together with a brand new car for Bonnier.

Jean went to great lengths to explain to me that the only way to get a good time at Monza in early September was to wait until just after 5 p.m. when things had cooled down a little. The engines gave more power, and it was not so late that the low sun was in your eyes coming through Lesmo. 5.30 p.m. was too late.

Ferrari was making a tremendous effort, with four cars entered and six to choose from. Hawthorn had a car with Dunlop disc brakes — a first for Ferrari. Vanwall had a complete perspex cockpit enclosure for Stirling, but he discarded it. He found it absolutely deafening, but he was easily fastest anyway. There was a terrific slip-streaming battle in the race between Moss, Hawthorn, Lewis-Evans, Behra and Tony Brooks. Cars were falling out like flies, and the centre propshaft bearing failed on Bonnier's new car. Nearly everyone stopped, including Jean, complaining about his brakes. We sent Jean out again, but eventually the clutch gave up, in protest at being used as an additional braking system. Poor Freddie Bothamley, the Lockheed man, went away and hid.

Jean told us he would not be driving for us next season as he was joining Ferrari, but he was persuaded to delay his decision. Back in England I was told Jean was taking a BRM to Le Mans for a demonstration run. I never knew why. I was told to set up an engine on nitro and anything else I could think of to get maximum possible power in a forlorn attempt to persuade him to stay. We were going to run four cars at Casablanca which struck me as crazy — the BRM death wish again.

However, I put the head from 2582, a five-bearing engine, on a four-bearing crankcase, high lift camshafts, 17.5 per cent nitro in BPK (50 per cent methanol) and saw 292 hp, with 240 at 6000 rpm. We left off the side fuel tanks and extra oil coolers, as running on alcohol there would not be an oil boiling problem. Behra's car weighed 1050 lb (477 kg). It was all to no avail. It poured with rain the whole weekend. On the way back from Le Mans with PB we were having lunch at the airport restaurant at Le Touquet, when Prince Chula came in, also on his way back from Paris but on a later flight. We had quite a talk. This was the last time I was to see him.

I was able to prove conclusively with the heat to oil figures that the missing power was wasted by the centre main bearing. PB and Weslake would have none of it; they had come up with a Norton inspired cylinder head, with a very odd squish deck cut deep into the hemispherical combustion chamber. The pistons had to be hand-fitted to the combustion chambers. Altogether it was a very impractical set-up, but their squish head on 2582 with 9.7:1 compression ratio gave 261 hp, that is 15 hp more than any other five-bearing engine. 2572, a four-bearing engine, with 10.7:1 compression, gave 279 hp next day. PB said get the compression up on the squish engine and you will really have some power. He was the boss, but there just was not time to do it his way. We compromised by taking two of each to Casablanca, that is two four-bearing and two five-bearing engines.

Our travel agents did a very good deal for us, finding a charter DC6 which would fly the four cars direct from Stansted to Casablanca. We were given a cabin plan and told how extremely important it was to correctly locate the centre of gravity of the load in the aircraft. Every box and crate had to be labelled with its weight. Two transporters, carrying spare engines and tyres went by road, via Gibraltar. I did some sums and decided that the only way to meet the centre of gravity requirement was to load one car on top of the other. We made a 'see-saw' out of loading ramps. The lower car held it down while we pushed the second car up the see-saw. It was a quickly assembled device, and we could load four cars in 20 minutes in a mock-up of the cabin at Folkingham.

To my extreme mortification, when the aircraft arrived at Stansted, we saw the cabin trim had been removed as well as the seats for the freight configuration. This made the cabin 4 inches (101 mm) wider, and by loading the cars in echelon, with soap on the tyres to slide them sideways, we achieved the correct centre of gravity without my see-saw. To rub salt in my wounds, when the French captain appeared, he walked round the aircraft, applied a plastic measure to the extension of the nose wheel leg, shrugged his shoulders and said: 'It's a long runway.' The flight took seven hours with full cabin service from two stewardesses for ten of us.

Behra was fastest in first practice, just inside Fangio's lap record. We narrowly escaped major disaster when Dick Salmon was being towed in Harry Schell's car by a local Moroccan driver who tried to pass beneath a temporary Bailey bridge with a truck two feet (61 cm) taller than the bridge clearance. The truck body fell around Dick, but apart from a few scratches and a broken windscreen Dick and the car were undamaged.

I had plenty of problems. Our rules were that the only person allowed to warm up an engine was me, so I was rushing up and down sand dunes from one car to the next like a demented camel. Jean became very disheartened in the race as he could not keep up with the battle, and gave up on lap 26 muttering about low oil pressure; but as he had the best four-bearing engine no one believed him. Stirling won and Mike was second. This made Mike World Champion.

It was interesting to see Lofty England from Jaguar looking after Mike, who was understandably very tense, alternating between violent fits of humour and black despair, and receiving no visible support from Ferrari.

After the race Jean confirmed he was definitely going to Ferrari and disappeared, and RM took PB and me to dinner at a seafood restaurant on the sea wall just under the light house. Mike and Lofty were there, having a quiet meal together. The Vandervell outfit had already left in their chartered Viscount to get the terribly burned Lewis-Evans home. It was a sad evening, yet we had Mike Hawthorn as the first English World Champion, and Vanwall had won the Manufacturers Championship.

I was full of plans for 1959, although AGB had clamped down on our budget. PB gave me a work programme to settle the controversy of four versus five bearings; bigger dampers; new cylinder heads with smaller valves and change to Dunlop brakes. He returned home via Paris where he was putting a deal together with Antony Lago of Talbot. The plan was that PB would design a BRM/Rubery Owen engine and BRM would build it to power a new small Talbot. Lorna Berthon thought this a terrific idea and set up a flat in Paris.

I soon established that the heat rejected to oil was the equivalent of 49.4 hp on the best five-bearing engine. The same figure for the best four-bearing was 30.8 hp. The difference (nearly 19 hp) was roughly the difference in power between a four- and a five-bearing engine, proving conclusively that the extra bearing cost us the power and Tres's dictum of 'balance weights where there are loads and bearings where there ain't' was entirely correct. PB fought hard, but he finally gave in, and agreed that we would use 1957 four-bearing crankcases with reworked 1958 heads for 1959. He launched me on a camshaft crusade. Lift was increased, and as expected we were back in valve spring and rocker trouble.

RM confirmed that he had signed Jo Bonnier and Harry Schell for 1959, and there would be a three car effort in some minor races. Harold Hodkinson of Dunlops came to check out our brakes. He was very scornful of ventilated discs and said they were a waste of time. He was adamant that we used hard linings, which hurt after our happy relationship with Ferodo. We rearranged the frame tubes, to give more de Dion travel with longer stroke dampers.

During the winter I built an air flow rig, but unlike Harry Weslake, who used a redundant gasometer, we used a large drum. When BRM closed down I bought the rig for Lotus Engineering. There is a photograph of it amongst the illustrations.

I started road testing the cars on 18 February and found the Dunlop brakes very much better. Absolutely consistent, sharp and very sensitive to front to rear braking ratio. I also investigated engine air intake ducts to see whether the Vanwall NACA duct would give us any more power. I found the old centre intake between the two halves of the radiator was good but we lost the ram effect through the long pipes. The best solution for us for power and ram pressure was a long duct, down the side of the car to the top of the nose. It was very ugly, and some of the extra power was wasted dragging it through the sky. We tried cutting it back a few inches at a time until we started to lose ram pressure. Finally with this intake we had pushed the indicated peak rpm at Folkingham up from 7800 to 7950 and had gained ram pressure equivalent to 6 hp.

I ran an engine for 27 hours on the test bed developing a new low level tapered exhaust tail pipe. After we had apparently picked up 5 hp I put the original pipe back and found we still had the 5 hp. An object lesson on the need for frequent back to back testing. Now we had laid the oil boiling bogey, we discarded the inefficient and leaky oil water/heat exchanger and replaced it with a large tubular oil cooler behind the main radiator.

Ron Flockhart took a car to New Zealand. He retired in the first race with a broken oil pipe, won the second race after a battle with Brabham, and in the third was second to Bruce McLaren, all on the same four-bearing engine. We did not see much of PB who was busy in Paris with his Talbot project.

We had a test day for Dunlop at Silverstone. I went in my Austin A35 to pick up Harry Schell at Northampton railway station, take him to Silverstone to test, and then back to Bourne. After his train arrived, there was a most impressive procession. Harry, with an expensive camel-hair coat slung around his shoulders, escorted by the stationmaster, preceded by a porter carrying a five-litre bottle of Courvoisier cognac, and another porter bringing up the rear with a trolley laden with baggage. Harry introduced me to the station master and explained the cognac was for me. All went well until they saw the A35. I think they were expecting at least a Rolls-Royce, but we got it all in somehow. We had a very good day's testing getting down to 1 min 38 sec, which pleased Harry. I suspected most of it was because of improved tyres. We ran for over 200 trouble free miles.

The Formula 1 scene for 1959 looked very different from 1958. Tony Vandervell had given up racing, but retained the nucleus of his team. I was trying to recruit Cyril Atkins, his Chief Mechanic. Stirling had joined Rob Walker and embarked on his career as a car designer. His first idea was a BRM engine in a Cooper chassis with a Colotti gearbox. RM had tried to persuade Stirling to join BRM without success. Tony Brooks had gone to Ferrari to partner Jean Behra. Mike Hawthorn sadly was dead. Maserati were in the doldrums. Coventry Climax had built a full 2.5 litre 4-cylinder which had plenty of torque, and there was talk of an F1 Aston Martin for Salvadori and Carol Shelby.

The first race of 1959 at a wet Easter Monday Goodwood was dominated by the Coopers powered with the new 2.5 Climax. Stirling first, Brabham second, Harry and Jo third and fourth. We were surprised and disappointed. Nothing wrong with the cars, plenty of power and good handling. What can be wrong? We found one of the answers next afternoon when Stirling drove both cars producing the first 100 mph lap at Goodwood, 2.5 seconds under his record.

The only trouble we had was when some of the Dzus fasteners pulled out of the air intake. I consoled myself that at least there was enough ram pressure in the intake to pull fasteners through the skin! Stirling agreed to drive for us in the Daily Express Trophy at Silverstone the weekend before Monte Carlo. Apparently Stirling told RM that he preferred Harry's car (257) to Jo's (258). RM never told me and I never knew the reason for Stirling's preference.

At Aintree Jean in a Ferrari and Harry shared the front row; Jo and Brabham the second; Stirling in the Cooper-BRM on the third. Jo had a magneto failure, Jean and Harry had a tremendous battle, until Harry retired with a stone through his radiator.

We prepared Behra's old car 256 for Stirling to drive in the Daily Express Trophy at Silverstone and Ron had 2511. All the other cars were ready to go to Monte Carlo on Sunday — Harry and Jo's regular cars 257 and 258, and 2510 for Ron. But Stirling objected to 256, claiming that RM had promised him 257, Harry's regular car. He tried Ron's car, decided he liked it best but recognized that the engine we had given him in 256 was much better, so we had to switch them over the night before the race. In the process we must have damaged the brake pipe from the front master cylinder. Stirling went into an easy lead but on the fourth lap sensed something was wrong and managed to spin the car to a standstill going into Copse with a broken front brake pipe. We found the tell-tale mark. If Stirling had driven either car, with the original engines as we prepared them with loving care at Bourne, he would have won comfortably. At that time he was on top of his form and easily faster than any other driver competing. How many races he threw away by his search for a little more performance when his natural skill put him head and shoulders ahead of his contemporaries in the late 1950s no one will know — perhaps enough to have given him the World Championship more than once.

Monte Carlo was a complete disaster for us. The three BRMs were in mid-field; Harry sixth having a go at Tony Brooks, then it all went wrong.

Jo Bonnier came in saying he had no rear brakes. Harry went into the straw bales in the Casino square, also with no brakes, and drove down to the Mirabeau pouring oil and water onto the road from his damaged radiator assembly, which did not make him very popular. Five laps later Ron was out at the Gasworks, also no rear brakes. All three cars had completely worn out their rear pads. I immediately hoisted the ventilated disc banner.

All hell then broke loose. There were rows everywhere. Ken Gregory, Stirling's manager had put forward a proposition that the Moss family should run a BRM on loan from the Owen Organization, who would also foot the bill if and when Stirling drove. The car was to be prepared and raced by the Moss organization, known as British Racing Partnership, and BRM would overhaul the engines. There was near mutiny at Folkingham. AGB's sister Jean and her husband Louis Stanley went to Monte Carlo for their first race. They became instant enthusiasts and were swept into the controversy.

Dunlop requested a test day at Zandvoort to resolve the brake problem, with Stirling driving. To add to our troubles we were given notice to quit Folkingham which was to become a Thor missile site. There was not time to get the car to Zandvoort in a transporter, so we loaded the Vanguard van with spares, and towed the car from the Hook of Holland to the circuit, where fuel and tyres awaited. We covered over 300 miles (484 km); found the best tyre set-up, and Dunlop solved the rear brake problems.

On our way back to the Hook of Holland for the ferry we were stopped by the police. We had three people in the front of the Vanguard which was illegal. The police had a novel solution, they took the third person in the police car, and escorted us all the way to the Hook, radioing ahead to have the ferry held up for us! Testing the spare car at Folkingham before the race I had third gear seize on the shaft while I was at full speed in fourth gear — Monza 1951 all over again. The car went into a violent spin in between a stack of steel tubes ready to build the concrete missile emplacements. I did not enjoy the experience at all.

At Zandvoort for the Dutch GP the atmosphere was electric. I was given a fistful of resignations by the mechanics, and Mr and Mrs Stanley were assailed on all sides. When practice began everyone, except us, was staggered by the rate of tyre wear. Coopers and Lotus with bolt-on wheels were particularly concerned. Stirling who had managed 1 min 36 sec during the BRM test day was fastest with 1 min 36.8 sec in Rob Walker's Cooper on the first day and 1 min 36.2 sec in final practice, but Jo beat him with 1 min 36 sec. We ostentatiously practised tyre changes; easy with our knock-off wheels. Harry Schell was in trouble. He had fallen off a bicycle and scraped most of the skin off both hands, so the best he could do was 1 min 37.3 sec.

Jo led on the first lap, with Masten Gregory second. He passed Jo at the back of the pits. Jo regained his lead and by lap 15 he was 7.8 seconds ahead of Brabham, Behra was well back holding up Stirling and Graham Hill. Stirling got by and started to make up lost time. On lap 30 Brabham took the lead for one lap. On lap 60 as Jo came up to lap Behra for the second time Stirling managed to nip by him into the lead. Three laps later Stirling's gearbox gave up and Jo was back in front well clear of Brabham. I had the very great pleasure of giving the slow down signal for the first time in eight years. Jo won by 14.2 seconds having had to fight nearly all the way. Harry dropped out with a completely seized gearbox — the oil pump had failed.

We found it very hard to believe that at long last we had won a World Championship race. Mr and Mrs Stanley laid on a terrific celebration dinner. Jean Behra came to congratulate me. I had a vague recollection seeing the transporter drive by, against a spectacular sunrise, with the mechanics sitting on the roof.

In an attempt to defuse the row over the BRP car, AGB authorized us to build a mid-engined car. PB ruled that as I had my hands completely full with the racing programme the Bourne Drawing Office would design the car, taking the existing front end and grafting a new engine bay onto it. The engine would be given belt driven magnetos similar to the Cooper-BRM, and the old BRM gearbox mated to the engine with a new bell housing. The drawings that came from Bourne showed a Chapman-strut rear suspension. This meant the rear damper housing was welded to the hub so the damper piston and rod took suspension side loads. There was a fabricated steel extension below the hub to a long bottom wishbone, with an even longer forward strut to take the thrust. It was the simplest form of rear suspension possible. The ball spline half-shafts and the single rear disc brake were retained.

The French GP at Reims was the first race with Stirling driving the pea-green 2510 for British Racing Partnership. He collected the 100 bottles of champagne for the fastest lap on the first day's practice after which Ferraris got going. It was an incredibly hot race and the track broke up. Stirling was in a safe second place behind Tony Brooks's Ferrari when something went wrong with his clutch linkage; not a serious problem on a circuit such as Reims. Unfortunately he then spun on soft tar and could not free the clutch to restart. Jo Bonnier had a cracked water rail and cooked his engine, Ron was sixth and Harry seventh.

It rained for most of practice for the British GP at Aintree, and when it was dry, tyre and brake wear were problems. We previously ran on 16-inch rear wheels, but since Zandvoort the car used 15 inch, so unlike other teams we could not look up previous Aintree data. Because of a metal workers' strike in Italy there were no Ferraris. Tony Brooks was to drive the lightweight Vanwall, and the new Aston Martins were going well. During a dry spell Harry managed to get onto the front row alongside Stirling and Salvadori driving an Aston. Stirling experimented throughout practice with all sorts of set-ups, including fuel location, full side tanks and little in the tail tank, and so on.

At the start Jack Brabham ran away and hid, while a fierce battle involving Schell, Bonnier, Masten Gregory, Trintignant, McLaren and Stirling developed for second place. We had made our drivers start on new tyres as we were worried about wear, but Stirling had started on part-worn tyres. He gradually caught Brabham, but just as he was about to overtake he had to come in for a new left rear tyre. Jo Bonnier had dropped out with a broken carburettor throttle lever, Flockhart had spun off when eighth but Harry was going great guns in fourth place. Stirling drove as only he could and then had to come in again for five more gallons (22 litres) of fuel which let McLaren into second place. The BRP mechanics having checked with us had put the same quantity of fuel in their car as we did, but they had filled the side tanks rather than the tail tank. Under acceleration the fuel had surged up into the back tank and in fact he still had plenty of fuel and had no need to stop. We were a little put out by all this. Harry finished fourth, but Stirling could have won.

The German GP was to be held at Avus in Berlin with its steeply banked South Curve. Before the race PB took Jo Bonnier who had driven there before to carry out some tyre tests for Dunlop. They left the car in Berlin for the race. I could not go as at the time I was busy working out a new, much shorter, exhaust system for the mid-engined car. We chartered a DC6 again, this time from Eagle. In practice de Beaufort went over the top of the banking landing right way up in the paddock and drove back onto the circuit frightening everyone but himself — apparently. A short time later Behra, who had fallen out with Ferrari and was driving his own Porsche single seater, did the same thing, but he was not so lucky, the car hit a building and he was thrown out and killed. We found that not all the data from the Bonnier tyre tests had been passed on, and we could have made a better suspension job had we known all we were up against.

The race was run as the aggregate of two heats. In the second, Harry's clutch had seized, so we push-started him about 100 yards (91 m) behind the line, as the starter raised his flag signifying five seconds to go. Harry then chugged up to the line and crossed it as the flag fell doing about 30 mph (48 kph) so he was well away. Unfortunately his clutch gave up soon after. Hans Hermann had a spectacular crash in the BRP BRM. It was blamed on a broken front brake pipe. I had a look at the wreckage, and all the pipes I saw were intact, except the flexibles to the wheels which had been ripped off. With proper handling I never saw a Dunlop-made machine-flared pipe ever break. The front-engined 2.5 litre car was coming to the end of its life.

I remained behind to test the new mid-engined car, while three cars were sent to Lisbon for the Portuguese GP where Bonnier had a fuel pump diaphragm split, Harry was fifth and Ron seventh. The cars from Portugal went straight to Monza and we sent a fourth out in the 'coal cart'. They stopped overnight in a village called Belley, close to the Franco-Swiss frontier, and they carefully parked in a cul-de-sac in the village square thinking the car would be safe. Next morning they found somebody had built a complete fairground in the square — dodgems, big wheel, rides and so on — and they were stuck. Fortunately it was only a one-day fair! Monza was a poor race for us. Harry seventh, Jo eighth, Ron 13th, but the police were on form — they would not let Fangio in, and they threw RM out.

There had been complaints of the power falling off as the engine got hot. I ran a series of tests to improve the water flow through the engine, particularly in view of the effect on flow because of the long pipe runs on the mid-engine car. I found some restrictions mainly across the head-block joint, caused by the mass of metal where the cylinder liner screwed in. After a tedious amount of detailed work we solved the problem. We found that the 1959 radiators, with more matrix area, did not flow as well as the originals.

We planned to send the front-engined cars to Argentina while the type 48s were kept behind for more development. The move from Folkingham back to Bourne was due to begin during January.

AGB charmed a Royal Tiger coach chassis out of Leyland, fitted with high axle ratios and long range tanks. Marshalls of Cambridge built its body at a special price. The Drawing Office having made a tenth scale model of the planned body, everyone concerned injected their ideas, and it was, as I recall, the only case ever of a successful design by committee. Delivery was promised in May.

AGB appointed Bertie Bradnack Team Manager. PB said it did not concern me when I asked if I would be working for Bertie at races. Peter Spear told me that AGB was concerned by lack of management control, and he hoped Bertie would correct this. I told Spear that Bertie had the wrong job. We did not make many management mistakes at races, it was back at Bourne where we produced the lulus!

I did not go to Argentina. The cars were quick, driven by our new team Gurney, Hill and Bonnier, who led at times, but they were dogged by valve spring trouble.

# CHAPTER TEN

# Making the mid-engined BRM work

IN AUGUST 1959 I started testing the mid-engined prototype. The first problem was clutch operation. Someone had done their sums wrong on hydraulic ratios, but panic work using cylinders from a Ford Anglia made pedal travel and loads acceptable. The car did not handle well, and had highly variable understeer.

We had developed the spaceframe Type 25 into one of the best handling cars of its day, according to no less an authority than Stirling Moss, but the Type 48 with a flexible chassis and widely varying rear roll centre had thrown away everything we had learned. The rear roll centre was generally well below road level. I just could not believe we were so stupid. I had sent written reports to PB on all my tests, as well as verbal explanations, but PB told me quite firmly not to interfere with Bourne. To be fair, he also told them not to interfere with me.

We took the prototype to Monza on a trailer made from a Rubery Owen test rig, purpose-built to test their new caravan axle which had leaf springs in torsion operated by long trailing arms. With a very low floor line, it made a very effective racing car trailer. It had a road level roll centre, and no dampers, so it rolled rather more than was comfortable, and the spring rates of trailer and load were out of phase. This produced a diabolical weave between 50 mph (81 kph) and 70 mph (113 kph) when towed by our Standard Vanguard Estate car. Fortunately it was quite stable at our cruising speed of 75 mph. After a few stops to feel the trailer hub bearings, we had a pleasant trip to Monza, enlivened by scaring RM to death when we saw him coming up behind us on the narrow bumpy stretch between Troyes and Val Suzon where we showed him a really lurid series of weaves.

The car had the best of our five-bearing engines for the tests. We saved a four-bearing to install if the car was good enough to race. After five laps the clutch failed, and the gearbox did not scavenge. Next day a fuel tank split, so we blanked that one off and continued using the other side. Then, with the score at 14 laps, the cylinder head cracked. It was time for official practice so we fitted the four-bearing engine. The car went quickly but not for long. It lost power badly as its coolant temperature climbed — and both fuel tanks split. I could not understand why we had abandoned our tried and proved system of threading the tanks on rubber hose wrapped round the frame tubes, and had chosen to strap long tanks at frequent intervals to a very flexible frame. No wonder they cracked.

The car was nowhere like fit to race, but we stayed on for some more testing. The rear brake disc was running at 600°C (1112°F), and it took me some time to convince PB this was to be expected. This car was heavier than the front-engined car, and carried 58 per cent of its weight on the rear wheels with driver and half fuel load. The front-engined car, with the same loads, carried 52 per cent. This meant instead of 70:30 front to rear braking ratio we needed 65:35, so the single rear disc was doing much more work. The solder melted in the gearbox oil filter. We could not tell whether it was heat from the brake or the box itself. Eventually the gearbox gave up — all the rubber seals were charred and oil leaked everywhere. Fuel tank temperature was 40°C (104°F); nearly the fuel's lower boiling point. It really was a disastrous expedition. I was totally disillusioned. All that we had learned and built up over the years just thrown away. However, I enjoyed the run back to England: measuring tunnels to make sure our new transporter could pass through.

PB went on holiday — while I got down to it. The frame was nearly as flexible as the Maserati's — only 650 lb ft per degree (90 kg/m). With a few additional tubes we improved to 1655 lb ft (228 kg/m). The rear suspension could not reach full bump, and the half-shafts bottomed due to excessive plunge caused by the geometry. We had to leave out two rows of balls before we could get full suspension travel. When we did we had eight degrees of negative camber per wheel. I thought it was excessive, and Dunlop's Vic Barlow had apoplexy. I left a sour report for PB and also went on holiday.

When I returned, PB had an engine programme waiting for me, but he had convinced Dunlop we needed ventilated discs. We discussed the idea of using aircraft rubber bag fuel tanks. The sums I did showed that we would get more fuel in a given space with them and, after talks with Fireproof Tanks at Portsmouth had convinced us they would not be prohibitively expensive, we committed all the new cars to them. AGB was keen to use British drivers. RM had signed Graham Hill and Dan Gurney, in addition to Jo Bonnier. Graham was as British as you could get, but Dan, although a very nice chap, seemed more like a Californian to me.

In the autumn of 1959 I started on what became a weekly Goodwood test programme with Graham and occasionally with Ron Flockhart. We could no longer use the track at Folkingham as missile silos were being dug in the runways. The routine was to telephone for a weather forecast at 2 p.m. and, if favourable, send the test crew to stay overnight in Chichester. I left Bourne at 5 a.m. in the A35, ready for a 9 a.m. start. We ran until something broke, or the light failed. At first we also took 2511, the newest front-engined car, for reference and tyre tests. Graham said it felt big, heavy and clumsy after a Lotus and the tail hung out a long way. PB visited us for one test, and as Coopers were also there he invited Brabham to try the mid-engined prototype. Jack said it understeered, but they all do at first. After 1000 miles testing, Graham and Ron agreed it rolled too much and the back end did the steering. I politely suggested to PB that this was a design problem.

I was in deep trouble at the time. Peter Spear had been conducting a terrible witch hunt, because I was quoted as saying the Type 48 was heavier than the Type 25. This was true, yet one of the key arguments used to persuade AGB to pay for the mid-engined car, was that it would be lighter. Peter Spear had not been much in evidence since the spaceframe cars appeared in 1958. He sensed my fury with the various stupidities. He had also had a going over from Dunlop concerning our retention of the single rear brake. I recognized he was collecting ammunition for another attack on PB, and I tried to keep out of it as much as I could. I had only given him indisputable numbers. The Type 48 frame was 12 lb (5.5 kg) heavier, the engine as set up for mid-ship mounting was 10 lb (4.5 kg) heavier, so was the gearbox with its new bell housing. The only weight we had saved was in the propshaft, at 7.5 lb (3.4 kg), which about equalled the hydraulic clutch mechanism and longer pipe runs.

At Goodwood early in 1960 — with all the cooling improvements, the front end stuffed full of camber and toe in, the thinnest front rollbar, and the stiffest rear springs — Ron managed 1 min 25.2 sec compared with Stirling's 1 min 25.8 sec in 257 at Easter. A valve spring failed before Graham had a chance to try 482, the first definitive Type 48 which had just been completed, using the front end from Harry's old 257. The new rubber bag fuel tanks fitted with no trouble, and held the calculated amount of fuel.

I returned to Goodwood with 482, and I found RM had sent all three drivers. Jo took an immediate and total dislike to it — one less to worry about. Dan Gurney said the handling was nothing like as good as the front-engined car he had driven at Cordoba. Graham said it rolled far too much, and the cockpit was too hot. The gearbox still failed to scavenge, and one magneto and several valve springs failed. On that happy note we went home.

A few days later we went to Silverstone with an even bigger gearbox scavenge pump. We managed 24 laps before it rained and the gearbox filled with oil. Graham's best time was 1 min 38.4 sec, although he said 1 min 37 sec was possible. Ventilated rear disc temperature was 515°C (959°F), fronts 565°C (1049°F). A few days later we repeated the whole performance at Goodwood: rain, and gearbox full of oil. I was getting desperate over the failure to scavenge. The system was fine at moderate speeds, and it did not give up until the final few seconds were cut from lap times. Graham also said there had to be a clue in that the car was good in the wet, but not so good in the dry.

The next outing was Goodwood Easter Monday. We had another new car for Dan — 483 using the front of 259. Graham kept 482, and fortunately Jo insisted on his favourite 258, our only GP winner (which AGB had decreed was to be preserved). We were soundly trounced by the Coopers and Innes Ireland's new mid-engined Lotus. Dan collided with Salvadori and Graham was fifth, with Jo sixth. Bertie Bradnack resigned before the race amid a flurry of press releases.

I realized that we had softened the car so much, to kill the understeer, that it was now quite lethal. It was impossible to change your line once committed to a corner. It was not so bad when testing with a clear track — no other cars to avoid — but when you were racing, and tried to change the line, you were in deep trouble.

Dan was staying with Pam and me. Pam thought he seemed extremely lonely, having left his wife and family back in California. She persuaded him to bring his wife over in June, and go to some races, while she looked after their children. Dan loved TV Westerns, English cheese and pickled onions. His idea of heaven was an evening laying on the hearth rug, watching a western and gorging himself on cheese and pickled onions.

When we returned from the disastrous Goodwood it was clear that PB did not intend to relinquish his hold on vehicle dynamics. He told me Bourne had the answers to our problems. I was given a lecture on becoming too familiar with the drivers and living in their pockets. I had stood with PB looking at the new Lotus. He was quite derisive: 'There must be something dreadfully wrong with it,' he said, 'it's got a roll bar each end.' I did not make myself very popular by saying that I wished our car was as far wrong as the Lotus. It was much faster than we were. He said there was no need to worry as he had the answer.

I found Stan producing new rear hub assemblies which dropped the wishbone attachment point 1.25 inch (32 mm). This raised the rear roll centre, but it still moved far too much — about 14 inches (356 mm) from bump to rebound. Longer rear wishbones to use all of the balls in the half-shafts had increased the rear track, which did not help the understeer. Following a long series of arguments I eventually succeeded in convincing PB that we needed a rear roll bar. We had so much rear grip that the front end just could not cope. Mercifully, we had cured the gearbox scavenge problem by moving the oil cooler and its back pressure to the pressure line.

Dan, his car, and Snetterton were the first available to test the new rear suspension, but we did not get there until late afternoon. There did not seem to be anything dreadfully wrong. We went straight to Silverstone the next day where we managed 100 miles before the Track Manager, Jimmy Brown, closed us down. The car looked good. Dan, with a time of 1 min 36.7 sec, said it was the best so far, and with the right gear ratios 1 min 35 sec was possible. Three days later we returned to Silverstone with Graham, 482 and the 'right' gear ratios. After stiffening up roll bars front and rear, he got down to 1 min 35.2 sec — four seconds under Brabham's Cooper lap record. So we began shaking hands with ourselves.

A few minutes later, just before Jimmy Brown closed down for the night, Coopers arrived, all of a heap, with their new 1960 car. It was much lower, with full wishbone and coil spring suspension instead of transverse leaf springs. After a brief stop to check for leaks and things about to fall off, they were down to 1 min 34 sec. Talk about instant mortification — we were absolutely stunned. There was a lesson to be learned. However much you may improve your car, someone somewhere may do even better.

There was no time to do much to improve our cars: the Daily Express Trophy was that weekend. It rained during practice, which stopped Jo whingeing when he, too, discovered that the car went well in the wet. In the race the special aircraft high temperature flexible pipe to the rear brakes split on Jo's car, and Dan had fuel troubles, but Graham finished third behind Innes Ireland in the new Lotus and Jack Brabham in the new Cooper.

Two days later the Team set out for Monte Carlo. I think PB had sensed how disgruntled I was, as he said: 'Why don't you drive down and take Pam; it will give her a nice break.'

New car build and race car preparation was now established in our new building on the site of the old gasworks. There had been a tremendous drama when the base of the old gasometers was filled in and concreted over. They had been full of oily water, and when this was pumped into the drains it had found its way into the local river, the Bourne Eau, which drained the whole district, some of which was below sea level. The Bourne Eau was a fisherman's paradise, until the polluted water from the gasometers reached it, when all the fish promptly died. There was then a colossal buck-passing session. RM had bought the gasworks site and leased it to Rubery Owen. The contractors who erected the new building had pumped the polluted water into the drains with permission from the local council, and the Air Ministry were footing the bills to compensate us for having to quit Folkingham. The row was over who paid to replace the fish?

There was another problem. We could no longer use Folkingham to see if we had put the cars together properly; neither could we start the engines in the new workshop as we were in the middle of a built-up area and the corrugated sheeting of the building reverberated with the exhaust noise. Part of T.W. Mays and Son — Raymond Mays's business — was an organization known as the 'Bovril', situated at the end of a long lane, called the 'slipe', leading east into the Fen. They were fell mongers (dealers in animal hide and skins) and their slogan was 'we will take any animal no matter what its state of decomposition' — in short, a genuine knacker's yard. We were allowed to run the cars down the slipe and, provided the wind was from the west (as it usually was), it was not too bad. If it was from the east we all hoped that the car started quickly!

The office layout had been changed. Sandercombe had moved into PB's office and I had been given Sandy's old office. The stores was now in the old Raymond Mays and Partners garage, shared with the engine shop. PB now had an office and conference room in the former stores area. I could walk to work in six minutes. I had no more leisure, just my availability had increased. The test beds had moved to a new site, but remained on the airfield at Folkingham, so I still had to drive there to run an engine. Willy, although fully competent and totally trustworthy, was not even allowed to run one in.

En route to Monaco, Pam and I parked the children on my mother; crossed the channel by Silver City and spent the night at Reims. The next day, filling up at Montelimar, I checked the oil level after cruising for several hours at 75 mph, which was not far short of the A35's maximum. There was no sign of oil on the dipstick. High speed cruising had increased consumption, even though there were as yet no such things as autoroutes. We stopped overnight in Avignon, visited the bridge, then lunched with Johnny Carl from the Bira days at La Napoule, and reached Beaulieu mid-afternoon.

The Scarabs made their European debut at Monaco, driven by owner Lance Reventlow and Chuck Daigh. Richie Ginther had a mid-engined Ferrari; the shape of things to come. We still had to qualify, as again only the fastest 16 could start. The time-keeping system broke down, so first practice did not count, which made Graham very cross. He had a wrist watch with an expanding metal bracelet which he did not remove when driving the racing car; unlike the other drivers who had me looking like a jeweller's shop with wrist watches half way up my arm. Graham did not allow for the BRM vibration; the watch strap broke, and the watch fell onto the track about four feet from the edge of the curb. This happened right opposite our pit, the pits being set up on the curving central strip between the promenade and Boulevard Albert 1er. Cars were serviced on the harbour side, with signals from the boulevard side. Anyone trying really hard hugged the curb at the back of the pits.

Graham saw his watch lying in the road and hoped no one would run over it. We saw it all, but no one dare try to pick it up as there was not enough warning of a car coming round the slight curve from the Gasworks hairpin. Eventually Graham ran over it himself, much to his disgust!

The Scarabs were in dreadful trouble. We lent them some road springs. They were on Goodyear tyres, the first time we had seen them in Europe, whereas everyone else was on Dunlop. Stirling took pole position, joined on the front row by Brabham and Tony Brooks (Lotus, Cooper, Cooper). Jo Bonnier and Chris Bristow (Cooper) had the second row, Graham with Innes Ireland (Lotus) and Wolfgang von Trips (Ferrari) on the third. The start was still on the harbour side, so the drivers were immediately confronted with the Gasworks corner. Rain threatened but had not started to fall. Jo led on the first lap, but by quarter distance it began to rain, Graham was sixth and Dan 12th. Brabham had gone off. It dried off at half distance, by which time Jo was second, about 14 seconds behind Stirling, Graham now fifth. Dan came in with the left rear wheel pointing in a very odd direction; the modified rear hub carrier, with the extension to raise the roll centre, had buckled very badly. Graham, still cross with the timekeepers, lost control in the wet and hit the timekeeper's box, doing both the car and the box serious mischief. On lap 78 Jo came in with the same trouble as Dan. Right at the end of the race, someone realized there were only four cars running, but there was prize money down to sixth place. Dan and Jo set off to try to become classified as finishers. Dan's car was so bad, with six inches toe-in on one rear wheel, that he could not keep going, but Jo was classified fifth.

There was much frantic telephoning to Bourne from Eddie Hall's flat above the Royal box. Eddie had been a very successful driver pre-war with MG and a Rolls-Royce built Bentley, with which he finished second in the TT three years running. During the war his Bentley was stored, with others, in Derby, and the apprentices, including me, cared for them in their spare time. He and his wife Joan, who used to run his pit, kept open house at Monaco. There the ladies could freshen up, and there was excellent food any time of the day — and a drink most of the night as well.

Zandvoort was only a week away, and the plan was for us all to travel there direct from Monaco. We spent Monday morning assessing our situation, and finally got the convoy away about midday. Another, even larger, job list had by then been telephoned to Bourne.

On the way to Zandvoort Pam and I had planned to drive the A35 to Gütersloh in Germany to see her sister, who was married to a New Zealand RAF pilot. We were at dinner with PB and RM at Bideau's in Villefranche when we received a garbled message to the effect that the workshop lorry had hit a horsebox in Frejus. It finally transpired that it had broken its gearbox, but they were continuing. I was sent off early next morning armed with various contingency plans, depending on what I found wrong and how far along the route they had travelled. We caught up with them in Valence and found the Commer had lost third gear. But they had already done all the right things; flushed the box out and removed most of the debris. Telephone plans were made for a working party to meet them in Brussels with the spares and travel on to Zandvoort. By using the two-speed rear axle, changing from high second to low fourth, the missing third gear was not too much of a problem. Fortunately there were no mountain passes to climb.

Pam and I left the convoy and reached Nancy that night, having covered 540 miles (871 km) that day in the A35, not necessarily the most comfortable vehicle for this sort of journey. We reached Gütersloh next day about 4 p.m., spent most of the night being entertained in the mess, then started out for Zandvoort at 5.30 a.m. with a detailed route plan and Forces map.

We were about two hours down the autobahn when we were startled by an RAF jet about 50 feet above us rocking its wings and banking right. A minute later there was another; then one head on, and we deduced there had been a change of plan and we should leave the autobahn by the next exit. We later found there was a traffic hold up at Rechlinghausen. We reached Zandvoort at lunchtime, where a new car for Graham, 485, complete with modified rear suspension, and two more sets for Jo and Dan were waiting. We had arranged to use the circuit from 5 p.m. to shake down Graham's new car. However, something went wrong. The caretaker did not turn up to let us in, so we lifted the gates off their hinges. We found, though, that we could not re-engage them, so we just propped the gates in place. When the gatekeeper finally arrived, on a stately two-crossbar Dutch bicycle, and unlocked the gates they fell on him, and he was not at all pleased. Graham managed a 10-lap shakedown run, and said the car was better than the 482.

We had numerous engine troubles in practice — valve springs and blowing valve seats. The only relief was Lance Reventlow's wife, film star Jill St John, wearing a white sharkskin suit complete with illegal poodle. The race organizers laid on a welcome dinner. I had the seat opposite Mrs Reventlow, and refused all manner of lucrative offers from various drivers to change places.

The night before the race, most of the Squadron from Gütersloh arrived — sleeping in their vehicles, parked on the beach. At first light on race morning I had to give a car a shakedown run following an engine change; there being no FOCA race morning warm-up in those days. (We have a lot to thank FOCA for.) Driving the car back to the pits, the rotating rear brake disc collected and severed the main TV cable, causing tremendous panic. When I got back to the hotel to clean up, I found the bath full of bottles of RAF duty-free spirit, and a scandalized housemaid lurking outside our room. Apparently the RAF had used our bathroom to wash and shave after their night on the beach. The maid had seen about ten personable young pilots staggering into the room loaded with bottles, later emerging perfumed and immaculate. I probably would have seen the joke if one of them had not made off with my razor!

Most of the British teams shared the same garage at Zandvoort. Colin Chapman came round and suggested that it was time I joined him at Lotus, as I was obviously not getting anywhere at BRM. I declined his offer politely as I had opened negotiations to return to Rolls-Royce.

The race, on Whit Monday, and thus attended by Sir Alfred, with a large entourage, was a disaster for us. Moss was on pole with Rob Walker's Lotus, Brabham and Ireland alongside, Graham and Jo on the second row, with Dan just behind. On the 10th lap the special aircraft pipe to Dan's rear brake burst as he was going into the hairpin at the end of the main straight. Dan went straight on into the sand dunes, unfortunately an 18-year-old Dutch lad had crept under the safety fence for a better view and the car hit him, killing him immediately. Dan was apparently just cut and bruised but very distressed. His wife was watching at the hairpin end of the pits with Lance Reventlow who took charge of things, and Dan. We debated whether to call the others in, but we were not sure what had happened.

Stirling also had a spectacular accident, he was having a battle with Brabham for the lead, when Jack ran wide on one corner throwing a large piece of curb stone into the road which Stirling's front wheel hit, smashing the rim and bursting the tyre. What with a bolt-on wheel and a borrowed Cooper jack, Stirling's pit stop cost him much time which he proceeded to make up in his usual inimitable fashion. Jack was then leading, Innes second and Graham had inherited third place. Jo had spun off, without much damage, on his own oil due to an insecurely fastened oil filter. Graham was 46 seconds ahead of Stirling, now in fourth place, we did not wish to press Graham because of our worries about Dan's failure.

We calculated that Graham could afford to lose three seconds a lap to Stirling. Stirling gained four seconds on one lap, but Graham speeded up and he only lost two next lap, so Graham held third place. After the race there was quite a business with the police, and we could not find the car. The police had taken it away, doing a terrible amount of damage in the process. Next day Dan was exonerated and we got the car back.

After dinner, while PB and RM left to attend a starting money meeting, the drivers requested a meeting with AGB, and I was dragged in by them as a witness. The gist of their argument was that they had lost confidence in the cars and would not drive them any more. AGB, an experienced negotiator, asked: 'What do I have to do to restore your confidence? Obviously there are circumstances under which you will continue to drive.' 'Nope', said Dan; but Graham did the negotiating. If PB did not interfere, and I was allowed to build and set-up the cars, with someone like David Yorke, the ex-Vanwall Team Manager, to run the team, then they would stay and drive. At this moment PB and RM returned. After much discussion the meeting eventually ended at about 5 a.m. AGB instructed that I would be in complete charge of the cars and their set-up at races and I was to build a new car in the Bourne workshop to my own design. No reference to David Yorke. It appeared to satisfy the drivers, but it did not move me up in the Bourne popularity ratings.

Back at Bourne we took stock. Repairs to Graham's Monte Carlo car were already underway. We had two very badly damaged cars (482 and 483), 484 was slightly damaged, 485 (Graham's Zandvoort car) was serviceable, and we had three good engines and eight days before we left for Spa. We had cut up all the Type 25s bar Jo's so there was no solace there. I wonder today where all the Type 25s now racing have come from!

We were going to be very lucky if we managed three cars for Spa, and there was absolutely no chance that I could get started on a new design of car. It was a good thing really, it gave me a chance to think out what I was going to do. Peter Spear, scenting blood, turned up to mastermind the new car planning and was very surprised when I said I could not talk about it for a week.

I took advantage of the repairs to modify the rear hubs to reduce the camber change, and made the new front wishbones longer, increasing the front track. We had one piece of good luck — the new Leyland transporter arrived. The entire Drawing Office was mobilized to sort out its teething troubles and stow the gear from the Commer mobile workshop. I was saddened by the passing of the workshop, where we had many a welcome cup of hot soup in the middle of the night.

The Leyland set off for Spa, on schedule, with its full complement of three cars. Stan and his team had worked absolute miracles. In 15 days they had made six car sets of rear hubs to two different designs, four car sets of front wishbones, also to two different designs, and had rebuilt two badly crashed cars.

I flew out to Brussels, took a hire car to Spa and a solitary hotel in Spa itself. The mechanics were staying at the Hostellerie Le Roannay in Francorchamps; an ideal arrangement, close to the circuit, a very good restaurant and a large garage at the back. Since those days it has grown much larger still under the same owner. RM and PB were in one hotel, and the drivers in another nearby, just outside Spa. I was obviously a bit of a leper.

After talking things through with Graham we came to the conclusion that whatever the consequences, we must stiffen the suspension and stop the car rolling so much. In 1956 Chief Draughtsman John Botterel and I had studied David Hodkin's paper on suspension so that we could understand vehicle dynamics. Our trouble was that there were plenty of textbooks on engine design but none whatever on suspension systems and vehicle dynamics. The only person who could have written one, Colin Chapman, had absolutely no reason to do so while he was supplementing his income designing the Vanwall and redesigning the BRM. It was before the days of pocket calculators and we relied on slide rules. In 1983, during my spell with Team Lotus, I had a pocket computer programmed to do all these sums in seconds.

Dan had gone on holiday with his wife, leaving their children with Pam as planned. A minor fracture was found in his wrist. If he was able to drive at all at Spa, he would have to do so with his forearm in plaster. There was chaos at first practice, the race organizers would only permit 15 cars to start on a circuit nearly nine miles round. It seemed to me that half of the entry was Coopers!

Brabham put in a lap of 3 min 50 sec compared with Hawthorn's lap record of 3 min 57.1 sec. Graham managed 3 min 54.2 sec, and Jim Clark in his first F1 drive in a Lotus, 3 min 57.5 sec. At least we were in the hunt. Next day Stirling had a fearful crash at Burnenville. One of his rear hubs had broken, and it took the ambulance 20 minutes to get to him. Around the same time Michael Taylor went off the road in his Lotus — well into the woods — and in the confusion was not missed for some time. People in the pits thought he had stopped at the Moss crash. Dan was not up to his usual form, but insisted he had to drive, otherwise he would never drive again.

The start was an absolute shambles; the flag falling before several drivers had started their engines, including Clark. On the first lap there were seven cars nose to tail, Brabham, Gendebien, Phil Hill, Graham, Ireland, Bonnier and McLaren. Dan was soon out, rather to our relief, the bolts holding two timing gears together having sheared. A little later Jo missed a gear and turned his engine inside out.

'Moleskin Arry' — Clarence Brinkley's nick-name for me because of the corduroy coat. Note the White Mouse lapel badge — circa 1949.

With B. Bira and Popski in September 1937.

# Fifty years of high performance

The International Aston Martin in May 1945.

**Top** *Test prototype of Rolls-Royce supercharger for the BRM — 1949.*

**Above** *BRM Team arriving home after the 1951 British GP at Silverstone. Left to right: Colin Atkin, Evans (or Cutler), Sam from the Standard Motor Co, Cutler (or Evans), Ken Aldridge, Gordon Newman, Jack North, Willy Southcott, Dave Turner, Cyril Bryden, the author, Sybil Ambrose, Arthur Ambrose ('Hammy').*

**Below** *Monza lap times. The circuit broken up into sections as suggested by Taruffi in September 1951.*

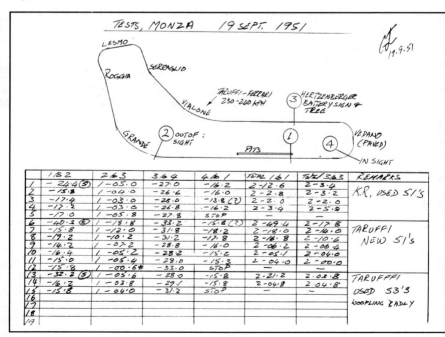

TESTS, MONZA   19 SEPT. 1951

| | 1 to 2 | 2 to 3 | 3 to 4 | 4 to 1 | Total 1 to 1 | Total 3 to 3 | REMARKS |
|---|---|---|---|---|---|---|---|
| 1 | −24.4 (5) | 1−05.0 | −27.0 | −16.2 | 2−12.6 | 2−3.4 | |
| 2 | −15.3 | 1−04.0 | −26.6 | −16.0 | 2−2.8 | 2−3.2 | K.R. USED 51's |
| 3 | −17.4 | 1−03.0 | −28.0 | −13.8 (?) | 2−2.0 | 2−2.0 | |
| 4 | −17.2 | 1−03.0 | −26.8 | −16.2 | 2−3.4 | 2−5.8 | |
| 5 | −17.0 | 1−05.8 | −27.8 | STOP | − | − | |
| 6 | −40.2 (5) | 1−18.8 | −33.2 | −16.8 (?) | 2−49.4 | 2−17.8 | TARUFFI NEW 51's |
| 7 | −15.8 | 1−12.0 | −31.8 | −18.2 | 2−18.0 | 2−14.0 | |
| 8 | −19.2 | 1−10.2 | −31.2 | −17.8 | 2−16.8 | 2−10.6 | |
| 9 | −14.2 | 1−07.2 | −28.8 | −16.0 | 2−06.2 | 2−06.4 | |
| 10 | −16.4 | 1−05.2 | −28.2 | −15.2 | 2−05.1 | 2−04.0 | |
| 11 | −15.0 | 1−05.4 | −28.0 | −15.3 | 2−04.0 | 2−00.0 | |
| 12 | −15.8 | 1−00.6* | −53.0 | STOP | − | − | |
| 13 | −32.2 (5) | 1−05.6 | −28.0 | −15.8 | 2.21.2 | 2.03.8 | TARUFFI USED 53's WOOPLING BADLY |
| 14 | −16.2 | 1−03.8 | −29.1 | −15.8 | 2−04.8 | 2.04.8 | |
| 15 | −15.8 | 1−04.0 | −31.2 | STOP | − | − | |
| 16 | | | | | | | |
| 17 | | | | | | | |
| 18 | | | | | | | |
| 19 | | | | | | | |

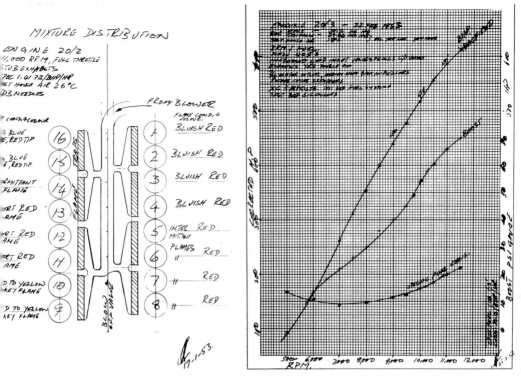

**Above left** *V16 fuel mixture distribution, before corrective action in 1953.*

**Above right** *Power curve for V16 20/3 terminated by backfire at 11,500 rpm — 22 February 1953.*

**Below** *Mark II No. 4 on the starting line at Goodwood, Easter 1954. In the foreground (left to right): Maurice Dove, Ron Flockhart, Dick Salmon (with the plug spanner), the author and a rear view of Peter Berthon.*

**Top** *The author driving the Maserati from the paddock to the start line at the Spanish GP, Pedralbes, Barcelona, in 1954, followed by Maurice Trintignant in a Ferrari.*

**Above** *With Mike Hawthorn at the BRM Supporters' Club Open Day in 1956. Mechanics in overalls: part hidden on left Reg Williams and on the right Gordon Newman.*

**Left** *High speed cine photograph of pot-joint rubber gaiter, rotating at the equivalent of 145 mph, showing how all the lubricant has collected on one side, deforming the rubber and explaining Hawthorn's crash at Goodwood, Easter Monday 1956.*

**Top** *Denis Jenkinson's photograph (reproduced from 'Motor Sport' Racing Car Review), taken at Monza on October 1956 showing the modified rear suspension, with transverse leaf spring and 'Connaught-link' axle location.*

**Above** *Stirling Moss making the first 100 mph lap at Goodwood in 257 — Easter 1959.*

**Right** *Jo Bonnier on his way to winning the Dutch GP at Zandvoort in 1959.*

**Top** *The mid-engined prototype during practice for the Italian GP at Monza in 1959. Left to right: unknown, Raymond Mays part hidden by Peter Berthon, the author, Maurice Dove (half sitting on wheel), Roy Forman, Dick Salmon (in cap), Pat Carvath, Jo Bonnier in the car, Villoresi wearing a hat, and extreme right with one foot on the wheel, Reg Parnell.*

**Above** *On our way home from Monza, with the prototype mid-engined car, at the top of the Simplon Pass. Left to right: Alan Ellison, Body Shop Chargehand, Dick Salmon and Maurice Dove.*

**Below** *Dan Gurney with 483 wearing a rear roll bar for the first time — Snetterton 1960.*

**Above** *The sad end to Graham Hill's epic drive in the 1960 British GP at Silverstone, when he stalled on the grid but took the lead 50 laps later.*

**Right** *Showing details of the outboard rear brakes and the double wishbone rear suspension.*

**Below** *The Leyland Transporter emerging from our second home of the '50s — the Albergo Ristorante Marchesi.*

**Top** *Stan Hope and Alf Martin with the nearly complete frame for 5781 in April 1961.*

**Above** *The partially-skinned complete chassis for 5781 waiting for its V8 engine in July 1961.*

**Below** *The Test House at 11 p.m. on 12 July 1961 just after the first run of the V8 engine.*

**Above** *Driving the V8-engined car for the first time at Witham Airfield in August 1961, with my Austin A40 in the background. The smoke is from burning stubble.*

**Below** *Aerodynamic test at Snetterton in July 1962. The photograph, taken from Graham's Jaguar, shows three wool strips on the nose of Richie Ginther's car. Whatever we did the middle strip persisted in coiling itself around the support, indicating some strange eddy.*

**Bottom** *The second World Championship victory in 1962 — the German GP — which met Sir Alfred's conditions for him to keep BRM in being. Denis Perkins with hat, rare smile and raincoat.*

**Above** *What it was all about — victorious 5783 at the Racing Car Show in January 1963.*

**Left** *The South African GP Trophy in my garden at Bourne in January 1963. (We had to send it back at the end of the year.)*

**Below** *The Rover BRM at Le Mans 1963. Peter Spear is in a white shirt on the pit counter.*

**Above** *Some of the Boardroom trophies in December 1963.*

**Right** *Prince and Princess Chula with their daughter in 1963.*

**Below** *The four-wheel-drive car in June 1964.*

**Left** *The Shell advertisement in anticipation of one or both of the 1964 World Championships.*

**Below** *A more light-hearted version of the Shell advertisement.*

**Top right** *Tyre testing for Goodyear at Riverside, California, with Dan Gurney in the Brabham — November 1964.*

**Right** *Wet track tyre testing at Riverside. Artificial rain was provided by the sprinklers on the inside of the track.*

**Below right** *Graham Hill in a nicely balanced drift at Silverstone in 1965.*

**Top** *Princess Chula in 'Romulus' in 1965 at the National Motor Museum, Beaulieu. Note the white mouse on the mirror fairing.*

**Above** *'Romulus' and friends at Beaulieu in 1965.*

**Left** *Pre-race check. Looking for oil leaks at Monaco in 1965.*

**Above** *Jackie Stewart's wheel-breaking spin at Monaco in 1965.*

**Below** *Jackie Stewart at the controls of the Learjet on our way from Watkins Glen to New York in October 1965.*

**Above** *Graham, Jackie and the author with the third US GP trophy and the Lear on arrival at La Guardia in October 1965.*

**Left** *Eddie Hall talking to Raymond Mays at Monaco.*

**Below** *Mike Spence and the H16 in 1967.*

**Above** *Jackie Stewart testing an H16 at Snetterton in 1967 — too much roll and too much understeer.*

**Below** *A typical shot of Willy Southcott — 1967.*

**Above** *Dickie Attwood's fine drive into second place behind Graham Hill at Monaco in May 1968.*

**Below** *Graham Hill's* 'This is your Life' *in 1971. John Coombs is between us.*

**Above** *The first clay model of the Lotus Esprit in 1972.*

**Below** *Giugiaro's first rendering of the Esprit in 1973.*

**Bottom** *The second version of the Esprit (with legal windscreen rake and part-productionized) at Ketteringham Hall in 1974.*

**Above** *Don Safety Award presentation, for contribution to vehicle safety by the Lotus Elite in May 1975. Left to right: Fred Bushell, Richard Morley (Managing Director, Lotus Cars), Mike Kimberley (Vehicle Engineering Manager, Lotus Cars), the author, Colin Chapman, Hazel Chapman, PRO Donavon McLauchlan.*

**Left** *An Esprit in Norwich Cathedral, in support of my address on 'Careers in Engineering'.*

**Top right** *Model of first ground-effect Lotus — which became Type 78 — in the wind tunnel (autumn 1975).*

**Middle right** *Another view during the same tests.*

**Right** *A very early Moonraker prior to the addition of the flybridge.*

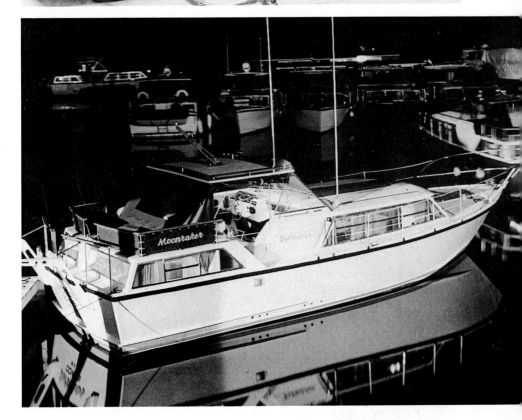

**Above** *The first Mistral at Cogolin, southern France, waiting for the Chris Craft party (and its own correct name plate!) in August 1977.*

**Left** *Jim Rochliss (second from right) 'Riding a Mistral' in the Bay of St Tropez in August 1977.*

**Below** *Sales picture of the Marauder running through its own wake — 1977.*

**Above** *The old BRM air-flow rig in its new home at Lotus.*

**Right** *Showing Prince Philip the 2-litre engine converted to proposed 4-litre V8 induction and water circulation systems in 1980.*

**Below** *Colin Chapman kneeling to get a better idea of the frontal area of the KFM 4-cylinder microlight engine in Bologna in September 1982. Peter Wright is behind the engine.*

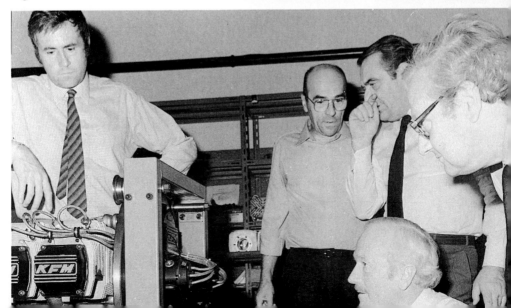

**Above** *With four Lotus Managing Directors at our Christmas party in 1981. Left to right: Fred Bushell, Mike Kimberley, the author, Richard Morley and Denis Austin.*

**Below** *Sunbeam Lotus, the winner of the World Rally Championship in 1981.*

**Above** *The first Lotus V8 engine showing long induction ram pipes crossed over top of engine — 1981.*

**Right** *The Lotus 4-cylinder 50 hp microlight aircraft engine. Note that the propeller is driven from the end of the camshaft.*

**Below** *Early Lotus Engineering project for Gloster Saro — Airport Rapid Intervention Vehicle. Project funded by the Department of Trade and Industry and administered by the Design Council.*

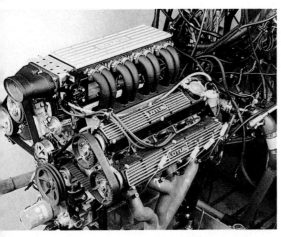

**Left** *The Lotus 4-litre V8 engine being used to test the Corvette LT5 induction system, with 11 throttle butterflies and 16 injector nozzles.*

**Below** *Showing King Hussein of Jordan and his staff the LT5 engine.*

**Left** *Sectioned LT5 engine exhibited by General Motors at Riverside, California, Dealer Convention in 1988.*

**Above** *The Corvette Indy 'Press Car' at the Detroit Motor Show in January 1986. This car, a non-runner, was exhibited to obtain Press and public reaction.*

**Below** *The judges of the Innovative Vehicle Design Competition at Vancouver in July 1986. Left to right: Kazuo Morohoshi (Advanced Vehicle Design, Toyota), Dr Gordon Campbell (Director Road Traffic Safety, Canada); Hideo Takeda (Chief Engineer Honda R & D), the author, Ted Elliot (Director of Engineering, Chrysler Canada), Frank Walters (1986 President of the Society of Automotive Engineers), Dr Bernd Strackerjan (Advanced Vehicles Daimler-Benz), Gail Halderman (Director Design, Ford, North America), Dr Ghazi Karim (University of Calgary). Not in the group, but an active judge, was Ted Robertson (Director of Engineering, GM Canada).*

**Left** *Site of the International Vehicle Design Competition — the University of British Columbia — taken during my helicopter trip.*

**Below** *The running Corvette Indy, at Lotus, before despatch to the US.*

**Bottom** *Another view of the Corvette Indy.*

**Above** *Starting another trip to Heathrow and the US with driver Joe Bedford and a ZR1 Corvette.*

**Below** *Among the Corvette ZR1s lined up at the Hotel Intercontinental, Geneva, before the drive to Mireval and Carcassonne.*

**Above** *With Arv Muller (left) Vice President Engineering Chevrolet Pontiac Canada Group of General Motors and Roy Midgley, Chief Engineer CPC 90-degree Vee Engines and thus LT5 Project Manager, during presentation of LT5 to the SAE in 1989.*

**Left** *Martin Donnelly's second engine change in Monaco 1990.*

**Below** *With Prince Albert of Monaco, Madame Deutsch and her daughter, about to introduce the winner of the Charles Deutsch Award in my capacity as Chairman of the Award Jury, at Monte Carlo in January 1991.*

**Above** *Colin Spooner's 4-valve model for my 65th birthday.*

**Below** *Colin Spooner's boat model for my retirement.*

*Albert Adams reading his farewell ode at my retirement party on 28 March 1991. The group includes (left to right) Chris Garrett, Ken Sears, Roger Mackrill, Warren King, Steve Green, Albert (performing), Gerry Doe, Fred Bushell, Patrick Peal, Oliver Winterbottom, Chris Dunster, John Sandiford, Colin Gethin.*

*Albert's actual ode.*

*Cutting Jennie's cake helped by Pam, with Hugh Kemp and Steve Green waiting with plates at the ready, while Avril Bishop, Mike Kimberley's secretary, holds our drinks.*

At half distance Brabham led by 12 seconds from Phil Hill who was four seconds ahead of the battle for third place between, Gendebien, Graham, McLaren, Chris Bristow, von Trips and Willie Mairesse. Bristow rolled at Burnenville and was killed. Shortly afterwards Alan Stacey, in another Lotus, went off and was killed; it was suspected that he was hit in the face by a bird. With two laps to go Brabham was still in front, but Graham was only 18.5 seconds behind, having got the better of Gendebien.

At the start of the last lap Graham coasted into his pit, still in second place — a pulled main bearing stud had broken the crankshaft. Seconds later Gendebien coasted in with a failed gearbox. Fortunately for him the Ferrari pit was ahead of the start line, so all he had to do was to push over and claim third place. There was no way Graham could push his car 8.77 miles to complete the lap. There was quite a witch hunt after the race. Opinions were canvassed over the three Lotus crashes. Mechanical failure was apparently to blame for two of them. I would have absolutely nothing to do with this, on the 'there-but-for . . .', basis, but some people gave the pot a good stir.

Back at Bourne I issued the British GP build specification and set to work on my new car, 486, to be known as the Mark II. It had a much lower line, with the driver leaning well back. The rear suspension had long bottom wishbones with a common centre pivot. The top arms were 'N' shaped to control toe-in. The vital feature was a brake at each corner, the rear discs were inboard of the hubs.

A.G.B. Owen had built Donald Campbell's Proteus turbine-engined Bluebird land speed record car in his Motor Panels group. As some of the funds set aside for aerodynamic consultancy and wind tunnel work had not been used, AGB decided that BRM could have the benefit to improve the F1 cars. Peter Spear had brought the aerodynamic consultants to Bourne in January, and very carefully I took them through the regulations. The wheels had to be exposed — the Mercedes and Lancia designs of 1954 were no longer permitted, the regulations being explicitly worded to exclude such cars. I obtained and sent to Spear an up-to-date set of the regulations with a covering letter.

When the party duly arrived, Spear having got the whip out so the new car could have the benefit of the consultant's aerodynamic improvements, with great ceremony they unveiled their ideas — which were fairings between the wheels! There was a fearful row. Only PB saw the funny side. Fortunately my covering letter, sent with the regulations in January, drew attention to the changes and specifically said you cannot put fairings between the wheels or enclose them. The only good thing that came out of it all was a new nose with better air distribution over the radiator.

PB decided to join the new car camp. His contribution was Lucas fuel injection. Lucas had developed a very good mechanical fuel injection system, used on the Ecurie Ecosse Le Mans-winning Jaguars. The Lucas Jaguar system seemed to be very efficient. Everyone agreed it was a good idea, although I would have preferred to have developed the car on a proven carburettor engine, rather than have all the problems with a new car and fuel injection as well.

I flew out to Reims for the French GP via Paris. We had more than the usual trouble with blowing valves and broken valve springs, but when the cars were running properly they were quick. I had started using stick-on white plastic numbers. International Regulations had long specified that British cars had to be green with white numbers, and we had a book of adhesive numbers which we stuck on the cars as appropriate. The valve problem got so bad that at one stage we only had one serviceable car between the three drivers. Each driver had to turn in three laps within 5 per cent of the time of the second-fastest man in order to qualify. We were distracting the pit marshal's attention and changing numbers on the unserviceable cars as well as the solitary serviceable one (it would have given the game away to suddenly have two cars with the same number). Fortunately we had the end pit furthest from the Dunlop bridge. When this highly illegal operation was completed we had Graham on the front row with a time of 2 min 18.4 sec. Dan and a rather indignant Jo, whose car it was, were both at 2 min 19.8 sec. I heaved a big sigh of relief, relaxed on the pit counter and said to my neighbour assuming him to be a BRM team member: 'I think we have got away with it.' I was talking to Denis Jenkinson, who as far as I know never ever gave us away.

There seems to be something about Reims which leads to higher spirits than usual. We were setting off for practice, led by Jo and Marianne Bonnier, in his new Mercedes. I was just behind him in a hire car, followed by Graham in a Porsche. We were stopped at an intersection by a traffic policeman. For some reason my car gradually crept forward and pushed Jo's car forward to nudge the policeman. Jo nearly missed practice altogether. Fortunately he was multilingual and could speak English, French, German, Italian and Spanish, as well as Swedish. He needed his best French that day. In the race all our efforts came to nothing; Graham could not get his car into gear on the line and was rammed by Trintignant who came from the seventh row which meant he was really moving when he hit Graham. The other two cars did not last long either before they were out, both with broken valve springs.

I did manage a wry smile at Reims. Colin Chapman had confided in me at Zandvoort that he could not understand why a Cooper with the same engine was so much faster in a straight line than his Lotus. He had asked my opinion as to whether it had anything to do with Cooper leaning their engine over at twenty degrees so that the carburettors were well within the body shell. Lotus mounted the engine vertically with the carburettors hanging well out. I did not think it had anything to do with it and pointed out that the Yeoman Credit Coopers had long intakes down the nose. For Reims, Lotus had one car with the engine inclined, Cooper style — it went no faster. Meanwhile Coopers, who could not understand why Lotus were faster than they were in a straight line, modified a car to have a vertical engine like the Lotus. John Cooper had worked it out that if the Lotus went so fast with a vertical engine, he did not need all the problems of an inclined sump, and it helped him get the engine lower. They both reverted to their standard arrangement for the next race, and probably cursed the drivers who gave them the false information which started the expensive witch hunt.

In the bar of the Hotel Lion d'Or after the race, Gregor Grant was the source of much merriment. Apparently he wrote his race reports from tape recordings of what he saw during the race. Gregor and his friend, Dunlop's Dick Jeffrey, were rather bored at Reims. They had, however, enjoyed Zandvoort immensely, so they decided to drive to Zandvoort on Saturday evening in Dick's Jaguar. It must have been a good night. Dick forgot that he was supposed to collect a Dunlop director from Paris on Sunday morning. They only just got back in time for the race, slightly the worse for wear. Gregor was bemoaning to all and sundry that he had forgotten to switch on his tape recorder and could remember very little about the race and was therefore in trouble with his race report. Everyone laughed and told him he missed this incident or that incident; and what about so and so? While this was going on Gregor had his tape recorder switched on in his pocket. The race account he eventually produced was one of his best ever.

Later in the evening I was having a beer with Wally Hassan and his wife Ethel in Bridget's, when things got a little out of hand and the police were called. They rounded up the revellers and loaded them into their Black Maria (a blue Renault). Someone — I suspect Innes Ireland — removed most of the wheel nuts, and they did not get very far before the wheels fell off. It began to look very ugly, so we discreetly drifted away.

Back at Bourne the new car was making good progress. I had planned the suspension geometry to have a constant distance between the roll centre and centre of gravity. It also had nearly zero scrub. Rolls-Royce had come up with three possible jobs, all attractive. I had to tell them which one I preferred after the British GP at Silverstone. I still enjoyed motor racing, especially the design side, but was getting extremely fed up with the Bourne set-up and the eternal politics and intrigues.

There were two Coopers and two BRMs on the front row at Silverstone for the British GP. We had a fearful panic just before the start. Part of our warm-up drill was to check each magneto in turn, and one of Graham's was dead — the one we could not change in the time available. Ever resourceful Willy spotted that the wires to the switches had been crossed, so it was the magneto we could change in time and we got Graham to the start with seconds to spare. When Stirling Moss, who, after his Spa accident was not yet fit to drive, dropped the flag, Graham stalled his engine and Tony Brooks from the third row hit him a glancing blow. After we had quickly checked there was no serious damage, we push-started Graham and he joined the race last and some 30 seconds down. Jo and Innes Ireland were fighting for third place behind the two Coopers. I had the watch on Graham who was gaining a second a lap on Brabham, the leader. His 30-second disadvantage was soon down to 24.5 seconds. We started from then on to give him his time behind the race leader every lap.

Graham said afterwards that it was our prompt recognition of the situation, and the introduction of a decimal point into our signals that encouraged him. Dan came in with a broken gear change, so we stuck him in top and he eventually finished. Graham was still going well, but having trouble picking his way through the back markers. However, by lap 40, Graham had moved into second place and was only 5.4 seconds behind Brabham. The Cooper pit had already spotted the challenge and had warned Jack. On lap 54 Graham passed him into the lead with a record lap of 1 min 34.6 sec. Jo was fighting Clark and McLaren for fifth place when his rewelded rear spring attachment broke away from the frame. Graham was now drawing away from Jack by an odd tenth, so that on lap 60 he was 1.2 seconds ahead; on lap 70, 1.8 and lap 71, 2.1. It looked as if Brabham was giving up, which was out of character, but on lap 72 coming up to lap two Ferraris at Copse, Graham was faced with the choice of waiting until after the corner, letting Jack close on him, or taking one of them before the corner. However his brake pedal travel had been increasing with the thrashing they were getting, and he was giving the brakes an occasional pump; on this corner it caught him out and he spun off. The crowd gave him as big an ovation as if he had won.

I told the Rolls-Royce people after that race that I would stick it out a bit longer. Peter Spear tried to goad me into going to AGB and complaining I was not getting a fair deal at Bourne — no drawing office assistance and so on. Such assistance was the last thing I wanted. On the way home, in the Austin A35 (for once no traffic jams) AGB overtook me in his Bentley and we stopped for a talk. He said he was very pleased with the improvement in our fortunes. He was impressed by Graham, and he enquired about Dan. I said Dan was still upset by the Dutch boy's death but was gradually coming back to his old form.

AGB gave me the 'British driver in the British car' lecture. I told him that much of our improvement was down to the inspiration from Graham who was getting better every race, but I did not know how much more there was to come. I thought Jo had reached his limit but Graham, I thought, given a reliable car, would continue to improve. I did not think that Stirling would ever come to BRM as he enjoyed his relationship with Rob Walker. I was sure he would recover his form following his Spa crash, as he knew it was not his fault. I said I thought Tony Brooks was very underrated. He was not as ruthless as Stirling, but just as fast when he was happy with the car. I thought two seasons in the wilderness away from a team like Vanwall may have taken some of the edge off him, but a good season in a good reliable car would put it all back. We parted on this very amicable note.

There was a race at Brands Hatch on August Bank Holiday Monday. The race organizers pressed very hard for Graham, although I was not very enthusiastic. We had brake trouble in practice and had to bring the car back to Bourne. I ran it with new brakes on Sunday at a local disused airfield — North Witham. Graham finished second four seconds behind Brabham. He did not seem to get into his stride until half distance, by which time Jack had too much of a lead.

We were making terrific progress with the new car, helped by the German GP being for F2. I was still too busy to go to the Portuguese GP at Oporto. Dan had pole; Jo had flu, Dan and Jo suffered broken valve springs and Graham gearbox trouble. Then on the return trip the Leyland was doing about 80 mph (130 kph) along a tree-lined road when a front tyre burst, and it took down four trees before coming to rest without hurting anyone. The whole right hand side of the vehicle was torn out, but only one car was damaged. It was just as well the British teams boycotted the Italian GP. We could not have gone as it took ages to get the crippled Leyland and its load back.

First runs of the Mark II were frustrating. The fuel injection system flattened the batteries every 15 minutes at Silverstone, and at Snetterton the car just would not start. So we hurriedly converted it to carburettors.

We took the converted Mark II and 484 to test at Oulton Park, where Graham established that the Mark II was 1.6 seconds quicker than a Mark I. A week later in practice for the Oulton Park Gold Cup race, Graham, Jack Brabham and Jim Clark all tied for second fastest time behind Stirling. However, we found blowing valves and broken valve springs in 484's and

486's engines, and Jo was complaining of gear change trouble. In the race Graham found the replacement engine would only pull 7600 rpm against the 8050 rpm of the original. Even so, he got the better of Clark and McLaren to finish third. Dan was in fifth place with a broken valve spring, and Jo was still in gearbox trouble.

Graham gave a very enthusiastic report to AGB concerning the handling of the car at Oulton. After some discussion it was agreed that we would buy Coventry-Climax 4-cylinder engines as a temporary measure to keep us racing until our own new F1 engine was ready. We were to build three Climax-engined cars, and AGB directed that I was to design them, and then the new car for PB's new engine, when that was ready.

I had been issued with an Austin A40 as my company car. Graham, who had an interest in Speedwell, gave me a Speedwell performance kit.

PB asked whether I thought we should take the Mark II car to Riverside, California for the American GP and then on to the Tasman series in New Zealand and Australia. I decided not to, although it would have been ideal on Riverside's corners, but we would not get the cars back from Australia until late March.

We all flew out to Los Angeles in a Pan American 707 for the American GP, with me in charge of the team. PB was too busy with his new engine, and RM hated flying. The engines had been converted to coil valve springs. We all had at least one set of springs in our luggage, confusing the American Customs at Los Angeles. The race organizers issued us with enormous Buick Le Sabre station wagons, and we stayed in the oldest building in California, The Mission Inn, Riverside. The cars were garaged with a friend of Dan's, Joe Vittone, the local Volkswagen dealer.

I was terrified that we would run out of serviceable engines — Graham was pounding round learning the circuit. June Wilkinson, the *Playboy* centrefold girl of the month, visited the pit lane. She was a great help. The drivers were so busy chatting her up that practice running was kept down and I had enough engines left. We were issued with American number plates so we could drive the racing cars on the road from the garage to the circuit, but someone blew a speed cop off, so then we had to travel in convoy with a heavy escort from the Californian Highway Patrol. Graham seemed to have a job getting to know the circuit and was way back on the grid.

In the race Moss led all the way. To start with, Dan was second, Clark and Surtees collided, and at quarter distance Stirling was leading, Dan second, Jo third, Ireland fourth, and Graham fifth, but it soon went wrong. A core plug blew out of Dan's cylinder head, and Graham had a timing gear failure. However, Jo held second place until seven laps from the end when he came in with a valve spring failure. I sent him back out to finish in the considerable prize money. We thought he was fifth, but his official placing was fourth. By the prize-giving enough people had protested, so he was finally classified fifth. Denis Perkins, our gearbox fitter, was also our chart keeper, and the best there was. Such was his reputation that I believe, if we had stuck it out, we would have been allowed to keep fourth place. But Denis's chart showed Jo fifth so we had to live with it.

The race organizers were unable to pay our start money. Somehow they had upset one of the local newspapers, and the gate was less than 20,000. I spent several hours each day with John Cooper and Stan Chapman (deputizing for his son who was busy with the London Motor Show) chasing the money. Not a very auspicious way to celebrate my first race in command.

We prepared the cars for shipment to New Zealand. We were not booked to fly back to England until the Friday after Thanksgiving, so for the first time in their lives the mechanics had it easy. They found a supply of draught beer in a Honkey Tonk called Diamond Lil's, and they spent the mornings packing, afternoons in the hotel pool and evenings in Diamond Lil's, while I pursued the start money. On Wednesday evening before we were due to leave I got enough to pay the hotel bill. It was about six months before we received the rest of it.

American hospitality was lavish. Visits to film studios, and a Hawaiian party at the Reventlow's with flowers floating in the pool; large numbers of unclad film starlets; underwater lighting; Hawaiian music — the works. For some reason I still do not understand, Innes Ireland had been voted one of Britain's best-dressed men, so he arrived at the party properly dressed, complete with bowler and furled umbrella. Later he decided to join the ladies, and nearly everyone followed him into the pool. It was not very warm.

I was also getting worried as to how many members of the BRM party I could assemble for departure to Los Angeles Airport at 6 a.m. on Friday. One mechanic was having a torrid romance with one of Diamond Lil's young ladies, and at 6.20 a.m. the minibus driver was getting restive: we were still one short — Arthur Hill. The large black lady who kept the all-night coffee shop at the local bus station then appeared carrying Arthur, very much the worse for wear, under her arm.

After Christmas I set out for New Zealand (once again in charge, despite the start money fiasco) via New York and Los Angeles, where we were joined by Reg Parnell, John Surtees, Dan Gurney and Innes. Most of them had been having a good time in Los Angeles. At Fiji we changed into an old piston-engined DC6 for the last leg. Among the other passengers were some people going to a religious convention and Miss Fiji 1960. It was all very quiet and decorous until Innes Ireland, a practising Scot, discovered he had missed New Year's Eve as we had crossed the International Date Line and would go straight from 30 December to 1 January. Innes thought it was a leg pull, and it took the complete crew including the captain several hours to convince him. When he returned from the flight deck he was wearing most of the stewardess's uniform with a blanket as a skirt.

Everyone in New Zealand was extremely hospitable. I was asked whether I would like to swim, drink beer or sail. They all seemed attractive to me, so I found myself sailing, swimming and drinking beer. Following New Zealand custom, a crate of beer from the car was transferred to the boat.

The circuit on Ardmore airfield began to break up, and we had to put wire mesh everywhere — radiators, windscreens and air intakes. If it had been a European race everyone would have refused to drive but the people were so friendly, helpful and enthusiastic that it would have been quite wrong. They were trying so hard to stage a good race and see that everyone had a good time.

The race was run in two heats and a final. Brabham won, McLaren was second and Graham was third (running on one magneto — a stone had destroyed the drive to the other). Dan was in great form. He lost some time due to gear change problems but was going through the field in fine style when the cylinder head joint blew.

Graham felt that we should return some of the tremendous hospitality we had received. He had been learning to water ski, most of the time under water. Every time he came into the garage and bent down, water ran out of his ears! We organized a barbecue around the pool at the Papatoetoe Motel. Half-way through the evening Graham said to me: 'It needs livening up, they are all too poh-faced. Park your car with its lights beamed on my chalet, but do not switch them on until you hear me yell.' When I switched the lights on, on cue, there he was running for the pool, absolutely starkers — no one was poh-faced after that.

I stayed on for a few days while we were getting the car ready for two races in Australia. These could be run on any fuel, so we were going to use the old BPK 50 per cent methanol. Unfortunately it was so hot at Warwick Farm that the methanol dissolved the jointing compound in the rubber fuel cells. At Ballarat we reverted to petrol and Dan won, with Graham second. This was on an RAAF airfield. The night before the race some of the airmen took Dan's car and hid it under some straw bales. Fortunately it was found in time.

The race organizers' travel agent put together my trip home. Before I left, the Shell representative took me to lunch at a very elegant club with Air-Marshal Sir Keith Park, who had been the commander of the key 11 Group during the Battle of Britain — a very great man in my eyes. After that I was taken to a 'plonk factory' — a winery producing sherry. I flew on a Qantas Constellation to Fiji, where I stopped off for 24 hours. On the next leg to Honolulu I sat next to an American working for Bell Helicopters and on his way home from Australia. We spent 36 hours together in Honolulu, Pearl Harbor, Waikiki Beach and a volcano. On to Los Angeles for 24 hours where the Rolls-Royce representative and the Reventlows looked after me extremely well. Then on to New York by American Airlines, flight 001. I was so well looked after by American Airlines that whenever I have to travel by air in America I have used them ever since. I now have a one million mile Gold Card. From New York to London I was in a Rolls-Royce-engined BOAC 707, arriving on time. I had cabled Pam to meet me at Heathrow, planning a big day out in London as it was her birthday. Unfortunately the cable got garbled and read p.m. instead of a.m. The last leg, bus, tube and train to Peterborough was an anti-climax after all that.

When I got back I found that Wilkie Wilkinson had been appointed Team Manager. Our drivers were Graham and Tony Brooks. I was to concentrate on development. As usual, neither Wilkie nor I had been briefed separately, or together, as to who did what, and neither had the drivers. It led to some running-in problems as Wilkie believed that once a car was sorted out it should never be 'mucked about with', and it certainly should not be changed to suit different circuits. Graham fiercely believed the total opposite, so we had all the ingredients for trouble.

We took the cars to Goodwood with Coventry Climax Mark I engines, which went well enough even if they were slow, being about 70 kg (154 lb) over the formula minimum of 450 kg (992 lb). I had not learned at that time that a kilogramme of excess weight costs one hundredth of a second a lap, so we were giving away seven tenths of a second a lap to Lotus who were certain to be down to weight. Wilkie and I went to the Goodwood Easter Meeting together, but I did not go to Aintree or to Silverstone where there were both F1 and Intercontinental races. We generally collected a third, with an occasional second. Wilkie considered that the cars were now sorted and there was no need for me to go to any more races. In any case I was concentrating on the new car for the V8.

Just before the Team left for Monaco, PB decided that I should go too. Wilkie's face when he saw the mechanics unloading umbrella racks full of roll-bars and boxes full of road-springs and bump-rubbers, was an absolute study. Graham had our first Mark II Climax engine, which gave another 6 hp and weighed another 12 kg (26½ lb). Stirling, in last year's Lotus, was down to 1 min 39.1 sec, and all four Ferraris and Graham were under 1 min 40 sec. Tony Brooks managed 1 min 40.1 sec. In the race, Graham had a fuel pump failure and Tony hit Dan Gurney's Porsche when trying to overtake and collected the centre mounted Porsche exhaust pipe in his radiator. The highlight of the race was a tremendous duel between Stirling and Richie Ginther in the experimental 120° Ferrari.

I flew home to get back to the new car, but was then sent out to Zandvoort with the second Mark II Climax engine for Tony Brooks. As usual we broke the circuit up for timing and found the new Lotus 21 with inboard suspension and 150 hp was much quicker down the straight than the 180 hp Ferraris. Graham was quickest from the starting line around the hairpin and out of sight at the back of the pits. There was a Ferrari front row but Graham and Stirling, again in a Lotus, were on the second, which I felt was about right. We could out-corner both the two Lotus cars, but Stirling could out-drive Graham. Stirling could not make up his mind whether to drive Rob Walker's Lotus or Cooper. Wilkie banned me from the garage and the pit, so I was able to walk round the circuit with my Leica and take photographs. All 15 starters finished. I was disappointed that we were only eighth and ninth.

Mr and Mrs Stanley were concerned by the problem between Wilkie and me. Several successful teams had a Team Manager and Chief Engineer — notably Ferrari and Mercedes. PB was not going to races, although the V8 engine was completely drawn and pieces were beginning to arrive in the workshop. RM sat on the fence, but finally it was agreed that I could go to races when I chose, but on race day Wilkie was in charge and any instructions I wanted to give to the mechanics were to be given through Wilkie. If this had been sorted out when Wilkie joined it would have made life a little easier, and the cars might have gone faster.

It was clear that we needed to find a little more speed, given our shortage of horsepower, so Tony Brooks and I took a car to Snetterton, where we picked up 5 mph on maximum speed by reducing rear toe-in and giving the car a new nose. It was my first test session with Tony for some years. He had become coolly analytical and had gained confidence from his Vanwall and Ferrari days. It really was a useful day's testing.

I went to Spa for the Belgian GP where, in practice, Ferrari discovered the advantages and disadvantages of rear camber. They ended up with eight degrees, much to Vic Barlow's horror, and started throwing treads. We were second and third among the also rans, ahead of Stirling. To our surprise Surtees was the leader taking a very unorthodox line through Eau Rouge corner after the pits. The race was not so good for us. Graham had a tussle with Surtees for fifth place, until Graham's exhaust pipe broke and Tony Brooks's magneto failed. I did not go to Reims for the French GP as the pace was hotting up on the V8. In fact my next F1 race was the GP at Monza with the V8, with Wilkie in charge of the Climax-engined cars.

# CHAPTER ELEVEN

# The birth of the V8 — and under new management

ALTHOUGH THE 1.5 litre formula due to come into force on 1 January 1961 was announced late in 1958, for most of 1959 the British took the attitude that if we ignored it, it would go away. It did not. By mid-1960 it was clear not only was it going to happen, but Ferrari was good and ready and Porsche was not far away. They were recruiting drivers like Bonnier and Gurney. A new engine took a year to design and build, so we had already lost most of 1961.

My relationship with PB and RM had changed following Zandvoort and AGB's (now Sir Alfred Owen) subsequent decision that I had a free hand to design the new cars. RM was very petulant and rarely came into the workshop, then only to show a visitor the old cars. His attitude changed a little when Taruffi told him at Spa in 1961 that the Type 57 Climax was the best handling car in F1. PB was very cordial, but rarely came into the workshops. I spent little time in his domain — the Drawing Office. I produced my design schemes on my own board in my office or at home; frames were dimensioned on the centre line and a print given to Stan who then made it. More complex components were detailed by the Drawing Office from my schemes. My routine — purely convenience — was a visit to the Drawing Office first thing in the morning (PB still did not arrive until midday), so our paths rarely crossed by chance. With the RAF taking over Folkingham, the Berthons had to move out of their flat in the control tower. Rubery Owen Estates Ltd bought the Old Rectory in Folkingham village for them, so Lorna Berthon reappeared and set in motion a very expensive redecoration plan. I don't think she was very happy about moving back from Paris. She liked the lifestyle, but the Talbot project had collapsed. Also, I suspect, their marriage was going through a rough patch. It would not be unfair to say they were both difficult people to live with.

I had the impression, never formally put into words, that Rubery Owen were exerting much stricter control over BRM's finances. The attitude that 'It's the Chairman's only relaxation, and we are making plenty of money', had been replaced by, 'What are we getting for all this money?'

Armed with the experience gained from 486, and the Climax-engined cars, I laid out the smallest possible car that could carry Graham. He and I had long talks about what we needed from the car. I calculated how much fuel a 200 hp engine would need, and arrived at some basic dimensions. I laid out the ideal front and rear suspensions, based on my limited knowledge. From this I calculated the loads and forces I had to deal with. On the 24-hour flights to and from New Zealand I calculated all the frame tube diameters and wall thickness. It all seemed to work. The chassis was very stiff, it survived many minor shunts and we never had a cracked tube. I spent hours discussing with 'Flash Alf' Martin, our welder, and Stan what they could and could not make. From this I devised myself some design rules.

The cars were BRM Type 57s, but to make a distinction between the Climax-engined 4-cylinder cars, the cars for the V8 were designated 578s.

I had a series of informal chats with PB (he was not one for formal meetings) in the autumn of 1960 concerning the new 1.5 litre engine. He said: 'I am thinking a V8, what do you think?' He asked me to tabulate all my air flow and port data so that they could be made into a series of charts and graphs. We had developed cylinder heads for the Ford Consul, the new 105E Anglia as well as the Zephyrs, so what with work on the V16, the Maserati, the 2.5 litre, the four-valve single and the Climax, we had a fair amount of data.

PB said he intended to use the V16 timing gear pack and roller bearing camshafts as none of them had given any trouble on the V16, but he favoured direct-acting bucket tappets. He also planned to use the V16 connecting rod which was the right size and had not given any trouble.

Sir Alfred Owen had decreed that the engine must be offered for sale in competition with the new Climax V8, so we had to face the need for several different gearbox mounting faces. We discussed the idea of separate gearbox adaptor castings on the back of the engine, which would also carry the rear crankshaft oil seal. PB was concerned that this would add weight and bulk, even though it made the engine more versatile. We had already committed extra metal and space at the front around the V16 timing gear pack. He believed the Lucas fuel injection system was the only solution for a V8. He had organized a year's exclusive contract with Lucas, so if there was any advantage we had it, not Climax or Ferrari. The only thing we could not agree on was the use of Norton type squish. 'Squish' was a term coined by Sir Harry Ricardo to describe an improvement to the combustion process he developed in the 1920s. A flat surface on the piston came very close to a matching surface in the cylinder head at top-dead-centre and 'squished' the charge towards the centre of the combustion chamber. As far as I was concerned it cost air flow and involved an incredible amount of hand fitting of the piston into the combustion chamber.

PB said the engine was planned to rev to over 12,000. I reminded him that the old Dynamatic was only safe up to 10,000 rpm. He said: 'You will have to catch it unawares, nip it up to ten five and extrapolate, you have done it before.' This was a dig at my V16 boost curve. They were all reasoned and constructive discussions, even if informal. He seemed to take my views quite seriously.

On my return from the American GP at Riverside Mrs Walker, his new secretary, called me to his office and he showed me the V8-engine layout drawings, saying they were not, under any circumstances, to leave his office. I could come and look at them at any time he or Mrs Walker were there, to obtain the dimensions from which to design my chassis.

When I got back from New Zealand I found on my desk a drawing of a valve spring test rig to be made up from welded steel plates. I was to use it to determine how much oil the tappet needed and from which direction — into the load or after the load? Soon afterwards oil pumps and water pumps were delivered to me for test. One day he politely asked if he could come and look at my chassis. He asked many questions but, apart from expressing surprise at the reclining driving position, there was no word of criticism. When he saw the detachable tubes over the exhaust cam covers to facilitate engine changing, he remarked: 'Make sure you have plenty of meat around the bolt holes, they will fret and wear.' He did not go to many races. He seemed to be keeping everyone's noses to the grindstone, including his own. There were also plenty of rumours about — that he had a serious girlfriend — but that was nothing new.

When we started to build the first engine PB was as exasperated as I was by the numerous silly mistakes; some of them costing much time and money. He rarely visited the old ERA garage where we were assembling the first V8 engine, and the first time he saw the engine run was on a Sunday afternoon when we were ready to run up to 10,000 rpm for the first time. I used to leave the data from the night before on his desk at 8 a.m. Two or three days later it was returned to me with handwritten comments, but no instructions. He sent for me one day and asked: 'When are you going to put an engine in the car and give it a run? How many days testing are you planning at Monza, before practice?' Peter Spear suggested that I was being set up as the fall guy in case anything went wrong, but I never really had that impression.

The first engine was nearly complete, waiting for its crankshaft, when we heard that it had been found to be cracked. The second shaft was fairly close behind, so we decided to build the engine with the cracked crank in order to find all the snags, as we suspected there might be plenty. We were quite right — the first snag list had 26 items, and with the second one the number rose to 48. Some could be excused, some were downright unforgivable. The cams were bigger than the outer tracks of the roller bearings so the camshafts could not be assembled. The tracks had to be reground, with fewer, bigger rollers. The worst blunder was in the squish calculations — the compression ratio of the first engine was 8.2:1 instead of 12.0:1! The mandatory starter motor had been forgotten; it ended up alongside the gearbox, which created problems for other teams using the engine.

On Sunday 9 July the first complete engine was sent to the test house at Folkingham, with its Lucas injection pump and one throttle butterfly per cylinder. It weighed 250 lb (113.6 kg). From then on there was a feverish rush to get it running. There was plenty of work and adaptation to get the engine onto the test bed.

By the evening of 12 July we were nearly ready. We motored the engine over to check that oil and water were in the right places. There was far too much oil to the valve gear, and water everywhere. The heads pulled down onto Cooper joint-rings on top of the cylinder liners. Ideally, when the Cooper ring was correctly crushed, the head would touch the cylinder block and make a water seal; another miscalculation. We decided to ignore the water leaks — at least we should have a good gas seal — and motor the engine for five minutes at 3000 rpm to see if the right amount of oil went to the right places. As the jacket temperature rose through cylinder compression the water leaks became less, although they did not entirely disappear. We connected up the injection system, fuel sprayed from all the injectors, and switched on. We had manual control of the injection pump stroke by means of a lorry speedometer cable and a big calibrated handwheel mounted on the dynamometer console. I gradually increased the stroke and thus the amount of fuel to the engine. At 0.0115 inch (0.29 mm) stroke the engine fired and settled down to run. It was 22.58 on 12 July.

Everyone was determined that the engine would not run for the first time on the 13th, so no one had anything to eat all day. We had not even stopped for the traditional cup of tea. The test house was an absolute shambles. We had some tea, while I wrote a job list.

Next day I went to Aintree, where it rained, for practice and to set the cars up, and I was back in the test house on the 14th ready to go. By Saturday 15th we had seized the crankshaft rear seal twice and learned how to make the injection system work properly. After long discussions with Dr Ted Jagger, Technical Director of Angus Oil Seals, a former Rolls-Royce graduate, we decided to replace the labyrinth seal with a silicone rubber seal. No one had ever tried it at these speeds before. We kept running with loads of clearance and a big oil leak while Angus made the silicone seal.

By the time the engine was a week old it had been to 9000 rpm, 144 hp, and had seized the crankshaft labyrinth seal five times. We sent it back to Bourne for strip and rebuild, with new pistons, which gave 10.0:1 compression. On 20 July it ran all day, a first for any BRM engine. It was very good-natured and reacted to every change we made. By the end of the day we were back to 9000 rpm and had seen 162 hp. After we had stopped to see why it had not broken, we found we could not open the throttles. This was the beginning of a long saga. Differential expansion caused them to seize.

We now had enough data to start making a proper exhaust system. The engine was a normal V8 with a two plane crankshaft, so it was going to be very difficult. Graham Hill rang me from the Nürburgring to describe the exhaust system on the new Coventry-Climax V8. They had joined the exhausts of the end cylinders on one bank to the middle cylinders on the opposite bank. This gave them a fat torque curve. This was something we could not do. Since the BRM engine was designed to run at much higher rpm, this meant the ideal length of the exhaust primary pipes was shorter and they just would not reach from one side of the engine to the other. We were going to lose at least 10 hp between 7000 and 8500 rpm. There was also some evidence of hot exhaust valves so we sent the engine back to Bourne to have the exhaust stem seals removed.

We then ran the second engine, working it up to 9750 rpm when it gave 165 hp. This was another low compression engine. We could not get above 9750 rpm as the engine misfired badly despite everything we did. We tried three different fuel injection systems and every Lucas ignition component available. Lucas were sure it was a fault with our test-bed installation, and the engine would work in the car. We therefore concentrated on developing a cam to control the mixture so we could put the engine in a car. We convinced Eric Downing, head of the Lucas Fuel Injection department that we could use Polypenco plastic fuel injection lines rather than Bundy (steel) tube. He feared it would harm the spray pattern but I was more concerned by all the trouble Vanwall had in their early days with broken metal injection pipes.

Anyway we put 5602 into the car and took it to North Witham airfield late one evening. Driving it, I was pleasantly surprised, the car did not feel mid-engined at all, unlike the Type 48s; it felt more like the front-engined 2.5 litre. I started to develop a theory about this being a function of the location of the driver's ear drums within the wheelbase. Graham tried it next day, when we all decided it was good enough to take to Monza. 5601 was rebuilt for the second car. We got away on schedule, two cars and a spare engine.

At Monza we found the misfire at 9750 rpm was still with us, much to the discomfort of the experts who had blamed it on our test-bed installation. The engine did not scavenge too well, but we just managed to keep the oil in the engine. The Lucas ignition people shouted louder than Eric Downing, their Injection Chief Engineer. Eric was sure there was nothing wrong with his injection system. Nevertheless, he checked and modified every last detail, removing the spill valve from the metering unit and mounting it downstream so all the fuel passed through the metering unit, to eliminate throttle lag and reduce the risk of fuel boiling in the pump. During the official practice run on the combined road and banked circuit Graham managed one flying lap before the misfire set in. Although he had got in amongst the Ferraris, we decided that until we could cure the misfire there was no point in trying to race the car.

After the race, and because of the von Trips accident, we were not allowed to use the road circuit, but we planned some testing on the banking. We modified the scavenge oil system and moved the ignition coil box out into the slipstream. I ran the car round the banking to make sure everything worked. It shook me to pieces and made me realize how fit a driver had to be. Graham then drove the car, but the injection system blow back caught fire and singed the back of his neck.

After Richie Ginther's much more serious accident the following year, while convalescing he was having his hair cut by Graham's barber in London who remarked: 'That's funny, I look after another gentleman with the same sort of scars on his neck.' 'Does he have a moustache?' asked Richie!

Back home from Monza we made absolutely no progress curing the misfire, but we got the oil system under control. While we were away the 12-year-old Dynamatic had been sent back to Heanan's, and Jim Fielding, their Managing Director — a great racing enthusiast — had it very carefully balanced and everything possible done, so we could run it to 10,500 rpm. It was late in October before we were ready, but we were no nearer a solution to the misfire. Lucas Electrical were absolutely adamant that it was nothing to do with the ignition system, while Eric Downing was tearing his hair out and saying he could not see any reason whatever for it to be a fault of the injection. All our instruments also indicated that the injection system was working properly.

Eric persuaded me to try Jaguar up-stream injection. He said that injecting against the incoming air flow made the engine more tolerant of variations in mixture strength, because it increased the time for the fuel to mix with the incoming air. It might lop a tiny amount off the top of the torque curve but it would increase the maximum power. With a mechanical fuel injection system, flow is directly proportional to rpm. Double the speed at which the metering unit rotates, and it will pass double the amount of fuel. I have never yet seen an engine with a torque curve that is actually a straight line. Our engine had its torque peak at 9000 rpm so with mixture strength correct for 9000 we were going to be too rich at 7000 and 11,000, if we ever got there. We made the conversion and found it was quite true; the engine would accept wider variations in mixture strength without any significant loss of power. We also found that injection timing was only critical for starting. Once the engine was over 3000 rpm it did not care when we injected.

We were still struggling to cure the misfire and beat 165 hp, and were getting worried. We heard that Climax had 175 to 180 hp on carburettors and Ferrari were over 185 hp. Lucas suggested that as we had tried everything and we were still convinced it was ignition, then it must be the sparking plugs. So we ran Marellis, but they made no difference. Then I had an idea and snatched two of the high-speed magnetos from the old V16. The engine ran up to 10,500 rpm, 186 hp, without a trace of a misfire!

While Lucas digested this we ran heat to oil tests, and a different exhaust camshaft which was worse. We had measured cylinder pressures at the point when the exhaust valve opened and found they were too high. When we counted up, the engine had been on the test bed for 16 days and had run for 42 hours so we gave it a rest and ran 5602 on the same magnetos. It immediately turned in 176 hp. Next day Lucas appeared with a completely new transistor ignition box which ran up to 10,500 but with a trace of a misfire and only 170 hp. Lucas retired scratching their heads and muttering. The engine then shook us out of our complacency by breaking a big-end bolt.

In the course of the investigation we discovered we had an Imperial big-end bearing at 2 inches (50.8 mm) and a metric crank at 50 mm! We were amazed that we had not had any trouble — running with three times the designed bearing clearance. The next engine up had larger exhaust ports and more exhaust flow generally, and gave 183 hp on its first run. It was removed to make way for the rebuilt 5602 with transistors everywhere. This engine also gave 185 hp immediately, then Lucas arrived with several ignition kits. We spent three days getting data for them, then converted the engine to carburettors. By then we were getting near to having to deliver customers' engines for which Wilkie had obtained five orders. They were to have Weber 35 IDMs. This took the shine off, only 176 hp. When we put the injection back, we saw 185 hp again.

Eventually I wore PB down and he allowed me to run 5604 with hemispherical pistons instead of squish. It had 12.0:1 compression, and after we advanced the ignition three degrees over a squish engine it gave 191 hp — it must have been someone's birthday. We then ran the slide throttle system, devised to cure seized butterflies. After we had developed an appropriate injection control cam we saw 194 hp. We also did some running for Eric Downing on a metering unit with a lead bronze core instead of steel to reduce the risk of seizure. We found the engine gradually gained power as it ran, up to about 10 hours. It stayed at the same power until about 18 or 20 hours, then it began to lose power badly. At 22 hours it was not worth running.

The racing shop had converted the three Climax-engined cars to take

V8s, and Wilkie had customers lined up for each one.

Sir Alfred had delivered his ultimatum. Either we got good race results and spent less money or he would close BRM down. Wilkie had sold four other cars, and RM and PB had convinced Sir Alfred and Rover cars that they could make a Raymond Mays head for the new 3-litre Rover that would considerably increase performance and earn money, although Harry Weslake had tried and given up. In vain I tried to convince them that performance was not limited by the head. This particular Rover engine had overhead inlets and side exhausts, the exhaust flow due to the ports in the block were the limiting factor and could not be enlarged. Everything we did made no difference. PB gave me a major Rover test programme which destroyed my carefully planned, interlocking engine and car testing programme, already delayed by the misfire which had cost us two months. I was running 3 litre Rover engines with three carburettors which did not give a scrap more power than the existing single carburettor set-up.

When Bruce Johnson from South Africa arrived out of the blue to take over car testing, I felt abnormally tired and quarrelsome, and I was quite unaware I was sickening for something. Bruce brought our new driver, Richie Ginther, up to the test house where I was fruitlessly running a Rover, and they both pestered me as to when there was going to be a car ready for them to test. In a few days I went from a state of high enthusiasm for the V8 to the blackest despair. I took to my bed. My doctor (actor Stanley Holloway's step-brother) was skiing: his locum diagnosed glandular fever, but by the time Dr Holloway returned I had developed all the symptoms of mumps.

While I was confined to bed they started car testing. The first thing found was the car would not pick up the last ten gallons (45 litres) of the 27 gallons (120 litres) of fuel it carried. An army went to Snetterton to try to solve the problem — Graham, Richie, Bruce, Wilkie, plus chief mechanic Cyril Atkins. By now the fever had gone and I was just uncomfortable and at the calamine-soaked cotton wool stage. Most of them rang me up and described the day's events to me in the hope that I would make some helpful suggestions. The only thing I learnt from the calls, was that they went to Snetterton and the car did not work!

Eleven days later, when I was up and about, PB suggested I went to Witham and watched Richie testing his car, 5782, with a modified fuel system and see what I could make of it. After a few laps we were horrified to see him heading towards us, trailing a stream of flame. The banjo bolt in the main fuel feed pipe to the injection control unit had slackened off and the leaking fuel had ignited. Instead of switching off, which would have completely cut off the flow of fuel at 7 Bar and probably extinguished the fire, Richie drove the car over to us so we could deal with it, as a result he was badly burned. He jumped out of the car with his petrol-soaked overalls blazing. Arthur Hill, an ex-Tank Corps sergeant ran after him, knocked him down and lay on top of him to extinguish the flames. While Arthur was doing this, I emptied one of the big extinguishers onto the car and put the main fire out. Denis Perkins had just arrived in his brand new Triumph, so I wrapped Richie in my overcoat, shoved him in Denis's car and said: 'Hospital, quick.' Denis drove onto the A1. Grantham was slightly nearer but he had to cross the centre strip, so he chose Stamford to the south, which was fortunate since Stamford had one of the best burns units in the district. Denis's new car was thoroughly run-in with this trip. By this time the neglected car had rolled over some burning debris and the fire restarted. I was using the second extinguisher when the tanks burst. I thought I saw flames coming out of my trouser pockets. The car was completely destroyed.

PB and I went to see Richie in the evening. He was lying on his stomach, heavily sedated. The hospital said he would not need grafts but they would keep him in for two or three weeks. Everything happened very fast after that. Richie had a constant stream of visitors, including Sir Alfred Owen and Mr and Mrs Stanley. Eric Downing showed me how to make a fuel collector pot, the basic design of which is still used today. This enabled us to wring the last drop of fuel out of the tank. Car 5783, nearly complete, was renumbered 5782 for Richie, and we issued an edict that banjos must not be used for high-pressure fuel connections. A wire-braided, high-pressure 10 mm bore hose is so stiff it is like a spanner — it can unscrew the banjo bolt. So we knew where the fuel leak came from but I was mystified as to what lit it. Finally we ran an engine in the dark and saw that the little metal clips securing the plug terminals over the leads were sparking to the jubilee clips on the water outlet connections. We replaced the clips with nylon fishing line.

Richie made good progress. I used to go to see him most evenings. When we had first met I was incubating mumps and was terribly rude and bad tempered, but now I found he was great fun and had a wealth of stories of his days as Ferrari's tester.

A week later I went with Graham to Snetterton to test the new fuel system and some other changes. Everything worked. Graham and I had developed a way of working. We would plan the session together before we started, to make the best use of the time. Graham would drive throughout at 9/10ths, and we inserted back-to-back tests to make sure that nothing had escaped or confused us. At the end of the day we would put the best set-up from the tests on the car and, to quote Graham, he would do three (laps) for Tony at 10/10ths to get me a time. In the middle of the three for Tony I was called to the telephone. It was Sir Alfred Owen's secretary, saying it was imperative that he saw me in Stafford, next day at 11.00 a.m., between two Staffordshire County Council meetings.

Snetterton to Stafford, was quite a journey. I had not the faintest idea what he wanted me for, but it was very obvious I had better be there. His meeting overran, and I had to wait two hours. He told me he had spent £1,000,000 on motor racing (£1,000,000 in the fifties was a lot of money. A front-line team's budget was less than £85,000 a year then; today it's £25 million or more) and had nothing to show for it. His brother Ernest was pressing him to stop wasting money on BRM, and he could see no sense or justification carrying on wasting money. He had told Mays and Berthon that unless there was a major improvement 1962 would be the last year. After Ginther's fire he could not justify to himself, even continuing until the end of the season. Even his sister, Mrs Stanley, as enthusiastic for BRM as he was, now agreed with him. However, his sister had persuaded him to give BRM one last chance. There had been so many, but Mrs Stanley believed that Hill and Ginther were the best driving team in BRM's history and the car was the best BRM ever. It would be folly to throw it all away when at last they were on the threshold of success. He went on to say that Graham,

Ginther and his sister all believed that, given sole control, I could run the team and achieve success. What did I have to say?

I waffled about stabbing people in the back, but Sir Alfred would have none of this, saying: 'If you do not agree here and now you will stab the 100 people who work for BRM at Bourne in the back, when they will be out of a job.' I came down to earth but, being an engineer, I asked for his definition of success. 'In the last ten years you have won one World Championship race. This year you must win two.' I replied: 'Yes, I can do that.'

He first instructed me to bring Mays and Berthon to see him at Darlaston on Monday, but when I reminded him of the race in Brussels on Sunday, he delayed the meeting until Tuesday, saying he would summon Raymond Mays but I was to tell Berthon. Peter Spear had sat in the background during all this, making notes. As we parted Sir Alfred said to Peter: 'See he gets something to eat.' Over egg and chips, I asked Spear if the old boy really meant it. If not, I had burnt my boats. I got no answer from Spear.

I went home and on to Mill Hill to stay with Graham on our way to Brussels via Heathrow. Next day I got a real wigging from Mr Stanley who told me I had blown it. Sir Alfred had told them what I had said to Spear and said it showed I did not have enough confidence to do the job.

The race at Brussels was a fiasco. After Graham won the heat, beating Moss and Clark, we were disqualified in the final for push-starting after the starter motor failed. The English text of the regulations said it was permissible, the French text said not. Graham reluctantly admitted that when the car was sorted it might be quite good and wished me luck on Tuesday.

At the fateful Tuesday morning meeting there was no RM. Sir Alfred was at the head of the table, with Mr Glover, the Company Secretary (a very tough cookie), plus Spear on his right and PB and me on his left. He waded in with a vengeance. There was none of the woolly, benign, remote old man. As from now I was Chief Engineer and Team Manager. PB was to become a consultant to the Rubery Owen Group and would work for Spear, an arrangement that would continue just as long as I did not complain to Sir Alfred of interference from PB. Spear was to introduce me to Messrs Holmes and Houston who, with Spear, formed the Budget Committee and who would monitor my expenditure. They met monthly. I was to call at Miss Ramsden's (his secretary) office before I left Darlaston to collect a letter of appointment. Glover took PB away. It had all taken about ten minutes.

Sir Alfred rang RM from the Boardroom and told him what he had done. He assured me I would get 101 per cent support from RM. As we parted he said he had every confidence I would succeed, and to demonstrate his confidence he was increasing my salary immediately by 50 per cent. Some comment was made that the few trophies BRM had won should be displayed in the Boardroom. Sir Alfred said he had never seen a trophy. I said for a million pounds you ought to have a Boardroom full; to which he replied: 'Go and get them then.' A photograph of that first year's collection is reproduced in this book.

I found Holmes and Houston very pleasant and helpful, but they gave me a shock by telling me that the 1962 budget allocation of £90,000 was virtually all spent or committed. The BRM financial year ran November to

October next year. The only money I would have to operate the team would be what we earned in start money, prize money or bonus. They had allocated sufficient money to pay the drivers and most of the known bills. Starting money, per race, on the Frankfurt scale for us was £600 for the first car and £500 for the second, as we were on the lowest rating based on World Championship points earned in the last twelve months. Now I needed at least £20,000 to keep us going for the rest of the season. My potential earnings as they saw them were about £12,000, and they would certainly ring the bell as soon as I went over the limit. I drove home in a very thoughtful mood and spent the evening visiting Richie in hospital.

Next morning I went into the factory as soon as the caretaker opened up, pinned Sir Alfred's letter of appointment on the notice board and went home to breakfast. When I arrived at my normal time the atmosphere was, to put it mildly, electric. I collected the Drawing Office together and told them anyone who did not think we would succeed should contact Peter Spear, who would find them a job, either within Spear's team or in PB's new consultancy. If they stayed I would expect 100 per cent effort and support, but I would bear them no ill will, if they chose to go. It was going to be a hell of a lot tougher than it had ever been before, but we had everything going for us. The only people who could beat us were ourselves. Only one chose to go.

I did the same with Les Bryden, Stan, Cyril Atkins, Colin Atkin, and the other foremen but I knew pretty well where I stood with them. Sandy came to see me. He had been briefed by Darlaston and pledged his full support, but did I know the till was empty? He could keep us going for a few weeks by sitting on invoices but not for much more than a month. I had jumped in at the deep end with a vengeance.

Our first race 'under new management' was at Snetterton. Richie was still not fit. In first practice Jim Clark, in a space-framed Lotus 24, did 1 min 34 sec. Graham was not far behind at 1 min 34.6 sec, and Stirling 1 min 35 sec. We found a major crack in the back of the crankcase, at the gearbox joint face, and had to take the car back to Bourne for an engine change, missing second practice, when Moss got down to 1 min 34.2 sec. This was the first sign of a major problem that dogged us most of the season, and nearly destroyed us. On the starting grid we noticed occasional puffs of smoke from No. 7 or 8 cylinders of Graham's engine, but he made a good start and built up quite a lead. Then, first Stirling and then Clark overtook him. His engine sounded very rough and gradually got worse, eventually going on to seven cylinders. He finished second after Stirling blew up — No. 8 plug was completely oiled up. When we returned to Bourne and put the engine on the test bed with a new plug the engine ran properly and after a few minutes gave its former power. The original sparking plug was defective.

At Easter Goodwood Richie was able to drive, although still not completely fit. It rained, and Graham's steel core fuel injection unit seized. I had made a rule that a metering unit change meant an engine change as we could not calibrate one in the car; it needed to be done on the test bed. Eric Downing talked me out of this; came down from Birmingham over the weekend and spent Sunday morning building up a new one from all the measurements we provided. Graham asked for a gear ratio change which I refused as there was no time to change back if we were wrong. John

Coombes then took us all to lunch at Birdham Yacht Club in his Jaguar, when we found why it was called a Mark Ten — because you can get ten people in it.

On Monday morning we were allowed a short untimed run, and everything worked well. Graham started on again about gear ratios — fourth was too low for St Mary's. I said: 'All right, you can use 10,500 rpm in third, but do not exceed 10,000 rpm anywhere else.' They both made bad starts, with Richie stalling his engine, but eventually Graham got into the lead and won.

The jubilation was spoiled by Stirling's dreadful crash which ended his career. Richie had finished well down, but what with prize and bonus money the till did not sound so hollow. We stayed at The Horse and Groom at Singleton at Graham's suggestion. I had become an enthusiastic member of the Bourne Flying Club, which had a Cirrus-engined Auster. The club doctor, Geoff Smith, joined us, and it was a thoroughly good weekend.

After the race Graham said that injection might give us the power, but the engine lacked throttle response, and he would like to run at Aintree on carburettors. I said that we would run Richie on carburettors. I did not say so, but I felt Richie was a more sensitive driver and much more observant than Graham, who looked upon the engine as a device which moved the rev counter needle.

We had been testing reticular tin bearings in engines on the test bed. They gave much more power, and we had seen over 200 hp, but there was a risk that with a temporary interruption of oil flow (surge in a corner) they would seize, and the seizure was pretty horrible. A lead bronze bearing would just smear the lead.

For Aintree, Richie had carburettors as planned. We took engine 5605 with tin bearings as a spare. The crankcase/gearbox joint face cracking problem was becoming serious. It had spread from crankcases to the gearbox, and Les Bryden had a programme of machining a crankcase a week. It must have been heartbreaking for him just machining crankcases, and knowing that they would crack within two races. Graham spun during practice, damaging the body, and we had to call for help from Bourne to repair it. Richie broke a tappet and had to take the spare engine with reticular tin bearings. The carburettor versus injection experiment was inconclusive. Richie reported injection was the best, but Graham was not convinced.

Clark ran away with the race. Richie followed Graham for a few laps; then found his engine was much more powerful, passed him and started to catch Clark, but at half distance the experimental bearings seized as we feared they would. We noticed an oil haze behind Graham's car, and he eventually gave up with the pipe feeding oil to the fuel injection unit broken. He said his engine was 400 rpm down throughout the race. The till was making hollow noises again. Both drivers complained about their brakes. Richie commented that Graham was blowing smoke rings at him. When we stripped Graham's engine we found the edges of the cut-outs for the valves in the hemispherical pistons were nibbled as if by detonation — explaining the lost rpm. We machined the cut-out right across the piston face, costing 0.2 of a compression ratio and picked up power. We rushed to Zandvoort for a planned series of tests. We learned much, and improved the brakes. As usual Zandvoort changes dramatically with the wind when it blows sand on and off the circuit.

Back at Silverstone everything seemed to go right for once. Graham was on pole, whereas Richie had a job getting to grips with the circuit in practice. So Graham towed him round for a few laps and got him on the front row. It did not work out quite as planned in the race — it rained and Richie lost it at Club and wrote off the second 5782. Clark was drawing away from Graham at a second a lap, and the megaphones were falling off our exhaust pipes at about the same rate, one per lap. This cost him power at the lower end of the range. Graham remembered that I had said the engine was designed to go to 12,000 rpm but there was no point as it did not give any more power, and just wasted fuel boiling the oil above 10,000 rpm. He knew what had happened from his mirrors, and so he took it up to 11,000 rpm in the gears and his lap times improved dramatically. Vacarrella, his Targa Florio Porsche team-mate, forced him on the grass in front of the grandstand, letting Surtees into second place. Fortunately, this made Graham good and mad, which always made him go. It rained harder, and Clark's lap times dropped from 1 min 36 sec to 1 min 50 sec. Graham went faster and faster and passed Clark on the line. Artists' impressions show Graham sideways, but in fact David Phipps's photograph showed that it was Jimmy who was sideways.

Sir Alfred left at the height of the excitement to keep another appointment, but not before Richie had suggested that a two-year-old Austin A40 was not the appropriate transport for the BRM Chief Engineer and Team Manager. 'Quite right,' said Sir Alfred, 'I will see he gets a new car.' Richie was staying with us then, as Pam said she could not bear the thought of a convalescent Richie sitting alone in the village pub. He was very grateful, and did all sorts of odd jobs, including the children's school run. One day he even took the television set to pieces and cleaned it, telling us not to worry because when he served in Korea in the USAF he was an electronics crew chief. It did not work at first but he finally fixed it! He even turned the stair carpet end-for-end one day.

Graham had just moved into a new house in Mill Hill and planned a housewarming after the race at Silverstone. Graham's parties were always good but this one was really terrific. I found myself in one corner with Shirley Eaton, the golden girl from the Bond film, *Goldfinger*, while Pam was being chatted-up by Roger Moore. On Monday morning the Rubery Owen Transport Manager rang up for my A40. He had a new car for me. Len Reedman, who looked after our transport, ripped off the Speedwell conversion, and took the car to Darlaston. Len appeared in my office late in the evening with a wry smile and said: 'You have a Hillman Minx!'

We did not manage to complete a new car for Richie for the Dutch GP at Zandvoort, so we put an injection engine into a 1961 Climax chassis, which Wilkie had already sold, and left him to make peace with the irate customer. I had my first Budget Committee meeting. Not too bad. Not only was the prize money from the Daily Express good, but so were the supplier bonuses, and I delivered a second cup to Sir Alfred for the Boardroom.

Zandvoort was noteworthy for the appearance of the Lotus monocoque — the legendary Lotus 25. Graham was soon down to 1 min 33.3 sec, benefiting from the earlier test session, and Richie was fourth fastest. In second practice Graham got another 7/10ths off his time; then we took the car away from him as he had already done 35 laps. There was a very strong wind before second practice on the second day. While Graham's car was

being warmed up, a passing car doused the engine and throttle slides with
sand. It took us most of the practice to safely free them, by which time
Surtees in a Lola boasted a time of 1 min 32.6 sec, a tenth quicker than
Graham. Timing round the back, Graham was quickest at 29.8, Clark 30.2
in the Lotus 24, and 30.6 in the 25. Surtees's best time was 31.0. Graham's
gearbox developed a very bad leak from the differential seal. He said it was
the best gearbox he had ever had, please do not change it. We did
everything we could to seal it; binding it with tape and all manner of crude,
terrible tricks. Both BRMs made bad starts, and Richie suffered from
misfiring most of the race. Clark jumped into the lead. We had made
Graham start on nearly-new tyres — based on our tests on a really clean and
dry track we thought we needed them — but once they were scrubbed he
started to haul Jimmy in, when Lotus started having gear selection
problems. From then Graham had it easy, winning his first World
Championship race, one of the two required by Sir Alfred, and also moving
us up the Frankfurt start-money scale. It was also a second triumph for Pat
Carvath, Graham's mechanic, who had also been Jo Bonnier's three years
before. The greater earning power plus the prize and bonus money nearly
took care of my financial problems.

The race was significant for development in the relationship between
Graham and me. He blew his top over the time lost by the sand in the
throttles before final practice, and we had quite a row. Afterwards, under
pressure from our respective wives, we made our peace. Graham said he
was sorry he blew his top but winning meant an awful lot to him. I said:
'Don't you think it means as much to me?' He held me at arms length,
looked at me for some time and said: 'I never thought of that.' From then
on our relationship moved into top gear.

# CHAPTER TWELVE

# Won one
# — one to go

PB HAD ORDERED some Colotti gearboxes in the autumn of 1961, and the first one had arrived, so we fitted it to the third car numbered 5782, for Richie. Although Graham was very good at sorting out a car's handling, Richie was very much better at engine and gearbox development, and we thought he would sort it quicker. It was 6 kg (13¼ lb) lighter than the old 2.5 litre box we were using. When I took the car down the Fen to start it I found there was no oil pressure. This was very mysterious as the engine had given no trouble on the test bed. I had an awful suspicion, and tried towing the car in reverse gear, when up came the oil pressure and the engine started. It was possible to fit the crownwheel and pinion either way round, and Colotti had built it the wrong way round — we had six reverse gears and one forward!

I practised what I preached and tried to cut out Sunday work at the factory. I had a Monday morning meeting with the foreman and charge-hands when we agreed the programme for the week and used Saturday afternoons and Sundays as an emergency reserve to pull the programmes back onto schedule. The only exception, of course, was the unfortunate test-bed crew because the engine shop would quite often have engines ready for test late on Saturday afternoon. There were always development and customers' engines to run. Cutting down Saturday afternoon and Sunday work reduced the wage bill, and we got just as much done and made fewer silly mistakes.

Willy Southcott was absolutely the ideal person to carry out the routine testing and quite a bit of the development. I would say to him that I wanted to run a certain test, and sometimes he would say quite politely that he doubted whether it would work, and give his reasons. Then he would carry out the test and put everything he had into making it work. He never, ever let his personal opinions or prejudices interfere with getting at the truth.

We set off for Monte Carlo in very high spirits. We had shortened the noses of both cars so that we were less vulnerable if we got into the usual shunting match. It was very hot and close for first practice, and the shortened noses reduced the air dispersal over the radiator face. Within a few laps both cars were in with their drivers' complaining that the engines were cutting out. Willy diagnosed the problem — fuel was boiling in the injection system's electric high-pressure pumps. We moved them outboard so that they were in the air stream and re-routed the fuel pipes so they were also in a cooling flow of air. Next day it rained, so we did not know if we had cured the trouble.

Colotti came to see his gearbox stripped after practice. Apart from the pinion being a little too deep in mesh, we could see nothing wrong. Graham and I agreed that we really did not want pole position since the start was still on the harbour side of the circuit, which meant crossing the crown of the road to get lined up for the first corner. Second fastest gave the ideal situation, so we had an 'after you' session in final practice and sat about waiting. We found the Colotti gearbox casing had cracked badly on Richie's car (a variation on the cracked crankcase theme) and we had to send him out in the 1961 spare car. An over-zealous pit marshal stopped us switching numbers, and we began to worry that we might not qualify. RTV Monte Carlo asked if Graham would do a lap with their TV camera, and during the excitement we managed to switch Richie's numbers. He got on the fourth row! Graham was in the desired centre of the front row. We were still worried about fuel vaporization, so I decided that, if we were safe enough, to stop for more cold fuel, but it was left to the driver's discretion.

Two hours before the race it started to rain, which cooled things down thoroughly. I told the drivers to drive through the puddles and splash the fuel pump. Vittorio Jano, the legendary Alfa designer, came and had a long talk with me in French. Like the great Rolls-Royce engineers, he was completely unassuming and easy to talk to and exchange ideas with — I used to look forward to my chat with him every year.

Louis Chiron made a mess of the start. He told the drivers he would hold up his left hand at five seconds to go and count down on his fingers to the fall of the flag. Instead he held his left hand up, dropped the flag in the road and ran. Mairesse tried to get between Graham and Clark and hit them both. Someone else hit Richie who also had his throttle stick open, and he was out before he reached the first corner. McLaren led away followed by Graham and Brabham, but by lap seven Graham was in the lead and pulling away. Jimmy got into second place but soon dropped out with multiple problems. Graham then drove on his thermometers. On lap 90 we saw a little oil smoke, and he stopped finally on lap 93 with a seized engine through lack of oil. It had all leaked out of the distributor because the seal on the drive had been fitted the wrong way round. Even so, Graham was classified sixth with one point.

I caught a very early flight back to England as the gearbox failure had thrown all our plans to convert all the cars to Colotti gearboxes after this race. Les now had to include new gearbox front halves in his machining programme, added to which the crankcase-a-week programme was delaying the build-up of engines for customers. All this was not helping my finances, and the customers were getting extremely restive. Graham tried Richie's car, with another Colotti gearbox, and said it was an absolute dream; which made it all seem worse.

For the Belgian GP at Spa we fitted a new low tail pipe exhaust system in place of the upswept chimney stacks. It gave a little more power from 9750 to 10,500 rpm — our new limit. There was another fearful row with the organizers about qualifying as they were only going to pay for 16 starters. Two of our customers dropped out because we had not delivered their engines. Graham had pole position, but as the race progressed he gradually lost power and there was a slight — increasing — misfire at the top end. Graham was lucky to finish second to Jimmy Clark. Richie, still using a Colotti gearbox, had trouble with it again. We had been taking English petrol with us to each race but, by Spa, Shell convinced us that the fuel we would get in Belgium was exactly the same as in England, and our precautions were not necessary. With fuel injection we needed a large and very efficient filter for scrupulous cleanliness. After the race, when we removed Graham's fuel filter, we found it was covered with green slime. We had filtered the dye out of the fuel and it had clogged the filter, causing fuel starvation.

There was a very lucrative non-championship race at Reims, followed a week later by the French GP at Rouen. My Monday prayer meeting considered the logistics and decided we could just manage both. Money was getting to me: some of my engineering principles were in danger of compromise. To do the two races properly we needed eight engines, but we only had five. Fortunately the RAC manager at Le Touquet airport was an absolute jewel, and Silver City Air Ferries were very helpful. We would use them to ferry engines across the Channel.

For Reims, the engines in both cars had the reticular tin bearings which gave more power. There were not many corners to upset the oil supply, which we had improved anyway. Richie agreed to give the Colotti gearbox one last try — while it was working, the car was much faster than with the BRM box. In first practice one of Wilkie's customers, Masten Gregory using a BRM engine in a Lotus 24, got down to 2 min 26 sec, which compared well with Phil Hill's last year's Ferrari lap record of 2 min 25.9 sec. Graham had a really big go with 2 min 24.4 sec, then the engine tightened up: No. 2 big-end had seized. Richie had stopped with overheating.

We sent Graham's engine back to England, by RAC/Silver City, and wound the tin big-end bearings out of the other engines. Thanks to Willy's ingenuity we did this without too much dismantling. We left the tin mains in place. In the race Graham, McLaren and Brabham had a slip-streaming dog-fight while Surtees led for a short while until he retired with valve gear problems. During the dog-fight Graham crossed the line in the lead 15 times, McLaren 17 and Brabham 12! On the run to the finishing line they all over-revved scandalously. McLaren took his engine to 9500 instead of the Climax limit of 8600 and just beat Graham, who was second. Graham had used 11,000 instead of 10,500 to beat Brabham. Richie had a very good run until the gearbox seized. I set off back to England in the ubiquitous Hillman Minx with a BRM V8 engine in the boot; there was an overhauled engine waiting at Le Touquet ready to be collected.

On Thursday morning I crossed to Rouen with another engine in the Hillman's boot. The mechanics had converted Richie's car to a BRM gearbox. Rouen was just as hot as ever. My 1962 snapshot of my race notes reads rather pompously, that: '. . . it became apparent, as expected, that our superior road-holding would pay dividends.' Although Graham was well out in front with 2 min 15.9 sec, we had all sorts of petty troubles in practice. Graham's car was jumping out of 4th, and Richie had an injection trumpet set screw come adrift, which fell into the inlet port causing an engine change. Eventually Jimmy screwed himself up and produced 2 min

14.8 sec to Graham's 2 min 15 sec. Graham said he wanted to stay in the middle of the road for the start and was not going to go out again, thank you. This was a more mature Graham, who would normally cover more than the race distance in every practice if we let him.

At the start Richie's starter motor would not operate. He pushed it down hill to his pit, as laid down in the regulations, where we found the main lead had broken at the motor. His mechanic, Arthur Hill held it in place, Richie pressed the button and was away, 75 seconds down. Graham led very easily and was pulling out half a second to a second a lap on Clark. On his 34th he had just lapped customer Jack Lewis for the second time when Lewis ran into the back of him. Graham spun round three times and jumped a 9 in (23 cm) high curb, the incident costing him 35 seconds and the lead. As usual, this really fired Graham up. He was pulling in race leader Jimmy at two to three seconds a lap, with 20 left to go, when Clark retired with a front suspension problem.

We had begun to count the prize money, when Graham stopped. He could not re-open the throttle after a corner. The fuel injection metering unit cam had rollers as full throttle and slow running stops. To adjust, you changed the diameter of the roller mounted on a clevis pin secured by a tiny brass split pin. These clevis pins rotated under vibration. So we always replaced the brass split pin with stainless. Unfortunately, when this pump was overhauled by Lucas they had replaced our steel pin with a brass one, which we failed to notice when we refitted the unit. The clevis rotated, wore away the brass pin which then fell out, complete with slow running stop. The injection cam fell right over-centre, so Graham could not open the throttle of an otherwise serviceable engine. He managed to chug into the pits, but we sent him back out to collect the bonnet and drive over the line to qualify for the 1000 francs for fastest lap (which only went to finishers). Meanwhile Richie had got going and was chasing Tony Maggs for second place when his throttle cable snapped. He finished in third place by pulling on the broken end!

Back home we changed ratios, made the necessary repairs and took both cars to Snetterton to try to find some more performance. We covered Richie's car with wool tufts and Graham drove his Mark II Jaguar alongside for me to watch, armed with my Leica. We learned all sorts of things. There was a peculiar back eddy over the nose. The wool tuft closest to the skin lay neatly in the streamline along the body but the middle one for some reason tied itself in a knot round the pillar. Nothing we did cured this. I have included this photograph. From these tests came a new engine air intake which gained us 150 rpm and reduced under-bonnet temperatures by 15°C (32°F) which helped the fuel system. I used to lurk on the corners with a long lens on the Leica and take photographs of the car coming through the corners. As soon as I got home I would develop the negatives and spend half the night sitting at my enlarger. I had a photograph from Thillois hairpin at Reims where I noticed that the outer front roll bar lever had twisted and gone over-centre. I commissioned some stiffer ones, with a solid section instead of the beautifully machined H section. I was frightened that one day we might actually break the roll bar lever.

I was getting worried, although the financial situation was under control. We did not seem to have the edge that our extra power should have given us, yet we had as good if not better road holding. There was nothing to touch us in fast corners. Our brakes were extremely good — better than most — but if anything we still lacked traction out of slow corners. When Lotus got the 25 really sorted they would give us a lot of trouble. Also I could not understand why our power dropped off above 10,000 rpm. It was actually a waste revving the engine to 11,000 rpm, which it could do quite safely. All running to 11,000 seemed to do was to increase fuel consumption and oil temperature. Added to all this was still the crank and gearbox cracking problem, which was taking up nearly all our machining capacity.

An even more worrying problem was that we had now built 13 engines and the power varied considerably between them. The best fuel injection engine with lead bronze bearings gave 193 hp, while the worst, to the same specification, only gave 172. Dimensionally they appeared to be identical, and the air flows of the cylinder heads on the rig were all the same. Neither Willy, Geoff Johnson nor I could find any difference anywhere. Air flow through the engine on the test-bed went up in a straight line, although the power dropped off badly above 10,000 rpm. The only clue we had was that the exhausts on 'bad' engines were much brighter red than on a good engine, and a bad engine was less sensitive to mixture strength. I asked Shell for help. They agreed to send a specialist, but they could not do this until after the British GP at Aintree.

We went to Aintree hoping for the best, but fearing the worst, which was not long in appearing. Graham's engine blew up in first practice. A big piece of the timing pack had broken away and gone through the scavenge pump gears. We sent it back to Bourne, and Colin Atkin and his crew got it back to us completely rebuilt within 24 hours. Californian Richie, with a bad cold and a high temperature, tried the original megaphone stubs and the lower tail pipes, but could not detect any difference. So we raced the Spa system as it was more reliable, being less prone to break up. We had built another new car, No. 5783, although it was really the fifth. It was slightly smaller in cross sectional area and had thinner frame tubes, so it was much lighter, but neither driver liked it.

Sir Alfred and the Rubery Owen management had realized the value of BRM's new-found reputation. We were leading the World Championship, which was something new for us. They arranged a big dinner party on Friday night for all their major customers. Attendance by Graham, Richie and me, plus wives, was compulsory. Before the dinner Sir Alfred gave me a big lecture that we were racing to prove the excellence of Rubery Owen engineering. Although winning was top priority, if we could not, he preferred finishing second and third, with both cars trouble-free, compared with one car winning and the second car of the team blowing up, as did Lotus. He also impressed upon me that if ever we killed a driver he would close down immediately. He gave me a very clear sense of direction. Mechanical integrity was vital, and do not take chances with drivers' lives.

On race morning Dunlop made my problems worse. It had rained during the night, cleaning the track, so tyre wear would be critical. Our tyre wear was 20 miles per mm of tread. We had 7 mm of tread and 225 miles to go. Cooper and Lotus were a little better at 22 miles per mm. However, although we could change wheels faster than they could with our knock on wheels, even so the stop would cost us 25 seconds. In the middle of all this I did an extremely stupid thing. The stiffer roll-bar levers arrived — the result of the Thillois photograph — hot from Bourne's machines. Without thinking, I said put them on; thus breaking the cardinal rule — never race on something you have not tested.

Innes Ireland was on the right hand side of the front row, Graham behind him and Richie behind him. Innes's mechanic walked back and said Innes could not find first gear and would be starting in second so would be getting in our way. It was not good news but it was typical of Innes to warn us, and we were at least able to avoid a shunt. By half distance Graham had climbed up to fourth and was closing on third-placed McLaren. Dunlop then told us that tyre wear on the cars that had stopped was nothing like as bad as expected and we had nothing to worry about. At three quarter distance Graham was getting ready to take third place from McLaren when he noticed most of the tread had gone from his left front tyre. Brabham then was five seconds behind when Graham eased off to think. He remembered I had told him that after the tread disappeared there were another ten laps left in the tyre, but as he had 17 to go he settled for fourth place. We did not know that both Coopers were worse off for tyre wear than we were and that McLaren had no brakes left. Graham could probably have taken third place and an extra point.

I drove back to Bourne conscious of the fact that we were still leading the World Championship; 19 points to Clark's 18 and McLaren's 16, but unless I was extremely clever and lucky, not for much longer. I cursed my stupidity in fitting the stiffer roll-bar levers. This had caused Graham's car to understeer much more, which is why the left front tyre had worn. If I had left the old lever in place he would have had enough tread to pass McLaren and would have had that one extra point.

Back at Bourne there was no good news and by mid-week I was beginning to think in terms of damage limitation. However, Pam gave me a very severe talking to, which had the desired effect. Dr Harrow from Shell Research Laboratories at Thornton, near Chester, then arrived, and we discussed our problems. He watched an engine run on the test bed, took data and a cylinder head away to instrument.

We then prepared for the German GP at the Nürburgring. Before I left, buoyed up by Sir Alfred's positive attitude at Aintree, I sent him a long letter setting out my plans for 1963. Harry Mundy, Technical Editor of *The Autocar* and a former ERA, BRM and Coventry-Climax engineer, paid us a visit. Harry pointed out that we had two crankshaft balance weights too many. He was right, we had. The crankshaft designer, no longer with us, had used balance weights to counterbalance balance weights! This explained the crankcase and gearbox cracking. There was a panic redesign of the crankshaft with pleas to our supplier to get some correctly balanced ones for Monza.

I drove to the Nürburgring in the Hillman Minx, taking Pam with me. We had all three cars out and were first and second fastest in the morning session. I took some comfort that my 1958 conclusion that wheel movement was the answer to the Ring's problems was proved correct. We had something like plus and minus 4½ inches (114 mm) wheel movement on the Type 57. In the afternoon Graham produced 8 min 50.2 sec in 5781 and said he could go five seconds faster in 5783. When he went out to try he came upon a TV camera lying in the road at the Fox Run — it had fallen off de Beaufort's Porsche. Graham tried to take it between the wheels and the hull of the car but it was too big. The camera ripped off the main oil pipe, and he went off on his own oil into the undergrowth at 140 mph (226 kph), followed by Tony Maggs in his Cooper. When Graham got back to the pits he was absolutely livid. He had a stiff neck and some bruises, but could still drive, so we sent him out in the old car.

It rained all through final practice, so the first day's times stood. German Dunlop had produced a special tyre known as the SP for the Porsche racing sports cars, and everyone knew they were incredible in the wet. As the grid formed up for the race there was a torrential rain storm which washed some of a track side bank onto the circuit. The start was delayed for an hour while it was cleared up.

Graham managed to persuade me and Dunlop to let him do his reconnaissance lap on SPs, causing the most tremendous consternation amongst the other teams. When they saw us on SPs waiting for the race to begin, they laid siege to Dunlops who had already given me a written warning they would not be responsible if we tried to race on them. I knew that we could not do so, as SPs reduced our ground clearance by 15 mm, which we could not spare. When the three-minute board went up, I nodded to Cyril Atkins; the jacks went under the car, and using the knock-on wheels we put standard Dunlops back. By this time the other drivers had stopped rowing with Dunlop and were back in their cars ready for the race.

Gurney led the first lap, then Graham took the lead and stayed there for the whole race. During the SP-inspired startline panic, Clark forgot to switch on his fuel pumps and stalled on the line, losing 20 seconds, and was never in the hunt. By the 12th lap Graham, with a seven second lead over Gurney and Surtees, thought he saw an oil patch and slowed down. Gurney and Surtees did not and caught him up. We had cut a hole in the wire at the back of the pits so we could push a signal board through to the drivers and show them their lead in front of the pits, so the information they got was only 30 seconds out of date, not ten minutes as it otherwise would have been for a full lap. This enabled us to keep Graham well informed, and he won by 2.5 seconds. Richie finished 8th, but both drivers said they had not enjoyed the race, although their cars gave no trouble.

We had a big champagne session in the Dunlop tent afterwards. This was my second win, as directed by Sir Alfred. We could now look forward to another year, and Graham now had 28 points to Clark's 21. I felt sorry for RM. After all, it was seeing the German cars win at the Nürburgring that started him on the BRM idea. After the race he had a furious row with Mr Stanley and did not join in the celebrations. It had been agreed that we could all clean-up and change in Jo Bonnier's room in the Sport Hotel under the grandstand rather than drive 30 miles to our hotel at Lochmuhle. When we got there the hotel water supply had failed. Fortunately Pam had an enormous jar of cleansing cream, which soon disappeared. Everyone was rain-soaked outside and champagne-soaked inside.

# CHAPTER THIRTEEN

# Fighting for the World Championship

AS SOON AS we returned to Bourne, we started on the Shell programme. Within four hours their instruments showed us that we were opening the exhaust valve too soon and we had too high a residual pressure in the cylinder. We fitted an inlet camshaft in the exhaust side which gave more lift and a longer opening time, although we had to run with enormous tappet clearances. This gave us 2.5 per cent more power from 9000 to 10,000 rpm. From a study of the pressure diagrams it appeared that the steeply domed crown of the piston was splitting the combustion chamber in two. We decided to cut the top off the piston crown to improve this. To avoid losing too much compression, we cut at the angle of the sparking plug to the cylinder centre line, which was 14 degrees. This dropped the compression ratio from 12.2:1, to 11.2:1. We lost a little power up to 9000 rpm, but by the time we were up to 10,500 we had picked up 4.2 per cent more power.

Dr Harrow said his instruments showed lower combustion temperatures and a much faster rate of burn. (Dr Harrow and his partner Mr Ireson, also from Shell, published their findings in 1964 as Institution of Mechanical Engineers papers.) Here, too, was the explanation for the difference between a good and a bad engine. A bad engine was a slow burner.

When it was all over we had 200 hp plus at 10,500 rpm from three engines, and all of the bad engines had became good ones. It meant, of course, changes in driving techniques and gear ratios.

We invited Graham to the test house to see one of the engines run. He was absolutely horrified. Indicating the red hot exhausts and the standing wave over the induction system, he said: 'How can you stand there a few feet from all that?' I replied that he sat with his back against the engine for hours on end and it did not seem to worry him then!

The next race was the Gold Cup at Oulton Park on 1 September. In preparation we organized a day's testing. RM was pressing for Bruce Johnson to be given a drive, so we took him and a customer's car that was the subject of complaints. This was always a problem. They bought a BRM and then expected to achieve the same lap times as Graham. Graham drove the customer's car and said he would have preferred it, or rather its carburettor engine, to the one he had in the rain at the Nürburgring.

For the race Graham had 5781, now known as 'Old Faithful', Richie had the third 5782, and Bruce the rebuilt Nürburgring crashed car. All three had modified engines which were to be run up to 11,000 rpm. We had risked a run on 5605 (Richie's engine) up to 10,750 rpm on the Dynamatic brake, and the power dropped from 202 hp at 10,500 to 201 at 10,750. We did not dare risk doing this again with the thirteen-year-old Dynamatic before Monza. The Owen family were at Oulton in force: Sir Alfred, Mr Ernest Owen, his wife and family, and Mr and Mrs Stanley. Ernest was overcoming his objections to motor racing. He asked me if we were going to win. I said: 'I do not know, but what we learn here will help us to win at Monza.' This struck him as cocky, and he said so! We let them do as much practice as they liked, Graham covering more than the race distance when he did the first 100 mph lap.

For once Richie was faster than Graham at 1 min 38.6 sec to Graham's 1 min 39.2 sec. Bruce Johnson managed 1 min 41.6 sec. Jim Clark also did 1 min 38.6 sec, but as Richie did it first he had pole. McLaren with 1 min 40 sec completed the front row. It was the first race for Jack Brabham in his own Brabham Climax, which did 1 min 40.4 sec. Graham and Richie missed gears — Graham's engine going to 11,800 and Richie's to 12,500 rpm without damage. Jimmy won, Graham was second (gradually losing power as the race progressed) and McLaren was third. Richie had a connecting rod failure about half distance, Bruce Johnson finished fourth, after a spin, but 3 laps down.

We put Graham's engine and all its fuel system onto the test-bed after the race, as he said he was losing rpm, and by the end of the race the engine was misfiring at over 8000 rpm. We reproduced it all on the test-bed. Using the race plugs it started to misfire at 7500 rpm, and with new plugs the misfire set in at 8000. The fuel pressure was only 88 psi instead of 105. When we replaced the car's fuel pump with the test-bed pump, fuel pressure went back up to 105 psi and the engine ran cleanly through the range, although some 3 per cent down on power (most of which it recovered with running). Increasing the power and, especially, rpm meant increased fuel flow and we were into or above the bottom limit of the flow for the fuel pump. It transpired that only one of our eight fuel pumps was on bottom limit and this was the one fitted to Graham's car for the race.

Lucas took them all away and reworked them, because the problem would be much worse at Monza. They also rushed through some 10-amp alternators in place of the 8-amp we had been using, so that the battery voltage would hold up for more of the race.

Richie's connecting rod bolt failure originated from a damage mark. The bolt in question had done 800 race miles, so we fitted each engine with new double checked bolts, with a life of 500 miles. Bruce Johnson had complained of low oil pressure, and when we ran his engine on the test-bed complete with its oil system, there was a slight restriction at high rpm so we increased the sizes of pipe to and from the tank.

The Italian GP was a full-length (500 km/308 miles) race. We therefore fitted an oil catch-tank above the gearbox (leading to the 1963 FISA regulation making catch tanks mandatory) which collected all the oil and fumes from the engine breathers. It had a non-return valve in the pipeline back to the sump, and this gave us nearly an extra gallon of usable oil.

I put Alec Stokes to work to design for 1963 a six-speed box using the

best features of the Colotti and our old gearbox. We had found all the
Colotti seizures were due to the internal oil pump cavitating above 9500
engine rpm. We were particularly attracted by the Colotti design whereby
the gear cluster could be built up on the bench, so you could get at all the
selector mechanism to adjust it, instead of poking about from inside.

We put the best engine in the lighter smaller 5783, shaken down by Bruce
Johnson at Oulton Park after its rebuild. I vetoed RM's suggestion that we
should also run Bruce at Monza, it would cost us our spare car. I wanted no
distractions from the Championship, and start money was not so vital to our
survival. I had quite a fight — a distraction I could have done without.

We arrived at Monza a day early to check tyre wear, car set-up and gear
ratios. Fuel consumption was just 12 mpg, so as we had 308 miles to go we
would need more than 25.67 gallons. We carried 27.8. I got the gear ratios
wrong again, which was completely inexcusable. In first official practice
Graham produced the fastest time in 5783. He said, although the engine felt
strong and powerful, he preferred the handling of his old car, which had
incidentally passed the 10,000-mile mark during practice. Graham said he
would like engine 5606 put into 'Old Faithful', please, for the race. Richie
had been running with full tanks, even so he was sixth fastest. He said the
car, if anything, handled better with full tanks, although it felt rather
cumbersome. After some wheedling from Graham, we agreed to switch
engines as we still had another practice to make sure we had put everything
back together correctly. We also rebuilt 5783 with the other engine, just in
case.

Next day practice was from 2 p.m. until 6.0 p.m., and we went out early
despite the heat to check we had put everything together properly, and also
the race would be run in the mid-afternoon heat anyhow. Everything
seemed to be satisfactory at first. Then I began to fret over fuel
consumption. With the gear-ratio change, and drivers trying harder, it was
now down to 11.1 mpg, needing 27.75 gallons, perilously close to our
capacity of 27.8. Then Richie complained of overheating, and we found the
head joint blowing. We wrapped Richie in foam rubber and put him in the
rejected 5783, set up for the much larger Graham. Poor Richie could just
see out, and hardly reach the pedals, but he did 1 min 42.1 sec and said it
was fine. We began to switch over as much of his cockpit set-up as we
could in the time. At the magic 5 p.m. when temperatures were just right,
they both went out. Graham tied with Jimmy for pole at 1 min 40.4 sec, and
Richie was third at 1 min 41 sec. After practice, when it was too late, the
time-keepers did their sums again and gave Clark 1 min 40.35 sec and
Graham 1 min 40.38 sec. Graham said: 'It's a long way to the first corner,
do not worry.'

Lucas checked through the fuel systems. The pump on 5783, which
Richie was going to drive, needed 9 amps instead of the usual 5 amps, so it
was changed amid much misgivings on my part. I hated changing anything
after final practice. There was no morning warm-up in those days to test a
last minute change. We applied 5 psi air pressure to the rubber bag fuel
tanks while in position and found we could get nearly another quart (1 litre)
into each tank, making 28 gallons. It was going to be touch and go. At the
final check, Graham should have 0.3 of a gallon to spare, and Richie 0.2. I
warned them they would have to walk back, as they would run out on the
Lap of Honour. Graham said he could put up with that!

Race day was cooler and the barometer had dropped. Willy and I debated whether we dare weaken the mixture, and decided not. We took a small funnel and a piece of plastic tube for each car to the line, with bottles of petrol, and we topped them up on the grid through the tank vents. We even shook them to squeeze in the last few drops and we wiped the fuel bays with wet cloths to cool them. Graham made a dreadful start, nearly stalling his engine, then he over-revved to 12,000 rpm, so Jimmy got well away. Graham said the engine felt all right, so on the back straight he just gave it the gun, pulled out passed Clark easily and led for the rest of the race. I had carefully briefed Richie. His job was to help Graham get clean away and then go for second place. Seeing from his pit signals Graham was well away, Richie was debating where he should pass Clark, when Jimmy retired with gearbox trouble. Richie settled down in second place. He was being slip-streamed by Surtees, and he decided to hold his speed so as not to tow Surtees into striking distance. He was also conserving fuel. He planned to lose Surtees when they were lapping the back markers.

His tactics worked, although not quite as he planned. By half distance Surtees's engine had failed, leaving Graham 30 seconds ahead of Richie who was 47 ahead of McLaren. Both of them eased off to lap at 1 min 48 sec. There was just a faint sprinkling of rain which helped cool us down and save some fuel. They finished with Graham 30 seconds ahead of Richie who was 28 seconds ahead of McLaren. Richie's engine cut on the Lap of Honour; coasting in with a dead engine, with about an eggcupful of fuel left. Graham had about half a pint, but said he had been taking it easy and nearly coasting round the corners at the end. The cars and engines were both sealed by the scrutineers, to be inspected by the RAC back in England. Even though we had our first one-two and laid the ghosts of 1951, we were an extremely subdued party that night.

Graham now had 36 Championship points to Clark's 22, and in the Constructors' Championship BRM had 37 to Lotus's 27. Graham also had the fastest lap in the race on laps three and four, which told a story. The only flight home I could get next day was via Paris, and it was after midnight when I reached Bourne to find I had just missed a number of my RCAF friends who had flown one of the last surviving maritime Lancasters over for the Battle of Britain celebrations. Pam had just shooed them out, saying he will be very tired — and I had arrived home spoiling for a party.

Rubery Owen gave an enormous dinner party at the Grosvenor House in London every September for their many customers and suppliers. This year I was commanded to attend. In the receiving line, Ernest Owen, after congratulating me, asked if we were going to win the World Championship. I replied that we were in with a chance. He bet me his Rolls-Royce we would not. Graham, on holiday in Spain, appeared on a giant BBC TV screen during the dinner. Sir Alfred made PB, RM and I stand up, with a spotlight on us, to be applauded — it got a bit heavy.

The World Championship situation was not as good as it looked. The marking system in those days required that from now on Graham had to discard points. If Clark won the last two races and Graham was second in each they would both have 40 points. Graham could then only count his best five races, Jimmy would take the Championship with the most wins.

For the US GP at Watkins Glen, at the southern tip of Seneca lake, in upstate New York, by agreement with the drivers we prepared 'Old Faithful' as Graham's race car. Richie was back in 5782, and 5783 would be the spare. It would cost an awful sum to take a spare car, but I preferred a complete working car on its wheels. We knew we then had absolutely every spare we needed. This race introduced us to the American system of large amounts of prize-money down to the last place, but no starting money.

Sir Alfred had approved my 1963 programme. When I got back from the Nürburgring I found a rather stiff letter saying that I had not won two races yet, but fortunately by then I had.

Nearly all the teams flew out to the USA on the same aircraft. During the flight Colin Chapman proudly showed us photographs of his new car, the Elan. I sometimes wondered who had the most problems, he with his car business as well as his F1 cars, or me with my engine and gearbox problems, as well as the cars and Rubery Owen politics.

Graham, Bette and I drove from Idlewild (now Kennedy) on the freeway, in a vast Ford Galaxy, for 400 miles via Albany, Utica and Syracuse to Watkins Glen. We arrived a day before the cars so we spent the day sightseeing, the Glen itself and from a boat on Seneca Lake. When the cars arrived, we found much transport damage, but we had escaped lightly compared with some other teams. Surtees's car had its front wishbones broken by over-enthusiastic chaining down on the trucks. The Kendall Technical Centre had yet to be built, so the cars were housed in Watkins Glen itself, and local enthusiasts carried them the 12 miles up to the circuit on trailers.

Richie arrived from his home in California slightly distraught. His wife was showing signs of an imminent addition to the Ginther family. First practice was dry, but the track was muddy with puddles. Richie, who had not driven at the Glen before, was second fastest to Clark, while Graham was pounding round and round and round. I noticed that the slow twisty circuits — Monte Carlo, Oulton Park, Watkins Glen — were really Richie's handwriting. Surtees crashed badly in second practice, and his car could not be repaired. We were very sorry for him, particularly as it was probably because of the transport damage. He asked if he could drive our spare car, which the race organizers already had their eyes on for Phil Hill, but I refused. With the Championship at stake it was a genuine spare.

Clark was fastest, 1 min 15.8 sec, on the 2-2-2 grid alongside Richie 1 min 16.6 sec, who was grinning from ear to ear and pressing cigars on everyone: he now had a son and heir — Brett. Graham was third, at 1 min 16.8 sec in 'Old Faithful', and Gurney fourth. Graham had done 1 min 17 sec in the spare car. He came and said he had to admit I was right after all, 5783 was definitely quicker. Please, could he have the engine from 5781, which felt good, put into 5783. I said: 'No, we have no chance to check the build, it's not like Monza where we had four hours of practice, after the change. We are a long way from home, and we do not have all the facilities I would like.' Graham and I had quite an argument while he was driving us back to our hotel, but I would not budge. In the heat of the argument Graham missed the 30 mph limit sign and was booked by a speed cop for doing over 70. The cop said he could fine him on the spot for anything up to 50 but he would have to jail him for 70! He let Graham off with a warning saying that no one would believe he could be doing over 70 anyway!

The plan was that Richie let Graham through at the start and Graham would keep the pressure on Clark all the way. We knew the Lotus was skittish and tended to oversteer on light tanks. Graham made a good start. Clark was quicker, but Graham got in front of him from the 12th to the 19th lap, when Clark got back in front. The strong wind had changed direction and it was bitterly cold. The leaders were going faster and faster. Clark was down to 1 min 15 sec and Graham 1 min 15.2 sec. The average speed for the race was faster than Jimmy's pole position time. Jimmy won and Graham was nine seconds behind, with McLaren a lap and 24 seconds behind, which showed how hard they were going. Richie dropped out with a blown engine. I expected Graham to complain that, if I had changed engines, and let him drive 5783 (a combination he estimated would be two or three fifths of a second per lap faster, or 15 seconds for the whole race) he might have won. Instead, he apologized for having given me such a hard time over changing engines and cars. I was quite right, he said. With the change in wind direction, he was using 11,200 rpm, which he would not dared to have done after an overnight engine change. Clark had made all his ground on the corner after the pits where he could hold a tighter line and get onto the power sooner. It was this sort of thing that made working with Graham such a pleasure.

Before the race Mrs Stanley asked me how many minutes to the start. I fished out my Lockheed key ring Timex to tell her. Soon after my return to England, a Rolex arrived with her compliments!

Afterwards we split into two parties, the Cyril Atkins group packed the cars and returned via New York, while I went with some of the mechanics, via Niagara Falls, to Toronto for a TV programme to help Rubery Owen, Canada. On the way back we were diverted to Prestwick because of fog, which gave me time to do some heavy thinking. The Championship position was now Graham 39, Clark 30 and McLaren 24, and for the Constructors' Championship, we had 39 to Lotus's 36. The next cloud on the horizon was that Lucas said they would now supply their injection systems to Climax for Lotus and Cooper. I protested that our agreement was exclusive for the year, but they said: 'The year was nearly up.' I argued that it was not over yet. Sir Alfred would not support me. He said it only made things fair and, anyway, Graham was always saying he would have been faster on carburettors.

Sir Alfred said Rubery Owen had many important interests in South Africa, so he and his eldest son David would go to the race at East London. The long-awaited rebalanced crankshafts had arrived, and we tried to convince ourselves they gave more power, but I do not think they did. The first decision I made was that we would do the two minor races at Kyalami and Durban, to get everyone acclimatized to South Africa for the final Championship race on 29 December. We would keep 5783 back in England until the last possible moment, lightening and improving it, with the intention of using it in that vital Championship event. Similarly we would fly its engine out at the very last moment.

Shell gave our finances a boost by saying they had learned so much from the running in August that they would like to give us a contract for high-speed combustion research. We would provide engines and so many test-bed hours per year. I was extremely pleased, but when PB heard about it, he said: 'Wait a minute, that's research, that's Weslake's job.' Sir Alfred agreed, and I lost that contract before I ever received any benefit. In September PB had persuaded Sir Alfred to buy a major interest in Harry Weslake's business and to install him as a director. As a result there were many arguments and distractions. Sir Alfred formed a BRM-Weslake Liaison Committee, chaired by Spear. PB and Weslake had already convinced Sir Alfred that BRM ought to have a 4-valve engine, but they did not convince me — certainly not one of theirs anyway.

I was obsessed by the torque advantage obtained by cross-coupling the exhaust, Climax fashion. We had run a test in August crossing the pipes under the sump showing us there was 15 hp to be gained at 7500 rpm. Richie suggested we crossed the heads over, so the exhaust manifolds were in the V, then it would be easy. Unfortunately it meant new cylinder heads. Our engine designer, Geoff Johnson, did all the sums for a single plane crankshaft so that we had, in effect, two 4-cylinder engines running on a common crankcase. Then we could couple the exhausts as two 4-cylinders with all the benefits. The downside was a horizontal cross-shaking couple, but from Geoff's sums the forces were so small that we could live with them. It meant the engine would try to shake the car from side to side in a horizontal plane. I decided to make some of these crankshafts as an experiment.

However, Spear, as chairman of the BRM-Weslake Liaison Committee, ruled that the single-plane crankshaft had to be provided by Weslake, and I could not spend money without Spear as a member of the Budget Committee finding out. I insisted that the Berthon/Weslake four-valve head had the exhaust ports in the middle of the V and the inlet ports between the camshafts. This meant we could make our proposed monocoque with fuel tanks alongside the engine, all the way to the rear suspension. Harry objected and said it would not work; there would be no port turbulence. I disagreed, citing the W196 Mercedes and Bristol 2 litre 6-cylinder engine. Spear ruled in my favour on this occasion — I was responsible for car design, if I asked for an engine of this configuration, I must have it. These liaison meetings, held in Rubery Owen's Head Office in London (wasting an awful amount of time and even more money) sometimes ran for two days. I managed to get Alistair Wadsworth of Shell added to the committee, as Shell were putting up a significant share of the money. Alistair and Shell were staunch allies.

Back at Bourne I tried to improve the car. We managed to lighten it by nearly 50 lb (23 kg) which almost brought it down to the formula weight. We made two lead plugs which we could push into the bottom frame tubes; so that if the car was weighed with Colin Chapman watching it would still appear overweight. We would remove them for the race when it would still be legal. I do not know whether the deception worked. Lotus drastically reduced their oil tank capacity to get down to the weight limit.

Sir Alfred had decreed the car must be all-British. When we ran a check we found a small needle-roller bearing in the gearbox was made in Germany. INA, its manufacturer, transferred the production of this bearing to their plant in South Wales so we met Sir Alfred's directive.

There were some enjoyable social events during the autumn. BRM were awarded the Ferodo trophy and Sir Alfred was delighted. The only snag was that all the current cars were either in South Africa or on their way, so the old Mark II V16 became the centrepiece. The BRM team were voted BBC

Sportsview Team of the Year — another problem, the working team were already in South Africa with the cars. Some of the backroom boys donned overalls for this function. The BRDC dinner became a bit hectic, as they could not award the Gold Star to the champion — they did not know who he was going to be. It did not seem to make very much difference to the fun. Graham was going through his stripping phase. He removed most of his clothes and cavorted about on the tables wearing his London Rowing Club cap and very little else.

I was flying myself to test sessions in the club Auster, and nearly came to a sticky end after one of our Snetterton tests. The weather forecast indicated that there was going to be an unpleasant front about 12 noon but it would be clear by 2 to 3 p.m. I thought that the front would have passed by the time we had finished and I would be able to fly back in reasonably clear conditions. The Auster was not the world's fastest aeroplane, it cruised at 85 mph. The flight from Cranwell to Snetterton took about 45 minutes. However, something went wrong about midday and being impatient to get back and get the remedial action under way I set off. After about 15 minutes it got dark and very unpleasant. I suddenly remembered the forecast, but by then it was too late, I was in snow flurries, crossing the Bedford levels at Downham Market. The levels are two parallel rivers, a very good landmark, so I flew up them to Kings Lynn and then tried to follow the railway line through Sutton Bridge and Spalding to Sleaford. Unfortunately somebody had dug it up. I applied one notch of flap, selected warm air to the carburettors to avoid icing, and at 40 mph followed the road at 100 feet. I went through rather than over Spalding railway station, and let down at Cranwell North. It was a fairly primitive aircraft — no radio, but that was legal in 1962.

In mid-December we shipped the car and the die was cast. In the first warm-up race Richie had gearbox trouble, Graham had a rectifier problem and both cars overheated, so I organized seven-row instead of six-row radiators. In Durban, Richie was third, Graham dropped out with the wire broken off the ignition trigger. They were obviously missing Willy, kept back to help with engine development. On the morning of Christmas Eve, as I was preparing to depart, Cyril Atkins telephoned on a very bad line asking for yet another spare engine. The engine shop turned out, and foreman Colin Atkin drove me to Heathrow with the engine as part of my luggage. I left tearful children saying: 'But Daddy you won't see Father Christmas.' Five o'clock on Christmas morning saw us refuelling in Brazzaville in the Congo to the sound of revolutionary gunfire. On my arrival in Johannesburg the local Rubery Owen people took me for a Christmas dinner of barbecued turkey by their swimming pool. At 5 a.m. on Boxing Day, when I tried to collect my spare engine to fly on to East London, I was told it was too big to go through the doors of the Vickers Viscount, and that it had already been sent on the old DC3 which carried the newspapers. When I arrived at East London I found it was still in Johannesburg. Mr Beizudenhout, the South African Airways Manager at East London was extremely apologetic; located the engine, got it on the next flight and asked what he could do to make restitution. I said: 'That is easy, get me home for New Year's Eve.'

I was booked home via Nairobi and Tel Aviv, arriving in London on New Year's Day. Pam said, she could face my being away for Christmas, but

New Year's Eve as well was a bit too much. The only other way was to charter an aircraft from East London to Johannesburg. Mr South African airways said he would get me on the Press Special charter to connect with the regular flight to London from Johannesburg, arriving 8.30 a.m. New Year's Eve.

RM had pressed me very hard to let Bruce Johnson, a South African, drive. I said we could not be distracted from the Championship, but he could have a '61 car. He must also find his own mechanics and, above all, they must not come near us. They played to my rules, we saw nothing of them.

There was an untimed practice on the afternoon of Boxing Day. Graham had trouble with the special engine in 5783 and carried on using the old car. Clark had a new Lotus 25 with fuel injection which gave much trouble, and so did his carburettor car. Next day, in official practice Richie came in telling me his engine was not running properly. I said to him: 'I should get out of it if I were you Richie, it's on fire!' He jumped out and ran down the bonnet without leaving a mark. Something was wrong with the alternator which fortunately we were able to fix. Graham kept pounding round in the old car, getting nowhere. The spare engine in 5783 blew up — a piston failure. Practice ended up with Clark on pole in the carburettor car at 1 min 29.3 sec and Graham 1 min 29.6 sec with 5783. Richie was further back at 1 min 31.7 sec.

The night before the race Willy and I took stock. We had a serious low oil-pressure problem on all our six engines, and not one of them was really filling us with confidence. We realized our only hope was to keep going; play the reliability card and wear Clark down. But which engines to use? All the engines had been removed from all of the cars, we arranged them in a circle, like the spokes of a wheel, and set to work to take the front covers off and build three good oil pumps for the selected engines. The other engine people examined bearings and did the pre-race check. While this was in full swing, Sir Alfred came to see us preparing to win the Championship. It gave him a shock to see the chaos in our garage. Fortunately, someone had the wit to take him to visit Lotus — it was the same scene except, chez Lotus, gearboxes were the centre of attraction.

Finally we got two cars together, and set off for the circuit towing the cars behind Grosvenor Motors' vans. I ran Graham's car on the road beside the sea and it seemed smooth and lively, with no leaks. So now all we could do was hope for the best. Graham was completely relaxed. When interviewed by an American TV reporter, who said: 'You seem very calm. With the World Championship in the balance, doesn't anything worry you?' Graham replied: 'Only berks like you asking bloody stupid questions.' This seemed to sum it all up. The Stanleys had not made the trip to South Africa over Christmas, so I had been commissioned to take photographs of everything for Mr Stanley. I had even deputed one mechanic to keep an eye on Willy to see that he did not take anything to bits, to check, that he could not get back together in time for the race. The tension even got to Sir Alfred who asked if there was anything left to check. I told him we had checked and double-checked, and showed him the pre-race check sheet, every box signed and even counter-signed.

When the race began Innes Ireland was first away, but Clark and Graham soon got by. Clark then started to pull away, but Graham, in second place, drove with grim consistency. Richie was in the middle of a dog-fight with McLaren and Surtees; Bruce Johnson came in complaining his car would not go; Roy Forman, one of our engine mechanics spotted that the wires were crossed on the ignition trigger, thus retarding the ignition something like ten degrees. He crossed them over, and got Bruce going well. Richie stopped with a misfire, so we changed his plugs and gave him a new ignition coil box, which fixed him. The Championship, which I had never dreamed of eight months earlier, seemed to be slipping away from us. By lap 60 Clark was 28 seconds ahead and there was nothing we could do. Graham nodded grimly when we gave him the time he was behind Clark. Then Jimmy came round trailing a thin stream of oil smoke from the top rear of his engine. Next lap it was even worse. Stirling, who had been walking up and down between our pit and Lotus, said to me: 'Don't get excited yet, they are all right while they smoke, it's when the smoke stops because there is no oil left to smoke, that's when they are in trouble.'

Next time round Clark pulled in, and everyone at Lotus swarmed over the car looking for the trouble. When Graham came round I stood in the road with his signal and pointed at the stationary Lotus. He nodded again. Next time he came round, Jimmy was out of the car and Colin Chapman was congratulating Sir Alfred and me. Now, whatever happened, Graham was World Champion, even if he did not finish. By some chance, all three BRMs came round together, so I showed them the race order board. Richie waved both arms in a boxer's salute and Bruce Johnson gave us a big thumbs up. Graham grudgingly slowed down as we gave him his lead on McLaren and laps to go. He finally crossed the line 50 seconds in the lead, with Richie seventh and Bruce ninth. Sir Alfred and Cyril Atkins went to the finishing line to wait for Graham. I just sat on the pit counter glad it was all over, feeling absolutely drained of all energy.

Graham turned up wearing an enormous wreath, which he called the privet hedge, and with an equally enormous trophy which I gave to Sir Alfred on the spot. I persuaded him to let the mechanics spend a week visiting the Kruger Game Park on their way home. Graham was rather concerned: during his slowing down lap a 15-year-old boy had run into the road. Graham had hit him and wanted to know if he was badly hurt, but fortunately there was nothing serious.

I now had a problem. The organizers of the London Racing Car Show wanted the Championship car back as the central exhibit. Now I had the problem of finding a way to get it back, which I had refused to even think about before the race. The race organizers had planned an enormous barbecue on the beach, including a whole roast ox — a really big party. There was no way I could manage it, as all I wanted was bed. I felt badly and thought I really ought to go and help the mechanics celebrate — they had done it all. I could not find Cyril but I found Willy, and asked him to make my apologies as I was beyond getting to the party. He told me not to worry as hardly any of them were up to going; all they could think of was a bath and bed. Richie drove Graham and me back to our hotel, saying: 'You are a miserable pair — you are acting as if you are going to a funeral — not two people who have just won both Championships.'

I sent Pam a cable giving her my arrival time at Heathrow so someone could meet me. As I went to my room I passed Graham's open bedroom door. Graham was in the shower and Stirling was lying on his bed, knuckling his forehead. I stopped to see if he was alright. Suddenly he snapped his fingers, picked up the telephone, dialled a number and started to make a date with 'Valerie', a local girl. No notebook, all memory! I had some sandwiches sent up and fell into a bath. I could not remember when I had last had my clothes off. I was in a deep sleep three or four hours later when I was called to the hotel switchboard to take a call from England. Apparently they could not switch it through to my room. In pyjamas and dressing gown I took the call which was from a very excited Mr and Mrs Stanley. On my way back to bed I was ambushed by journalists who said: 'You can't go to bed, you have just won the World Championships.' I do not remember the rest of the evening. When I went into the breakfast room the following morning, there was Graham finishing off an enormous 'trek' breakfast, a plank of wood with a mixed grill, potatoes, fried eggs, the lot, and supervising the preparation of a large jug of black velvet, in which I participated. He had also managed to get on the Press special. In Johannesburg I was taken by the Rubery Owen people to see a gold mine, but I do not remember a thing.

I sat next to Gregor Grant for the flight to Nairobi. I can remember wandering around the airport shop having just heard that Europe was in the grip of a big freeze-up, London airport was closed and we might have to stay in Nairobi for some time. Hazel Chapman gave me a severe ticking off for looking miserable — 'You have just won the Championship.' Eventually we got to Rome and sat around for a few hours, then we were told they could get into Amsterdam which, at least, was getting us nearer to London. We had only just got off the plane at Amsterdam when we were called back again — Heathrow was open for one hour. I was carrying films of the race for the TV news, and after being entertained by them and calling to see Bette Hill, I finally arrived home and flopped into an armchair. Pam said: 'You need not think you are going to sit there tonight my lad, we are going to a party to end all parties.'

There was a week of parties. Mr and Mrs Stanley invited everyone from BRM to their home in Cambridge, several busloads of us. They gave a big dinner party in the Dorchester Hotel penthouse suite. Then there was the Racing Car Show. The Bourne and District Council gave a civic reception for the BRM team. Lots of speeches. I thought I would get out of having to make one, but there was a tremendous amount of foot-stamping, whistling and shouting, so I thanked them all for what they had done. Then came Graham's celebration party. This surpassed all his previous efforts. The highlight was when a policeman arrived and said the neighbours had complained of cars parked in their drives. He was soon swept into the party, Innes wearing his helmet. An hour later a police sergeant arrived looking for him. The sergeant had been in the local Boy Scouts with Graham — he had no chance. The door bell rang again. Barrie Gill (then Motoring writer from *The Daily Herald*, for whom Graham had been providing a weekly column) said: 'I bet this is the inspector, looking for his policemen.' Sure enough, it was. He was polite but very firm.

At the presentation of the World Championship Awards at the RAC, Tony Vandervell took me into a corner to congratulate me privately and split a bottle of champagne to celebrate. He implied that it had been easier for me than it had been for him. The Italians had not been so much of a problem. I did not convince him that Clark and Chapman were not all that easy to beat either. However, I valued his personal touch when he was not in the best of health. The celebrations concluded with a BRM supporters' club (Owen Racing Motor Association) party. Then it was time to get ready for 1963, it was not very long until the first race.

# CHAPTER FOURTEEN

# More V8

THE FIRST DASH of cold water came very early in 1963, when Sir Alfred called a meeting with RM and me. RM had a very bad cold, so we met in his bedroom at the Berkeley Hotel. Sir Alfred told us that Rover wished to run at Le Mans to try for the special prize for the first turbine-engined car to average 150 kph for 24 hours. He had agreed to provide the car. I was to design it, and Bourne were to build it. Berthon-Weslake would design the transmission. Motor Panels Coventry, a part of Rubery Owen, who had just finished the second version of Bluebird for Donald Campbell would build the body. Wilkie would manage the team, under Peter Spear's direction, using Bourne mechanics. He handed us Peter Spear's programme. I said it was crazy. There were six weeks for this, eight weeks for that, and yet we had to have the car running by the middle of March, just nine weeks away. Sir Alfred asked: 'Why? The race is not until the end of June.' I said: 'The test weekend is the end of March. With such a revolutionary car, if you do not go to these tests, you are imposing an impossible handicap! It was clear that none of the planners knew of the test weekend.

The next item on the agenda was my new car. Ernest Owen had bet me his Rolls-Royce we would not win the Championship, but Sir Alfred suggested an E-Type Jaguar would be a better idea. I explained that with two young children I needed a four-seater. We settled for a 3 litre Rover.

Spear reviewed his Le Mans timing, Weslake trimmed their share, Motor Panels would not budge from their original time to build the body. Rover sent us a turbine engine which weighed 90 lb (41 kg) complete — no radiator or oil cooler. We cut 57/3 down the centre line, and made it into a two-seater. We estimated the weight of a BRM Elektron 0.05 inch- (1.25 mm) thick body, found we needed loads of ballast to reach the regulation weight and poured lead into the lower frame tubes. Motor Panels, without reference to anyone, ignored the specification and made the body in 0.08 inch- (2 mm) thick aluminium. The body was double the estimated weight and the car now well over the minimum permitted. We had a terrible job extracting the lead.

At the Le Mans test weekend Richic found that the aerodynamic lift of the flat rear deck nearly lifted the back wheels off the road. His Ferrari sports car experience saved us. He recognized the problem and knew the answer — an enormous duck-tailed spoiler. It then handled well and, with the 150 hp turbine, reached 150 mph (202 kph) and a respectable lap time. It had the most incredible throttle lag — measured with a calendar not a stop watch. There were many tests in the MIRA wind tunnel to develop the new body.

I estimated that all this activity delayed our 1963 monocoque car by at least two months. Not only staff and facilities were diverted, but there were many distractions. It did not end there either. During official Le Mans practice there was an awful panic. All the wonderful roadholding from the test day had disappeared. I had to fly out to Le Mans in a chartered Piper Comanche to find out why. As I walked around the car, it was easy to see. We had set the car up on Dunlop 'green spot' tyres; their softest racing compound, normally used on a wet circuit. With such a light car and so little power I was quite sure there would be no problem and I had briefed all the BRM people accordingly. But now Dunlop had issued them with the hardest possible long-distance racing sports car rubber and they said not a word. I managed to get it put back on 'green spots', under violent protest from Dunlop, despite them having all the test weekend data. Graham found the handling had returned, and produced a worthwhile lap time, while happily Dunlop found wear and temperatures were acceptable. During the race the car ran well, averaged 173.546 kph, covered 4,172.91 km, and won the prize.

We always realized that we would have to race the old cars in the first two or three races until the monocoques were ready but, with all the turbine distractions, the three races became six. The first single-plane crank arrived from Weslake in February. The engine seized on its first run, and we found that the oil ways did not line up and were not drilled in the right places for the loads. The ever-invaluable Les Bryden re-drilled the supposedly glass-hard nitrided crank. After this experience, I had Geoff Johnson check the balance calculations. We discovered four surplus balance weights which when removed saved about 6 lb (2.7 kg) if nothing else. There was the hoped-for satisfactory increase in mid-range torque and even top-end power. Shell had produced a new oil for us and it all looked good. Every engine was giving over 150 hp at 7500 rpm and over 200 between 10,000 and 10,500 rpm.

I had a quiet word with Harry Weslake concerning all the blunders on the crankshaft, which was not like his own people, and also asked if he could guarantee the 4-valve heads on time. I was building cars around the engines, and BRM would be in a dreadful predicament if the engine did not turn up on time or did not work. He said delivery was no problem, but he was less happy about performance. My downdraught ports still worried him. He could guarantee 10 per cent increase in peak torque but probably only 2 or 3 per cent more power, which I thought was fair. During Spear's October 1962 liaison meeting, PB had promised the first 4-valve heads ready to race in the first F1 event of 1963 — Monaco in May. Spear asked for a critical path analysis, and when it was produced the date had slipped to late June. I believed the old cars with flat crank engines, would be good enough to win at Monte Carlo (which they did — another 1-2) but we needed something better for Spa in June. We had to hope for the best, and everything right first time, which, knowing some of the people involved would be another first.

I had been designing the BRM P61 monocoque along different lines from

Lotus. Despite Graham's size compared with Jimmy Clark, it was going to be smaller than the Lotus 25 and a true monocoque — just a tapered oval tube with a hole for the driver. I had planned to carry eight gallons (36 litres) of fuel alongside the engine, which also helped weight distribution. We had moved the oil system alongside the engine, and put rubber bag oil tanks in the monocoque and the oil cooler behind the driver's seat to save the weight of oil-filled pipes and to move weight towards the back wheels. The suspension geometry was to be more of the same from the Type 578s, but the spring characteristics were to be radically different. The basic theory is that the lower the spring rate the higher the cornering power. No one could live with the wheel movements that went with extremely soft springs, although Colin Chapman did a better job than most. I went for an 'S' shaped spring rate curve. As the suspension drooped, the effective spring stiffness was increased by the system geometry. In the other direction — bump, compressing the springs — after a certain point the springs became stiffer because of the way they were coiled and also by the bump rubbers. That meant the car would always ride at the softest spring condition, which could be adjusted to control ground clearance — one of the objectives of today's active suspension systems. I was also trying to get air to flow between the wheels and the body. The central exhaust pipes removed one obstruction. The variable rate rear suspension put the rear springs and dampers inside the body, so I had a clear flow path. We tried it in the MIRA wind tunnel and it worked although, of course, the rear wheels were not rotating which makes a significant difference.

I was rather worried that if I committed the car to this new suspension system and it did not work, I would have gone down a blind alley with no escape route. I also feared that the Berthon-Weslake 4-valve head might not come up to expectations. To cover these contingencies, on the first car, I made a tubular structure to carry the engine, instead of the planned full monocoque. This was a mistake which ruined the original 61s. The monocoque was fine, and the steel tube space-frame not too bad, but I made a hash of the joint between them. Transmitting the high-point loads from the space-frame into the monocoque, where you need low stress levels spread over large areas, caused the monocoque to distort and flex. It was some months before we understood this.

I was itching to get the car tested but turbine car problems kept getting in the way. Spear made all sorts of promises to Rover without consulting us. If BRM failed to keep them I would get a snotty message from Sir Alfred's secretary, of which Sir Alfred later denied all knowledge.

When we started running the monocoque we had problems with the oil system, which we put down to the new Shell oil reacting with the rubber in the tanks and causing the oil to foam. Fireproof tanks had tested them and cleared them to 130°C (266°F). The skin would also conduct some heat away. It was in fact nothing to do with the rubber tank or foaming, but we wasted a month solving this problem. We took the car to the Dutch GP at Zandvoort with the intention of racing it, but the brake fluid boiled — something we could not immediately cure.

At Reims for the French GP, a week later, still with a 2-valve engine, the car began to perform. Despite many teething troubles, Graham qualified second to Clark. 2 min 20.2 sec to 2 min 20.9 sec, with Richie in the old car at 2 min 25.9 sec. It must have had some effect on Lotus, as Colin Chapman and Jimmy came round to our garage and asked if they could have a look at the car. Something had attracted Jimmy. Graham would never admit that it was faster in a straight line than a Lotus 25. However, some three years later Jimmy told me that although he could hold Graham out of Thillois on initial acceleration, it would then draw away from him and he had to pull out of the slipstream as he was in danger of over-revving. It would have helped to have known where we were losing time, but at Reims our biggest problem was how to get the missing extra 8 gallons (36 litres) of fuel in it for the race. Because of the delay with the centre exhaust 4-valve engine, we could not carry the planned fuel alongside, as with the 2-valve engine the exhaust pipes occupied the space. Danny Woodward, one of our sheet metal workers, made aluminium fuel tanks to fit in every nook and cranny. We eventually finished third, penalized 60 seconds for push-starting under the instructions of starter Toto Roche after the engine refused to start on the starter motor. We also had slight clutch slip due to the fluid boiling, which must have cost us time.

After a disappointing test session at Silverstone we decided not to race the car until the 4-valve heads arrived. However, they were never good enough to use in 1963, but we had to use the car at Monza where its variable-rate suspension would be a great advantage. We had terrible trouble at Reims with the centre electrodes dropping out of the spark plugs. Sometimes they just went straight through the engine without doing any damage, other times they would get under a valve and wreck the engine. I began to get desperate about this as it was getting worse and costing us engines and races — the suppliers did not seem to be able to cure the problem. Fortunately one of Mr Stanley's golfing friends was a director of Champion Spark Plugs, and over lunch at the Dorchester he was persuaded to bring Champion back into Formula 1. It would take time, until 1964 in fact.

We also had Stokey's new 6-speed gearbox which did not produce the anticipated performance advantage. There were some teething troubles with the change mechanism. The quill shaft, that went right through the box and permitted us to use smaller and narrower gears, also gave trouble.

Fortunately the old cars lived up to expectations. Graham won the first race at Snetterton. Lotus lost the race at Aintree with a flat battery on the start line, so Graham had another easy win. At Goodwood we had trouble with the new ultra-low viscosity oil getting past the piston rings, so had to abandon the oil and the extra power it gave us. In the race Graham had a very peculiar failure. His car was fitted with the fuel tanks repaired after the Nürburgring crash. Unfortunately one of the pads used in the repair process was left in the tank and it eventually blocked the outlet pipe. Graham retired with symptoms of fuel starvation even though there was plenty in the tank. We had electrical problems in the Daily Express Trophy race, both cars dropping out with alternator rectifier troubles.

Monaco was our first Championship race. Graham again had symptoms of a low oil level towards the end of the race, so he was taking it very easily around the corners. Richie was going well and catching him fast. I did not want them to get into a dogfight, so I just showed Richie his lead over third place man McLaren — eight seconds. Suddenly Richie spotted the helicopter ahead, filming the race leader, he realized he was very close to Graham. When he knew, after the race, of Graham's problem and realized he could have won, he had something to say. Fortunately he did not bear me too much ill will, and we had a very pleasant lunch together at Bideau's on Monday before I flew back to England. It was a very pleasant easy weekend, I wished all races were as easy. It was our second one—two, and surprised the 'experts'.

At Spa, for the Belgian GP, it was very wet. Graham got 5783 on pole but he dropped out, suffering from trouble with the old gearbox when in second place. Richie was third for most of the race but finally lost it to McLaren and finished fourth. It poured with rain throughout the race. Colin Chapman and I tried to get the race stopped as it was so dangerous, but no one took any notice. Three cars were wrecked as a result.

At Zandvoort Clark had an easy win. During the race Graham's engine, 5606, developed an internal coolant leak, but it appeared that Graham could still finish second, so we kept him going. Unfortunately the engine seized with about ten miles to go and it was destroyed — the only one of the V8s we lost in the whole of their use by the team. Richie was fifth. At Reims Richie had a stone through his radiator when in second place. Graham, third in the race with the new monocoque, as already recounted, blew an engine during practice in 5783 — a broken tappet which began to be a problem.

For the British GP we started taking the cars back to Bourne instead of using a garage at Brackley. We had to load the cars into the transporter wherever we went, but less than two hours to Bourne against half an hour to Brackley was more than balanced out by all the facilities at Bourne. Ernest Owen wanted us to paint the cars orange with black numbers — Rubery Owen's colours. I explained that under current international regulations British cars had to be green with white numbers. We compromised on an orange band round the nose, and the mechanics wore 'dayglo' orange overalls. The British GP saw the whole new scheme for the first time. Graham had another tappet failure in practice. We were not sure of the fuel consumption on the replacement engine so we filled the tanks, resisting temptation to weaken it on the line. Graham ran out of fuel at Abbey on his last lap and coasted over the line, losing a certain second place, and was third, with Richie fourth.

At the German GP the new monocoque again had brake trouble. Wilkie had sold 'Old Faithful' to Scuderia Centro Sud, and Bandini, their up-and-coming driver, caused a colossal upset by being faster than Graham in practice. Richie led the race for a while, Bandini and Innes Ireland collided, doing much damage, and Graham's gearbox quill shaft broke when he was in third place. Eventually Surtees won, Clark was second and Richie a good third.

The Italian GP at Monza was on the combined circuit. This is where the new car really had to perform. I caused a stir by predicting a lap time of less than 2 min 30 sec on the combined circuit and the Italian Press were incredulous. The fastest lap, which was set in 1961 by von Trips was 2 min 46 sec. I thought I was pretty safe. On his fifth lap of official practice Graham was timed at 2 min 28.8 sec! The 'S' shaped rate curve was really working at Monza; the circuit I had in mind when it was designed. The problem was that you needed a very hard suspension for the banked circuit, which made the car quite undriveable on the road circuit. The Type 61 suspension system coped easily with both circuits. Unfortunately, for all my planning, other teams had a series of crashes because of suspension failures. The stresses on the banking did the damage, but the suspension did not break until the car was in the woods, which was very dangerous. Eventually the race organizers abandoned the banked circuit; first practice times were cancelled and we had to set up the cars for the road circuit only. Surtees made pole with a time of 1 min 37.3 sec to Graham's 1 min 38.5 sec, all done by horse power. Clark and Richie shared the second row. In the race Surtees led until lap 17, when he blew up, and there was a fearful slip-streaming battle between Clark, Gurney and Graham — changing places every lap until Graham's clutch and Gurney's fuel pump gave up. So Jimmy won, Richie was second and McLaren third. Richie was so pleased that he drove his Fiat Topolino up the steps of the Hotel.

By this time I had confirmed that the joint between the monocoque and the temporary steel sub-frame was the basic problem with the Type 61. I put in hand the full monocoque structure with a simplified variable-rate suspension for 1964, broke up 61/1 and decided to finish the season with the old cars, although I came under fire from the Owen family for abandoning the monocoque.

At Watkins Glen Graham put 5783 on pole with a time of 1 min 13.4 sec to Clark's 1 min 13.5 sec. Surtees and Ginther tied with 1 min 13.7 sec. The new Tech Centre was now open, and I struck up a friendship with Bill Milliken, Clerk of the Course, which has lasted to this day. We had a fairly easy time. Clark had another flat battery on the start line, which cost him over a lap. Graham led; Surtees and Gurney passed Richie, then the Ferrari blew up, Gurney dropped back and Graham's rear roll bar link broke, but the bar was only like a bicycle spoke, and it did not really trouble him. Graham won, 34 seconds ahead of Richie. Clark was third, one lap and 46 seconds behind. When I collected the prize money — $100,000 for first and $75,000 for second, all in $100 bills, Cameron Argetsinger, the race organizer and his staff were very concerned that I had planned to drive back to the Glen Motor Court by myself. I had not given it any thought, so I was relieved to get back, pay the hotel bills and share the money out. After this there was not enough left to worry about. I did not go to Mexico or South Africa. Both races were won by Clark who was already World Champion, with Graham and Richie in joint second place.

I had stayed at Bourne to run the Berthon-Weslake 4-valve head, on which so much depended. Ferrari had a colossal upheaval in 1962, when most of the team management left, and Mauro Forghieri was appointed their Chief Engineer. Actually he and I had something in common; we had both been dropped in at the deep end at the same time! We became good friends and since he spoke quite good English we could chat with one another. He was beginning to get their new V8 monocoque really competitive. We also heard that Climax were going over to flat cranks. I could not understand this; they had their cross-coupled exhaust working so well. All that a single plane crank would do would be to give them a lighter engine by a few pounds, but no more power and it would not be as smooth — pressure from their customers, I suspect: BRM had them and went faster.

The 4-valve head had all the usual crop of stupid mistakes. We built it onto a two-plane crank engine as it had that firing order. We were disappointed to find it gave less power than the 2-valve up to 9000 rpm. It was about the same at 9500, then the power just vanished. Harry Weslake blamed my stupid ports and proposed a side-port version. After some work we got the same power, between 9000 and 10,000 rpm, as a 2-valve, then the power dropped off badly. We did several runs to collect data for PB before sending the heads back to be reworked.

Graham had been driving the Ferguson 4-wheel-drive car, P99, and was very impressed. He suggested that BRM should build one. I said we were too busy. Graham replied: 'You will be left behind if Chunky builds one.' (Graham had christened Colin Chapman 'Chunky', and if you look at photographs of him between 1958 and 1960 you can see why.) I told him I was not sure it would work. Sir Alfred settled the dispute by ruling that as BRM raced to demonstrate Rubery Owen's engineering competence we should go ahead. 'How much will it cost?' he enquired. I said '£30,000 to £35,000.' He said to give him a costed proposal and he would think it over. I flew the Auster to Silverstone in pouring rain to see Graham test the P99. It was even worse on the way back, and I had another grope around Ketton's 600 foot chimney. Sir Alfred finally authorized £10,000 for design work with Ferguson and Tony Rolt. It emerged later they were also working with STP and the Granatellis to make a 4-wheel-drive Indy car. This made more sense to me; all the corners at Indianapolis were of a similar nature so it might be possible to balance the car.

Jim Fielding, Managing Director of Heanan and Froude, invited me to lunch, saying: 'Bring a racing car with you.' He had waiting the prototype Rolling Road, a road wheel dynamometer. We found that the Colotti gearbox transmitted 92.8 per cent of the power put into it. The old BRM box gave 90.9 per cent, but our super new quick ratio-change 6-speed box only 88 per cent. The power was lost in the ratio change gears at the back. Stokey was set to work on a completely new gearbox where we could have six first gears if we wished. He was and is an odd chap. He looked and acted like the village policeman — not surprising really as his father was one, and Stokey was a sergeant in the Special Constabulary, but he designs the most elegant and efficient gearboxes. The result was the Type 72, one of the lightest and most efficient boxes of the 1.5 litre formula; dead reliable, transmitting 94 per cent of the power it received, and its gears lasted a season. It only wilted when we started putting 292 hp from the Tasmans through it. I told him it must have been over-engineered.

In the middle of all this activity Peter Spear played a Joker. At the end of November I was instructed to meet him at the Ariel Hotel, Heathrow for a highly secret trip — 'bring your passport'. It was to be a visit to Chrysler in Detroit, where they were developing a V8 engine for Indianapolis — 4.2 litres unblown, with four valves per cylinder and downdraught ports between the camshafts. Their intention was to install it transversely rather like the, as yet, unrevealed Honda. Our mission was to critique the engine and design the car. Lotus and Jimmy Clark had very nearly won the race that year with a push-rod Ford Fairlane engine. So now Chrysler were going to show Ford how to do it. Chrysler had nearly as big a market share as Ford in 1963. I was stunned, I wanted to say 'Yes', but what about our F1 programme? Spear arranged that we should work out a time and cost programme before committing ourselves. On the way home he suggested that I should take on the extra staff to work under my direction to design and build the car. Graham had been very impressed with John Crosthwaite, an English designer working for Mickey Thompson, so we did a deal with John and Chrysler and I started transatlantic commuting.

There was a flight from Heathrow to Detroit getting in around 3 p.m. I would collect an envelope from the airline desk at Detroit containing a car park ticket and the keys to a car. Sometimes this was a Chrysler turbine. I drove myself to the Monterey Motel on Woodward Avenue, a few blocks from the Chrysler factory at Highland Park. When I arrived I rang my contact at Chrysler, generally Bob Cahill, who would come to the Motel and take me through the agenda. Next morning we would start work at 7.30. Sometimes this was all day Friday, sometimes I would fly out on Friday, we would work Saturday until about 3.30 or 4.00 p.m. when they would drive me to the airport and put me on the flight home, arriving early Sunday morning.

I did this once a month for most of 1964, including a visit to Indianapolis where Lotus and Dunlop had a tyre problem and withdrew. Chrysler decided to cancel the project; there was now no longer a need to beat Fords. However, they kept the relationship going and I became involved with the fearsome Hemi, a 7 litre V8 with enormous push-rod operated valves in a hemispherical head which was dominating the American racing scene in the middle sixties. I made a number of friends; Bob Rarey who designed the racing V8, Willem Wertman, his right-hand man and later a senior member of their Powertrain Engineering team in 1985, when I again renewed my relationship with Chrysler.

Sir Alfred, having heard from Spear of the Chrysler project and their interest in 4-wheel-drive, gave us the go-ahead to build a complete 4-wheel-drive-car. I had by then acquired a graduate number cruncher, Mike Pilbeam, who produced tables of suspension set-ups for the monocoques, using the very new Rubery Owen computer. He seemed very bright so I gave him the 4-wheel-drive project. He is still producing successful hill-climb cars in Bourne.

Towards the end of the year I was saddened to learn that Prince Chula had died at the early age of 55. He had followed my career with interest and written occasional letters of congratulation, which were very much to the point.

Dunlop came up with a major new tyre development on 13 inch instead of 15 inch wheels which were much wider. This also meant a major brake redesign, as they would have to be much smaller. Graham was very concerned over the dilution of effort by the external projects — first Rover, now Chrysler — so Sir Alfred invited Graham and me to discuss this over dinner at the Carlton Club. I had just survived a major brush with him earlier in the year. Rubery Owen and BP were funding Donald Campbell's Bluebird Land Speed Record attempt. The car was already in Australia, but there appeared to have been a number of incomprehensible delays. The idea was that I should become Team Manager, with full authority, to run the record attempt, with Stirling Moss at the end of a telephone as reserve driver. I politely but quickly declined, saying I had organized my domestic life around motor racing, my wife was due to produce our third child in February and I did not wish to be the other side of the world when this happened. It was bad enough for her with me away all summer. She never complained but there had to be a limit. There was some discussion but finally Sir Alfred said he understood and would not press me.

Graham's theme at our meeting was that too many people were trying to run BRM. He had every confidence in me, but my efforts to win the Championship were being diluted — we should give up any idea of Le Mans and Indianapolis and concentrate on the Championship. Sir Alfred said he wanted some return for all the money he had poured into BRM; now he was beginning to see results, and Graham wanted him to stop. He was ready to put all the profits earned by Bourne back into facilities which would benefit Graham and the racing team. It was agreed that it had been a useful meeting and that we should continue to meet once a month at the Rubery Owen head office in London, to review BRM plans and programmes. He gave Graham an undertaking that if any external project looked like jeopardizing the BRM F1 effort we would have a chance to speak up. The meetings were useful, but the projects came in thick and fast. Finally the pressures led to my leaving BRM for Lotus, where ironically I built up Lotus Engineering into a large and prosperous engineering consultancy business, just as Sir Alfred had wanted me to do at Bourne!

# CHAPTER FIFTEEN

# Enter the real monocoque

I HAD STARTED to design the new monocoque, with fuel tanks alongside the engine as originally planned, with assistance from the youngest member of the design triumvirate, Alec Osborn. This car embodied all the lessons we had learned from the first, and was numbered 261 (the 2 prefix being added because it was the second version). In late February 1964 we sent it to Silverstone for Graham to try, but at the last minute I was called to Dunlop to sign the 1964 racing contract and could not get to Silverstone until after lunch. When I arrived everyone looked sheepish. Graham had said he could not drive the car because there was not enough shoulder room. He had asked the mechanics to beat out the cockpit, but they had refused so he had taken a hammer and done it himself, rather brutally. He said to me: 'Before you blow your top, look at that.' He pointed to the signal board, which read '1-32.8'. Clark's best time from 1963 was 1 min 34.4 sec.

Unfortunately this car could not use 13-inch wheels, so I gave John Crosthwaite the job of redesigning 2613 for them. After some discussion he managed to convince me that he could get my geometry with a four-link system. One of the arguments he used was that if 13-inch wheels required a different geometry it would be easier to change with a four-link than with double wishbones.

I realized with a shock that 1963 had slipped by. It had been a very unfortunate season. We started off well enough, running the old cars as planned. Then the turbine car disrupted our activities until the middle of the season. The single-plane crankshaft engine gave the old cars a new lease of life but the first of our monocoques was a great disappointment. If we had had it sooner I might have recognized some of its problems in time to get some useful racing out of it. Fortunately, the second attempt made up for all the grief and pain of the first.

Passing on to the 1964 season: there are several pages in my snapshot album of 2612 being destroyed at Snetterton by the famous aquaplaning accident. We never got to the bottom of this. I do not think it was Graham's new-fangled spinning visor, but Graham was very distressed and upset over the accident. He told Mr and Mrs Stanley it was the best BRM ever. Richie, whose wife was ill, had asked if he could stay a little longer in California. We agreed as we only had one 261 ready. At Goodwood,

Graham in the first 13-inch wheel car (2613) led for most of the race from Brabham and Clark, until the distributor rotor came unbolted — a new failure.

For Aintree we had 2613, 2614 and Richie. He rolled his car at Melling Crossing in the wet and travelled a long way inverted. He had some damaged ribs, cuts and bruises which kept him out of action for a while. The car survived the accident remarkably well. Graham took pole position from Brabham, whose cars were becoming a force to be reckoned with — 1 min 52.8 sec against 1 min 53 sec. Graham led to start with but his high-pressure fuel pump got tired, rather like it had at Oulton Park in 1962. He recognized the symptoms and nursed the car home. Clark crashed at the same place as Richie had done, fortunately with no injuries.

The next race was the Daily Express Trophy at Silverstone where the Brabhams went even better and had the first two places on the grid, plus Graham and Clark. Graham set about the Brabhams in the race, Gurney dropped out with rear-suspension failure and Graham passed Jack. But his brakes were fading — the 13-inch wheels shrouded our brakes too much and we were in serious trouble. BRM used Dunlop and Brabham used Girling. Jack pipped Graham on the line much as Graham had done to Clark two years earlier. Richie was not up to driving but he joined in the worrying. If we were in brake trouble at Silverstone, what would it be like at Monaco, which was very hard on brakes?

In the middle of all this we completed the new Rover BRM Coupé, which Graham tested. It employed a new variable-geometry turbine. It worked very well on the test day, but on the way back aboard the articulated Land Rover transporter the car was very badly damaged in a jack-knifing accident in the wet. No one dare ask me to try to rebuild it in time for Le Mans.

We put our brake troubles to Dunlop, who came up with some ideas; but I had a better one. I resurrected the old 2.5 litre ventilated rear discs and found we could just get them on the monocoques as front brakes with the exercise of much ingenuity.

We crossed our fingers and set off for Monte Carlo. Graham said we should keep what we were doing very quiet. He thought it might give us a big advantage. We were not the only team in trouble, and we did not want everyone getting in on the act, which turned out to be very perceptive. We used standard brakes with Dunlop's recommended fixes for first practice, and had a big worry session. Graham was third to Brabham and Surtees in a Ferrari. For second practice on Friday morning we had both cars on ventilated discs. Clark had arrived from Indianapolis and got into the act. The disc temperatures were 80° to 100°C (176° to 212°F) cooler and pad wear was much less, so we started shaking hands with ourselves. Final practice was a waste of time as the track had become very dirty from the heats of the F3 race. Brabham and Clark had the front row, Graham and Surtees the second while Richie was on the fourth row.

I watched the F3 race from Eddie Hall's flat above the new start line. It was the perfect way to go motor racing. The ladies could freshen up, there were wonderful things to eat and absolutely fearsome gin and tonics. As I watched the race, which had got underway before I arrived, one car was either very badly last, or an awfully long way in the lead. I borrowed Eddie's binoculars and watched. It was a certain J.Y. Stewart. He was very smooth and obviously in a class of his own.

On my way back to our garage, the Auto Palace at Beausoleil, and now replaced by a tower block, Dunlop gave me a written and carefully worded disclaimer of responsibility for the brakes. They argued they had no experience whatever of our proposed installation; they believed the duties were much more arduous than the older and slower 2.5 litres, and they had no experience of the discs, or the materials from which they were made. It was all very true, but I believed that unless we did something we might as well not compete as we knew we would be out after a few laps with brake failure. As I continued on my pensive way I met David Phipps, a photographer and journalist, who said he thought we would win tomorrow. 'You have your brake problems licked. Everyone else will be deep into it.' I forbore asking him how he knew.

I had been summoned to have dinner with Mr and Mrs Stanley, who also had been given Dunlop's letter. Some other members of the Owen family, who had come to watch were also very concerned by the furore. I said it was my responsibility; that I had consulted the drivers who knew the risks; and that I was paid to win.

I had reorganized the pre-race checks. Amongst other things, when the engine was still warm we washed it down with petrol, then soapy water and ran the engine with the car on a lift to check for leaks. In view of our experiences the previous year we had fitted a bird-bath type extra oil tank in the scuttle above the driver's legs. We debated whether to fit the extra fuel tank under the driver's knees, because we were still using 2-valve engines due to the shortcomings of the Weslake 4-valve. The exhaust pipes passed through the boxes intended for the side fuel tanks, but we decided we had enough fuel without the knee tanks.

Before the start I had my usual chat with Vittorio Jano. He was very interested in, and curious about, the ventilated discs. He told me Ferrari had tried a 4-bearing crankshaft in the flat-12, but it had broken. Graham made a brilliant start; so did Richie. *Autosport* had a wonderful picture of Graham trying to get between Clark and Brabham, but they shut the gate on him. They all three touched. Clark was so determined to do his usual disappearing act that he hit a bollard at the Gasworks hairpin on one of his opening laps. His rear roll bar eventually came adrift. It should not have mattered much — we hardly carried any rear roll bar at Monte Carlo and Lotus were very much the same. Clark led with Gurney second; Graham third; Brabham fourth; Richie fifth. By half distance the first three were nose to tail, then Graham took the lead. He said afterwards he took them down the hill from the Casino towards the Mirabeau, where they least expected him, using his superior brakes.

By lap 80 Graham was well in the lead and we were pushing Richie to overtake Clark, which he did, then the Lotus ran out of oil. Graham's engine missed once or twice. He thought he was out of fuel and took it very easily, as he was able to do since he was a lap ahead of Richie, who was three laps in front of Arundel in the second Lotus. Clark, whose engine had failed, was still classified fifth. Graham also had the fastest lap. There were still two gallons of fuel left, plenty of oil and the brakes were only half worn. The first people to congratulate me were the Dunlop brake technicians armed with a large bottle of champagne. Richie did well to finish; he was still in some pain from the Aintree crash. We had the usual problem at the

Prize Giving Banquet, hosted by Prince Rainier in the Hotel de Paris — dinner jackets were required. We had been caught out in 1963, and this time Graham and I discussed whether to pack them. Graham said it would be asking for trouble. We were finally admitted, and later we retired to the Tip Top, where Graham entertained us until dawn.

The distractions then set in with a vengeance. John Crosthwaite and I went to Indianapolis via Detroit — meetings morning, noon and night. Some of my time at Indianapolis's gasoline alley was spent trying to snatch a photograph of Tony Rolt (always an immaculate dresser) in STP overalls, which looked like over-sized pyjamas covered with enormous pink STP logos.

He was equally determined not to be photographed. I was intrigued by the one-car-on-the-track-at-a-time to qualify, and the way the order was determined. The crew chief would take his tool box and park it at the track entrance, rather like the poolside procedure on European package holidays.

I had to leave before it was all over to get ready for Zandvoort, which turned out to be a disaster. The cars went well in practice — little to choose between Graham and Clark. The old cars had been sold, 5782 and 5783 had gone to Mimo Dei's Scuderia Centro Sud, who in turn had sold 5781, 'Old Faithful' to Trintignant. Tony Maggs crashed 5782 in practice, and Mimo wanted us to mend it. I had quite a battle to convince him that we could not with the resources we had at Zandvoort, and we would not do so anyway. Although full of charm, Mimo was as sharp as a needle.

In the race the electric fuel pumps overheated. They were mounted horizontally in the cockpit under the driver's knees, with an air duct to cool them. We reasoned that as they were so close to the driver, the driver would tell us about it if they got warm. But it did not work like that. We could hear them burping round the back of the circuit, so we brought them in and threw a bucket of water into the cockpit which cooled them down for a short time. Richie stopped out on the circuit. Graham finished fourth, Richie eleventh. Baghetti in 5783 was tenth. We could not understand why we had overheating fuel pumps at Zandvoort, when we had no trouble at Monaco. If we were going to get it anywhere, Monaco was the place. We mounted the pump vertically on Lucas's advice, with a larger air blast and a small fuel cooler in the return line. We also put a double skin with an air-draught between the fuel tanks and the engine.

The next distraction was the 4-wheel-drive car. We intended to run it in the British GP at Brands Hatch, to be driven by Dickie Attwood. He had shown promise in the other formulae and did well at Goodwood in one of our older cars, standing in for Richie. There were business ties between his family firm and Rubery Owen. Richie did most of the initial testing at Snetterton with 2613 as a reference car. We found we were about 8 mph down on maximum speed, but no quicker around the hairpins. There were a number of minor teething troubles — nothing serious — but plenty of questions needing answers, such as tyre sizes and brake ratios. It was intriguing that Graham, who had been the instigator of us getting into 4-wheel-drive, had completely lost interest.

The castings for our own 2-valve heads with central exhaust ports and inlets between the cam boxes had arrived, and Les had started to machine them. We only had conventional machine tools and, working two shifts, it was going to be a month before we had an engine set. We were building a new and better-shaped car, based on more wool tufting and sessions in the MIRA wind tunnel.

After another quick trip to Detroit I arrived at Spa confused and jet lagged. I was becoming worried about Richie — he seemed to be losing his enthusiasm. The tiger in him that so attracted me when he was chasing Moss at Monte Carlo in 1961 had nearly gone. The drivers nearly always seemed to confide in Pam, and she said he was worried about his wife, a devout Roman Catholic, and that they were arguing over religion and their son's upbringing. Pam suggested that Richie brought Jackie and Brett over for the summer. She would look after Brett, and Jackie could go to races with Richie.

It seemed to work. Jackie joined him at Spa for the Belgian GP where he went well in first practice, but the old problems appeared in the race. The front row was Graham sandwiched between the two Brabhams. Clark had trouble and was on the second row. Gurney led with Graham, Clark and McLaren fighting for second place. Graham had the hardest suspension setting we could get. Clark would overtake Graham around the hairpin at La Source, Graham would get him at Eau Rouge at the bottom of the dip and draw away up the hill. Just what you would expect, hard versus soft suspension. Graham said afterwards he could go round the long 150 mph corner at Burnenville on the outside of the Lotus; no trouble at all. With two laps to go, it was Gurney, Graham, McLaren and Clark; then Gurney came in for fuel, Clark for water, and on the last lap Graham was well out in front. The first car that came in sight was McLaren coasting to the line with a dead engine, then Richie a lap behind. Suddenly Clark appeared going well and passed McLaren on the line. Graham had stopped at the beginning of the uphill stretch, apparently out of fuel like McLaren. Clark ran out a mile beyond the line. When we got Graham's car back to the garage we found there were still three gallons in the knee tank. The Bendix electric fuel pump which should have transferred the fuel from the knee to the main tank had failed, so had Gurney's. McLaren's battery was flat. Richie was fourth, a lap behind, no troubles to report.

I was able to draw breath before the French GP at Rouen. The new car and its cylinder heads were making good progress, and Mike Hall had joined us to act as John Crosthwaite's counterpart on the engine side. There were now 11 customers' engines in circulation. We started to design a 997 cc F2 engine, effectively half a V8. I gave design responsibility for this to Alec Osborn as I was saving Geoff Johnson for the new F1 engine. We raced Stokey's new gearbox, Type 72, at Spa — no problems. It had met all its targets.

I have never managed to explain to my own satisfaction how there came to be such a wealth of engineering talent in Bourne, a small market town on the edge of the Lincolnshire Fens. It was not the place where you would expect to find a group of locally born, world-beating racing car designers. When, many years later, the government gave a reception at Lancaster House for British motor racing, I managed to find convincing reasons for Mrs Thatcher as to why most racing cars were built in England and why British mechanics were the best in the business, but why Bourne produced such talent still has me baffled. Geoff Johnson left soon after I did, for a senior position at Austin Morris, then Cosworth and is now back at Lotus.

Alec Osborn is a senior engineer at Perkins diesel and Alec Stokes spends his retirement writing textbooks. John Crosthwaite and Mike Hall were imported, like me. John went on to be Technical Director of Reliant, then Hyundai and was last heard of producing 4-wheel-drive recreational vehicles in the Seychelles. Mike Hall retired as a Director of Cosworth. Unfortunately we all lived in the era before engineers' salaries followed the drivers' upwards.

Rouen 1964 puzzled me — it still does. The cars had suited the circuit in 1962, yet in 1964 they were just as powerful and handled as well, relative to the opposition, but we had a struggle to get into the third and fourth rows. We were well down at half distance when Graham lost more ground with a spin; Clark was leading chased by the two Brabhams and Arundel in the second Lotus. Finally, Graham decided it was all in his mind and fought his way into second place, with Richie fifth ahead of McLaren.

I had spent the Friday evening aboard a boat on the Seine trying to talk Jackie Stewart into joining BRM. Colin Chapman was also on his track. BRM's cause, as far as Jackie was concerned, was not helped when I introduced him to RM next day, as drivers contracts were his responsibility. He did not even know who Jackie was! Fortunately Mrs Stanley did.

Things improved a little for the British GP at Brands Hatch; somehow a circuit that has never inspired me. Silverstone was lacking in ambience and facilities but it had some sort of aura. Monza was fraught with problems, facilities were poor, the police and officials nearly as much of a problem as Lotus or Brabham, yet there was some sort of brooding magnificence about the place. But Brands did nothing for me. Maybe it was the difficult journey from Bourne. This year there was plenty of excitement: 100 bottles of champagne for the fastest lap of first practice, and the beginning of the topless fashion for ladies. Gurney, virtually a teetotaller, won the champagne. The front row was Clark, 1 min 38.1 sec, Graham 1 min 38.3 sec and Gurney 1 min 38.4 sec. Richie was on the fourth row behind several customers. Attwood, in the 4-wheel-drive car, at 1 min 45.2 sec was not fast enough to qualify.

Clark led, challenged by Gurney and with Graham third. Richie was mixed up in a backmarkers' shunting match, without damage. Gurney's ignition box went up in smoke, several people put oil down and Graham closed right up on Clark. He said afterwards that he could have passed him quite easily as, with the oil down, his car handled very much better than the Lotus. What he could not explain to me was why he did not pass Clark and build up a lead. I suspect Graham felt he was better at applying pressure than taking it. Clark gained a little while picking his way through the backmarkers, then the track cleaned up, reducing some of Graham's advantage. They went at it harder and faster taking turns to break the lap record. Clark eventually won by 2.8 seconds. If Graham had passed him when he had the chance, when the road was oily, he might have kept the lead, which might have given him the Championship. Richie was eighth, saying there was no feature he could pinpoint to explain why he was three laps down. We made Jackie an offer, which he said he would think over.

I had another trip to Detroit before the Nürburgring, and we started to build the first centre-exhaust engine. Port flows were disappointing, but we needed the car. Everyone was curious to see how Honda performed. I thought they were very brave starting at the Nürburgring with Ronnie Bucknum an American driver who had never driven in Europe. On my return from Detroit I had more distractions. Jim Hall of Chaparal asked if we could fit Lucas injection to one of his big GM V8s, and Peter Spear and I had a meeting with Vauxhall to discuss building a front-wheel-drive prototype for them.

At Nürburgring we had trouble, both drivers missing gears and breaking tappets. Two engines to change and we were not even in the front row, which consisted of the two Ferraris, plus Clark and Gurney. In the race the usual bunch started fighting, Surtees leading Clark, Gurney and Graham. Richie stopped, complaining of a misfire, so we changed his ignition box and plugs. By half distance Clark was out with a broken valve, and Gurney with overheating. Graham's engine was cutting out over the bumps. After the race we found one of the wires from the ignition trigger (which replaces the contact breaker, triggering the ignition) was broken, only held in place by the insulation, which explained the cutting out. Surtees won, Graham was second, Bandini in the other Ferrari third, Richie seventh, behind both the old Centro Sud BRMs. To our surprise, Graham was now leading the World Championship by two points.

I organized a test session at Snetterton to try to find out what it was that Brabhams had that we had not, and to try to put some spark back into Richie. We already knew what Lotus had — a Scotsman called Clark — but the Brabhams had outboard suspension, space-frames and none of the latest modern gimmicks. As I arrived, Graham was going round having set his mirrors so he could watch his rear suspension. After two laps, the inevitable happened and he spun off at Coram, damaging the car, but he said he was all right. I said that until he let Jim Russell take him to Norwich Hospital, I would not retrieve the car or repair it. After quite a row he duly went, and returned several hours later wearing a neck brace, but highly amused. After having an X-ray, the doctor appeared and asked him: 'Mr Hill, when did you first break your neck?' They had found traces of a fracture several years old! I drove him home to Bourne in his Jaguar, to stay the night, but eventually he decided he would drive himself home to Mill Hill. He assured me he would be fit for the Austrian GP.

The airfield circuit at Zeltweg for the new addition to the calendar, the Austrian GP, was dreadfully bumpy and, in practice, Richie had a front wheel break due to a defective casting — which did nothing for his morale. Several cars had suspension failures. Graham, despite his inflatable rubber collar, was on pole, completely destroying my assessment that he was slow to learn a new circuit. Richie managed to put his act together and was only half-a-second slower. Graham made a very bad start, and Clark missed a gear. However, together they stormed through the field, but not for long. Graham's distributor rotor broke again, Clark had a half-shaft rubber doughnut failure, as did the other works Lotus. Gurney's suspension broke, and so did that of Surtees. It really became a case of the ten green bottles hanging on the wall. At half-distance Bandini was leading, with Richie second 17 seconds adrift. Richie pulled some back, but not enough and Bandini won by 5.8 seconds. It helped BRM's Championship position, but left the drivers with Graham at 32 and Clark at 30 points. It would have been 35 and 27 if Graham had taken his opportunity at Brands.

After practice I had a long debate with Rob Walker and Gregor Grant as to who of the three of us had been in motor racing longest. We were staying at a rather bleak motel with all the other teams except Ferrari. The local wine, at 37p a bottle, probably prolonged the discussion. We finally agreed it was Rob, then me, with Gregor third.

After the race we went to a very formal Prize Giving and then back to the motel. There seemed to be no night life, but it was much too noisy to go to bed. Two young Scottish Boy Scouts in kilts appeared, asking for the autographs of their fellow Scots. That was the trigger. Jimmy and Innes donned their kilts and danced a Scottish reel on the billiard table, which had a light plywood cover. Some of the audience felt that the dancers were not getting their knees up high enough, so cactus plants were used to get the desired results. The cover collapsed, then the table, and the place was generally wrecked.

Next morning I was up early to drive the 100 miles to Vienna airport. I apologized to the landlord and offered to pay for my share of the damage, which he computed to be £5. At the airport everyone kept pressing £5 on me, saying that the motel owner had told them I had paid for the damage, and here was their share. What with this and the backwash of the attention lavished by the cabin staff during the flight home on Laurie Hands (of Champion Plugs), who sat next to me with his arm in a sling. I arrived at Heathrow somewhat confused.

The new engine gave no trouble. It had already been up to 9000 rpm, and the heads had been removed for a check — no problems. Power was about the same as a standard engine. Then consternation. Above 10,000 rpm the power fell off badly so that by 10,750 rpm we were 4 per cent down. Nothing we tried improved it. The engine politely responded to mixture and timing but not in the right direction. We rushed through some venturi valve seats for the second set of heads, in case Harry Weslake was right and I had destroyed the port induced turbulence. From our previous work there was no such thing, so how could I destroy it? We put the first engine into the new, slimmer car, 2615. There were no problems, we were well into our right-first-time mode and sent it to Monza for a day's testing before official practice. The second engine was a little better on the test-bed but not as much as I had hoped. With Pam, I rendezvoused at Basle airport with Mike Hall, who had brought the checked-over engine as his luggage. We had a very pleasant run in my Rover through the Alps to Monza.

Next day we were in the thick of it, but I postponed telling Graham that the engine we had been waiting for all season was down on power. We now had the Championships to worry about. When he came in after his first run with a time of 1 min 38.6 sec, against Clark's last year's lap record of 1 min 38.5 sec, he pulled my sleeve and whispered: 'It doesn't half go.' My confusion can be imagined. Obviously the aerodynamic improvements we had striven for worked. Then we were told that the race was to be shortened from the published 500 km (310 miles) to 450 km (280 miles). All our efforts to gain enough fuel capacity and a simple fuel system were no longer necessary.

Richie had his wife and son with him, and he was on a circuit he liked. We had already done a deal with Jackie Stewart, apparently under Colin Chapman's nose, so now we had to determine Richie's future. There was much slip-streaming in practice. Bucknum, in the Honda, did 1 min 40.4

sec, as did Richie, a fourth-row time. We put the second engine in Graham's car on Friday night. It poured with rain on Saturday and only Gurney and Clark broke two minutes, and then only just. Race day was dull and overcast. When the flag fell Graham was left on the line — the clutch withdrawal race had seized in the out position. He did not actually cross the line, but the Italians paid the start money anyway.

Surtees led Gurney, Clark and McLaren with a colossal slip-streaming battle behind them, including the Honda and Baghetti in Centro Sud's old BRM. Clark broke a piston, while Richie got the better of the second mob, but towing Bandini with him. Graham, who had been rather gloomy at the back of the pit, perked up when Clark retired, as this left him still in the lead for the Championship. Then Gurney blew up, leaving Surtees with a secure lead from McLaren, with Richie and Bandini fighting for third place. Richie got the drop on him and was behind coming out of the Parabolica, which gives you the advantage in a slip-streaming rush for the line, providing you do not do it too soon. This was the old Richie but, when he made his move, Bandini turned into him. It would have got Bandini disqualified in England. They were all over the wide road at Monza, and it had to be decided by a photograph, but eventually Richie was classified fourth, Bandini third, and Surtees was now in the Championship hunt. Mike Hall flew home with a formidable job list, while Pam and I drove to Venice for three days holiday.

When we got back, the hunt for the missing power was well underway. Skimming the heads to raise the compression ratio — on the low side at 10.8:1 — produced more power than we expected, which should have given me a clue. We had previously found that going from 10.5:1 to 11.0:1 compression ratio was worth about 2 per cent in power, providing nothing else was changed. But this time we had gained 4 per cent — why? We had recovered most of the loss between this head and a side port — it was a great relief — but I would have liked to know the reason. We now had a third engine with central exhausts. Should we convert Richie's car for the US and Mexican GPs?

I had long been obsessed by chassis stiffness as the foundation for good handling. The stiffest component in the car was the engine. Lancia had shown us the way in 1954 with their D50. Earlier in the year we had run an engine on the test-bed bolted down solidly at the front, and supported — but free to rotate — at the rear. A long arm applied torque to twist the engine. We held the engine at peak torque for long periods, while we applied and re-applied a twisting moment of up to 2500 lb ft (344 kg/m). The dynamometer needle did not waver. The same at full power; no change at all.

One of the features of car 2615 and onwards was that the engine imparted stiffness to the structure. The crankcase was bolted solidly front and rear to the two legs of the monocoque. The blanking plugs between the cylinder head and the rocker covers, through which we bored the cam shafts, were replaced by double eccentrics (to cope with dimensional variations) with a split collet like a Merlin aero-engine mounting. We bolted the cylinder head through these to the front bulkhead and, at the rear end, to the hoop carrying the spring-damper units and top wishbone. It made a dramatic increase in stiffness from just under 6000 lb ft (826 kg/m) per degree to 8000 and, although a bit fiddley, never gave any trouble, either through oil leaks or head joints.

It meant that although we could fit a centre-exhaust engine into an old car, we could not use it to stiffen the monocoque as it did not have the pick-up points. We could not, of course, put a side port engine into the new cars. There were four gallons of fuel where the exhaust would have emerged. We finally decided to put the engine into Richie's car to learn as much as we could, the centre-exhaust layout owed much to him, so he was entitled to the benefit.

The Lotus 23 had recently electrified small sports car racing, particularly with Clark's performance at the Nürburgring. Brabham had made a similar car. Richie found an American backer who bought one, for which they wanted us to stretch a BRM V8, so Geoff Johnson came up with an 1880 cc version, which gave no trouble on the test-bed. Geoff and Mike Hall did a very good job. In the car there was an initial problem; performance with its 240 hp BRM engine was down on similar cars with 190 hp Climaxes. In fact the engine would only just run, and it appeared much too rich. I told Richie to try it with the cowling removed. This did the trick; there was something wrong with the engine air intake. It became a very good car, but it was taken to America and we lost track of it.

I also had a long talk with Richie about his future. He realized he had lost his edge, but he was still an invaluable development driver. We got valuable information from him, such as Graham blowing smoke rings! He had helped us with the Rover BRM and gearboxes; but I had to win races. Finally Richie talked to Honda, RM and I talked to Nakamura and it was agreed that we would release Richie to Honda where he was invaluable and won their first race a year later.

Between Monza and Watkins Glen, Goodyear Tyres asked us if we would send a car to Riverside California after the Mexican GP to test tyres for them. They would pay $25 per mile and hoped for 1000 miles testing from us. They would pay all travel and hotel expenses from Mexico City to Riverside and back to London. They would also 'take care' of our team drivers. I liked Riverside, 1000 miles would take a week, and we might well learn something. I said I would need to consult Graham and Richie. No problem, they said, they had already done that — so I was sold. We would use side port engines so as not to interfere with our development programme.

At the Glen we seemed to have difficulty getting a quick time; everyone was very friendly and relaxed as usual. Ferrari were running their cars painted blue and white, and Bandini had the flat twelve. We improved on the second day, Graham being third fastest, 1 min 12.92 sec to Clark's pole time of 1 min 12.65 sec and Surtees's 1 min 12.78 sec. Richie was on the seventh row. Graham was extremely relaxed on race day. I had to send someone to fetch him from the pit to his car waiting on the start line, he was so engrossed in a paperback! But within a few laps the old gang were at it — Surtees, Clark, Gurney and Graham fighting for the lead. On lap 30 it was Clark, Graham, Surtees, Gurney; then Graham got by Clark who dropped back, stopped, and then took over Spence's car, but that too had injection problems. Surtees led for a few laps, but by half-distance Graham was comfortably in the lead and gradually drew some 30 seconds ahead. Siffert in a Brabham BRM was third and Richie fourth. Trevor Taylor in a BRP BRM was sixth. We thus had four BRM engines in the first six in three different cars which particularly pleased Sir Alfred. This result gave Graham a slightly better hold on the Championship — 39 points to Surtees's 34 and Clark's 30. Ferrari led the Manufacturers Championship with 43 points to our 42. The 1964 scoring system ruled that only the six best results counted, so Graham had to finish in the first three in Mexico.

The cars went to Mexico by road from Watkins Glen. It cost less to leave the mechanics in America than to fly them home for a week, as they could not work on the cars, so they spent the week in Acapulco. Graham and I had a long session in Lord Snowdon's studio being photographed for a Shell advertisement to exploit the Championships. I held up a blank signal board, so that Shell could paint in the race results. We both wore Mexican sombreros! I suggested to Graham that his relaxed attitude at Watkins Glen meant he knew he had the edge on the opposition. He said yes, but he did not want to give the game away. I said I would not have told anyone.

I flew out to Mexico by Air France via New Orleans, arriving late at night. The altitude seemed to hurt us and Ferraris more than the Climaxes, indicating that their engines were more efficient mechanically than ours and did not waste as much power in internal friction and pumping losses. Gurney and Clark had the front row, the Ferraris the second row, Graham and Spence, in the second Lotus, the third row, and Richie was on the sixth. The start was delayed — the usual dog on the course. Clark made a lightning start, but the strap of Graham's goggles broke, which cost him several places. By quarter distance Clark was leading comfortably, Graham was third, Bandini fourth and Surtees sixth, which was fine for the Championship, but on lap 31 Bandini ran into the back of Graham's car going into the long curve at the back of the pits and pushed him off. Brabham, in fifth place, who saw it all, said overtaking at this part of the circuit was totally out of the question. Jack's comments were confirmed by the experienced Bernard Cahier and the TV films. Graham limped into the pits, with the rather vulnerable exhaust tail pipes bent down around the gearbox. Willy levered them up with a jack handle. The other damage seemed to be cosmetic, so we sent him out again in 13th place. It looked as if the Championship had gone to Clark who was pulling away from Gurney and Bandini, with Surtees now fourth. Graham worked up to 10th but the accident had damaged the throttle-cross shaft, which eventually broke and that put him out of the race and the Championship. It looked as if Clark and Lotus were 1964 World Champions. Graham and I agreed that it was no good lodging a protest, it would not change anything and it was not the way we liked to go racing.

Then, consternation in the Lotus pit, a negative sign from Clark with two laps to go. He was creeping round with no oil pressure and no oil either. He had seen a trail of oil going into a corner and had taken a different line next time around to avoid it, but to his horror the oil trail had taken his new line so he knew who was putting the oil down. This let Gurney into the lead, Bandini second and Surtees third which put us back in the Championship lead. Colin had just come up to congratulate me when I pointed to the corner. The entire Ferrari pit staff was in the road, blocking Bandini's way to force him to let his team-mate Surtees into second place and of course, the Championship. It looked as if he was going to ignore them but he finally got the message, just in time. No one took much notice of Gurney winning in all this. Richie was eighth, Clark classified fifth and Graham 11th.

Although Graham had 41 points to Surtees's 40, he was only allowed to count 39 of them under the marking system, which gave Surtees the Championship. We had 51 points in the Manufacturers Championship but could only count 42, while Ferrari had 49 and could count 45 of them, so the Shell advertisement was wasted.

Mauro Forghieri, Ferrari's Chief Engineer came to commiserate and apologize. We were absolutely besieged by the Press. I said I did not think Bandini did it on purpose, he was just a bit stupid. All I wanted to do was to forget about it and prepare for 1965. Nearly all the journalists pointed to his tactics against Richie at Monza, which could have caused a major crash. On my way up to my room in the hotel, who should I share the elevator with but Bandini, who was very apologetic and said we had been good to him when he drove the Centro Sud BRM; the last thing he wanted to do was to deprive us of the Championship. There were numerous phone calls to and from England; including Sir Alfred, and Mr and Mrs Stanley, who were unable to come to Mexico. They all agreed it was best to forget it, even though according to the regulations we had until 9 p.m. to lodge a protest but, as I said, what difference will it make? At the Prize Giving the mechanics plied me with whisky as its effect of making me quarrelsome was well-known!

Next day I flew to Detroit, via Chicago, to talk gas turbine cars for Le Mans with Chrysler. The plan was to build a prototype powered by a fuel-injected hemi, the second car would have a 550 hp regenerative turbine, hopefully for the 1966 race. We sketched layouts, fuel tanks under the doors, a centre box to stiffen the car and contain the air intake to the mid-mounted turbine. After a 24-hour-day we had enough for me to prepare a plan, from which Peter Spear would quote. I never knew how much Chrysler were charged or for what.

On Thursday I flew from the old Detroit airport at Willow Run to Los Angeles and drove to Riverside, where I found a mad hatter's tea party. The cars, both ours and Brabham's in the Shelby Cobra transporter were stuck at Laredo, Texas on the Mexican border because of paperwork problems. The mechanics were enjoying the sun and the pool at the Mission Inn, Graham was staying with film director John Frankenheimer, who was planning his film *Grand Prix*. Richie was at home with his family, so I did not have much support when I complained to the Goodyear people. They told me to enjoy myself; there was no chance of the cars arriving before Monday. I flew a friend's Bellanca with 'tail feathers' (three fins) to San Diego and spent the weekend sailing his boat.

On Monday the cars had arrived and we got to work. I was tremendously impressed by Goodyear's organization. They must have had over 50 combinations of tread and compound to try. They separated us from Brabham, so we could not compare opinions, and provided lavish trackside meals. Frankenheimer had lent Graham his Ferrari in which we took turns to drive around the circuit. Joe Vittone had a VW-based dune buggy, and he took me out into the Mojave desert. I was amazed it did not turn over. I went to the Champion spark plug engine test facility at Long Beach and became involved with Rolls-Royce Merlin engines in racing powerboats.

Goodyear even set up an irrigation system to simulate a wet track in the middle of the desert. We passed the 1000-mile mark when the rate changed to $27 per mile. Finally the second engine began to get tired at 1760 miles, so we called a halt. Goodyear then made a very attractive offer for us to race on their tyres in 1965, which I recommended to Sir Alfred who had the final word. Next day was the Presidential Election. I stayed overnight at Los Angeles airport, before flying home with Graham.

Charles Goodacre, whom I had known from his days driving 750 cc blown Austins before the war, was now a well-respected consultant. He sold me the idea of long connecting rods to reduce side thrust and he showered me with pages of calculations, with which none of us, Geoff, Mike or Alec Osborn, could find fault, so Alec's F2 engine was given connecting rods 0.5 inches longer (12.2 mm) than the V8, which cost us much money and performance both in the F2 and the two-valve H16. The theory was that reducing piston side loads released some 4 per cent more power. What none of us appreciated at the time, was the effect of rod length relative to stroke on the kinematics of piston acceleration and the combustion process. This knowledge made a lot of money for Lotus Engineering in later years, so it really was an 'ill wind' situation.

Back in England Champion invited all the teams to a lavish lunch at The Savoy and proposed that we should participate in London's Lord Mayor's Show. Arrangements were made for the F1 cars to be driven through the City of London. We had two cars; one carried on a lorry in the procession and the other one driven in advance of the main procession by Graham. It was an intensely cold day and we could not get Graham's engine rich enough to start. Willy disconnected the throttle mechanism so he could over-ride the injection control, and sat astride the car facing backwards, while I steered and Len Reedman towed us with my Rover. Team Lotus had exactly the same problem in 1978 when they were driving their cars through the streets of Norwich to celebrate their Championship. While we were waiting to start driving the cars through the streets, Graham complained to the incredibly senior policeman in charge that he was cold. The policeman knocked at the door of a pub. The Landlord opened up and served brandy all round! I never saw any money change hands.

Champion had arranged for gangways to be set up from the lorries carrying the static cars into the window of a hotel in a side street off the Strand. This was to enable us to go in, warm up and have lunch while the Lord Mayor was being sworn-in at the Law Courts. We were very sympathetic towards the Connolly Leather girls wearing minute leather bikinis. It really was incredibly cold. There was a reception in the Guildhall crypt and we all agreed that it was a most worthwhile event and should be added to the racing calendar, when we would all compete for no start money!

During the original Savoy lunch I found myself next to Colin Chapman whilst visiting the toilets. 'The very man,' he said. 'How would you like to build all our racing twin-cam engines?' In 1965 we produced four versions, a fuel-injected dry-sump, giving 185 hp and that was never out of gasket trouble for long; a 165 hp wet-sump, carburettor racing engine, a 140 hp engine, the basis of the SE version and a 125 hp, which eventually became the 1971 Lotus 'Big Valve'.

Spear had got us into the front-wheel drive Vauxhall prototype, and we were making 100 stick-shift 4-speed racing gearboxes for Chrysler, the

latest American trick 'four on the floor'. So it was hard to find any time for
F1 and the Championships. I never knew what the external projects earned
but, from the attitude of the Budget Committee, it must have gone some
way towards the £90,000 per year the F1 programme cost. Fortunately we
did not have to pay Weslake — just the cost of building our own cars and
engines, paying the drivers and staff and going to races. 1963 was about
£10,000 less than 1962 as we only made two new cars and three new
engines, and our earnings as World Champions on the Frankfurt scale had
increased considerably. 1964 was back to 1962 costs, but I anticipated 1965
would be much less. No new engines, just some new heads and a new car,
2616, for Jackie Stewart.

Dean Delamont, Manager of the RAC Competition Department managed
to get the interested parties — Brabham, BRM, Cooper and Lotus as well as
Coventry Climax — invited to the FIA deliberations on the future of F1,
due to change in 1966. This was a significant policy change by the FIA to
consult the people who ran the teams and built the cars before making a
decision. Dean warned us that it would be a total waste of time to keep on
saying we wanted things to stay as they were. F1 was the ultimate form of
motor racing. The big 7-litre Can-Am sports cars were breaking F1 lap
records by large margins and we had to face, as an absolute fact, that engine
sizes were going to increase. He hammered this into us at meetings in
England and again before we met the FIA.

We discussed how to get there, for despite the racing rivalry we were all
good friends and were in close communication with one another, including
Wally Hassan of Coventry Climax. The first plan was to travel out in the
Lotus Twin Comanche from Panshanger, but Cooper and Brabham said they
would have to drive past Heathrow to get there. It was late November and
likely to be foggy, so we might as well go commercial. We decided to go on
the 10 a.m. BEA flight, and over lunch have a final get-together with Dean
who was already in Paris and Wally who wisely kept clear of our travel
adventures. When the flight was called I was the only one who had checked
in. Jack Brabham arrived soon after, Colin Chapman at the last minute, and
Cooper who had the shortest distance to travel to Heathrow missed the
flight altogether!

Over lunch we confirmed our agreement that if we could not stay with
the 1.5 litre formula, what we would like would be two litres. The BRM
engine and the Climax would stretch. All Climax had to do was to put the
1962 long-stroke crank in the 1964 short-stroke engine. BRM already had
a 1880 cc engine. These engines would fit the existing cars and we were
quite sure that the Ferrari 12-cylinder would stretch. The question was
how to sell it to the FIA. We agreed that whatever we asked for the FIA
would reduce. It would be a waste of time asking for 2.5 litres, as we had
just had such a Formula. Someone said let's ask for three litres, they will
cut that down as they always do, they cannot make it 2.5 so they will give
us two litres. We all agreed the tactics and that Colin should do the
talking.

We sat around for ages waiting to be invited into the meeting. There was
a long rambling introduction, then the FIA President asked: 'What would
you gentlemen like?' Colin said, 'Three litres.' the President looked round
his colleagues, nodded and said. 'Done, thank you for your time
gentlemen.' That was that. We filed out, absolutely thunderstruck. Dean

went back into the meeting. Wally said: 'You've done it now, I don't think I can get the funds for a 3 litre.'

After a slight delay because of fog, we all sat together in the back of a BEA Vanguard playing liar dice. The stakes included the Cooper factory, which Colin Chapman eventually won. We then got serious and said we ought to work together more often. Colin had a big go at me over Monte Carlo qualification, as I felt — so did Sir Alfred — that if we could not qualify at Monte Carlo, we had no right to even try to compete. This was a sore point between us. Colin took the line that you never knew when you would have a major problem or a shunt, followed by a wet practice and you might not make the race. He argued that if we all stuck together we could eliminate a lot of the stupidities of the FIA; reduce our costs and increase our earnings. We should invite Ferrari to join in, and we could all contribute towards the cost of a secretary and call ourselves the Formula One Constructors Association — which is how and when FOCA was born.

We were diverted to Manchester because of the fog, so we hired a Ford Consul which Colin drove. When we reached the Newport Pagnell service station in the middle of the night we went in for soup and coffee where members of the local motor club, on the way home from their annual dinner dance, were surprised to see the four of us sitting together, and we were asked for autographs. I eventually got home just as Lesley, my middle daughter, whose birthday it was, was opening the front door to the postman to receive her birthday cards. This fixes the date of the formation of FOCA, the 27 November 1964, and the first secretary was Andrew Ferguson. Ferrari said it was his policy not to join Trade Associations, but please keep him informed. The first non-founder member was Ken Tyrrell. It worked well and was effective, but really took off when Bernie Ecclestone, having bought Brabham, became their representative. Colin Chapman said he was always cast as the villain, so let someone else have the flak for a change. Bernie became FOCA's spokesman and negotiator at the time sponsorship was coming into the sport, and FOCA grew to its present position under Bernie's leadership.

Jim Fielding told me Heanan and Froude had built a version of their gas turbine dynamometer which could run up to 14,000 rpm and handle 1000 hp, especially for Ferrari, known as a G490. It was basically mechanical, with no complicated electronics, but Ferrari did not like it. Jim offered it to BRM, free of charge for a year. If we liked it, then we paid them its value as a two-year-old machine. It took us about a month to find out how it worked, plus a lot of hard work from Willy and his crew, and with someone from Heanan's permanently on the road between Bourne and Worcester. We tried to run an engine up to 12,000 rpm and were dumbstruck when we found it did not generate enough power, even to turn the dynamometer with no load applied. From 205 hp at 10,750 rpm it dropped to 200 at 11,000 and it was down to 155 hp at 11,500. The air flow went on up, the heat to oil and heat to water fell off with the power. It was time for another call for help to Geoff Harrow of Shell, Thornton.

He confirmed what I should have realized from the effects of raising the compression ratio on the centre-exhaust 2-valve engine. Above 11,000 rpm the flame just could not keep up with the piston. He found more for us to worry about. The variation in power between one cylinder and another and between one cycle and another was as much as 6 per cent. He believed that these variations came from the fuel injection system. As usual the Lucas competition department said it was absolutely impossible. Eric Downing had by then retired. For a time we sank into complete confusion. Then I found most engines behaved like this.

# CHAPTER SIXTEEN

# 'Scots wae hae'

I HAD LONG discussions on the future with the designers and engineers: Willy, Cyril, Colin Atkin and Stan Hope, together with Les Bryden (who thought meetings were a waste of time and that I should just say what I wanted). I was growing more and more concerned by the distractions caused by external projects. I vividly recalled how, by extreme effort and attention to detail, we had managed to win at Monza in 1962. Now I had a really strong team with no weak links, I thought I had the basis whereby we could apply this attention to detail to every race, without me being so completely involved. Each car was in the charge of one mechanic; Alan Challis ('Dobbin') (now Chief Mechanic at Williams) looked after Graham's car; Jimmy Collins, Jackie Stewart's; Pete Bothamley looked after the spare; Denis Perkins gearboxes, and Willy engines at races. Cyril Atkins was Chief Mechanic, while Len Reedman drove and maintained the Leyland, being encouraged to treat it as his own, and he also looked after the spares. We developed a good system of sharing out my responsibilities throughout the factory, and it was agreed that we would go for total reliability. Rumour had it that the Climax 4-valve would give Lotus 210 hp, and the Ferrari 12 would have even more. John Crosthwaite and I agreed that the only advantage the Lotus had was slightly better traction out of slow corners, while on fast corners we were better, so John was to look at anti-squat and anti-dive which seemed to be the only difference between the two makes of car.

The season began early in the New Year with the South African GP at East London. Sir Alfred had ruled that we were to stay with Dunlop for tyres, but I had mixed feelings as I was very impressed with Goodyear, yet we had enjoyed a long and successful relationship with Dunlop.

It was Jackie Stewart's first race for us. He had done enough testing to encourage us and, as I found later, he listened intently and stored away everything I told him. Clark, Surtees and Brabham were on the front row, and Jackie was on the fifth row with a respectable time. We noticed that Spence, the Lotus No. 2 driver was developing and was nearly as quick as Clark when his car held together. Clark went into his usual lead followed by Spence, Surtees, Brabham and Graham. Someone dropped oil, and there was a light rain shower. Spence spun and Bandini nearly took Surtees off, which seemed to prove something. At the end of the race, Jackie, in sixth place, appeared to us to be jumping up and down in his cockpit. The Bendix fuel transfer pump had failed, just as it did at Spa last year. We had cut a big hole in the panelling above the rubber bag tank so that the driver could squeeze it and force fuel into the main tanks. Jackie remembered what I had told him, and this was what he was doing. His reward was his first world Championship point in his first race. Clark won by 29 seconds from Surtees who in turn was just two seconds ahead of Graham.

The Frankfurt scale provided money for the driver based on the number of points he had acquired in preceding races. As Jackie, starting in F1 had no points, I had guaranteed him a minimum payment, but I told him that I did not expect to have to pay him this for long.

When we got back to England John had his anti-squat schemes ready. We tried them at Silverstone and it seemed to work, but at Brands Hatch for the Race of the Champions, run as the best of two heats, with everyone running in both, all manner of strange things happened. Clark crashed, and both Brabhams and Graham had engine failures. The new boys came into their element: Spence won with Jackie second. We found anti-squat and anti-dive did not work when you had to mix it in racing conditions. It snowed again at Easter Goodwood. Clark gave the 4-valve Climax its first outing — Jackie had pole position with Graham and Clark alongside. Graham led for the first six laps and then lost power, while Jackie's electrics failed, and Clark won with Graham a very sick second with a broken tappet. We had been in tappet trouble before, Shell had rescued us by reheat-treating the tappets. We had a solution that made me rather nervous — chromium-plated steel tappets against a cast-iron camshaft. We had made a set and given them to Jackie for the race; they looked good, although the roller tracks were slightly pitted.

On the way back from a Silverstone test session I was mulling over the apparent need for a little more valve-to-piston clearance, which would cost us power. It looked as if the higher rpm we were now using was causing the valves to float and lag behind the camshafts. Geoff Johnson, now an expert on polydyne and polynomial cam forms, had come up with better camshafts and springs. We also had Geoff Harrow's report, which showed that the speed of combustion flame travel (rate of burn) in the centre exhaust port engine was slightly less than on the side port engines, and we knew the power tailed off badly over 11,000 rpm. The new steel tappet-iron camshaft combination looked as if, for the Daily Express Silverstone we would be able to safely run the engines up to 12,000 — but how to find more power up there?

Driving round the last corner on the A43 before Kettering, it all came to me — make a much smaller combustion chamber and take the tops off the pistons. As soon as I got back I collected Les Bryden and Geoff Johnson and put the idea to them. Slide rules and planimeters were nearly red hot, but by 10 p.m. Geoff had calculated that we could build up the combustion chambers by depositing weld metal and re-machining. The valves would remain in the same position, in a deep pocket with a big radius to prevent shrouding and interference with gas flow. We could then cut most of the dome from the top of the piston and reduce the hemispherical sides so we then had a 0.15 inch- (4 mm) wide squish deck all the way round the piston. It took us a little time to find the right profile of the cut-outs to avoid any gas flow losses from the shrouding. Hepworth and Grandage, our piston suppliers, had kittens about the proposed sections, but agreed that we dare run for a few minutes to prove the theory. They would make us some new pistons which were thicker all over, in about three weeks. Les, gloomy as always, started to machine another set of heads, in case the idea did not work and we had ruined an engine. Finally, when we got it all together, the engine seemed rather rough and down on power, but when we retarded the ignition away it went. Power increased all the way up to 11,000 rpm, and then gradually up to 11,500 when the power curve flattened out. We had obtained nearly all the data we needed, before Geoff Johnson reminded me that we had exceeded our self-imposed limit of five minutes at full throttle. When the engine was stripped, we found that the pistons had sunk visibly at the thin sections.

We managed to build two of these engines in time for the Daily Express Silverstone, geared to run to 11,500 rpm, and we permitted the drivers to use 12,000 on the run from Stowe to Club to save a gear change, if they were really racing. 'Try not to do it too often,' was my instruction. Clark and Gurney were at Indy, so we had Graham and Jackie sharing the front row with Surtees and Bandini. What time Clark would have done I cannot guess, but Graham managed 1 min 31.4 sec, Jackie 1 min 31.6 sec, Surtees 1 min 32.1 sec. Graham led away, with Brabham second and Jackie soon overtaking Surtees for third place. It was not long before Graham was out with a broken camshaft because of a badly pitted bearing track — we still had something to learn about the new materials. Then Jackie started to hang on to fifth gear between Stowe and Club. Everything held together, though, and he finally won, three seconds ahead of Surtees with Spence in third place. Jackie's first F1 win, although not a Championship race. The new combustion chamber worked and we had managed to prove it without risking Championship points.

I had a very pleasant Sunday at the Montagu Motor Museum, taking Pam, Brinkley, Charlie Davey and Jack Wyldes, the old ERA mechanics, to see Lisba, Princess Chula, hand over Prince Chula's old ERA 'Romulus' which Bira had given back to him, on loan to the museum. There were seven other ERAs in support. I was most impressed to see Lisba climb into 'Romulus' in a smart skirt and drive him at the head of the procession.

We had little time to take stock and sort ourselves out before Monte Carlo. Graham had won the first race at Snetterton with our new F2 engine, but we were in absolutely dreadful trouble with the OPUS ignition system. Jackie had also led the same race, until his ignition failed. We were really in desperate trouble. At one race meeting (Oulton Park) Jackie used seven ignition sets in practice and the race, and even then he did not finish. Clark and Gurney were still at Indianapolis as Colin Chapman had decided to miss Monaco and concentrate on Indy, which meant that Spence was out of a drive. (FOCA would not let that happen today.) I began to feel some pressure at this race, after a one-two for the last two years. We were expected to produce something special, particularly with the American Navy at Monte Carlo in force that year.

Graham was on pole with Brabham alongside him, while Jackie and Bandini were on the next row. Surtees and Attwood, in Tim Parnell's Lotus BRM, were on the third row, ahead of Denny Hulme standing in for Gurney in the second Brabham. I spent a long time briefing Jackie about keeping well back behind Graham, who I expected to jump into the lead. I went through the history of first-lap multiple shunts and the risks of following too close behind so that you did not develop your own cut-off points and line. I was therefore somewhat put out when the race began and Jackie went round glued to Graham's exhaust pipe in second place. There was much fist-shaking from me and signals to spread out. On lap 25 my worst fears were realized. Coming into the chicane Graham found the road full of Bob Anderson with a transmission failure, and all he could do was to take to the escape road. He could not find reverse, so he jumped out, pushed the car round and got back in again. Miracle of miracles, it restarted on the starter, and he rejoined the race 33 seconds down and absolutely livid. This was a sure way of getting the best out of Graham. Jackie then had a lap in the lead but, of course, as he had no line of his own, or cut off points, he spun coming out of San Devote, mounted the curb and badly damaged a rear wheel. It was the left one, so we could not see it from the pits; just as well — there was an enormous piece of the rim missing.

We were now fourth and fifth. Brabham was leading — but not for long — with Bandini following and Surtees close behind. We showed Graham how far behind the leader he was, then next time round the race order. Drivers did not have time to assimilate much from the Monaco pits. Ferrari seemed slow to spot Graham's charge, and he had Surtees in sight before they realized and speeded him up. Graham took him under braking at his favourite place, down to the Mirabeau. He had quite a job getting past Bandini, as he was very wary of him, but he managed to sell him a dummy and was back in the lead on lap 60. Surtees then speeded up but Bandini got in his way, so Graham was able to get well clear. He made two attempts to find fourth gear coming out of the Gasworks hairpin right at the end of the race, which frightened us silly. He said afterwards it was his own fault. Surtees ran out of fuel and the last lap was a procession. Jackie came third. We were horrified to see the size of the piece missing from his rim. Jackie said it did seem a little out of balance! I suggested that after winning three times in a row, we were entitled to keep the circuit, but I was gently reminded it had been done before. Both cars had plenty of oil and brake lining remaining, and between 1 and 1.5 gallons (6.7 litres) of fuel. I think it was Graham's finest drive in a BRM. He was equally polite and said it was our rapid response to the misfortune, recognizing he could still win, that fired him up. The car never gave him a moment's anxiety and he had hammered it!

It was then back to Detroit, followed by a major Weslake liaison meeting, plus Alistair Wadsworth of Shell. The agenda was the new engine for 1966. Weslake argued that it was for them to specify and design. They conceded I was allowed a say in the installation connections and layout of accessories. Flushed with the success of Monte Carlo I began to chuck my weight about. Eventually it was decided that Bourne would build a 2-valve H16 and Weslake a 4-valve V12. Arguing had taken five of the 17 months until the first 3 litre F1 race.

I became involved with the Rover BRM again. Rover had improved on last year's coupé. It had extremely good aerodynamics, but its regenerative engine still suffered badly from throttle lag. It was more economical, though. The screen wiper blades blew off the screen above 130 mph. We used Boeing fluid to break up the water droplets, and the rain then just blew off the windscreen. Having satisfied myself that the car worked, I left Wilkie and the Rover engineers to get on with it.

At Spa for the Belgian GP the opposition was heavily reinforced by the Indianapolis winner Jimmy Clark plus Dan Gurney. Graham drove Jackie, who had never been to Spa before, round the circuit in a VW Beetle. Jackie was now developing his own driving style and knew exactly what he needed. Graham's car was virtually a go cart with stiff springs and bars but Jackie's was four steps in our range of springs and bars softer. There was a fearful qualifying row concerning the non-FOCA members. Mr Stanley spent most of practice mediating in this dispute, a role I think he enjoyed. We had Clark in a BRM sandwich with Graham on pole, Clark was having trouble with the 4-valve so he ran a short-stroke flat-crank 2-valve Climax. It rained before the race and there were more showers forecast, but even so we could not talk Graham out of his rock-hard suspension settings. Gurney also liked a stiff car so they were both all over the wet road. Graham gradually dropped back, leaving Clark a clear run with Jackie his only possible challenger. Clark won, with Jackie second 45 seconds behind, Graham fifth, and Richie earned Honda their first Championship point with sixth place.

Next was the French GP on the Charade circuit at Clermont Ferrand, a new circuit for us but one that Jackie had raced on before. Jackie was now referring to Graham as 'Grandpa'. On the way to the Hotel from the airport I came upon Colin Chapman, Jimmy Clark and his girl friend Sally Stokes, climbing out of the ditch having rolled their hire car. Sally was cut about the face, and they were all bruised and shaken. Sally's father, an ex-RAF Group Captain, had been seconded to the Rolls-Royce liaison flight during the war so I knew him quite well.

During practice Clark had another crash when his rear suspension collapsed. Graham had a worse one. There were many loose stones about and one jammed his throttle wide open. The car was badly damaged and Graham's old neck injury was aggravated. Although we could repair the car we could not do the same for Graham's neck. The front row was Clark, Jackie and Bandini with Surtees and Gurney behind them. Graham was a long way back in the fifth row consoling himself that 'you meet a nicer class of driver back here, more polite, less pushing and shoving'. It was terribly hot and most cars were overheating. French Prime Minister Pompidou attended the race, and to our surprise was booed. Clark won, Jackie second again (26 seconds behind) and Graham fifth again. Clark was leading the Championship with 27 points and Graham and Jackie were joint second with 17.

I had trouble at Silverstone. The mechanics wanted to take their wives, and most of the factory wanted to go. But I felt this was all a big distraction, and I still do. Rolls-Royce lent me a Bentley Mulliner Flying Spur for the week. Pam was going with me, but would watch the race from the grandstand. I compromised, wives can go but they must keep out of the work area, and we provided seats for them in the grandstands. The front row was Clark, Hill, Ginther and Stewart. Clark led all the way, with Graham second, but towards the end of the race we spotted that Clark was in trouble. Graham reacted, but Clark managed to hold him off. Graham finished 3.2 seconds behind. Jackie was fifth, with deteriorating handling — we never really found out why.

Zandvoort was a dull race, apart from Colin Chapman thumping a policeman. Graham had pole from Clark and Ginther but Clark won, Jackie was a brave second (8 seconds behind), having fought and beaten Surtees and Gurney to claim his place. Hampered by a failed rev-counter, Graham was fourth. After the race Colin was carted off to jail. Even though he was severely provoked there are very few countries in the world where you can get away with thumping a policeman. It took all Mr Stanley's powers of diplomacy to get him out after a night in jail celebrating another Clark victory. I made the comment: 'I hope no one gives him a slide rule while he's in the pokey!'

For the Nürburgring, Mercedes lent me a very nice car which Jackie borrowed to learn the circuit. He felt his hired VW Beetle would not have enough steam. I could not believe my eyes when it was returned, neither could Mercedes. There was not a mark on it, or much tread on the tyres, and the oil just did not leak, it poured out. It had also lost several speeds in its gearbox, but it was all in a good cause, because Clark had to work really hard to beat Jackie's practice time. The front row was Clark, Jackie, Graham and Surtees. Another win for Clark, who led all the way with Graham in close attendance. Jackie went off on the third lap in third place, damaging his front suspension.

I started a big hunt to find some more performance and horsepower for Monza. The F2 engines had been disappointing; in addition to the ignition failures they were down on power. Cosworth, who used the same ignition, had the same trouble but not as badly. Graham kept arguing that we should give his engine, in John Coombes's Brabham, a three hemisphere head like the F1 cars, and we could then expect 145 hp, which would have got us closer to the 150 of the Brabham Hondas. The F2 engines were leased, teams did not receive the same engine each time, so we would have had to build every engine to this standard as Sir Alfred had given an undertaking that everyone would get the same specification and performance.

The only bright spot in our F2 problems was at Reims where Beltoise was driving a Matra BRM — a horsepower race if ever there was one — and he managed to go faster than the Brabhams. As Rubery Owen were very anxious to do business with Matra, I had to devote quite a bit of time to them, and I got to know their Chief Engineer Martin quite well and Jean Luc Lagardiere, their Managing Director. They told me that they had put a vibrating reed in the air-intake opposite the mouth of the induction trumpets, similar to the reed valve used in some high performance two-stroke engines. This had magnified the air intake pulses at high rpm. It only worked over a limited rpm range but it was fine for Reims which did not require a wide range of rpm.

We did a great deal of port flow experimentation, centred on the valve seat and shrouding, in the three hemisphere combustion chamber. We found with a seat formed by two intersecting radii, one of which ran out as an involute into the head, we had a significant gain in air flow — as much as 5 per cent. The benefit gradually disappeared as the narrow, soft seat hammered in and the tappet clearance disappeared; then the valve started to blow. We established that these seats had about 500 miles useful life in the engine, as we used the equivalent of 100 miles on the test-bed, this meant 100 miles for practice and 300 miles for the race. For Monza, we built three engines with these valves seats which we put into the regular two cars. The spare car had unmodified seats and the third engine was the spare.

I briefed the drivers. They were not to give the game away in practice — flat on one straight (about 11,700 rpm) roll off the throttle on the other straight at 11,000, never use full power on both straights on the same lap. They must understand that they only had 30 laps of practice in their race car engine. Any handling experiments must be done with the spare car. Jackie understood at once, but when Graham found he was not in the front row using these tactics, he suggested three laps at full bore all the way round. I said: 'No, absolutely not. What's more you are not going to use all the power in the race until you see *me* giving you the sign x laps to go.'

Willy was fretting about heat getting to the eight gallons of fuel in the tanks alongside the engine in what promised to be a very hot race. I had worked out that we should not transfer the auxiliary fuel, which included 3.5 gallons of fuel under the driver's knees, until lap 30 and only then if race circumstances permitted. To transfer fuel the driver, on instructions from his pit, switched on a Bendix pump which pumped fuel from the auxiliary tanks into the main tanks. After the calculated time had elapsed — another signal — switch off the pump and acknowledge: very important as the pump running continually dry would eventually flatten the battery and waste fuel by aeration. We had noticed, in some races, that the lap times sometimes dropped by 0.2 of a second while this was going on. I also planned to delay changing fuel if they were in the middle of a slip-streaming battle. I did, however, let Willy fit a duplicate pump and circuits, having made sure that fuel would not leak back through one while the other was pumping.

The race started from a dummy grid. For the first 25 laps it was difficult to know who was leading as they would come by in a slip-streaming bunch, changing order as they approached the start-finish line. According to Denis Perkins's chart, Stewart led for 43 laps, Clark for 18, Graham 14. At first, Surtees, Gurney and Bandini were in close attendance plus Spence and Siffert. By lap 30 they had split into two groups. Clark and the two BRMs, then Gurney, Surtees and Bandini. By the time they started to lap the back markers, Willy began to whittle about fuel temperature, but he got a short answer. Surtees's clutch then failed, Bandini dropped back, and Graham had a turn in the lead. Then I saw a clear spell with no backmarkers, and we gave them both the signal to transfer fuel on lap 43, Willy convinced that the fuel had all boiled away. On lap 47 we gave them the 'fuel pump off' signal. Graham just nodded, but Jackie gave us a rude gesture.

After all the worrying, they did not lose any time at all during the changeover. Gurney lost the tow and began to drop right back. It was then just Clark, Graham and Jackie. Willy and I conferred, and decided that Clark was not going to drop out, so we would have to help him. I donned the special signaller's orange waistcoat and on lap 50 gave them 25 laps to go. Jimmy Clark said afterwards when he saw me giving Jackie a signal instead of the usual mechanic, he wondered what that could mean. Jackie was leading Clark in the sandwich, with Graham very close behind. Jimmy was geared for about 10,250 rpm. In the three car slip-stream he was seeing 10,350. Now on the back straight he suddenly saw 10,600, and then he knew what my signal meant — use full power or at least go faster. He was surprised we had that much in hand. Next time round it was 10,800 and his engine stopped. Graham said he dropped back a little because if Jimmy had trouble he did not want to run into the debris. He saw two puffs of grey smoke from Jimmy's exhaust, then there was a great big grey cloud, he ducked, swerved and Clark had gone. The official story was that the fuel pump had failed.

After two more laps, when it was clear Gurney could not catch them, we gave them both the slow down signal. Jackie seemed to, but Graham took the lead, and I realized they had not slowed down at all and were racing each other! We tried everything to slow them down. We stopped giving them pit signals — just laps to go. On the last lap, lining up for the Parabolica, Graham put a wheel onto the loose stuff and had a little slide which let Jackie get three seconds ahead.

After the race, instead of a scene of absolute triumph we were all furious with each other. Graham thought I should have slowed Jackie down to let him win; after all he was our No. 1 driver. Jackie, delighted to have won his first World Championship race, was bewildered and cross in return. He had done nothing wrong. He had slowed down when instructed, and he had not gone onto the loose stuff. Why was everyone mad with him? I was livid with them both. They could have either blown their engines or taken one another off. However, things had cooled down by the Stanleys' celebration dinner in Milan. We visited the other teams at the Hotel de Ville in Monza, where Lotus were into their usual bread-rolls dipped-in-red-wine act, with Cooper retaliating with the fish from the fresh fish tank. When I finally reached my room at the Marchesi, now called the Parco, there was a fearful scuffle in the corridor. The enormous blue and yellow banner I had last seen across the track at the start-finish line, was pushed under my bed and someone said 'the cops are coming'. I dived into bed, half-dressed, hearing an altercation outside my door. The landlord was telling the Caribineri that the Inginere would never get mixed up in such activities and that I had been in bed for hours. The door was gently opened, I feigned sleep, there was a muttered apology and they went on their way. The banner was still over the racing shop at BRM when I left.

Photographer Gunther Molter had given me a large folder of close-up photographs of various team members. I also had most of the start and prize money in enormous yellow 10,000 lire notes tucked into the same folder. I was talking with John Cooper and Rob Walker at the airport, waiting for our flight home, when Cooper was called to the phone. He came back laughing, telling us that Chunky had filed an instrument flight plan home, the authorities had asked to see his licence to check that he had an instrument rating, to find that the actual licence was out of date, so they had grounded him. A few minutes later Colin called me, could I fly the plane home using my licence, but I, like Cooper, had left mine in England. As we boarded the BEA Trident there was a large group of policemen rechecking passports. They took my passport and ticket and locked me up in a waiting room where I was joined by Cooper, Rob Walker, Barrie Gill and others. After an hour they took us, one at a time, to another room where all our luggage was laid out. They searched my case, my briefcase, then me, and locked me in another room, where I was joined by the others after they, too, had been searched. After a couple of hours, Barrie Gill, who had been incarcerated with us for asking too many questions, discovered half the story. Apparently, Colin had left his briefcase containing his and Brabham's start and prize money outside the phone box while he phoned around for assistance with his flight plan and licence problems. The briefcase had been stolen. We assumed we were suspects, and were all very indignant. Fancy Chunky thinking we had pinched his loot!

Eventually BEA officials took us out to the plane and assured us our baggage was on board. The captain had refused to leave without us. Laurie Hands, of Champion organized a resuscitation ward in the Trident centre cabin, starting with champagne cocktails. Pam had brought my mother-in-law with her, to meet our flight at Heathrow. They were very worried by the five or six hour delay, however, a very cheerful bunch of journalists disembarked first, telling Pam: 'Your old man's been in jail.' Geoffrey Charles, of *The Times*, finally got the full story. Apparently it was then an offence to take more than 500,000 lire in Italian currency out of the country, and there was Colin Chapman with nearly 10,000,000. It occurred to police that the other team managers might be doing the same thing, hence the search. How they did not find all my money baffles me. These days FOCA handle it, but then I did not know it was illegal.

Graham and I had a very long meeting with Sir Alfred. I had been approached to send two cars to be driven by Graham and Jackie for the ten race Tasman Series in early 1966 — generous starting money, twelve free air tickets, free transport etc. The races of 100 miles each, were for cars up to 2.5 litres, running on Avgas. I had already mentioned to Sir Alfred, in a routine newsletter, that I had declined the invitation because we did not have a 2.5 litre engine. Our cars were too big and heavy, as they carried enough fuel for 300 miles, and I did not want to be away for a vital two months in the middle of the change to the 3 litre formula. Also Lotus were building special cars (there was no minimum weight limit, and only fuel tankage for 100 miles was required) using the old 2.5 litre Climax 4-cylinder engines of 250 hp, with its legendary Climax torque. We would not stand a chance.

Sir Alfred told us that the Austin-Morris group were going to build cars in New Zealand. These had to have a minimum percentage of local content, and he wished to set up a plant in New Zealand to make the same components for these cars as he did in England, to meet this requirement. He needed New Zealand business partners, as the plant had to have a majority of New Zealand capital, so he saw racing the Rubery Owen BRMs as a means of finding these partners. He was not interested in our excuses; just find the best way of doing it and putting up a good show, I was to apologize, reverse my decision and enter for the Tasman series.

Graham and I argued long and hard that our stretched V8 now at 1918 cc would be giving away torque to the Climaxes, and the cars would be 200 lb (90.72 kg) overweight. Sir Alfred was not interested, and said to let Tim Parnell manage the team and use his mechanics. All I had to do was prepare the cars. He was absolutely adamant. Graham need not do all the races; let Attwood do the others. I went back to the Tasman organizers, who significantly increased their offer. Shell offered to pay treble bonuses if we raced on local petrol and not Avgas. This gave me an excuse if we got soundly beaten!

Geoff Johnson went through all his figures and managed to squeeze a few more ccs out of the engines, and I set the programme in motion. Jackie, of course, thought it was a wonderful idea; he was completely irrepressible. There were still two races to go of the 1.5 litre formula. Clark was already

World Champion, and there was no chance of our beating Lotus for the Manufacturers' Championship. I left Willy behind to start on the Tasman engine programme, while I went to the US GP at Watkins Glen, taking Glen Foreman from the engine shop in Willy's place. Mike Hall was about to leave us to join Cosworth.

I flew to New York in a BOAC VC10 which I preferred to a 707 — it was quicker and quieter. At La Guardia I joined up with Brabham and Innes Ireland for a Mohawk Convair 340 to Elmira, via Binghampton. At Elmira I went to collect my car. The hire car people who were handling all the race loan cars, said: 'We have been waiting to see how you cope with three cars! Rolls-Royce have a white Silver Shadow for you, there is a Plymouth Superfury from Chrysler, and a Mustang from the race organizers.' I took the Shadow, and as there was not a car for Innes and Jack, they each took one of the other two. Then the laugh was on me — no luggage. I had checked it with Mohawk at La Guardia. Mohawk told me it must have been off-loaded at Binghampton or had gone on to Buffalo. 'It will turn up tomorrow, do not worry. Here is a voucher to buy what you need tonight.' However, it did not appear next day. Mohawk seemed surprised and provided another voucher for me to spend at Fred's Clothing Store in Watkins Glen. It was bitterly cold, but Graham showed Jackie round the circuit, and Graham ended up with pole position from Clark, with Jackie on the third row. Surtees was in hospital following a terrible crash at Mosport the week before.

I kicked up a tremendous row with Mohawk, telling them that I could manage without my clothing, but all our race data was in the lost case. If we did not win I would sue them for the lost prize money, but this had little effect. Eventually Mohawk sent a Passenger Relations Officer, an immaculate and efficient lady, to try to talk me out of some of my more militant ideas. She was impressed by my Rolls-Royce, and took me shopping. I chose a large fur-lined suede coat which I still have; a new suit case, sweaters, and generally proofed myself against the bitter cold. The mechanics served hot Bovril on cold days, and practice was very cold. The Mohawk lady got one with a large tot of brandy in it — a completely new experience for her!

Mr Honda spent nearly an hour talking to me through an interpreter. By the end of it I realized he had given nothing away and had collected quite a lot of information from me. He also extended a very cordial invitation to visit their Technical Centre when in Japan.

For the race the track was as slippery as glass, and it was still bitterly cold. Clark was out after ten laps with a piston failure in the 4-valve Climax, and Jackie was pushed off in a shunting match, damaging his front suspension too badly for him to continue. Graham did about 200 yards on the grass in front of the pits which let Gurney into the lead, but Graham soon got it back and won by 12 seconds from Dan and nearly a minute from Brabham who was third. I turned to the Mohawk lady and said. 'Well, that's got you off the hook.' It was the first time I saw her confidence crack. She realized it might have been a real threat to sue for the prize money.

Mr and Mrs Stanley gave an even more impressive celebration dinner than usual at the Glen Motor Court. I think this was the year someone's car went in the swimming pool. I drove to Elmira in the Rolls-Royce with the Passenger Relations lady who had said she would escort me back to New

York, but I said: 'No thank you, Executive Jet have laid on a Lear for me.' She thought I was bluffing. However, Executive Jet were very keen to get F1 teams interested in a sharing arrangement in Europe, and they had laid on a demonstration, taking Graham, Jackie and me to the Piper factory at Lock Haven in Pennsylvania, and then on to New York. We took turns in the second pilot's seat; looked after by ex-USAAF General Perry Housington.

Three months later, a letter arrived from Mohawk saying they were going to pay my claim for the lost luggage according to their standard terms, and herewith the cheque. A few minutes later, BOAC rang up to say they had got an urgent package for me, where could they deliver it. As I was going to London that night to an Esso party at the Hilton for Lotus, I said the Hilton please. They delivered the missing case to me containing much sand and dust. Apparently it had fallen off the conveyor at La Guardia, which Mohawk shared with Aeronaves di Mexico and had spent two months or more in Mexico City. I sent the cheque back but kept the fur-lined coat!

Willy went to Mexico and I stayed behind to deal with the Tasman Problems, where we spoiled our record of total reliability as both engines broke connecting-rod bolts. Jackie, Bandini, and Pedro Rodriguez had a shunting match at the same corner where Bandini had Graham off the year before. However, Jackie came off best, both Ferraris losing three laps. Jackie also had clutch trouble, and Richie won their first race for Honda and Goodyear. We finished second and third in the Drivers' Championship — Graham with 40 points and Jackie 33 points, but Clark had 54. As Graham said about the Scots: 'There are not many of them, but they certainly are a bloody nuisance!' In the Constructors' Championship we had 45 points to Lotus's 54. Only the best six races counted with nine points each, so Lotus hit the jackpot. It was the end of the 1.5 litre Formula but not the end of the cars or their engines.

I took stock of my situation. We had two of the very best drivers, but I feared problems as Jackie matured. He was improving with every race, while Graham, although still a wily old bird was getting no younger. Jackie was still ready to accept Graham as No. 1, but for how much longer? The potential problem was vividly illustrated during a test session at Snetterton. Peter Spear had provided an embryo on-board data system using light-sensitive paper tape, and we had light beam timing round a selected corner.

Analysing the data, I showed Graham that his technique of going deep into the corner; braking hard and late; taking it fairly easy around the corner until he was clear, then giving it everything the engine had, was not the quickest way. Jackie braked earlier, but not so hard, his car was stable in the apex and able to hold a higher speed. He then fed in a little throttle earlier, gradually increasing the amount, so that he was some 0.4 seconds quicker round this corner. I explained to Graham that Jackie had been looking at the data and had changed his methods and had improved his time. Would he like to do the same? 'No he would not.' This was unlike Graham, who, as he lost no time pointing out, was quicker round the whole circuit. Then there was the windscreen problem. Jackie nearly always pulled 75 to 100 rpm more than Graham. They had individually moulded windscreens — Graham's, of necessity, being much bigger than Jackie's. We put Graham's big screen on Jackie's car, and there was the 100 rpm. Happily there was never any ill feeling. Graham went to a great deal of trouble to teach Jackie and pass on his experience. It was just the law of the jungle — the younger challenging the older member of the herd.

In addition, my delegation policy did not solve all the problems created by the external contracts. The intense effort that produced results at Monza could not be sustained. The various members of the team worked wonders but someone had to co-ordinate their efforts. It was a full-time job for 24 hours a day; not something I could pick up and put down between trips to Detroit and meetings with customers.

By this time I was in deep trouble with the Tasman engines. The first came off test giving 256 hp, about right for Geoff's 1930 cc, but the next one broke several piston rings. By trial and error we deduced it was a running-in problem so Mr Stanley arranged for me to meet Cambridge Professor Dykes, whose ring design we used, and who made a number of helpful suggestions, some of which I later employed on the Lotus 2 litre engine. The only fix we could find in the time available — with engines queuing up at the test house door — was to add oil to the fuel for running-in. We had been using chromium-plated steel liners, but late in 1964 I had tried chromium-plated duralumin. This gave us a little more power but an increase in oil consumption. We had to fly the spare engines out to New Zealand, after the cars, while we sorted out this problem.

I realized that I had missed the chance of ever achieving one of my boyhood ambitions. I would never ever design a World Championship racing car from stem to stern. The 1.5 litre had been my last chance, the new 3 litre cars were going to be so much more complicated it would take three or four designers. For instance, in the case of Lotus, it was Colin Chapman for the chassis, Duckworth the engine and Hewland the gearbox. At BRM, I specified the cylinder head and engine layout which Geoff Johnson drew; the gearbox, which Stokey drew. I myself had drawn the suspension layouts and front and rear cross members and the monocoque structure which Alec Osborn then turned into working drawings.

Tim Parnell, supported by 'Dobbin' (Alan Challis), took the cars out to New Zealand and Australia, where they won nine out of the ten races. The only race they failed to win was Warwick Farm, near Sydney where Lotus's Firestone tyres really suited the circuit. This led to Tim's famous remark to Graham: 'I should have thought you could have done better.' This was one of the few races in which Graham competed. Jackie completely dominated the Championship, ably supported by Dickie Attwood. Sir Alfred was delighted and never let Graham and me forget that he forced on us the decision to compete. The ensuing financial bonanza, boosted by treble bonus from Shell — for the cars being filled at the nearest Shell roadside pump — helped offset the heavy expenditure on the H16, made all the more obvious by a very economical 1965 financial year. We had spent very little money, and with the Watkins Glen, Monaco and Monza wins and second place in nearly every race, we had a very good income. The financial success of 1965 came to haunt me in later years.

I realized I would need a back-up for the H16s in the early races, particularly at Monte Carlo. Car 2613 had already been sold to a team that had Bob Bondurant as their driver. Our first race in 1966 again at Monte Carlo, saw us with the first H16 — one week old. We took the best Tasman cars as a back-up.

It was my custom to drive myself to one of the European races to get up-to-date ideas on travel costs. We paid the mechanics a fixed daily expense allowance, which they could spend how they liked. If they had caviar for breakfast and could afford it that was fine. It greatly simplified bookkeeping, and Sandy had cleared it with the tax people. The mechanics felt they were being treated like reasonable human beings, but it did mean that I needed a good idea of the cost of living and travel in each country before Sandy and I set the daily rate for the season — Monte Carlo was always very expensive; Zandvoort was cheap; while France, Germany and Italy were half way between the two extremes.

I drove out in my 3 litre Rover with Pam and Baggy Sach of Shell, hoping to get from London to Monte Carlo in a day. However, our Bristol freighter had radio trouble at Southend, so we were two hours late taking off, and there was a major strike in France — no Customs and no electricity. There was also a smallpox scare in France. Pam had to be revaccinated and was very uncomfortable. Then it poured with rain. We had lost so much time that at Beaune we gave up trying to get there in a day, but could not find a hotel. 'Navigator' Sach in the back said: 'I don't care where we stop as long as we get a good meal.' So I told him to look for a place in the Michelin guide with a rosette. When we reached his choice — the Lameloise in Chagny — we saw Rob Walker's Facel Vega parked outside, and we knew we had made the right choice! Pam and I had what must have been a conversion of the top floor landing; two single beds, foot to foot in a very long narrow room, but a fabulous meal! Next day on the Route Napoleon we were blown off by French journalist 'Jabby' Crombac in his Lotus Elan. My Rover, well-modified, was no slouch because of the Rover BRM relationship, but I could not keep him in sight.

At Monaco I told Jackie to concentrate on the Tasman car, Graham having so much experience of the circuit could afford the distraction of trying the H16. Frankenheimer was making his film *Grand Prix* in Monaco at the same time, which was a bit of a nuisance, but it probably cut both ways. Phil Hill was acting the part of a TV commentator, and when he saw Pam filming him with her new cine camera he did a double take and stopped to talk to her, which ruined the scene. All the ladies had new Eumig cameras, there was a row of five of them on our pit counter. How they sorted out whose films were what and whose camera was which I do not know. The climax came when one of the film company executives rang me up at 11 a.m. race day to enquire when he could collect the cars. 'What cars?' I asked. Apparently one of the drivers (not one of ours) had sold him our Tasmans. The arrangement was that they could take delivery of them after the race, as from then on we would be running H16s. I was not particularly helpful, and we had quite an acrimonious 15 minutes before he realized that he had been had.

Jackie won easily after disposing of Surtees. Graham had an intermittent slipping clutch and finished third to Bandini after Surtees's gearbox failed. Bob Bondurant in 2613 was the only other running finisher. The garage proprietor laid on his usual champagne party for us. I left my Rover, as usual, for the garage to park after we had vacated the workshop and left for the circuit. They parked it satisfactorily but left it switched on. When I finally got the car running, it was much too late for the Banquet, but still in time for the party at the Tip Top.

One of our rules was that one of the two transporter drivers stayed sober at the party. It was Denis Perkins's turn (although it did not show) and they had to be on the road at 6.30 next morning. Pam and Baggy offered to drive on Monday afternoon so that I could spend the morning by the swimming pool to relax and our concierge booked rooms for us in the same Hotel at Chagny so we could arrive late. I was awakened after about two hours sleep by the most fearful blast from the Leyland's multiple horns to let me know they were on their way, on time. They used to make phenomenal average speeds. It had enough fuel tank capacity to make the run from Bourne to Monaco non-stop, and they would change drivers without stopping. There was a large winking green light at the back. I was never quite sure whether it meant it was safe to overtake, because the road was clear or that no one was attending to the calls of nature at high speed. There were few speed limits in the 1960s.

After a pleasant morning and a very good lunch, we left about 3 p.m. with me fast asleep in the back, and reached Chagny in time for dinner — 380 miles — at 7.30 p.m. The Lameloise was full of journalists; we had sung its praises loud. We had another very good night, and one of the major magazines carried an apology later in the week saying that so and so's Monte Carlo technical report had unavoidably to be held over until the following week.

We ran the Tasmans at Spa, where they went better then we expected, although Graham blew an engine in practice. The mechanics shared my irritation with the film crew but they had their own methods of showing disapproval — they wore white overalls on the first days practice, blue overalls the second day and standard 'dayglo' orange race day. The continuity girl, I understand, went raving mad. People who have seen the film *Grand Prix* will know that BRM was an essential part of the story.

In the race it began to rain heavily on the far side of the circuit, so as the leaders came down the hill to the Masta Straight, Jackie aquaplaned off, striking amidships a large stone buttress of an even larger and very solid stone barn, and wrapped the car round the buttress like a banana. It then bounced off into a ditch with Jackie trapped in the car with a crushed tank leaking fuel all round him. Graham and Bondurant went off in the same area for the same reason a few seconds later but without such disastrous consequences. Just as Graham was getting back on the road he saw Jackie's car and stopped to help him. It took nearly ten minutes to get him out of the car and another 20 minutes before the ambulance arrived. He had been sitting up to his waist in petrol, so the drivers helping him, stripped off his fuel-sodden clothes and wrapped him in a spectators rug. To quote Graham later — sowing fear and confusion amongst the female spectators. Graham finally arrived back at his pit full of apologies for having given up with a serviceable car as he explained: 'I could not leave him there like that.' It took some time to get Graham to understand that we never expected him to.

I went to see Jackie in the little medical centre at the back of the pits, where his wife Helen was with him. He was shocked, but did not appear too badly hurt. He seized my arm and said 'get me home'. I said 'leave it to me Jackie', and went out into the Spa paddock, rain still pouring down, to set about it. It was obvious that an aeroplane was required but how on earth did I get one? By an incredible stroke of luck, General Perry Housington of Executive Jets walked by. I grabbed him and asked if he had one of his Lears in Europe. Perry was a man of a few words: 'Yep, two.' It was soon arranged for a Lear to collect Jackie from Liège at 7 p.m. and take him to London.

Back at the medical centre I found them getting ready to take Jackie to Verviers Hospital, so I told Mr Stanley the plan and left him to get Jackie to the airport. Helen wanted to stay with him, so Denis Perkins and I ran through the rain across the fields to collect a car, and retrieve their passports and belongings. I had already phoned Sir Alfred; told him what had happened and asked him to get Jackie into St Thomas's Hospital, where there was an extremely good orthopaedic surgeon — Mr Farquhar — who had done wonders for Surtees. I told him I did not think Jackie was badly hurt, but until he had been X-rayed we could not be sure. I thought it was mainly shock, but as he had sat for ten minutes in petrol his skin was burning. We arrived at the airport at the same time as the ambulance containing Jackie, followed by Mr and Mrs Stanley's usual enormous Cadillac. 'Where is the plane?' demanded Mr Stanley, and it taxied in. There was no bed in the aircraft for Jackie, so Mr Stanley commandeered the stretcher from the ambulance. We flew to London at 41,000 feet on a beautiful evening, taking just 35 minutes.

At Heathrow Sir Alfred had laid on two ambulances, one with special burns facilities as he had misunderstood my words that Jackie's skin was burning. Customs waved the ambulance away while I dealt with the formalities and luggage. When I arrived at the hospital, Jackie had settled down for the night, and was quite cheerful. I then had to find a hotel for Helen and myself. I rang Charles Fonara, Manager of the Berkeley who said they were full but would fit us in somehow. Only one journalist, Michael Kemp, had kept up with us. I told him what I could. Next morning we were told Jackie had a hairline pelvic fracture; was badly bruised and sore, but would be up and about in three or four days. Graham had been awarded a BRDC Gold Star for his victory at Indianapolis, so most of the guests en route for the presentation called in to see Jackie. The ladies changed into their finery in his room, which seemed to cheer him up immensely. Jackie would obviously not be fit for Reims, so Graham ran alone, breaking a camshaft in his Tasman car after slip-streaming Parkes in a Ferrari for most of the race.

One day I was looking out of my office window, when I saw a BRM-green Rover coupé being unloaded into Raymond Mays and Partners Showroom. I tried to find out who it was for — RM would never have a green car and Mrs Stanley had preferred a Rover saloon. This car had the treatment, lowered on its suspension and so on, but I could not get a whisper as to who it was for: then it disappeared. I was then invited to Eastgate House for tea with Sir Alfred on Sunday afternoon. Sir Alfred had arrived in a new T series Bentley which he invited me to try. The green Rover coupé stood alongside. When he was about to leave he said: 'I have a new car, and so have you, the Rover is yours!' It was very quick, and wore out a set of Dunlop R5s in 5000 miles, but fortunately Dick Jeffrey always replaced them.

We ran Tasmans at Brands Hatch, Zandvoort and the Nürburgring. Jackie was still very stiff and tense at Brands Hatch, but back on form in Holland and the Nürburgring. Spear was busy doing a deal with Matra to provide a batch of engines for their proposed gull-wing Le Mans cars. These had to be 1998 cc. Strangely enough these engines gave no more power than the 1930 ccs. Geoff found a way of stretching the engine a little more to 2070 cc. We built two of these and eventually saw 292 hp from one and 287 from another. They were used by Jackie at Monte Carlo in 1967 but the gearbox gave up when he was in the lead. Even then the Tasmans refused to lay down. We ran one of them in the French GP at Le Mans later in the year.

It took me a very long while to understand the reason for the power differences from the various so called 2 litres. The best 1930 cc gave 262 hp which is 136.6 hp per litre; the 1998s only gave 129 hp per litre, with 258 hp, yet the 2070s gave 287 hp which is 139 hp per litre. Alec Osborn's 997 cc F2 engine gave 129 hp per litre. Frank Starke, designer of the Rolls-Royce sleeve valve air-cooled engines, tried to interest me in his 'bifurcated' port engine, which had two inlet ports for each valve. We provided a F2 engine which he had modified and we tested. Apart from many water leaks from the welded-up head it nearly worked. I began to suspect that the ratio of connecting rod length to the stroke was more important than we thought. We cut 0.5 inch from the block of Frank Starke's F2 engine and fitted it with the shorter connecting rods from the F1 engines. Fitted with a standard head the power went from 128 hp to 136 hp, which explained the disappointing performance of the F2 engine and the 1998 cc V8s. The 2070 cc engines had a longer stroke, hence the 139 hp per litre.

We received a request from the Army for a constant speed 250 lb weight 250 hp engine to run on military MT80 fuel. We made an injection 2 litre V8 with long ram pipes and a plenum induction system based on the original 'Queen Mary'. We were well on the way to meeting the other requirement — 300 hours between overhauls — when Mr Callaghan, then Chancellor of the Exchequer, cancelled the vehicle for which the engine was intended. He decided the taxpayer could not afford it. It took much time and effort and it had its own project team. From the income we were able to buy another G490 dynamometer.

The V8s were undoubtedly the most successful BRM engine, measured in terms of race wins, earnings and reliability. When Stokey and I called the roll, many years later, only one of the 30-odd engines was no longer around. That was 5606, which I deliberately destroyed at Zandvoort in pursuit of Championship points.

# CHAPTER SEVENTEEN

# Three litres — H16s and V12s

I HAVE HAD mixed feelings about the H16, from conception right up to the present time. I have always believed (and preached) that there are optimum dimensions and proportions for a specific engine duty, such as a Formula 1 racing engine. In the Winter of 1964/65 I believed that we were close to the ideal with the centre-exhaust 2-valve 1.5 litre BRM V8. It is significant that, after two attempts, the Coventry Climax V8 used the same bore and stroke as we did.

I was therefore driven towards keeping and building on what I saw as a successful cylinder and combustion chamber. There was, I reasoned, plenty of development potential left in our 187.5 cc cylinder. However, 3 litres meant 16 cylinders. How to arrange them? How to take the power out of the engine? — two vital questions. I was not (although I should have been) frightened of gearing two crankshafts together. I was fully aware of — and had already developed — the technique of using the engine as part of the car's structure. This also drove me towards an H16, in the form of two flat-8s, laying one on top of the other. However, historical precedents were not good, and I was aware of the problems of 'flat' engines. There had been a number of 'H' formation aero-engines, none of them very successful. Only one, the 24-cylinder Napier Sabre became a volume-production front-line engine, and then only after politics and plant capacities played their part.

There had only been one fairly successful F1 16-cylinder engine — the single-camshaft V16 Auto Union engine of the mid-1930s. There had been many less than successful attempts, and I bore the scars of one of them!

The other alternative was a 12-cylinder. We were making these far-reaching decisions before we had any experience of the highly successful Tasman 2 litre V8 with its 250 cc cylinder. The V12 Rolls-Royce Merlin aero-engine had loomed large over my formative years, but with a 2.25 litre cylinder and turning at only 3000 rpm it was hardly in the same category.

I could see, however, that a 12-cylinder could be a comparatively simple, inexpensive and reliable engine. It would be difficult to use as a stressed part of the car structure (too long and narrow) unless built in three banks of four — a broad arrow like the Napier Lion of the 1920s. This would be a problem in an F1 engine. Would you put three connecting rods side by side on the same crankpin and face the torsional and other vibrations that the inevitably whippy crankshaft would cause? Or would you pivot the two outer connecting rods on the central master rod, giving less capacity to the two outer banks of cylinders? No, two banks of six cylinders would be the way to go, if we opted for a 12-cylinder, accepting the inevitably long wheelbase this would cause.

Weslake was pressing very hard for a 4-valve V12, but our experience with Berthon-Weslake was not encouraging because of missed delivery dates and performance targets. Somehow I and my team began to associate 4-valve V12s with trouble. I was acutely aware of time slipping by as Spear's BRM-Weslake Liaison Committee argued, politicized and wrangled from December 1964 until April 1965.

My leanings towards an H16 were reinforced a little by knowledge of the Coventry Climax 1.5 litre flat-16 with central power take-off. If a designer of Wally Hassan's ability and sense of manufacturing requirements contemplated one, why not BRM?

I therefore accepted, with relief rather than joy, Sir Alfred's decision that BRM at Bourne would build a 2-valve H16 and Berthon-Weslake would build at Rye a 4-valve V12 and we would race the 'best' one in 1966. Weslake were also to build two single-cylinder research engines, a 250 cc for use in developing their 4-valve cylinder proportions and the other, funded by Shell, of 187.5 ccs to be used to develop a 4-valve cylinder for the H16. I suspect Sir Alfred was motivated by a desire to show the world that a 16-cylinder would work, and thereby vindicate the 1940s decisions.

Spear announced Sir Alfred's decisions at the May 1965 meeting of the BRM-Weslake Liaison Committee. It will surprise people that we had been arguing for so long, but this was the nature of things. Weslake was pressing his case to design and make the engine, and suffering the upheaval that attended PB's departure from Weslake & Co. PB and Harry were both very strong personalities. Harry believed (quite wrongly) that PB had extra clout as Rubery Owen's nominee and a confidant of Spear, whereas PB neither trusted nor confided in Spear. I have only Harry Weslake's version of what happened, so it is not fair for me to comment.

At this time I was extremely busy with the centre exhaust V8 and Chrysler operations. I had probably made the situation worse by my reluctance to pass on all our combustion technology to Weslake who, after all, were in the same business of selling technology as we were. I thought there was a risk that all we had learned, dearly bought by Sir Alfred, would be passed on to other people. Peter Spear shared this view and had become much less enchanted with the Berthon-Weslake set up. There had been far too many expensive stupid mistakes, which was embarrassing for Spear, who had said that under his control they would be eliminated.

During late 1965 Alistair Wadsworth and I received glowing reports that the Weslake 4-valve single-cylinder (the 250 cc version for the V12) was giving nearly 40 hp — 158 hp per litre. We were also told that the 187 cc was only giving 26.7 hp — 142.8 hp per litre. We both wanted to go to Rye to see it, but it was never convenient. Eventually Harry bought-out the Rubery Owen interest. He was building engines for Dr Savundra's racing power boat at the time. With the break with Weslake the V12 engine slipped into the background. Sir Alfred was also very keen to build a less complex

3 litre engine for sale, and he directed that when H16 work eased off we should build a V12, primarily for sports car racing. It had been agreed in July 1965 to supply H16 engines to Lotus.

I was very concerned by the H16's problems of getting water from the lower to the upper cylinder heads. When I look at the drawings today and see my solutions, I cringe and wonder how I could have been so naive, and how remarkable it is that Albert Bolton, Technical Director of Aeroplane and Motor Castings, who made them, is still a good friend!

We were superstitious, and invited *Autosport* to take some photographs of the H16 starting up in February 1966, about a week behind schedule — just as their photographer George Phillips had done for the V8. I wrote a paper ('Transport Engines of Exceptionally High Specific Output' — IME 1969) for the Institution of Mechanical Engineers on the many problems that beset the H16, especially the three months from our first run to its first public appearance at Monte Carlo. The problems ranged from broken camshafts and ignition trigger disc drives, stripped teeth on rubber belt drives to injection metering units and all the consequences of violent and destructive crankshaft vibration.

Lotus, in addition to their F1 engines, had asked for 4.2 litre engines for Indianapolis. I agreed to supply 3 litre engines in line with Sir Alfred's policy. It just meant making some more engines without any additional development. However, an additional 4.2 litre alcohol-fuelled engine would more than double our workload, and I vigorously opposed it. Spear and I formed an alliance, supported by members of the Budget Committee, who saw it as an expensive diversion, and all funded by Sir Alfred. There was a meeting in the Rubery Owen Boardroom at Darlaston with Colin Chapman to resolve the matter. Colin Chapman and Fred Bushell sat forlornly one side of the big table facing the scowling opposition battalions. Colin played all his cards superbly, stroked every one of Sir Alfred's pleasure points — the little man doing it for Britain against the might of America — and got everything he wanted! Many years later Fred told me that Sir Alfred must have been convinced he had a world-beating engine if Colin Chapman wanted it so badly, which is why he agreed to make the 4.2 litre for Colin.

When I drove the first H16 car my first impression was the lack of exhaust noise — more a mechanical frenzy; rather more vibration than I had expected, but a pleasant sensation of inexorable acceleration. At this time it was only developing 410 hp and running up to 10,500 rpm. It had inertia weights bolted and welded over crankshaft balance weights which were, we later discovered, prone to fly off if the engine was over-revved.

We decided to take the car to Monte Carlo and run it in practice as part of its test programme. The gear-change was by push-pull cables consisting of a metallic strip with pockets containing small steel balls, working in a flexible tube. This cable system soon got us into trouble. Graham would do about five laps and then complain the gears were no longer where he expected. The cables were stretching, and the resulting over-revving did not do the engine much good either.

Back at Bourne we hurriedly reverted to a tubular universally-jointed gear-change. Fortunately we had designed two large holes from front to rear of the engine in case we ever needed to pass a shaft through for 4-wheel-drive, which provided an easy route for the gear-change tube.

We delivered an engine and gearbox to Lotus which nearly destroyed the small van they sent to fetch it. They were absolutely thunderstruck by its weight. With all the modifications the engine weighed 555 lb (252 kg) plus 118 lb (53.5 kg) of gearbox and clutch. Lotus also had gear-change problems, and Colin Chapman spotted that we had the clutch the wrong way round. We had to accelerate or decelerate the whole drum and starter ring instead of just the plates to match the dog and gear speeds, which meant a slower gear-change. This led to another major panic modification, so we raced the 2 litres until Monza when all the modifications arrived.

At Reims, minus Jackie Stewart following his accident, we thought a slow gear-change would be worth 420 hp on the two long straights. Graham really wound his car up in practice. The engine was behaving properly. Everyone stopped to watch and listen, and for a few minutes we really took big chunks off the lap record. What really impressed me, however, was that as we listened to the exhaust note as the car went round the long corner after the pits, it never wavered, and there were many people looking at each other wide-eyed and saying 'he has not lifted off!' Some of the experts said he was not going fast enough to need to, but as he was lapping at 2 min 09.2 sec, the fastest of the second session, Graham was not hanging about. Most of the other quick times were achieved by slip-streaming. Eventually we had to call it a day, Graham's efforts to beat the slow gear-change had damaged the gearbox. Good came of this, however. When we took the damaged dogs to our friends at Rolls-Royce they showed us how to make gears that would stand up to anything. By August we had it all together — new gears, and clutch reversed. Stokey's inside-out clutch became the basis of Borg and Beck racing clutches for many years.

At Monza Jimmy Clark got the H16-engined Lotus 43 on the front row with a time of 1 min 31.8 sec, to the Ferrari times of 1 min 31.3 sec and 1 min 31.6 sec. He had tyre trouble in the race but went well otherwise and finally retired with gear-change trouble. Graham had a valve failure early on. Jackie had a fuel tank leak but soldiered bravely on until his engine developed a serious misfire.

Just before Monza I had a Budget Committee meeting followed by one with Sir Alfred where I reported that we could make a 400 hp 2-valve V12, weighing 325 lb (147 kg) for sports racing cars and, based on a batch of 20 engines, we could build them for £2,200 each. It was agreed we should proceed. Geoff Johnson set to work on what was effectively a 12-cylinder Tasman minus some of the more expensive features. It had chain-driven camshafts which reduced the length of the engine; and saved weight and £200. Chain failure cost us some vital races in 1968. Plain-bearing camshafts saved £350 per engine, but cost us 12 hp.

I hoped we were getting the situation under control for the US GP at Watkins Glen. Clark got the Lotus 43 on the front row but the engine blew up in the process. Pole went to Brabham with 1 min 08.42 sec, with Clark at 1 min 08.53 sec and Graham 1 min 08.87 sec. Much was made of our generosity in lending Lotus a spare engine but they had a lease agreement whereby we kept them in engines. In the race Graham's crownwheel and pinion failed; Jackie dropped a valve through a missed gear, but Clark won by nearly a lap, having had an easy time for the last 30 laps. There was not time to do much for Mexico, and I spent several days at Chrysler. Clark was again on the front row with a 1 min 53.5 sec to Surtees's pole time of 1 min

53.18 sec. In the race he had another gear-change failure (not one of our pieces). Jackie had a scavenge connection blow off when in third place and Graham a broken camshaft.

It was a poor end to what was Graham's last race with us as he had decided to go back to Lotus, with a generous retainer from Ford and the promise of the new Cosworth V8. It was all rather sad; we had suffered and achieved much together. I do not think he could see us quickly solving the H16 problems, whereas Jackie, with the eternal enthusiasm of youth, could. Graham was also wondering how he would cope with the developing Stewart. However, I was consoled by our new driver Mike Spence who had shown flashes of brilliance in 1965. In our early days together Graham had played a tremendous part in developing our good road-holding. He used to come to Bourne at least once a week; spend the day in the workshop and drawing office, and come home with me for supper. He made a tremendous fuss of my daughters, who would send messages like: 'Tell Uncle Graham to stop playing with our trains.' They had a very elaborate electric train set up in the room below their bedroom (their mother's idea, not mine!) We would look through my testing photographs, talk and plan until about 10 p.m., when he would drive home.

During 1965 and 1966 Graham had spent less time telling me what the car was doing, so I could prescribe treatment; he just told his mechanic Alan Challis what he wanted. I complained that if he did not tell us what was happening, we would stop learning and improving. He said it saved time and he always told Dobbin why he wanted the change.

One of my cherished snapshots of Graham will always be the way he would look for me after he had won a race, while we were standing at attention for the National Anthem and the hoisting of the Union Jack and then give me a tremendous wink. We had a very good relationship and understood each other very well. Once or twice, in the early days, I gave him a faster signal, but after that I just told him what was going on, and he could deduce from the sequence of the information what I was thinking, while I could always anticipate what he wanted to know. He would wonder what is so and so doing, next time round, there was the signal telling him. When he later began to build up his own team he complained to me of the troubles he was having with his drivers. I said: 'Now you know what you used to do to me.' He replied: 'You might have warned me, you berk!' We remained good friends until his tragic death in a plane crash in 1975.

After the first unfortunate H16 season, we launched a winter reliability programme which was fairly successful. The new crankshaft solved the vibration problems but the gearbox became the weak link. The cars were 250 lb (113 kg) overweight, so there was less stress-reducing wheelspin. With the clutch at the rear of the box our system of reducing shock loads with the quill-shaft was less effective. We built a lighter more compact car, the Type 115, but events overtook us after we had built the first, and we never built another. The project number was a measure of the multiplicity of external projects performed by the Engine Development Division of Rubery Owen — our proper name — BRM engines and cars were just one of our products. The first H16 car was Type 83 the second Type 115, with just a year between them.

One of our problems in 1966 was the effect of oil on our Dunlop tyres, and when the track became oily, Firestone always had the edge. We had to invoke the clause in our contract which permitted us to use other makes of tyres if Dunlop could not supply us with a competitive tyre. Dunlop fought back and organized a series of tests at Kyalami after the first GP of 1967.

I had noticed a lack of toe steer stiffness in our rear suspension during late 1966. I devised a modified rear suspension. The upper link was a massive 'N' structure, one triangular leg took forward thrust, the remaining trailing leg could be varied in length to control the amount of toe-in. A short lever, on the inner side of the pivot reacted on the damper, spring and roll bar, to give inboard rear suspension. There was just one long stiff lower link, and a long forward thrust rod. It was much easier to make, and it solved the problem, as we found when we tested it at the Dunlop Kyalami tyre tests. It also saved some 25 lb (11 kg).

Tim Parnell and I got together (self interest on my part) to transfer some of my peripheral problems to him. We put the idea to Sir Alfred that Tim should run some of our older cars with drivers we designated as having worthwhile potential, and this would give us a training and evaluation second team. It could only have worked with someone as good-natured and reasonable as Tim.

At Kyalami for the South African GP and the first race of 1967 there were four H16s, all running too hot. Clark on the second row, Jackie and Spence on the fifth. Graham had not succeeded in getting away from the H16 engine — he was driving a Lotus 43 with one, and was back on the eighth row. Jackie was the first to fall out, with engine failure; Graham spun off, Clark succumbed to overheating and Spence had gearbox problems.

During the tyre-testing after the race I got to know Mike Spence well, while Jackie was away at a much less successful Tasman series — the gearbox wilting under the increased power, where we were now putting 160 lb ft of torque through a gearbox designed for 125. Mike was the ideal development driver. He was able to give me a graphic word picture of exactly what was happening, then he would add detail to the picture by giving me his ideas to solve the problem, prefacing his remarks with: 'For my money I would change . . .'

On the way home I met several of the Rubery Owen South Africa people, on their way to England to Ernest Owen's funeral. This was the first I knew that he had just died suddenly.

Gurney put the cat amongst the pigeons with the Eagle-Weslake at Brands Hatch for the Race of the Champions. Lotus were not competing, neither was the official BRM team, but Tim Parnell ran Mike Spence in an unmodified H16, who was fifth behind Bruce McLaren (fourth) with a 2 litre BRM-engined McLaren. Bruce was the first customer for the V12. Meanwhile I was busy at Bourne as Spear had done a deal with Matra for us to design a 4-valve V12 for them. They would contribute to the head design with ports and valve sizes, but we had to design camshafts, drives, tappets etc., together with the rest of the engine. I had a high regard for George Martin their Chief Engineer.

We had finished designing our V12 and were waiting for the parts to arrive to build the first. Geoff Johnson and I had learned much from designing it and there were many basic similarities between the two engines; except Matra's pump assemblies were alongside the engine to get it as low as possible, whereas our pumps were buried in the sump and their camshafts were gear driven.

General de Gaulle had allocated large sums of money for the construction of a French Championship winner. Matra were leaders in the French aerospace industry; car manufacturers and a logical choice. Sir Alfred was thoroughly briefed on the sensitive nature of the project and how it must be kept absolutely secret, but speaking at an important dinner in London he told his audience how well BRM were doing — they were even designing a F1 engine for Matra. By 10 a.m. the next day the whole project had been cancelled. Matra were livid and in dead trouble. I believe some of their funding was reinstated, but we were definitely out. The contract to supply them with 2 litre V8s for Le Mans also vanished in the same puff of smoke. Commercial projects were taking most of my time particularly the military 2 litre engine and the various Chrysler projects. I seemed to be reorganizing the place from top to bottom every few months with major projects being cancelled and new ones substituted — the Matra affair was just one example.

Oulton Park in April marked the inauguration of the International Grand Prix Medical Services Mobile Hospital, largely because of the efforts of Mr Stanley who had been particularly concerned by the lack of facilities when Jackie crashed in Belgium. Now FOCA and Professor Syd Watkins have an incredibly efficient service, but in 1967 the mobile hospital was a major step forward and I had become one of the directors of IGPMS.

In practice Jackie gave us a morale-booster by getting the heavy H16 with its new suspension on pole, sharing the front row with Denny Hulme with a Brabham and Surtees in the new Honda. Spence was not far behind either, sharing the second row with Brabham himself. I think the reason the ponderous H16 went so well at Oulton was that there were so many similar corners close together. The car had exceptional road holding, but the problem was it was so dreadfully heavy, which made it sluggish under acceleration. Unfortunately, in the race it rained oil and we were in trouble with the Dunlop tyres. The lack of adhesion caused Jackie to have a fearful spin which damaged his suspension. McLaren, still with a 2 litre BRM engine, was fifth, and Spence sixth.

I tried to convince Sir Alfred that we would be better off with Goodyear tyres. They were nearly as good as Dunlop on a clean dry track and not much worse than Firestones when the oil was down. 1967 was the year it literally rained oil in every race. I argued that if we stuck to Goodyear we would learn to get the best out of them and the car. We were getting nowhere switching tyre suppliers every race, as permitted under the Dunlop non-competitive clause. Sir Alfred felt that he had some sort of responsibility to Dunlop and Jackie had a personal contract with them, so it all became very involved.

Exactly the same thing happened at Silverstone in May for the Daily Express Trophy. Jackie had pole, sharing the front row with Parke's Ferrari, Mike Spence and Denny Hulme, but as soon as the oil was down we might just as well have gone home. Graham, in a Lotus with a BRM 2 litre engine, was fourth. McLaren and his 2 litre BRM-engined McLaren, was fifth and Spence, who kept it on the island despite sliding about in an alarming fashion, was sixth. Jackie had a gearbox problem for good measure. The finishing order was Firestone, Goodyear, Goodyear, Firestone, Goodyear, Dunlop.

We ran Jackie in a 2070 cc Tasman car at Monte Carlo. We had put all new gears in the old gearbox, but of course we could not resist the temptation of screwing a little more power out of the engine. The gearbox failed again, Mike Spence was sixth, with an H16, and Graham second, with the same 2 litre BRM engine in his Lotus that he had used at Silverstone. McLaren, in the McLaren BRM, was fourth. He should have learned a lesson here; he had to stop for a replacement battery which cost him at least one place. This was the race where Bandini had his fearful accident and fatal burns. Pre-race socializing was enlivened by cocktails with Mr Stanley's guests, Richard Burton and Elizabeth Taylor, and I feared we would not be able to move in our pit because of the media attention, but they watched from their boat. After this race Mike and I went to Monza at Dunlop's request for some more tyre testing, which just proved that on a clean dry track Dunlop were best — which we already knew.

Jackie had taken Graham's place at the regular meeting with Sir Alfred. He talked Sir Alfred into building a V12-engined car in parallel with the H16s and, recognizing the tremendous amount of work going through Bourne, suggested we sub-contract the design and build of two cars to Len Terry's company. The jigs etc. would revert to us so we could build some more if they were successful. This should not interfere with the H16 programme and we could make 2.5 litre versions of the V12 for these cars for the 1968 Tasman series. Sir Alfred agreed; then all the Rubery Owen procurement and supply people dropped the H16 and concentrated on Sir Alfred's new project. Everything suffered from then on; John Wyer's Mirage engines for Le Mans, most of our V12 parts and H16 spares. I thought I had hit rock bottom at Zandvoort — Lotus, Eagle and Brabham had all got their cars working, while we were relegated to the fifth row. Jackie had brake problems; Spence spun and finished eighth, and our best finisher was Chris Irwin in one of Tim's cars.

Spa slightly soothed our wounded feelings. It was clean — no oil or rain. Jackie spent much time trying Tim's Tasman, so he was only in the third row with his H16, but on the first lap he came round second to Clark in the Lotus Cosworth and when Clark had engine trouble Jackie sailed into the lead with Spence sixth. Then Jackie's fifth gear started jumping out. He tried to avoid using fifth as much as possible, but at Spa fifth was essential for the three mile climb from Stavelot. Gurney caught him, so he was second after a brave drive (for some time holding it in fifth with one hand, while steering with the other) and Spence was fifth.

The French GP in 1967 was on the Bugatti circuit at Le Mans and, as I liked to take Pam to new races, we flew out to Paris a day early and visited Mont St Michel as tourists. It was incredibly hot. Jimmy Clark had his Indianapolis trophy, a Ford Galaxy with air conditioning, and nearly all the ladies took refuge in the cool Galaxy. Chris Irwin, in Tim Parnell's Tasman, was quicker than Jackie, with an H16, in practice so they did a swop. Then, just to make life more difficult, Irwin went even faster in the discarded H16. Right at the end of the race, the Brabhams were first and second, Jackie was third in the Tasman and Irwin fourth in the H16. On the last lap a piston ring failed in the H16 and dropped him to fifth, nursing the engine. Spence retired early with a broken half-shaft flange.

We were back in tyre trouble at Silverstone for the British GP. Jackie, in the Type 115, had suspension trouble. One of Spence's ignition coil boxes caught fire, and Irwin was seventh. Raymond Mays gave a fantastic party at his home in Bourne for the Ancient Pilotes. The guest list read like a Who's Who of motor racing. Fangio, Chiron, Amherst Villers, de Graffenried, Moss etc., and an auctioneer's mouth-watering yard full of BRMs.

At Nürburgring the H16 'yomped' fearfully. I thought their weight would have kept them down, but they 'yomped' the furthest! Jackie was third on the grid, pushing Gurney into fourth, but in the race he and Spence broke crownwheels and pinions — too much time airborne — the shock on landing was too much for them. Before we left for the Nürburgring the Type 101 V12 engine had a very uneventful first run, producing 389 hp at 10,000 rpm. That was nothing special, but 300 hp at 7000 rpm and 312 at 7500 compared with the H16's 280 at 7500, certainly was. The first V12 weighed 328 lb (149 kg) less clutch. A two pin crank H16, 7506, weighed 508 lb (231 kg). This particular week we also ran a 2.5 litre V12 (Type 121) which gave 217 hp at 7000 rpm, 314 at 10,000 and 330 at 11,000, and later that week a 1998 cc V8 weighing 258 lb (117 kg) which gave 212 hp at 7000 rpm, 250 at 9000 and 255.3 at 10,000. The test-bed set-up had to be changed from V8 to V12 and H16. The number of tests on so many different engines should serve to show the complexity of the operation.

The first V12 was sent to McLaren as planned, and having run a 2 litre, which it resembled, they got it into their new car in double-quick time. But they were a little too clever; they discarded the alternator — either they did not have the space, or thought it was not necessary. Whatever the reason, after their recent Monte Carlo experience, it was inexcusable.

Mosport, for the Canadian GP was a new circuit for me. Franco Lini, Ferrari's Team Manager and I stayed in Toronto and drove the 60 miles each day to the circuit, where it rained most of the time. The H16s gave trouble and were difficult to set up. It also became obvious that Jackie's interest was fading and I realized then we might lose him. McLaren were very secretive and refused Willy's offers of help, but in the race McLaren found the wide torque spread of the V12 just right for a wet Mosport, whereas Jackie was having to use all his skill with the H16. McLaren was just about to pass into the lead when he had to stop as his battery was flat — no charge — no alternator! Jackie spun, jamming his throttle slides with mud; the dependable Spence was fifth, and McLaren seventh in a race he could have won.

Alec Osborn was now spending all his time with Len Terry and the V12s, which had to use Hewland gearboxes much to Stokey's disgust. Alec reported the cars were well-made and well-designed but there was nothing revolutionary about then. The only small feature that troubled me was that most of the suspension parts were bright-plated, which did not sit well with my Rolls-Royce training. The plating process could cause hydrogen embrittlement which meant extra heat treatment. There was a risk of plating acid being trapped in welds. I preferred my cars to be like a gun; scrupulously clean, with all the steel parts wiped over with an oily cloth, but we were moving into the showman and sponsor era and I was probably out of tune with events.

We started building a lightweight 4-valve H16 with a target of 500 hp and 400 lb (181 kg) in weight. It had a very narrow included-angle valve gear of 13 degrees. This was made possible by saving space around the sparking plug boss. Instead of surrounding the deeply recessed plug with cast aluminium, to retain the coolant, we used a very thin stainless steel sleeve pressed in place. This enabled us to move the pair of camshafts 1.25 inches (32 mm) closer together. It had a large squish deck, with half the combustion chamber in the piston. Roller-bearing steel camshafts were carried in magnesium alloy trays. The crankcase was two large magnesium castings, sandwiching five titanium blocks which carried the main bearings. The whole structure was held together by long bolts which passed right through the engine from one cylinder head to the other and, having learned our lesson, it had short connecting rods. It met the weight target, but the separate stainless-steel tube and plastic inlet-manifolds and slides cost us our power target. We learned there was a relationship between port length and where they diverged. The Honda solution was to use two valves in one big port. We did not see much over 420 hp, although at 398 lb (180.5 kg) it met the weight target. I had spent nearly £40,000 on this engine — about 40 per cent of my budget!

The balance of power at Rubery Owen had gradually shifted during the year following the death of Ernest Owen. It had thrown more load on Sir Alfred who had less time for the minutiae of BRM. So Mr and Mrs Stanley took a larger part in BRM decision making. In the early days Graham and I could help and point them in the right direction — as Graham said: 'Aim Big Lou, pull the trigger and duck!' Now, having collected information from widely differing sources, they were pressing their ideas on Sir Alfred.

Bourne was getting extremely fragmented, with far too many projects on the go. I could walk round the machine shop and pick up pieces on several machines that I did not recognize, and meet people in the build shop who I did not know yet who were commercial project customers. Because of FOCA, the twin-cam engines and the H16s, I saw more of Colin Chapman — much to Mr Stanley's disapproval. We had managed to disentangle ourselves from Lotus and the H16 without too much acrimony. I was invited to both the foundation stone laying and the opening of the new factory at Hethel. Colin and I started shooting together both in Norfolk and Lincolnshire and in the course of these contacts Colin told me it was vital to the success of his F1 racing programme to keep F1 and racing cars for sale absolutely separate — different people in different buildings.

Dr Harrow paid another visit and we had a long session with H16 and V12s, calculating optimum bore/stroke and rod length ratios. There was enough information from the 64-valve H16 to show that this combustion chamber was the way to go; the rate of burn was 18 to 20 per cent faster than the next best engine, the 1966 three hemisphere 2070 cc V8. I was appalled at the internal friction in all the engines, although the 64-valve H16 was nothing like as bad as we expected, while the 2.5 litre V12 was easily the worst.

In the middle of all this Jackie told us he was going to join Ken Tyrrell who had a very good Ford Cosworth engine deal plus a Matra chassis, obviously an attractive proposition.

Monza was just an interlude amongst all these goings on. Surtees won in the Honda. McLaren got the V12 on the front row, but the engine blew up totally when fighting for third place. It looked like shortage of oil to us, although McLaren assured us that all the pipe sizes and capacities were as we recommended. As usual Spence was fifth, and Jackie was reported to have lost a tyre tread. Anyway, he certainly had a sticking throttle and the engine blew up at half-distance. I was aware that Mr Stanley was negotiating with Pedro Rodriguez and RM was talking to Surtees. I managed a meeting with Sir Alfred who told me that Spear had done a deal with Cooper to use our V12s next season. He wanted to know why McLaren's engine was only giving 365 hp and weighed 385 lb when I had told him 390 hp and 330 lb. I said these were the figures when it left Bourne, and asked who told him otherwise? He said it was Bruce McLaren himself. Apparently Sir Alfred had been negotiating direct with Bruce to drive in the Tasman series. I was also worked over for failing to meet delivery dates on a number of projects that I knew little about. I started to make progress on my 1968 plans, when he produced a diversion.

Apparently Sir Alfred had become involved in some Manx charity and was anxious that BRM should produce a motor cycle engine. I tried to explain that the Japanese motor cycles were up to 200 hp per litre, and there were even rumours of a 128 hp 500 cc Honda. I could see my way to 150 hp per litre, but I just did not know how to get much more, so he would be in for an expensive accelerated research programme. He reminded me that I had been too pessimistic about the Tasman engines, when he had been absolutely right, so I was told to go and produce a costed plan — which blew Peter Spears's mind when he saw it. I left the meeting feeling I had got some of my difficulties across to Sir Alfred, with the exception of the motor cycle engine.

Both H16s had transmission problems in the American GP, while McLaren had a chafed water hose. In the Mexican GP Spence was fifth as usual, just beating his new team mate Rodriguez. McLaren had problems with the car oil system and Jackie had a very rough engine. Sir Alfred decided that we should run V12s next season in the Len Terry cars, with a reduced budget. He also said he had given instructions, concerning commercial work at Bourne, which would reduce my commitments and give me more time to concentrate on what I was good at — F1. I was very mystified by all this, but Sir Alfred said I tried to do everything myself, and I should delegate more. He had never refused a request from me for more staff: I should have a deputy, why had I not appointed one? He had agreed that McLaren should drive and prepare the first Terry car for the Tasman series, and he was considering whether Tim should join them as Team Manager. Eventually Tim took charge of the Tasman series with McLaren and Pedro Rodriguez. The second car was to go to South Africa in early 1968 for Pedro, with Mike Spence in the H16.

I was sorry we were losing Jackie. We had given him the car for his first World Championship win, and he had stuck with us loyally through a very miserable season. He started as very much the new boy in a team dominated by Graham, but he soon developed his own style and personality, and became very much one of the team. Following his crash at Spa he became a little more sober, but the irrepressible sense of humour was still there.

Jackie was not so articulate as Graham at first, and used a different vocabulary. In fact it took me some time to understand what he was driving at. Things improved significantly during one Snetterton test. After trying unsuccessfully to explain what was wrong with the front end, he told me to try it myself, clapping his helmet on my head — so off I went. I soon realized what he meant, but he could not understand why I just sat in the car looking profoundly wise. When he realized I was stuck and could not get out, he had hysterics.

He became very vociferous on safety and, in fact, the champion of this cause. I could never understand why he was attacked for whingeing. Racing drivers of his calibre or even of a lesser standard are in very short supply, and the waste of human life when it could so easily be avoided was indefensible. There is a fine difference between dangerous and wasteful. In the days when he was with BRM we fitted seat belts for him: now everyone had them. I never minded Jackie's search for increased safety because once the flag fell he gave you 101 per cent — his performances in the wet at the Nürburgring, for example. On one occasion we found a small fuel leak in the tank breather on the startline at Monza. I told him we could not fix it in time, but that it should clear up after two or three laps when the fuel level dropped; but it was up to him. He just shrugged his shoulders, got in the car and got on with it.

It was this quality, in particular, that to my mind set him above Jimmy Clark, although you could argue for weeks as to who was the quickest driver. Under ideal weather conditions and equal cars, there was not much to choose between them on pure ability. However, as Clark only drove Chapman-designed cars, and Chapman's cars went best with Clark driving them it was difficult to decide how much of the performance came from Clark and how much from Chapman. Jackie drove three different cars superbly, BRM, Matra and Tyrrells. The prime difference was when things were not quite right, such as a wet Nürburgring: Jimmy would hold back a little — there was always another day and another race — but Jackie would give every race his maximum effort. He was a great ambassador for the sport, nearly up to Graham's standard, whereas Jimmy was painfully shy until he got to know you. Graham spent a lot of time in the garage and the workshop encouraging his mechanics, while Jackie believed that after showing interest and appreciation they worked better without him looking over their shoulder. Jackie and I have kept in touch. His father's last words to me still ring in my ears. 'Tell the wee bugger to get his hair cut!'

After the cars had set out for their various destinations in the southern hemisphere, I had talks with Tim Parnell to set up a communication link. Tim would be in Australia and New Zealand with two untried cars and engines and two new drivers. I would be in South Africa also sorting similar engines and cars, and racing them a few days before Tim, so we needed a system of rapid exchange of information. We even considered running Tim's cars on one make of tyres and the works team on another, but Sir Alfred discouraged it. Alec Osborn and Geoff Johnson went out to Kyalami a few days before me to do the initial sorting of the Terry car and V12 engine, so that by the time I got there only the really difficult (or easy depending on your point of view) problems remained.

I realized I could not keep going at my present pace. I was slowing down, getting stale, and taking longer to reach decisions. I accepted that there was not going to be the time or money to develop the H16 into a reliable race winner and we stood a better chance with the V12 and the Terry cars. Neither Alec nor I could identify what was different, that would give them an advantage over a BRM-designed car. Sir Alfred said that until we had generated a certain sum of money (which equated to the sale of 23 V12s) we could not have any money to spend improving the V12 engine. I wondered what would have happened if we had built the 390 hp 2-valve V12 first. We would have had it ready for Monte Carlo or Spa in 1966. It would have given the 360 hp Repco Brabham a good run in 1966. We might even have been strong enough to challenge the 420 hp Lotus Cosworths of 1967 and still have had Graham and Jackie. I also realized if I had had more courage designing the H16 it would have been much lighter and it would have been ready to race three or four months earlier.

# CHAPTER EIGHTEEN

# V12s and
# ground effect

BY THEN IT was time for South Africa, where the combination of heat and
altitude caused the fuel to boil in both the V12s and H16s. Tim had reported
similar trouble with the Tasman cars. We put the H16 away and
concentrated on the V12. I was staying at a different hotel from the usual
Kyalami Ranch, sharing a suite with Pedro as there had been a mix-up over
his reservations. I found the comings and goings of his very spectacular
lady guests somewhat distracting but eventually we settled down. The V12
was not picking up all the fuel as the tanks emptied. We made a rear-
mounted collector tank with non-return valves to catch the fuel as it surged
back under acceleration, and put a cooler in the return line. The next
problem was aerodynamic lift from the long flat nose. I had known about
ground effect right from the days when I saw the first Stirling aircraft with
Gouge flaps and stork-like undercarriage. I had treated ground-effect as a
nuisance and deliberately gave the monocoques a V-shaped bottom like a
boat. This reduced ground effect and consequent drag, hence the
considerable speed advantage we enjoyed over the similar Lotus 25 and
33s.

After the race at Launceston in Tasmania in 1966 Jimmy Clark asked me
what power our 2 litre cars really did give? He would not believe 260 hp,
saying his Climax had 245, yet after Jackie passed him he just could not
stay in the slip-stream, and at the end of the straight he was 200 yards
behind. I did not realize that I had anti-ground effect. To combat the lift we
cut holes in the nose and fitted some large, steeply inclined spoilers each
side of the nose — they were the beginning of front wings.

With some minor adjustments to suit Kyalami we produced good lap
times so we could start on the Dunlop tyre test programme, as Dunlop were
paying for the trip. Mike Spence was very encouraged and, as agreed, we
passed all we had learned to Tim Parnell in New Zealand. Whether it was
coincidence or not Bruce McLaren then won at Teratonga. I commuted the
6000 miles back to Bourne nearly every weekend, where we were building
the first Type 133 in Len Terry's 126 jigs. There was a press release on the
Matra V12 — with photographs. Not surprisingly it looked like a 4-valve
version of our engine, inlets between the camshafts. Willy eventually found
some of the parts were interchangeable. I sensed that Rubery Owen was not

as profitable as it used to be!

The season opener at Brands Hatch cheered us up considerably. McLaren led in his McLaren Cosworth but with Mike Spence chasing him hard. Hopefully my pre-race pep talk had got through — 'You are a better driver than he is; the car is as good. Get in front and stay there.' Unfortunately the car was rolling and bottoming, and it wore through both the skin and the oil pipe below. Pedro stalled on the line, then carved his way through the field to finish second. Mike had won the 100 bottles of champagne for fastest practice lap, which also helped.

We spent Easter sailing the children's dinghy on the Broads with Mike and Lyn Spence, plus Roger Enever and Baggy Sach. Mike, Roger and I, none of us lightweights, sailing the dinghy, passed through a sailing club race at Thurne Mouth, in a great cloud of spray and with the mast bent like a bow, going about twice as fast as they were. During the holiday Mike confessed to a yearning to drive at Indianapolis. I also gave him another pep talk on the lines of: 'You are too much of a gentleman for this business, get in there and do some pushing and shoving.' We also hatched the Spence Elan programme that weekend, basically a BRM green Lotus Elan, with Spence suspension improvements and a BRM-built phase two Lotus twin-cam.

In April, at Dunlop's expense, we tested tyres at Zandvoort. It all worked out as planned. While Mike put in over 600 miles, we went to work on Pedro, teaching him the difference between stiff and soft roll bars, the effect of camber and toe-in changes. He was incredibly grateful; saying no one had ever taken the trouble to help him get the best out of himself and the car before.

We were all devastated by Jimmy Clark's death at Hockenheim later in April. It seemed absolutely inexplicable to me at the time. Colin Chapman, as one would expect, was shattered but realized he had a large number of people in his new factory depending on him, and he fought back.

I gave Mike yet another pep-talk at Silverstone for the Daily Express Trophy. The front row was two McLarens (Bruce and Denny Hulme) and two BRMs (Mike and Pedro), with Graham Hill and two Ferraris in the second row. Mike did not make a very good start but eventually overtook both the McLarens in quite hairy places, holding the lead for a while until the car developed understeer. Then the timing chain broke. Pedro who was fourth, stopped when an ignition wire came loose. He put it back, but the coil was damaged and he was out. It was all very encouraging, and not only for me. Sir Alfred agreed that we could make 4-valve heads for the V12s.

We went back to Silverstone a few days later to find out why Mike's handling had deteriorated suddenly and so badly. Lotus were there with Graham testing their four-wheel-drive Indy turbine car. Just before lunch Colin approached me saying: 'When you wrote to me (after Jimmy's death) you said you would do anything you could to help. Graham has to go back to London and 'Flame out Fred' (the nickname of the Pratt and Whitney engineer) also has to return to the States in a few hours. Could Mike drive the turbine for a few laps to get some data for Fred?' I agreed, if Mike was willing, which he was.

When we had finished testing and were loading up, as I feared Mike sidled up to me. I said: 'I know, you want to drive it at Indy.' He said: 'Yes, I will not let it interfere with Monte Carlo.' I had some difficulty convincing Mr and Mrs Stanley that we should release him to drive at Indianapolis, but no driver with red blood in his veins passes up that chance. I hoped that it would give him a little more confidence in himself. I cautioned him about jet-lag and not arriving for practice after an all-night transatlantic flight. I knew all about jet-lag and disorientation, having done it so often myself.

The next race was the Spanish GP. The cars had left Bourne on the morning of first Indianapolis practice, when in the middle of the night Andrew Ferguson rang me from Indy to say Mike was severely injured. He had got the Lotus turbine on pole, but as the similar STP cars were not going as quickly, Mike was asked to try one; which he did. It had a different front-to-rear drive ratio so its angle of drift through the curves was also slightly different. Whatever the reason, he touched the outer wall at the exit of one of the turns. The front suspension was torn off, as it was designed to, but the telescopic steering damper did not break away, so the wheel restrained by the damper hit Mike's head. A few hours later Colin rang to say that Mike had died. Then I had a phone call from Cyril Atkins to say they had just heard the news. They were at the Franco-Spanish frontier and asked what they should do? I told them to carry on. I then spoke to Sir Alfred, and we agreed to run Pedro alone, providing he was willing, with the mechanics wearing white overalls with black arm bands. I had lunch with him as soon as I arrived in Madrid. He said he would still like to drive, but he realized how close we were to Mike, and if we wished to withdraw the whole team as a mark of respect he would fully understand. I felt, and told Pedro, that we could not sit around and mope. The best thing to do was to get on with it and try to win.

Next morning Pedro put his car well on pole, ahead of Graham and Chris Amon's Ferrari. Beltoise was standing-in for Jackie Stewart who had hurt his wrist. Pedro was eventually pushed off the pole by Amon. On race morning Pedro got up very early and went to Mass. I had breakfast with him, sensing he was very tense. I told him there were several new cars in the race — the Honda, fresh from Japan, and the new Brabham, fresh from England by charter aircraft — so he should watch out for blow-ups and oil all over the track. We would feel that he had done well if he finished close behind such experienced campaigners as Graham, Surtees and Hulme. Finishing the race in a reasonable position would provide us with much vital data. Pedro made a splendid start and was well away, then Beltoise got by him on lap 10, trailing oil and smoke and soon blowing up. In the confusion Amon got by at the same time. By 20 laps Pedro was second, well ahead of Graham and lining up to have a go at Amon, when he spun on some oil and into the catch fence. We were all glad Graham won. I had to get back for Mike Spence's funeral, which was awful. Mike's death seemed to have affected Colin Chapman much more than Jimmy's. He looked gaunt and grey. He and Hazel sat alone in the church, so I persuaded them to join the large BRM contingent. I think he had mentally prepared himself for the possibility that Jimmy might get killed one day, but Mike's death so soon afterwards really hurt him.

It was decided that we would run Dickie Attwood in the second car at Monte Carlo and, if he did well, keep him for the rest of the season. He had a very good record at Monte Carlo and was acceptable to the Owen family.

Mike had described the Chaparral to me in great detail, especially its moveable wings, and the benefits of the GM 2-speed automatic transmission. But I was a little nervous about all the forces we would unleash with wings. Air Marshal Sir Geoffrey Tuttle, Managing Director of the Vickers Division of the British Aircraft Corporation at Weybridge, was an old friend from wartime days when he commanded the RAF Photographic Reconnaissance Unit with Spitfires and Mosquitoes. He arranged for me to meet Sir Barnes Wallis, and we would try to persuade him to design a wing for us. I had just acquired a personal assistant, one Peter Wright, a Cambridge graduate with an aerodynamics degree. I gave him the task of working with Barnes Wallis to devise a suitable wing.

Pam came with me to Monte Carlo. She had sensed Mike's death had gone deep, not helped by such remarks as 'his death will be forever on your conscience'. It was much harder to re-motivate myself and the team, than after the various BRM disasters and the departure of Graham and Jackie. Much as I liked Pedro, he still had some way to go. His social secretary somehow got his affairs mixed up at Monte Carlo! He spent much time and energy keeping his wife and other guests apart, so I was not very surprised when he hit the Armco at the Mirabeau. Attwood went incredibly well. He started amongst the toughs, alongside Rindt and behind Surtees, but by lap ten of the race shortened from 100 to 80 laps, he was fourth, and by lap 20 he was second. He finished 2.2 seconds behind Graham, with a new lap record of 1 min 21.8 sec. How much faster Graham could have gone I do not know, but it was a good race. I did not slow Dickie down, even though the two Cooper-BRMs that were third and fourth were a long way back.

We had a pleasant lunch to celebrate Hazel Chapman's birthday at Beaulieu on the Friday before the race. I think the wives were working hard to revitalize their husbands. I do not know whether Colin and I spoiled their plans by having a very long discussion on oil tank design, with the ensuing sketches covering the whole of the tablecloth! We drove back via Geneva and Switzerland as there was a serious fuel strike in France.

I was caught up in another Vauxhall project, and the engine shop was getting a little frayed around the edges; 12 of them having rebuilt 12 engines in seven days, with all of them being properly power tested and checked. I had fitted in three meetings — FOCA, the SSMT sporting sub-committee, as the formula was due to change at the end of 1969, and an RAC Committee trying to devise a better formula of equivalence between gas turbine and piston engines onto which I had co-opted Dr Hooker (SGH), having a sabbatical from Rolls-Royce at Bristol aero-engines. I also had a day at Rubery Owen to meet the new owners of Cooper who wished to renegotiate their agreement. I do not know why the meeting had to be at Darlaston, instead of Bourne, giving me a six-hour drive. Sir Alfred was not involved in any way.

At Spa for the Belgian GP, Ferrari and Brabham had fixed aerofoils, and as usual it rained. In common with most drivers from tropical countries, Pedro did not understand that wet roads were slippery and dangerous and that you should slow down. I realized that we were in deep trouble when Piers Courage in Tim's 126 was quicker than either Pedro or Dickie. They could neither of them tell me what their cars needed, so we could not change the set-up to help them. Mr Stanley had to lean on the race organizers to get some sort of sense into their plans in the event of rain.

On race morning I saw a rather glum John Cooper breakfasting with his team's new owners. As we walked out I told him I had been watching them and wondering who was Marks and who was Spencer. In a flash, he replied: 'I know who I am, I am St Michael!' In the race Attwood was forced wide at La Source, and tore out a water pipe, but Pedro gradually worked his way up by a combination of blind courage and attrition. He took the lead on the last lap only to suffer fuel starvation, which he tried to alleviate by coasting. If he had accelerated, fuel would have surged back into the collector tank which would have kept him going. We had briefed him on this, but he suffered from the red mist problem that afflicts many drivers. So McLaren had pipped him on the line. We found his front roll-bar had broken. When I asked him when it failed, Pedro said: 'Roll bar? What is a roll bar?' So much for our Zandvoort training!

Dan Gurney had split with Weslake and was by then running his Eagle operation on a shoe string. He had no test-bed facilities, so we let him use ours at Folkingham while we were away at Spa. They were most disappointed to find their engine now only gave 385 hp. I tried to work out how to set the cars up for Zandvoort, hoping that our Dunlop tests early in the year with Mike Spence, when we got down to 1 min 24 sec, would read across to the Goodyears we were now using. I was disappointed. Amon (Ferrari) had pole with 1 min 23.54 sec. Pedro's best was 1 min 25.50 sec. Fortunately for us, it rained. Jackie won, Pedro was third, Attwood seventh but five laps down.

I could not hope for such luck in the French GP at Rouen. Lotus were wearing enormous moveable wings, and we had top exit radiator ducts which provided some free front down-force. Jackie Oliver in the second Lotus escaped from a fearful crash relatively unharmed when he hit the turbulence from Attwood's slip-stream. We started on dry tyres, but it began to rain on the third lap. Pedro was in the middle of a battle for the lead with Ickx and Surtees when he ran over the wreckage of Schlesser's Honda causing a puncture. After a pit stop he finished twelfth and last, but with fastest lap. Attwood was seventh.

In practice for the British GP at Brand Hatch we could not improve our time from earlier in the year. I spent some time trying to decide whether it was going to rain. Sir Alfred said 'Pedro is good in the wet; start him on rain tyres and, if it does rain, you will have an advantage — if not you will still not be much worse off.' It made sense, except that it did not rain and the car fell off the jacks during our pit stop to change to dry tyres! HRH Prince Charles toured the starting grid. He said I looked calm and relaxed, should I not be worrying about something? If only I'd had enough time to tell him! Pedro broke a camshaft as a result of missing a gear and Dickie's engine was cooked because of a broken water pipe. We went to Graham's party that evening at his cottage on the Brabourne estate in Kent where I spent some time reminiscing with Lord Louis Mountbatten.

At the Nürburgring for the German GP we were in more trouble. It also rained heavily most of the time and Pedro finished sixth. Attwood, three laps down, was 14th and last, so he was told by Mr Stanley that his services were no longer required.

I was told to organize a familiarization session for Indianapolis winner Bobby Unser, who did not arrive at Snetterton until late in the evening. It took some time to fit him into the spare car — he was much bigger than our other drivers. Next day we went to Silverstone where it rained. Bobby seemed happy with the car, produced some good times and said he would see me at Monza.

Mario Andretti was due to drive the third Lotus in the Italian GP, but he and Bobby were also due to run in the Hoosier '100' on Saturday in America. It meant a few minutes practice on Friday, over to the USA, back overnight — in contravention of FISA's 24 hour rule — for the race on Sunday. FISA duly applied their rule, so Pedro started alone on the sixth row, wearing wings for the first time. In the race he had a sticking throttle. Piers Courage in Tim's 126 was fourth. One highlight of Monza was a dinner given by John Player Gold Leaf for Graham Hill's 100th GP. On the flight home I worked out it was my 186th!

I spent Monday at a FOCA/FISA meeting in Milan when it was agreed to extend the 3 litre formula for another three years. When I thought about the 186 races, I thought maybe it's time I gave up. I could not work up any enthusiasm for 200. Pam suggested we took a holiday and let somebody else take charge in Canada, so Alec Osborn went with Pedro and produced a well fought third place with very little coolant in the engine. I had ten days in the sun, which helped confirm 200 was too many.

It rained for the US GP at Watkins Glen, an event which underlined my conclusion that 200 was too many when Unser and Courage crashed in first practice. Unser's car was a write-off, Piers's should have been. Pedro and Courage both spun in the race eliminating both of them, and we blew up five out of our seven engines, mostly through severe over-revving. When I made my usual post-race phone call to Sir Alfred he must have sensed how I felt. He invited me to go to see him at his home, New Hall, Sutton Coldfield — now a hotel, by the way.

I went to the Mexican GP to keep faith with Pedro. He met me straight off the aeroplane and I never went near Customs or Immigration; just sat in his air-conditioned Pontiac Bonneville while my luggage was unloaded straight into the boot. Graham was then fighting Jackie for the Championship. During the race Graham's wing-feathering mechanism broke, leaving it stuck in the high drag, high down-force position, but Jackie had almost terminal fuel-injection troubles. Pedro was out-fumbled by Jackie Oliver in a dash for the line for third place and finished fourth. Next day Pedro took Tim Parnell and me to his country home at Cuernavacca for lunch and then to dinner at a very elaborate restaurant where different coloured fountains formed the cabaret.

When my return flight landed at Heathrow I had to go straight to Chrysler UK at Coventry for a meeting on a proposed 4-valve conversion for the Hillman Avenger engine to be developed for rallies. Ten years later the Lotus 4-valve-engined Sunbeam won the World Rally Championship, prepared in and operating from, the same buildings.

I duly had my meeting with Sir Alfred, who offered a compromise which I accepted. It was mainly noteworthy for how much he managed to convey to me without actually putting it in words. He said I would be letting him down personally if I left; having supported me at Bourne through thick and thin. His intention was that the Engine Development Division at Bourne should be self-supporting. We could keep all the profits to spend on the cars. He thought I should take more interest in the commercial activities.

He also implied that he was going to let his sister and brother-in-law take a more prominent part in BRM affairs. This might mean less interference with the running of the mainstream Rubery Owen business. He further implied that as I was on good terms with the Stanleys this would not present me with any problems. He repeated several times that most of the sales appeal came from having the work done by me and my team alongside the F1 cars. I felt that I had got through to him and I owed it to him to have another try. Two days later Colin Chapman rang me before breakfast and offered me the post of Director of Engineering at Lotus Cars. I had to tell him that I had shaken hands with Sir Alfred on a compromise and I could not back out now.

During our routine budget meetings planning for 1969 it was agreed that I would set aside 30 per cent of the money for drivers, even though I did not know who they were going to be. This did not leave much for new cars, but I felt we could extract more power from the engine and get more performance from the existing car. I assumed, incorrectly, we would keep Pedro, but apparently he already knew he had been transferred to Tim Parnell for 1969. I had asked Raymond Mays who our drivers were to be — I knew that he had been negotiating with John Surtees — but all he said was: 'You had better ask your friend Mr Stanley.'

I had a big meeting with myself as to why Mike's death had destroyed so much of my enthusiasm for racing. In the early days Graham Hill stimulated, prodded and generally kept everyone up to fever pitch with his enthusiasm. Graham inspired us to make his car go faster. Later, when he became involved in other activities, he would still come and fire everyone with the same enthusiasm. Jackie Stewart had the same urgent will to win. He would take as much interest in the preparation of his car and in new ideas, but he took the line that, once the idea had been accepted, how we did it was up to us. He would, though, keep pressure on us to make sure it was done as quickly and efficiently as possible. Mike Spence was rather like Richie, deeply interested, with a depth of engineering knowledge and ability, and able to paint a vivid and accurate picture as to what the car was doing, complemented by his ideas and opinions.

I still think the driver-engineer-manager relationship is absolutely vital to success, from Chapman with Clark and mine with Graham. Chapman and Team Lotus also suffered when they lost Rindt, but they had enough momentum and Colin enough ability to keep it going for a few years. It really needed the Andretti input to make the Lotus 78s and 79s into winners and then it sank back again. When I became Chairman of Team Lotus in 1989 Nelson Piquet tried to put this relationship back, but too much of my time was spent on Lotus Engineering affairs, which were my prime responsibility. McLaren would not be as strong as it is today without the Dennis-Prost and Dennis-Senna relationship. You could give them today's equivalent of Rodriguez and their cars would not be as good. It does not have to be a love affair, just mutual respect. Mike Spence did not apply the same intense pressure that Graham and Jackie did, but he came to Bourne and walked round and talked through with me how to make the car faster, just as they did.

I think this is what I missed. I could tell what the engine was doing, and needed, from running it myself on the test-bed. I learned from having my hand on the throttle. I could sense engine loads and stresses but I could not drive the car as fast as the drivers. I got some ideas from driving them myself, but I needed the drivers' input. In any case Rubery Owen finally forbade me to drive the cars. Pedro was charming and polite but he had absolutely no idea how the car worked. He was quite a good race tactician and far from stupid, but I could not obtain any technical feedback from him. Dickie Attwood felt very much the new boy and appeared to believe that any suggestion would be treated as criticism. The Bourne set-up with its political groups he found intimidating. I felt it all slipping away from me and concentrated on the V12's new 4-valve cylinder head.

The V12's head was very similar to the 64-valve H16 narrow angle valve gear exhaust in the V. The only aspect of the design we were not quite sure about was blending of the port into the throat around the valve seats. The first engine had the port centre line coincident with the valve and seat centre line. We also managed a very encouraging run on the 64-valve H16 with individual inlet ports all the way to the throttle slides which gave 484 hp (161 hp per litre) before the lash-up induction system fell off and started a fire. I told Willy to keep quiet about this and our run on a Berthon-Weslake 4-valve converted to a 'haystack', that is inlet and exhaust systems both sides of the same head, which gave 168 hp on a 997 F2. I was afraid that this might revive interest in the motorcycle project.

One of the good things to come from FOCA was a revised Frankfurt scale of start money. We all went to the meeting in the new Lotus Piper Navajo, followed on our return by a very hairy landing in a strong crosswind on an icy runway at Heathrow. We had another meeting in Paris where I introduced FOCA Secretary, Andrew Ferguson, to Fouquet's restaurant on the corner of the Champs-Elysées and the Avenue Georges V. I also managed to persuade Alex Blignaut who ran Kyalami to move the date of the South African GP to early March. Later I went with Mr Stanley to conclude the deal with Surtees. On the way I told Mr Stanley how much of the budget had been allocated for drivers, but I did not suggest a fee. I was startled, therefore, when he offered Surtees the entire drivers' budget, which Surtees accepted. On the way home I enquired how we were going to pay for his choice of No. 2 driver, Jackie Oliver, and got no answer. I was wondering what we would have to cut out of the programme when I remembered the extra start money we would get on the new Frankfurt scale. It would not exactly make Jackie Oliver rich, but the Budget Committee had impressed on me, not a penny more.

The first 4-valve V12 was ready to run. We agreed to strip it after reaching 9000 rpm to avoid risking the premature blow-up of a valuable prototype, due to be air-freighted to Kyalami in a few days. After running it in we took the first power curve at 3 a.m. on 13 February. It gave no trouble up to 8000 rpm but not much power either, being well down on a 2-valve. The exhaust note was flat, but as I opened up to 8250 it changed to a much louder and harder sound. We shut down, fearing something had broken, but we could not find anything wrong. We tried again. The needle went round the dial in a most satisfactory fashion. Even more at 8500, 8750 and 9000. Torque was climbing — we were over 400 hp. A good 2-valve would be about 375 hp at 9000 rpm. Geoff wanted me to stick to the plan and strip the engine, but I twisted his arm for one quick run to 9250 where we found the torque had flattened but we were up to 413 hp. The engine was in the engine shop when they came into work at 8 a.m. — still warm, and back on the bed 36 hours later, to give 444 hp at 10,750. Back to the shop for a strip examination, and three days later we saw 464 hp and just got it away in time to South Africa.

In first practice the bevel gears in the drive to the vertical fuel-injection metering unit failed. After some frantic telephoning, Geoff got us a replacement via the BOAC VC10 by 12-noon next day, 6000 miles away, in time for afternoon practice. John Surtees got down to 1 min 21.8 sec compared with Brabham's front row time of 1 min 20 sec using a Cosworth engine and 1 min 20.2 sec from Rindt in his first race for Lotus and 1 min 20.3 sec for Denny Hulme in a McLaren. We had switched cars for Surtees, notifying the officials in case the gears did not arrive. They did not record our notification of the change back, so we had to start from the back row.

In the race a high-silicon-content aluminium tappet bush broke up, which let the tappet loose, mangling the valve gear. Jackie Oliver had a broken iron camshaft in his 2-valve. I caught the helicopter to the airport and was back in Bourne for breakfast next day. The second 4-valve V12, with the inlet ports tangential to one side of the seat gave 2 per cent more torque, but was about 1 per cent down on maximum power, so we settled for this layout. We were able to play these tricks quite easily, as Les Bryden had developed a technique of reaming the ports.

Also on my return I found Peter Wright in a state of suppressed excitement. He had been running a wind-tunnel test programme and had been investigating aerodynamic section side-pods as eventually used by March a year later. He had gone further and tested a quarter-scale model shaped like an inverted wing, with the wheels slightly inset and a long thin fairing underneath for the driver, crankcase and gearbox. It gave very good results in the Imperial College tunnel, but I was rather sceptical that he had managed to get so much from an open-wheeled car, and suggested further tests which he rushed off to perform.

I went to Brands Hatch for the Race of the Champions with John and the 4-valve. He went off the road in practice, breaking a rear wishbone — nothing serious but it put an end to our practice. Pam and I were staying with him and his wife at his home in Surrey. While warming up for the race the engine went on to 11 cylinders and we discovered that one of the small steel balls from the self-aligning ball-race at the inner end of the broken wishbone had gone into the induction system and damaged an inlet valve, so he was a non-starter. When I asked him, in practice, how the car was going, he said it was early days yet, and when I asked him later he just tapped the side of his nose. I could not tell whether he had no idea or was just not going to tell me. Fortunately Jackie Oliver seemed to have plenty of ideas, as a result of his Lotus experience, rather in the Mike Spence tradition.

Peter's results from his second set of tests were even better than the first and I had to decide what to do next. Obviously we had to build such a car. We had two new cars, Type 139s, in the programme to make the best use of the very slim 4-valve engine, which was about 22 lb (10 kg) heavier than the 2-valve because of the extra 24 valves, 48 springs and the gear drive to the camshafts. The new car also had to carry more fuel for the more powerful engine, and we had been caught at Spa the year before. Stokey's new gearbox for the V12 was ready, it was 11 lb (5 kg) lighter than the Hewland, and smaller.

I cancelled the second Type 139 car (fortunately the first was nearly finished), picked a small team, mainly sheet metal workers, and sent them off to the Chapel — a building we rented on the other side of Bourne where the Raymond Mays cylinder heads used to be assembled — telling them all to keep their mouths shut. If the car was as good as the wind tunnel results, we would have a few months to make a killing before everyone copied it.

I was tempted to save it for 1970 when we would have a whole season ahead, but such was the state of BRM affairs we needed to get it to Monza and win two or three races, so I told Peter Wright that Monza was to be its first race. I told Sir Alfred very briefly what I was doing and the danger of any leaks. I was aware of his inability to keep quiet, but it was his firm and his money, so he had a right to know. He asked if anyone else knew, and I told him no one other than the people working on the car. He said — no doubt remembering the Matra debacle — to keep it that way, at least until our next meeting, due in a month. At that meeting, when he enquired as to progress with the new car, I told him we might even have it ready in time for the German GP, but I did not think it wise to run such a revolutionary car for the first time at the Nürburgring. He agreed and asked how I was funding it. I said I had cancelled the second car so I did not need additional funds. 'Have you told anyone else?' he enquired. I said: 'No.' 'Not even my sister?' he asked. I said: 'No' again, to which he replied: 'Good!'

For the Spanish GP at Barcelona we had trouble with the new gearbox selectors. I was very disappointed by the performance of the 4-valve engine in the car, it did not seem to be realizing the test-bed powers, which we traced to a scavenge problem. High cornering loads from the ever larger wings meant that the oil surged away from the scavenge pump pick-ups, the oil was left in the crankcase causing power losses through churning. We were given a clue when Jackie Oliver's car blew a scavenge pipe off, on the starting grid. John finished fifth, well down, after losing much time because of a defective ignition coil box. This was the race when the Lotus wings failed, with Graham and Jochen Rindt having major crashes. After Barcelona I had to go to Paris, as the FOCA representative, with Dean Delamont to an FIA meeting to discuss action on limiting wings. As BRM made their own engines and gearbox as well as their cars, I tended to be the spokesman for the British FOCA teams. It looked as if the FIA would sit on the fence until after Zandvoort when a major meeting was convened in Amsterdam. I suspected that the immediate problem might be pushed on to the Monaco organizers and warned the other teams. While I was away Geoff Johnson managed to squeeze a second scavenge pump, in tandem with the first, into the sump to cope with the oil surge.

I had, in view of my continued interest in automatic transmissions, borrowed a Morris 1300 fitted with the new Automotive Products gearbox to drive to Monaco to see how it worked. In view of my problems I debated whether to fly but decided against it. Pam came too and shared some of the driving. On the newly-opened autoroute from Arras to Paris it was a bit painful; the maximum speed being only 90 mph but it went through the pre-peripherique Paris in fine style, and on the very twisty pre-autoroute stretch from Fréjus to Nice I had a rare old battle with an Aston Martin DB6. It also took about eight of Graham's Indianapolis friends to the Pirate's Restaurant in Menton!

As expected, the Monaco race organizers banned wings. Tyrrell protested, so the FIA stepped in and confirmed the ban. Surtees began to go as I had hoped, and was fifth fastest. Jackie Oliver had trouble with the new scavenge system and started well back, but it did not matter. Up the hill on the first lap he collided with Attwood standing in for the convalescent Rindt in a Lotus, not even getting as far as he had the year before when he shunted in the tunnel on his first lap. Surtees and Brabham collided on the tenth lap, so we had two crashed cars to mend. In view of our troubles, I decided to go home that night, but I could not get out of the circuit, and traffic on the way to the hotel delayed us so much it was not worth it, so we set off at first light in the morning.

I had been very impressed by the new high-silicon aluminium-alloys and had arranged for a set of ventilated brake discs, as well as solid discs, to be made from this material which would save some 26 lb (12 kg) per car. Ferodo made some special linings and tested the aluminium discs; they also were very enthusiastic. The new slimmer Type 139 was ready, and I planned to shake it down at Zandvoort followed by two days testing at the Nürburgring. We had not learned anything the previous year because of the rain. I believed that one of the keys to good road-holding at the Ring was plenty of wheel movement which the 126 and 133s did not have. We had designed plenty into the 139. The plan was to travel to the Ring on the Monday after Zandvoort; maybe get a shake-down that evening, with serious testing Tuesday. I had to represent FOCA at a major FIA meeting in Amsterdam on Monday, but planned to reach Adenau late on Monday evening — it was autobahn nearly all the way. Peter Wright added to the fun. He had tested his model with large side-plates and a hinged flap at the tail, greatly increasing the downforce for very little increase in drag. He hoped to have the car on its wheels by the end of the month (June) incorporating these improvements, and he did not anticipate any delays. He had tested small side-pods to give downthrust, with end-plates, and they worked in the wind tunnel where there was no turbulence from the rotating wheels. He wanted to try a set on a car, and he thought they might be a temporary answer to the imminent ban on wings.

We then had a visit from John Surtees for a fitting in the new car. He did not say much, but it was obvious he was not impressed. He kept asking who did what, and it was clear that he had noticed the absence of some of the key people now in Peter Wright's team. I felt rather deflated because John queried why we injected fuel against incoming air flow. I explained why, with all the details of the early days with Eric Downing and the later spinning system on the H16. He made no comment, but soon I had a peremptory instruction from Mr Stanley to inject with the air flow. It did not make as much difference on the 4-valves as it did on the original V8 and H16. It was too much trouble to argue, but bad for Bourne morale.

So it was with mixed feelings that I set off for Zandvoort and the Nürburgring, planning to test the aluminium brake discs on the short circuit. I was rather amused by the appearance of 4-wheel-drive Matras and Lotuses. Graham later told me that it was just like the 4-wheel-drive BRM five years ago. They did not go as fast and you could not tell why. Surtees would not drive the 139, neither would Jackie Oliver, who said if he did life would become unbearable. Both cars were right at the back of the grid, and Surtees finished three laps down.

Later that evening I was summoned to Mr and Mrs Stanley's suite where I found John Surtees, and was told to cancel the Nürburgring tests — they were a waste of time. Whatever project I had running in the Chapel at Bourne was also to stop at once and the staff returned to their regular work.

A work and development programme was being prepared which would be sent to me in due course. I found Cyril Atkins, called off the Nürburgring tests and got him to phone the factory to try to set up a test session for the side pods and aluminium brake discs.

As I left the Hotel Bouewes to go to the Prize Giving next door I found myself walking alongside Colin Chapman. I asked if the job he offered me last autumn was still going. He replied it most certainly was, so we agreed that I would phone him as soon as I was back in England. Cyril had managed to arrange with Peter Wright and Jackie Oliver to test at Snetterton next Wednesday afternoon. The side pods had little effect, and the aluminium brake-discs broke up, much to Jackie Oliver's discomfiture.

When the tests were finished I drove over to Lotus where Colin Chapman asked me if I wanted to stay in motor racing. I replied that I could take it or leave it. 'Fine,' he said, 'I want a Technical Director for the car company. First, he must turn us into an engine manufacturer and then get our new four-seater car into production.' He showed me their new 2 litre 4-valve head on a cast-iron Vauxhall block and said: 'When can you start?' I told him my service contract called for three months notice, which he said was acceptable, but I had to get myself out of Rubery Owen as Lotus bought a lot of material from them, especially wheels and petrol tanks. Sir Alfred and 'Big Lou' had been very good to him and he did not want to fall out with them. I said I could extricate myself without difficulty and we agreed to meet again when I had resigned from Rubery Owen to finalize contract details.

When I got home — to find Eddie Hall from Monte Carlo had arrived unexpectedly to stay the night — I rang Sir Alfred and requested a meeting, which was set for 9 a.m. on Friday. I realized it was going to be a wrench for Pam who had lived in and around Bourne most of her life. I was uprooting her, and the children from their schools. She just said: 'Where you go, we go' — which settled that.

I kept out of the way on Thursday, and when I got to Darlaston on Friday I was asked to wait in Sir Alfred's outer office for about half an hour. I was then summoned to the Boardroom with its double row of motor racing trophies down the long table, and Raymond Mays, John Surtees and Spear were all sitting one side of the table. Sir Alfred asked me what I wanted to see him about. I said: 'The arrangement we made last autumn is not working, I would like to be free to look for another job at the end of the season.' To which Sir Alfred replied: 'If you feel like that I think it would be better if you go now.' To which I replied: 'Right.' And that ended my 19 years with BRM.

We agreed to say nothing to the Press until we had a mutually acceptable statement. Sir Alfred said he did not want to lose me altogether. He understood that after 20 years I might have had enough motor racing, but there was still plenty I could do for the Owen Organization. I was not particularly polite and said that selling washing machines did not appeal to me. He went on to say: 'Do not do anything hasty; I will have some proposals put together for you to consider.' It all took about ten minutes. I never knew why Raymond Mays and Surtees were there, or why the Stanleys were not there. I got home for lunch, rang Colin Chapman and told him I had resigned but that Lotus were not mentioned. I did not think I would be free before September. I rang Sandercoombe and said I had quit, and I would like to come in late in the evening and clear my personal effects. He was very surprised, but said he would get Mrs Walker to do it for me.

We had a share in a holiday home at Bacton on the Norfolk coast, so we collected the children from school and went down there for the weekend. Max Boyd published part of the story in *The Sunday Times*, but where he got it from I still have no idea. Monday, back at home, was very quiet, but all hell broke loose on Tuesday. Basil Cardew of the *Daily Express* rang me to say Mr Stanley had issued a press statement to the effect that they had demanded my resignation, which had been immediately forthcoming. What was my version? I told him I had nothing to say, and that there would be a joint press release in a few days. He said he was giving me a chance to put my side of the story, and I was stupid to keep quiet. He said, and I quote: 'They have crucified you.' There never was a press release, draft or any other sort. Sandy advised me that I could keep the Rover, my petrol account was still open, and I was to be paid as usual.

I had another meeting with Colin Chapman, who said there was some resistance to my joining immediately as Technical Director. No one had questioned that I could manage the engine side of the business; that I would soon learn about emissions, and I could handle chassis and suspension systems, but heating, ventilation and electrical systems might take me a little time to assimilate. He proposed I started as Powertrain Engineering Manager, with additional responsibility for planning the machine shop to make 150 2 litre engines a week. I would gradually assume more responsibilities so that I joined the Board after about a year.

Eventually Peter Spear wrote suggesting that I ran Rubery Owen's United States operations, as 'I got on well with the Americans'! — an offer that I declined. Meanwhile, I had written to Sir Alfred chasing up the press release, which must also correct the story that I had been fired, and reminding him that it was me who had resigned. I had several letters from Sir Alfred but he never touched on this issue. Eventually Spear came to Bourne to see me and said I must know that Sir Alfred could not get the press statement retracted. I told him that this was one of the reasons why I had resigned. After two months my financial affairs were all settled, most generously.

I was very surprised that after nearly 19 years my principal reaction was one of relief. In the last few months, apart from developing the 4-valve V12, most of my time was spent on meetings and so on for commercial projects. I tried to keep clear of the 4-valve Avenger engine, but Leo Kusmicki, Head of Chrysler UK Advanced Powertrain Engineering and an old friend, kept dragging me into the arguments. I never really found out if the 4-valve V12 ever did realize its full performance in a car. In late September, after I had joined Lotus, Graham Hill asked me how much power the 4-valve BRM engine gave. I told him about 465 hp, but I did not know what had been done to it after I left. He commented that that seems to be about right, because at Monza, as he emerged from the Parabolica, Surtees went by him in a BRM as if he, Graham, had been painted on the wall! Some years afterwards, Willy told me they had built a short stroke version of the engine in 1971 which only gave 425 hp and seemed to me to be completely the wrong thing to do in view of our theories on short connecting rods.

I had already arranged back in April that Tony Southgate from Dan Gurney's American operation should join BRM in July to take over racing car development. He must have had a shock! Aubrey Woods came from Rye to take over engine design and development, while Tim Parnell obviously took over as Team Manager. Within weeks Cyril Atkins, the Chief Mechanic had left, so had Denis Perkins from gearboxes. Geoff Johnson left for British Leyland, Alex Osborn went to Perkins Diesel, and Peter Wright to Specialised Mouldings at Huntingdon.

While the children were on summer holiday from school we went again to Bacton and I spent many days sailing up and down the Norfolk coast, all very pleasant and therapeutic. The story that I was going to Lotus had still not leaked out, although no one seemed very surprised when I appeared there. In retrospect I probably should have left BRM six months sooner and not let Sir Alfred talk me out of it. I enjoyed the motor racing, engine and car development tremendously, and met all manner of people, such as Jano. We built up a terrific team at BRM. I do not think there was a weak link anywhere, and looking at the successful positions most of them now hold, other people must think so as well.

I had heard that when PB parted from Weslake, he had opened a garage business in Rye. Then, shortly after I joined Lotus, I met him at a Dealer Seminar at Ketteringham Hall, which was used for this purpose before it became Group Lotus Headquarters. We had a long talk about old times. He really was a strange mixture. He had a unique ability to read a failure and a good appreciation of what made a good engine. I think he was, in some respects, badly served. Having no formal engineering training other than that he received as an RAF cadet at Cranwell, he had to rely on his draughtsmen for stress work and that type of thing, and some of them let him down badly. He did not seem able to adapt to the rapid pace of suspension and chassis development, although, quite often, he came up with bright ideas such as increasing the air volume of the air struts to change the spring rate. In many respects he was extremely kind and considerate to me, but at other times I might never have existed. He was tough, very independent and yet completely dominated by RM. This was something I could never understand. He did not start work early in the morning, although he was quite happy to continue late into the night. He resented any interference with his activities and had to be in complete control. He also tended to be rather secretive, to avoid any challenge to his engineering decisions. You could have a lucid engineering discussion with him and he could hold his own in any company.

RM was even more complex. One could say he invented sponsors, back in the days of his Bugatti with the Cordon Bleu and Cordon Rouge, cognac and champagne, and his arrangements with Englebert and India tyres. He also had tremendous charm. He always wanted to win but was not prepared to change his lifestyle in the slightest to ensure it happened. His Tuesdays in London at the Berkeley, theatre and dinner were absolutely sacrosanct. After I had joined Lotus, we used to go back to Bourne for Pam to visit her parents and family. We quite often used to go to see Pam's Aunt Anne, who was RM's mother, and RM as well. After Aunt Anne died, we still went to see him. He always seemed very friendly and interested in what I was doing. I think he resented the way he was finally eased out of BRM. His strength had been his close friendship with Sir Alfred and this vanished when Sir Alfred died. During the meetings with Graham Hill and me, Sir Alfred was always obviously aware of RM's limitations. Looking back, I am still glad I went to BRM. I enjoyed nearly all my time there, although there are a few things I would do differently a second time around.

# CHAPTER NINETEEN

# Powertrain Manager to Group Engineering Director at Lotus

I ARRIVED AT Lotus on 3 September 1969. Reg, the uniformed security officer, greeted me with a 'Welcome to Lotus' and showed me my newly painted slot in the main car park. I reported to Denis Austin, Managing Director, ex-Ford and Harvard Business School, was shown round and introduced by Gerry Doe, Safety and Legal Manager and installed at my new desk right in the middle of the open-plan office. My other snapshot from my first day, was a Managers' briefing, conducted by Denis Austin in the canteen after work. He told us about the turnover and profit problems from last month and what we had to do during September to improve. I realized that Lotus was completely different from both Rolls-Royce and BRM, and extremely professional in many respects. Because of my background and known friendship with Colin Chapman I was highly suspect.

I had been issued with a personal Lotus Plus 2S, the first non-director to get one, and had — as I was assured I would — run it into the back of the car in front! I was ordered to present myself to Chunky on Monday for sentence. As I drove in I noticed a Lotus Cortina wrapped about the iron signpost at the top of Potash Lane. One of the finger posts was right through the roof and nearly touching the gear lever. Chunky said he was not in a strong position, as he had just stuffed his Cortina. However, he would make the punishment fit the crime, and from now on I was responsible for the issue of Company Driving Permits: in an attempt to ensure drivers were competent, and to reduce the appalling cost and number of insurance claims. No less than 31 of the company's 53 cars had been the subject of significant claims, and the insurance companies were getting a bit tired of us.

I found the 2 litre 4-valve engine programme well under the control of a competent team. All they needed from me was to fight their political battles for space and money. I began to get the feel of emission problems: for FIA read EPA, the American Environmental Protection Agency. I took the Brabham-Viva with an iron block Type 905 engine to Shell Research at Thornton, where they put it through an emission test for me, showed me how it all worked and encouraged me in my naive belief that an efficient combustion meant low emissions. We embarked on a programme to determine optimum squish — a compromise between maximum power and not too much quench and excess hydrocarbon at low speeds.

My arrival coincided with a strike in the paint shop. Chunky said it was because they heard I was coming. I never found out what it was about, but the sole entrance to the factory was picketed and we could not get fuel and raw material in. I acquired Ian Bennett from Production Engineering who was making the plans for creating Lotus's own engine build facility. The Twin-Cam cylinder head was machined on antiquated multi-spindle pillar drills which they had inherited. These did not have enough stroke to drill right through the head for the holding down bolts, so the head had to be turned over and the hole completed from the opposite side. The two holes generally met somewhere near the middle, although often not quite.

I agreed with Ian that with a planned production of 7000 engines per year we need not think of a transfer line. Therefore it became a decision between conventional machine tools — possibly second-hand, in best Lotus tradition — or Numerically Controlled (NC — the industry name for computer control) dedicated machining centres. In 1969 the perceived wisdom was that anything over 50 sets should be produced by high-intensity tooling on conventional machines, rather than by NC. This was not the Cosworth philosophy, who thought 500 was nearer the mark. I visited Reliant who were making 80 very simple 4-cylinder engines per week by means of conventional machines. My old friend Sir Geoffrey Tuttle arranged for me to visit the British Aircraft Corporation's Filton plant where they had a line of NC machines producing wing panels. I also visited most of the NC machine suppliers: Kerney Trecker, Cincinatti, Milwaukee (favoured by Cosworth) and Marwin (favoured by the British Aircraft Corporation).

Chunky used to invite me to his home in Cringleford for dinner one night a week. We discussed the new F1 car, the Type 72, with variable rate torsion bar suspension, which he was drawing on his board at home. We used to shoot over the estate and lakes at East Carleton, where his new house was being built. After an early morning assualt on his duck, he told me the story of Putnam's leap. There was a hollow in the road followed by a pronounced hump on the way from the A11 to East Carleton and Hethel. Colin was driving into work along this road following an Elan driven by salesman Roger Putnam (now Sales Director of Jaguar Cars) when the Elan leapt off the hump higher than usual. It got out of control and went a long way into the field on its roof. As Chunky reached the wreckage, Roger crawled out from underneath and said: 'It's all right Sir, it's my own car.' Roger's version is different — the preliminaries are the same, but as he was crawling out Chunky asked: 'Whose car is it?' Roger said it was his, and Chunky said: 'That's all right then' and got back into his own car and drove off.

During these evening conversations he outlined his long-term plans, which I helped refine. First, the capacity to machine aluminium castings for engines and car parts. Second, capability to machine steel and other ferrous parts, such as crankshafts and camshafts. Third, we would set up our own aluminium die-casting plant. Fourth and last, introduce our own gear-cutting and heat-treatment plants. We realized this might be a ten-year-plan.

Colin displayed a lack of confidence in their ability to manage a manufacturing business. There had been two invasions by major management consultants to advise him. However, in my innocence it seemed to me that the original plan he and Fred Bushell had devised several years before was extremely effective. It ran on cost ratios: so much of the retail selling price was set aside for design and development, so much for manufacturing labour, so much for material, and so on. There were also a number of management systems, introduced by Denis Austin. I was most impressed by the whole set-up. However, the first team of consultants had advised the separation of the various operating functions — manufacturing, sales and servicing — making each of them a cost centre under its own director. (Team Lotus was not part of Group Lotus as, when Group Lotus became a public company, they were advised that an F1 team was not something the Stock Exchange would understand or accept.)

The next influx of consultants advised that Managing Director Denis Austin should rule Lotus Cars through three super managers, who had to be recruited. David Lane for Production, Richard Morley for Supplies, and a third for Engineering, which was me. There were still problems. Lotus Cars (Sales) were only supposed to order cars from Lotus Cars (Manufacturing) when they had a covering order from a dealer. Yet we had several hundred unsold cars stored in hangars and lined up alongside the runway. On 28 November 1969 I submitted my recommendations for an engine manufacturing facility — dedicated NC. One Marwin MinEcentre to prepare the big castings, two Marwin Twin Spindle MaxEmills to machine crankcases and heads, and three Moogs for smaller components. It took some time to arrange the funding; the growing stock of unsold cars was causing cashflow problems. The plan also required a detail redesign of the engine to equalize head and crankcase machining times, otherwise we would have made more heads than blocks.

The strike convinced Colin of the need to improve labour relations. It was clear that one of the problems was the many rates of pay, particularly in the laminating and paint shops, who felt they were the poor relations compared with the assembly line. So Chunky appointed a working party charged with formulating a standard pay structure, where everyone was to be paid by the week, not by the hour, with a profit-share structure that must be easily understood by the man on the shop floor. To my surprise I found myself chairing this working party, which also included David Lane and Richard Morley. I suggested to Chunky that this was not a job for an engineer, but I got short shrift. 'If you are going to be a director of this company you need to know how it works. You need to know how it makes the money you are so ready to spend on research and plant,' he said.

After several months the system that Fred Bushell formalized in a staff handbook and operating procedures, providing for elected staff counsellors to form a Staff Council in place of Trade Union negotiating systems to deal with problems, was put to the vote of the entire staff and accepted. It worked successfully and is still working. It was much more effective for Lotus people to negotiate direct with their management, to deal with Lotus's peculiar problems rather than through several levels of union representation, either from London or the Midlands, who had little or no knowledge of how Lotus worked. The system stipulated that when agreement could not be reached on matters of prime concern (pay and working conditions), these were to be referred to a Joint Negotiating Committee (JNC) consisting of six members from the Staff Council and two from management, under the chairmanship of the most senior director available, which for many years was me. Another key element was the '24 hour rule', the right to appeal on a personal matter to your sector director. If this did not resolve the problem, then the most senior director present, who was generally me again, had to settle it within 24 hours. It was not all perfect, but it certainly worked, and there have been no serious labour relations problems since 1970.

In the spring of 1970 Production Engineering and Quality were added to my responsibilities. A large new building, known as Factory 9 (the Laminating Shop), was being erected with a very elaborate ventilation system to cope with the toxic styrene fumes produced by the normal glass-fibre process. Styrene was heavier than air, so the foul air was extracted through ducts in the floor. Commissioning of this building and its equipment became my responsibility. Colin told me that there was only one thing I had to do to ensure success, and that was to make sure that the artificial ageing process was rigidly adhered to for every single component. This involved the component spending 30 minutes in an oven at 210°F (99°C) and he had a remote display panel showing the temperatures and cycles in this oven mounted on my desk so I could monitor the activity. In just 30 minutes this ageing process burst bubbles of trapped air, provoked sinks and all the other unpleasant faults that developed in the first six months of normal life. Then I noticed that there was a major drop in temperature around 12.15 p.m. every day. I went to look, and found that the ovens were being opened up to warm up the lunchtime meat pies. Having found a diplomatic way around this, it all worked.

Quality was a major problem. There was a very effective system to ensure that the production plan was achieved each week. A monetary value was assigned to each major operation after it had been signed-off by inspection. The gross value this gave per week was divided by the weekly wage bill which gave a percentage, hopefully about 15 per cent. This became that particular work area's Quality Bonus. If they worked overtime, this increased the wage bill and reduced their bonus. Chunky would come into a working party meeting saying Kiss! Kiss! (Keep It Simple Stupid). The bonus system worked for many years.

To learn how the warranty system worked I traced the history of some cars. I found one that had had its body painted in the factory, but inspection had rejected its finish, so it had been repainted by a sub-contractor. The dealer concerned rejected the paint standard and claimed for a repaint under warranty. I found that he had also been paid by the customer for a special colour scheme. The car had been painted three times and someone had paid for it to be painted four times. I began to reduce the warranty costs if not the problems.

The third phase of the management consultancy cycle was under way, this time conducted by consultants Urwick Orr. Their assessor was known to us as Berty Braces. They advised that with an Executive Chairman (Chunky), a Managing Director was not neccesary and might be disruptive, as there was bound to be duplication and overlapping of duties. There should be an Engineering Director, responsible for design and specification of the product, planning how it was made, including facilities, and ensuring through his quality system that the factory produced what he had specified. An Operations Director then made the product with the facilities specified by the Engineering Director. I never knew whether this was verbatim Urwick Orr or Chunky's own interpretation. However, I was appointed Engineering Director and Denis Austin became Operations Director. David Lane became Colin's assistant, helping with the major reorganization this involved. My responsibilities also included the New Model programme, which I had to define for approval by the Board.

Colin had now moved into his new home — East Carleton Manor — where we had long sessions in his garden while he outlined his plans for the company model line up. David Lane helped me to formulate the long-term programme. David had a gift for precisely describing anything with the absolute minimum number of words — he was incredibly succinct. The programme started with the M50 (the new Elite), the M51 (an Elite with a 4 litre V8) and the M52 (a 2+2 version of the 4-seat Elite to be known as the Eclat and later the Excel). The M53 was the 2+2 with a V8. The M70 'a wedge theme' mid-engined Europa replacement with as many common parts with the M50 as possible, including the 2 litre engine. This became the Esprit. The M71 was, of course, a V8-engined Esprit.

Before my euphoria had evaporated we had to make 30 per cent of staff redundant and cut production by 50 per cent. We were in the middle of a private Lotus-only recession. The cars were not selling, just piling up around the airfield causing a major cash flow crisis. I had to axe my new empire before I knew who everyone was, or what they did.

Rindt was killed at Monza in a freak accident. I had not been involved in the development of the Type 72, apart from occasional discussions with Chunky. Flying back from one of the 72's first unsuccessful races at Silverstone, sitting alongside Chunky, after 20 minutes without saying a word, he suddenly turned to me and said: 'What do you think is wrong with it?' I recalled my unfortunate experiences with anti-dive and anti-squat at BRM in 1965. He did not seem very convinced. However, most of the anti-dive and anti-squat was removed from one car which performed very well at Zandvoort, its next race. All I knew of Rindt's crash was that a broken inboard-brake front driveshaft had been found in the wreckage which the authorities had impounded. Brake failure did not make sense to me since the place where the accident happened, the approach to the Parabolica, (close to the scene of the 1961 von Trips accident) had a large run-off area. If Rindt had lost some of his brakes he could have brought the car to rest in the run-off area without damage. There were even rumours that Chunky was going to be charged with manslaughter. He was dreadfully upset and shut himself away in his new house, refusing to see anyone or even go to work. Hazel asked Pam and me over one Sunday evening to try to cheer him up. I took the Vauxhall VX 4/90 fitted with an iron-block 4-valve engine. Chunky took it for a run — eleven-tenths everywhere as usual. He said the engine seemed rough, but he certainly cheered up.

Throughout autumn 1970 there were several ineffective recovery plans. One, floated by Marketing, was to paint the Elan red and white with a gold stripe, the colours of Gold Leaf Team Lotus, and call it the Sprint. I felt very much the new boy at Board meetings, so I did not say much. Chunky collared me after this one and said I obviously did not agree with the Sprint idea. I said: 'No, what is needed is an honest increase in performance, not go-faster stripes.' He said he agreed with me, but supposed it would take me a year and cost him a million. I said: 'No, I could do it in a week, and you would not notice the cost.' He did not seem to believe me, but said: 'Go and get on with it then.'

I collected Stephan Williams, who I had appointed Powertrain Manager in my place, and described the BRM Phase II 'Spence' engine to him. Within a week he had an improved version running. I realized that increasing the torque would totally destroy the rubber-doughnut universal joints in the rear driveshafts, and failures of these were already top of the warranty claim list. A new and stronger one was already under test, so I specified this for the new car. Another problem was that there was a risk that the extra torque would accentuate cracking of the cast aluminium differential housing mounting legs, another, though lesser warranty problem. We tied them together with a rather crude sheet steel reinforcing beam. Late in the evening, ten days after my conversation with Chunky, my internal telephone jumped in the air. It was Chunky, who enquired: 'Where's that engine of yours?' I told him we were just putting it into the car. 'Fine,' he said, 'put it in my bay in the Directors' Garage, I'll take it home tonight.' I protested that it had not turned a wheel yet. He ignored me and repeated: 'In my bay; I will go home in it tonight.' We complied with his instructions. One side of the Directors' garage was exclusively Chunky's, except for my corner. The opposite wall, with space for five cars, was the parking area for the other, non-engineer, directors. Next morning there was no Chunky. I posted spies to watch, but he did not arrive until mid-morning. The car seemed to be still working, and no oil underneath, so we waited with bated breath until noon when the phone did its characteristic jump in the air. The voice the other end said: 'You go home to lunch don't you?' I replied: 'Yes.' 'Take your new Elan then.' 'How does it go?' I enquired. He replied: 'Use all of the power in all of the gears, all of the time' then hung up. I did as I was told. It certainly went — power had increased from 105 to 128 hp. Chunky intercepted me as I drove in and said: 'Well, now for the bad news — how much?' I told him 10s (50p) per engine, the difference in cost of the larger inlet valves.

We worked out a scheme to combine converting engines with reworking the stock of unsaleable cars (the prime cause of which was body and paint defects). I suggested we gave the Plus 2 a silver roof — to identify the increased performance — since most of its body problems were on the roof, and I proposed we painted the belly of the Elan white, as this was the area of most of their paint and body defects. By this means we could rework the unsaleable cars, freshen them up and fit them with more powerful engines, which would make them attractive enough to start selling again. Chunky said we must also identify the new engine, so Stephan came up with a ribbed cam-cover with the inscription 'Big Valve'. We set up an urgent proving and durability programme, for which there was no shortage of volunteers for the driving — and planned the stock rework. I nearly lost my newly-awarded medal when I referred to the rework area as the mushroom factory. Sales christened the new Plus 2S as the S130 — salesman's licence on 128 hp. The Elan was known as the Sprint.

While I was still organizing my new engineering team, I had found a bright young man, ex-Jaguar, running Continuous Engineering (the engineering needed by cars already in production). His name was Mike Kimberley. I gave him a project to put the Lotus twin-cam engine into the Europa in place of the Renault, eliminating its most serious problems at the same time. Magazine test reports and criticisms, with customer complaints arranged in cost priority order, created his job list.

The M50 was in the doldrums. Its body design created large amounts of aerodynamic lift, and the specified AP automatic gearbox did not have a delivery date. Worst of all, Chunky was not happy with the idea of making its body by the traditional hand-lay process.

I had told the Assembly Line Manager, John Pettifer (known as the 'Petrifier'), and my Chief Inspector that if ever there was a quality problem stopping the line, they were to fetch me. I was, as a result, spending many hours on the assembly line redefining standards and getting the engineers to fix urgent problems. It was very disruptive of the new engineering programmes, but very good for quality in the field. I was enjoying myself immensely. Early in 1971 we were ready to launch the Big Valve. Colin told me to make the Press Presentation, saying: 'It's your idea, you go and tell them.' I told the Press very proudly that the new engine gave 130 hp. 'So what's new?' they asked. 'All your engines do, so we have been told,' they added darkly. I had to flannel round this and say, wait until you have tried one. As a result of this exchange, Chunky added the preparation and presentation of cars to be tested by the Press to my growing job list. Fortunately, the Big Valve got a good Press. We had a new Sales Manager, an ex-Navy pilot called Barry Carter and we were soon selling more than 70 cars a week (35 new Big Valves, 25 reworks, and the rest Europas) instead of 35 at the depth of the 1970 crisis.

Around this time Graham was set up for a *This is Your Life* programme. I used the Big Valve prototypes to get to rehearsals after work. I was asked if they would need the 'Bleeper'. I assured them they would. It took place at the Park Lane Hilton during the launch of the 'Lobster Claw' Brabham. We were smuggled in via the kitchens. The organizers allowed us one drink before the performance. John Coombes was very nervous, and we managed to get him a few more gins, without him realizing, disguised as water. It was a good night, except that Jackie arrived from Kyalami and told me of PB's death.

Chunky then sent me to Washington to the Crystal City conference on vehicle safety standards for small volume vehicle manufacturers and importers, organized by the American Department of Transport, where I met Pete Pulver, the largest Lotus importer into the US. There, I made a plea for a mechanism to give exemption from a particular standard for a limited period, for small volume manufacturers on the grounds that we were the innovators. If they helped us innovate it was in the long-term public interest. Eventually it became part of US law. On the way home I visited Pete's operation in Millerton, New York, where he gave me a good working-over concerning our lack of quality in paint and body finish.

Soon after Exemption for Small Volume Manufacturers became law, we needed to use it, because the Europa could not meet FMVSS 204 — door side intrusion. We had developed for the next generation of cars an extruded aluminium door beam which passed the tests with a 100 per cent margin. Denis Austin and I made the usual epic trip to Washington to argue our case. We were fogbound at Heathrow for 24 hours. It looked like being another 24, so our pilot Mike Hamlin took us to Paris in the company Piper Seneca to catch a TWA flight, which in turn was diverted. Also, Doug Toms, the Transport Secretary, had fallen off his motorcycle, which added to the complexity of the problem. I recall sitting up all night drawing diagrams to illustrate Denis's pleas. We were there for over a fortnight, and eventually we were granted our exemption.

A few vehicle engineers left us, to join the Clan Crusader operation, so I took the opportunity to reorganize the Vehicle Engineering team again, putting Mike Kimberley in charge. His work on the Europa Twin-Cam being nearly complete, it had been decided to build the first batch with standard 105 hp engines until we had reduced the stock of components made redundant by the Big Valve, and a Renault gearbox with a suitable fifth-speed, made by Mike Hewland, became available.

As an essential part of pre-production sign-off, it was agreed that Mike Kimberley and I would drive the prototype Europa Twin-Cam to Rome and back during a weekend. I told Mike I would look after money, paperwork, travel arrangements, etc. but he was to look after tools and spares. Pam, who had a malicious sense of humour, knowing Mike had little or no experience of overseas motoring, plus a tendency to be always nibbling, told him he was in for a dreadful time. I never ever turned back if I lost my way, and worse, I never ever stopped to eat during the day. The factory was, at the time, shut down for the Whitsun holiday and essential maintenance — when the fire alarm sounded. I suddenly realized I was the only director on site and was therefore in charge. The paint shop was well alight, a spark from welding up a damaged grid in the paint booth having ignited paint overspray. It took two local fire brigades three hours to extinguish the blaze.

As a result, Mike and I were late starting — missing the Hovercraft and finally reaching our planned overnight stop in the early hours of the morning. The car was festooned with temperature sensors, from which we noticed that the battery was picking up heat from the exhaust. We improvized the aluminium base of Mike's notepad as a shield and reached Reims next morning at about 10.30. I told Mike to fill the car up while I cashed travellers' cheques. Mindful of Pam's advice he looked for something to eat, but the only thing he could find was cherries. He bought two kilos, not being too familiar with French measures, while I returned with a picnic lunch including a bottle of wine. We continued over World War I battlefields to shake up the suspension. When we stopped for lunch we found there was no corkscrew in the tool kit, so we pushed the cork in. Late in the afternoon Mike was holding the part-consumed open bottle of wine between his knees with most of the cherries at his feet in the passenger side foot well, when one of the rear tyres blew on a bumpy twisty descent into Belfort. We were doing about 90 mph (145 kph) at the time. After we stopped alongside a cemetery, I realized that Mike was a nervous passenger. While 'helping me with the braking' he had relaxed his grip on the wine bottle, which released its contents into the cherries, and he had stamped the wine and the cherries into a purée. The burst was due to a faulty inner tube. The roadside garage who replaced the tube did a poor job of rebalancing, and the car was undriveable. We pressed on through Zurich, with odd-sized tyres at the back — the spare was a small front — taking in the Susten, Furka and Grimsel passes, stopping to eat in Andermatt, and for midnight coffee outside Milan.

The early hours of the morning found us in a thick pre-dawn mist on the Autostrada di Sol south of Bologna. Mike claimed he was awakened by a rhythmic thumping. The right hand wheels were rubbing on the curb, as I had also fallen asleep. I do not remember any of it, other than the fog. We reached Rome, but failed to get Barry Carter his photographs of the Europa with the Coliseum in the background. We just could not find it, and started north planning to follow the Mille Miglia route rather than the autostrada. We got lost somewhere between the Futa and Raticossa passes, still seeking a garage to rebalance the rear wheel. I had been worried about the effect on the differential, running fast on odd-sized rear tyres. After a detour in a dried-up river bed we found ourselves back on the autostrada. As we descended in the dusk into Menton from Piacenza and Genoa, a violent thunderstorm broke out. There was a power cut, all the street lights went out and we went the wrong way down a one-way street and dived into The Metropole at Beaulieu for the night.

The night-porter called us with strong coffee and we were on the road, still in heavy rain, by 6.00 a.m. Somewhere between Avallon and Auxerre with the fuel gauge dangerously low, but enough for 25 miles (40 km) (Mike said), we came to a 'deviation' where the autoroute was still under construction. When we got back on it we ran out of fuel. Fortunately a passing Frenchman rescued us with five litres and we were back to Hethel at 00.30 on Monday morning with 3221 miles on the clock and no trouble apart from the puncture.

We had embraced, through Urwick Orr, Management by Objectives and monthly reports — 'trial by magic lantern', someone called it. It meant that by the 5th of the following month we had a fairly accurate idea of the previous month's finances. Our trading position improved and Chunky was very bullish at our Annual General Meeting in London. We had made a profit of £1,127,000 on a turnover of £5,593,000.

I continued to attend the Thursday Club dinners at the Saxon Mill just outside Stratford-on-Avon — the 155 miles home taking a few minutes over two hours. During one of these evenings, Kevin Beatty, Chief Engineer of Jensen, mentioned the troubles they were having with the engine they planned to use in their new Jensen Healey. I suggested they looked at the Lotus 907 engine, which would meet US emission laws and had all the power they required. A deal was quickly struck. We had the capacity to make the 150 engines per week they needed, as we had delayed the introduction of the new Elite by one year for a complete rethink of body shape and processes. This freed up engine manufacturing capacity. The company aircraft knew their own way to Birmingham airport. We had a good relationship with Kjell Quavle, Jensen's majority shareholder. He was also the West Coast Lotus importer. Alf Vickers became Managing Director of Jensen. Alf was an old friend, who had been Quality Manager of the Ford plant building Merlin aero-engines during the war.

Jensen launched an intensive road test programme, using six of our sand-cast prototype engines. We planned to make production 907s from gravity die-castings. The prototypes gave very little trouble, but the arrival of the die-castings coincided with the 1973 coal strike and power cuts. With green operators, new NC machining centres, untried castings, power cuts (even voltage drops upset the machines), it was an absolute nightmare. We generally worked from midnight to 5 a.m. when there was less risk of a power cut or voltage drop. One night, after a power cut, we failed to return one of the big tool-changing machines fully to zero. It seized its biggest cutter, set itself to maximum speed and attacked the tool magazine with all the power of its 75 hp motor. When the pre-production engines reached Healey there was more trouble. Various differences in the castings meant that oil did not drain so effectively from the cam boxes, so above 6000 rpm there was a loss of oil pressure. The oil was being retained in the cam boxes, not in the sump.

We used the autoroute from Arras to Paris to test the various cures. There was much aerial commuting to Arras via Birmingham to collect Kevin or one of his engineers. While our aircraft was being serviced, we used a loaned Piper Aztec which had trouble with its nose wheel retraction, but fortunately I was not on this trip. After trying to fix the problem in France, they set off back to Hethel. Lotus security, who also acted as airfield controllers, called me to the radio to say that the pilot had reported he could not get the nose wheel down. I told him to 'shake it about a bit', but no luck, so I sent him off to Norwich where they had full emergency facilities. He landed with the wheels up, severely damaging the aircraft in the process. Chunky was not amused.

We still had many teething troubles with the machine tools, but finally it all settled down under the control of an ex-Rolls-Royce engineer from their Middlesbrough factory. The profits from 150 Jensen Healey engines per week helped us through our money problems in late 1974 and 1975, because of the first oil crisis and loss of volume through the introduction of the Elite.

By late 1971 we could afford to strengthen our Quality and Production Engineering teams, so Alec Bailey, my old Rolls-Royce boss, arranged for me to interview some of the victims of their 1971 collapse. Martin Drury, one of their trainee Quality Engineers appealed to me and I hired him, along with a few others, and he quickly rose to manage our Quality Department, where he did a first-class job. I would listen, with wry amusement, to the impassioned pleading of long-term Lotus production managers. Martin, just 25 years old, dourly said: 'You are wasting your time, it's not good enough, you know it and I know it. I will not have it.' It was a great loss when he left us because of a family bereavement. By then warranty costs per car were down to less than 1 per cent of the retail selling price, which compared well with the other cars below 1 per cent — the Ford Escort and Rover 2000.

I also recruited Jim Dougan and Ken Bell as Production and Deputy Production Engineering Managers. This completed a first-class engineering team, some 80 strong. I still sat right in the middle of the main open-plan office with Mike Kimberley, controlling Vehicle Engineering, on my right, together with Albert Adams, glass fibre and composite development. Stephan Williams, Powertrain Manager, sat opposite, and Jim Dougan and his Production engineers, on my left hand.

We were practising simultaneous engineering long before the term was invented. There were innumerable engineering problems, but we took them all in our stride. We even coped with Chunky seizing the first person he came upon and instructing him to reverse our previous day's decision. Whenever possible he was referred to the right person and I was told. He caused most mayhem in the composite area. This was very much Chunky's speciality, he and Albert being old friends dating back to their Hornsey days. There was a tremendous amount of development in this area, which influenced 50 per cent of our labour costs, glass fibre and composites being extremely labour-intensive. We tried wrapped edges, in an attempt to avoid having to trim the moulded components which was very messy, dusty and involved diamond cutters. This was overtaken by other processes, and today we use extremely high pressure water jets. There were diversions into self-colour bodies, discarded because of the difficulty in hiding the join during field repairs. Finally we settled on VARI (Vacuum Assisted Resin Injection) which required a tremendous amount of detail process development, including resins, tool design, etc. Chunky believed this process had so much potential that it should become a separate business. He asked me to find a suitable Chief Executive to run this company, to be called Technocraft. I got in touch with Peter Wright, still working for Specialized Mouldings at Huntingdon, and Peter was soon in the thick of it all.

I had another Department of Transport Conference in Washington, this time to learn about US government-sponsored developments in the field of safety, including anti-collision sonar. I was treated, in some quarters, rather like an unexploded bomb. I think they suspected I might organize another new law for the exclusive benefit of Lotus! I stayed at the Hotel in the Watergate complex.

The new Elite was taking shape. Oliver Winterbottom had been recruited from Jaguar to style the body. The last piece of the jigsaw was put in place at Monte Carlo in May 1972. It was gradually dawning on us that the AP automatic gearbox we had chosen would not be available in economic quantities at our torque levels, and we had to find a five speed manual box. But in 1972 there were very few of them. I sat next to Dick Perry, then manager of BL's Longbridge plant, as a guest of GKN at the Monaco GP. I mentioned I was going to Fiat next day to meet Aurelio Lampredi to try to buy a Fiat 5-speed box. Dick suggested we put the gears from the BL 5-speed box into our own casting. I knew it would work as I had drawn 'Jackie Stewart' in Claude Burch's sweep at lunch, and Jackie had obliged and won. Lampredi was very friendly, but Fiat would not sell us the box.

We came to an agreement with BL, and quickly made a 5-speed box for the S130, for which we needed a very cramped and complicated linkage to get the gear lever and gear knob into the right place. The box was basically designed for the Elite which had a much simpler arrangement. We were assured by BL engineers that the gears had adequate torque capacity, but in service in the Elite second gear used to wilt. It is strange and I still cannot explain why — nearly all the gearboxes we have used from Renault, Gertrag, Citroen and so on, have all had second gear problems with either the gears themselves or the synchromesh. Stokey's explanation is that when people use second they are more often than not in a hurry, and cram it in, using plenty of power, but I do not think this is quite the answer. The box served us well, despite it being rather too easy to go straight from fifth to second bursting the clutch in the process.

While all these events were reverberating around us, Chunky bought Moonraker Boats from David Buxton, an earlier Lotus Sales Manager. I had discussed with him diversification into boats during our 1970 product meetings, but he wasn't interested, saying that boats are crude and primitive, and have not progressed beyond Noah and the Ark. So I was extremely surprised when the purchase was made. He sent David Lane to Brundall to run Moonraker. David had completed his part in our restructuring and was absolutely the ideal man for the job. He completely reorganized the build process, delaying fitting the superstructure until the last possible moment. David reasoned that many man hours were wasted, once the superstructure was in place, while people queued up to get in and out through the few hatches. David soon had Moonraker profitable, building two boats a week. Chunky told me that the Moonraker typified all that was wrong with power boats: noisy, rough and crude. He just saw it as a launching platform for his concept of what a luxury motor yacht should be like. He planned a 15-metre twin-diesel superboat. He was, as usual, reading voraciously everything he could lay his hands on, and had engaged Don Shead to design the hull. He started to build a wooden prototype, planning to exhibit it at the Earls Court Boat Show and obtain market reaction. I was not involved in the boats, although Chunky ran his ideas before me on various occasions.

Neither was I involved in F1, although he frequently discussed problems with me, such as the Type 72's early handling problem. I noticed that, following Jochen Rindt's death, he had changed from the cheerful exuberant character I knew in the 60s to a harder, more cynical person. The criticism and suggestions that Colin Chapman made unsafe cars had hurt him very badly, although he tried not to let it show. I went to several races with him, and we visited Mercedes together on our way to the German GP at Hockenheim — to try to buy their 4-speed automatic gearbox. They were quite willing to sell, but at an unacceptable price. I found that I had lost some of my enthusiasm for F1. Whether it was the settled existence I now enjoyed at Lotus, 8.30 a.m. until 7 p.m., occasional Saturday mornings, generally with the weekend off, I cannot tell. There always seemed to be a certain amount of pandemonium at Team Lotus that I tried to avoid at BRM. People expressed great surprise that I was still at Lotus and apparently enjoying it, Keith Challen of the *News of the World* in particular.

Everything which Colin promised me when I joined had arrived and I never had to remind him of anything. He was equally good to my children. My eldest daughter Carolyn took her horse to East Carleton when our grass supply ran low and was encouraged to ride around the estate. She even had a return invitation after her horse Rufus had chewed several of the newly planted trees. Chunky brought her home one Christmas Eve on the pillion of his 750 cc Honda motor cycle, which he insisted I rode. We evolved a way of working together. Engines, transmissions, castings and forgings were mine, while composites, body styling and interiors were his — but we could argue about suspension systems until we were blue in the face. There was, despite my suspension experience at BRM, a tendency to hang an engine label on me. Chunky insisted that I was treated with the same respect as himself and would send people to consult me, with the comment: 'He has the mileage ingredient.'

During the Geneva show we met up with Giugiaro of Ital Design — very much the coming man. He wanted to apply his design skills to a glass fibre car, and had chosen the Europa. However, Chunky soon steered him onto the M70. We cut and stretched a Europa chassis, crammed a 2 litre engine into it and sent it to Turin. I frequently drove one of the Elite prototypes to

Turin to see how the M70 was proceeding. Oliver had been installed as the resident Lotus man at Ital. Sometimes Mike Kimberley came too, other times we flew out. When the programme started to slip there was a high level visit — Chunky, Fred, Mike and me, now in the company Piper Navajo. On the way back, with a temporary pilot (Mike Hamlin was away) the cabin heating failed over the Alps. So we sat huddled together wearing oxygen masks with a blanket wrapped around four pairs of legs. Mike asked me if the moon should keep passing his window — we were gently orbiting the Tour de Pin beacon north of Geneva every five minutes, because of mishandling of the automatic pilot. Some days later Fred's toes began to itch. He went to see his doctor in mid-June, who said: 'You are not going to believe this, you have frostbite.'

Whenever there was a major change made to one of the Elite prototypes I would drive it to the south of France during a weekend, for assessment. Pam joined me at the factory, with overnight bag and picnic, on the Friday evening. We stayed the night at a motel near Arras, and were on the road again by 7 a.m., passing Le Bourget soon after 8 a.m., Orly runway lights by 9 a.m., Lyon by 12 noon, and picnic lunch at Tain l'Hermitage. I would drop Pam off at The Metropole in Beaulieu while I drove on to Monte Carlo; photographed the car in the Casino square with that day's *Nice Matin* newspaper trapped under the screen wiper for the benefit of a suspicious accountant, then back to Beaulieu, hopefully in time for a swim. We would start back at 5.30 a.m. on Sunday morning, to beat the traffic jams at the Paris toll booths, which developed after 4 p.m., and with luck we would be home at midnight with over 2,000 miles on the clock.

On one occasion, after meeting Giugiaro in Turin and lawyer Dr Monaco in Milan, and with Lesley my middle daughter as navigator, I drove round Italy, via Bologna, Pescara, Bari, round the Amalfi Drive to Naples, Rome, Portofino, Monaco, Marseilles and home.

Chunky decided on yet another major reorganization just before the Elite was launched. We had in 1973 made a profit of £1,156,000 on £7,344,000 turnover. Sir Leonard Crossland, ex-Ford Europe, succeeded him as Chairman of Lotus Cars but in a non-executive capacity. Chunky remained Executive Chairman of the Group. Richard Morley became Operations Director in place of Denis Austin, who went to Brussels as the head of ITT Europe's automobile team. I was to become Group Engineering Director responsible for all engineering, Team Lotus, Lotus Cars and Boats. Of course, Chunky was very much Team Lotus Chief Engineer. I was to design and build prototypes of new products, using the GM project team system, picking an appropriate team from all areas within the Chapman empire. I was rather loath to leave the hurly burly of Lotus Cars, but my job as Chief Engineer, Lotus Cars went to Mike Kimberley. I had just engaged Jack Phillips who designed all the post-war Rolls-Royce car engines, to help design our V8. Jack, who was born a few miles from Hethel, wanted to retire to Norfolk.

My first project was the M70, now known as the Esprit, although Giugiaro wanted to call it the Kiwi. It was during his antipodean era; the Boomerang and so on. He did not speak English so we conversed in French. Explaining why it could not be called the Lotus Kiwi tested my conversational powers to the absolute limit. In 1974 we were feeling the beginning of the first oil crisis, and I had to produce the Esprit on a shoe-string. Colin said: 'Things are a little bit iddley umpty, you must do the best you can. I know I can rely on you.' So ended my first five years at Lotus. BRM had all but vanished, Willy and Sir Alfred were dead. I had taken roots in Norfolk, an Elizabethan Manor House, six acres of land, horses and ponies — I was quite happy.

# CHAPTER TWENTY

# Lotus — Group
# Engineering Director

I PICKED MY Esprit team — Colin Spooner, back from his Clan venture, his brother Brian, pattern maker Charlie Prior, fitter Ted Fleet and car mechanic Denis Jewell, plus my secretary Chris. We installed ourselves in the stables at Ketteringham Hall and started work. The Hall — former home of the Boileau family, Headquarters of the Second Air Division (the B24s) of the Eighth USAAF in the second half of World War II, and finally a boys' boarding school (which left it very run down) — had been acquired in 1968. We needed several meetings with Giugiaro to reconcile his styling with what could be made by the VARI process. There could be no re-entrants — the body had to be withdrawn from the tool after moulding, just like a sand pie from a child's seaside bucket. He was very reasonable and there were no major problems. I planned that we would build the car by working groups, Volvo fashion, rather than on an assembly line. We estimated an eight-man crew, given a dressed engine with transaxle, body and chassis, could assemble a car in eight hours, that is 64 man hours in all.

Chunky visited us once a week. Colin Spooner was an enthusiastic model maker and made a one-tenth scale model of the chassis and body which helped us solve many problems. We planned to complete the running prototype by the end of the year, from an April start, but late delivery of some of the components just beat us. Chris had taken over our procurement function, and I heard suppliers being given hell over the phone. It was agreed that I would meet Chunky at Heathrow, with the prototype, off his flight from the first race of 1975 in South America. There was only one argument with him during the whole programme, and that concerned a sheet-steel strut joining the lower rear wishbone anchor points together. These were a pair of complicated aluminium castings bolted onto the Citroen gearbox, carrying the rear mountings of the assembly, brake calipers and lower wishbones. The M70 specification called for the fixed-length driveshafts and lower wishbones, from the Elite. Our scheme was to use the strut to share high cornering loads from the outer wheel across to the more lightly loaded opposite bracket and wheel. Chunky said it was unnecessary, throw it away!

We had chosen the Citroen-Maserati gearbox, as for some reason the Maserati engine rotated anti-clockwise unlike most engines. So when fitted in the back of the Esprit, the gearbox rotated in the correct direction for us. We devised some very crafty machining techniques, developed from my BRM experience, to match our front-half casing and bell-housing with the Citroen rear-half. Sir Leonard Crossland negotiated the supply of gearboxes from Citroen, with me in support. I soon saw why he had been made Chairman of Fords — they nearly gave us the Eiffel Tower as a bonus. We used our Piper Seneca for the trip. A very strong wind developed on the way back, and after landing at Stansted for Sir Leonard to disembark, we took off almost across the runway and we had not got far when the port engine blew up with a nasty thump. As we had a 60 mph tail wind, pilot Mike Hamlin decided to make for Norwich rather than Hethel. The wind direction for our active runway was not good; better at Norwich where emergency facilities were also superior. When we turned into the wind on finals we were only making 50 mph over the ground. It seemed to take a long time to get down.

We finished the car on the Friday, before we were due to meet Chunky on Monday. I decided that we must run the car for 250 miles before we risked a trip to London and back. So Colin Spooner and I took it in turns on the Hethel test track. Approaching Baldock on our way to London some enthusiast in a Jensen decided to have a closer look, so we had to lose him. On the way back to Norfolk (with Chunky driving), passing Hatch End tube station, the left rear suspension casting on the gearbox broke. We had brought Chunky's Elite with us, just in case, and as he drove off his only comment was: 'You had better put your lump of old iron back.' The steering was not particularly good, but improved with detail development. We had fitted Teves non-servo brakes, as used on a production Alfa Romeo, which were effective, light and not expensive. We had some problems with the radiator mounting and its ducting because of the bulk of the spare wheel in the nose. I chose a long shallow radiator and a pod similar to the Spitfire under-wing arrangement. Finally, we filled the boot of the prototype with drawings and sent it to the car company development engineers. Colin Spooner and the two fitters went with it to preserve continuity, and explain why we had done it like that. The development engineers spent some of the money we had saved and wasted most of the time we saved trying to change it to conform to their ideas. They fitted Girling servo brakes, which might have been an improvement, but made the steering problems worse because of the change in king pin offset. They tried a top-exit radiator duct which did not work, and eventually had to revert to our Spitfire pod. Colin Spooner resigned and moved to Lucas Marine in Hampshire.

I was then given the job, with Brian Spooner's assistance, of reviving the gearbox (the 'queer box') from the 1959 F1 Lotus. Chunky insisted that we design it around the ZF crownwheel and pinion and differential assembly from the 4-wheel-drive Indy turbine. He argued that the Pratt and Whitney PT6 turbine had much more torque than a Cosworth engine so it would have adequate strength, and it would not require development. I warned him that turbine torque was different from piston engine torque as it was constant, whereas with a piston engine it was the average of a fluctuating amount. After Chunky and I had talked the design through, we came up with the idea of using balls in tangential holes to lock the desired gear in place, activated by pulling a cone through the driveshaft to select the gear needed. ZF were very polite, but said they were too busy, so we went to see Getrag, next door to Porsche, who smiled politely and produced an exact model of what we were talking about. It was the transmission they had developed for the Messerschmitt mini-car built just after the war.

While we were working on the gearbox I had a trip into the boat world. Chunky was determined to avoid the use of a generating set weighing some 500 kg (1102 lb) in his new 15-metre Marauder. He specified a hydraulic drive from the port engine to the alternator plus a special exhaust system which came into action when the engine was in the charging mode. After much effort I made it all work, except that the big 6.5 litre diesel shook the whole boat when it started up. Once it was running at 900 rpm the alternator charged correctly, with the exhaust making a hissing noise, damped by the cooling water. In service the ZF exhaust brake valve, that we used as our bypass valve in the exhaust, corroded and eventually seized.

By this time I had been appointed a director of Team Lotus and JCL Marine (the company producing Chunky's big luxury power boats) as well as Lotus Cars; and I had been allowed to choose my own personal Elite colour scheme. I chose a banana-yellow body with no bright work — everything anodized black instead of chrome. Chunky had a fit and said: 'Don't ever do that again' and promptly made me responsible for ensuring that people issued with product cars took care of them and, more to the point, did not modify them at all. I was intrigued to see that the Marauder he exhibited at the Earls Court Boat Show was banana-yellow, with the erstwhile bright work anodised black!

I retained my responsibility for emission work and certification. Jack Phillips had organized a very efficient and well-equipped emission laboratory. Its first task was to prepare for certification of the 2 litre engine in the Jensen Healey. The 50,000 mile durability proving went smoothly with no major problems. Jensen had good relations with Chrysler, and used their engines and emission equipment in their big cars. They wanted us to use as much of the same equipment on the Healey, so I renewed relations with my old friends at Chrysler.

I became involved in motor racing again, but not in a very pleasant way. Chunky had been charged in connection with Rindt's accident. The Italian club had retained a first-class Milan lawyer, Dr Monaco, to defend him. Dr Monaco quickly discovered some technical flaws and had the charge dismissed, much to Chunky's annoyance, who said he wanted to be cleared of the charge that he made unsafe racing cars, not to prove he had the best lawyer!

The local Italian authorities reopened the case, and made Dr Colombo — a director of Magneti Marelli in nearby Sesto san Giovanni — a Magistrate, with appropriate powers to investigate and decide whether there was a case to answer. Dr Colombo had spent some time with Ferrari, so he knew what he was talking about, although he was no relation to the designer of the same name. Unfortunately we did not hear about all this until Dr Colombo's investigation was nearly complete. Then there was a panic. Peter Jowitt and I were rushed off to Milan to see Dr Colombo and make sure he had our side of the story. Peter was an investigator from the Royal Aircraft Establishment at Farnborough, with an impressive reputation, and a local Magistrate — an ideal man to have.

We flew out to Milan in the Navajo, landing with 45 minutes fuel left, to find the airport refuellers were on strike. Leaving pilot Mike Hamlin to sort this out, Peter and I went to see Dr Colombo, whom we found to be reasonable, very intelligent and well informed. Dr Colombo said some of the information we had brought was new to him and helped explain discrepancies in his evidence, and filled in some of the hitherto unexplained gaps. He would need statements from the persons we quoted, duly notarized, and copies of our photographs by the following Monday, when he was due to complete his report.

It was the weekend of the British GP so, with luck, all the people we needed would be there for us to interview. First, though, we had to get back. We decided to stick with the Navajo — there were no commercial flights — no hire cars and the trains were packed. Mike Hamlin believed we had enough fuel to reach Lugano, but not in the dark. Next morning was a typical Italian July day. We were soon letting down in the early morning mist, on to a grass strip, on a tongue of land in the arms of the 'Y' of the lake, surrounded by mountains, when the Italian radar, talking us down, went off the air — breakfast and change of shifts. We probably had enough fuel to divert to Malpensa, where we would have been stuck, then at the last minute radar cover returned and we were down. It was gin clear for the rest of the flight. We managed the interviews at Silverstone, Norwich and London, with a Notary Public in attendance. The works photographer, Ron Middleton, did his stuff and I was back in Dr Colombo's office first thing Monday morning.

His report concluded that the chain of events leading to the accident began when the car ran without wings, and at the same time being fitted with a more powerful engine, and the gear ratios raised two steps. The car, in an unfamiliar configuration to the driver, became aerodynamically unstable — Denny Hulme said when it passed him at high speed, approaching the Parabolica, it was weaving and looked very unstable. The car slowed, veered to the left and struck the Armco barrier at about 45 degrees. Because of recent construction work there was space for the front wheels to pass under the Armco at the point of impact. The car continued in its basic trajectory, but rotating, from the restraining effect of the front wheels and the Armco. This first impact caused the driver, who was not wearing the crutch straps, of his six-point harness, to slip or 'submarine', through the harness, and his feet became entangled below the pedals. The car, slowed by the impact and restrained by its front wheels under the Armco, was now travelling nearly tail first. It struck a tall post carrying a loud speaker, and the impact ripped the front from the car, restrained by its wheels under the Armco. The driver was, therefore, pulled by his feet entangled in the pedals through the seat harness, inflicting fatal wounds to his throat. The front brake driveshaft failure contributed to the car's instability, and was probably the cause of it veering to the left. We saw no reason to disagree with these conclusions. The failure of the driveshaft being only one link in an unfortunate and long chain of events. If any one of these had not occurred, Jochen would have survived. The driveshaft failure was also attributed to a combination of factors, the removal of shot-peening, a protection against fatigue, by emery cloth, which also left a deep scratch from which the fracture originated. It was suspected that this happened during a routine radiological inspection by a subcontractor. I think Chunky was satisfied with the outcome, and no charges were brought.

Chunky then had me writing Policy Directives and a Group Engineering Manual. I wrote a three-page directive on how to design an inlet port, and when I sent it in to Chunky for his approval he burst in on me and said: 'Let me see you burn that. Don't ever let anyone see it, it must be worth millions.' I had to define a Lotus product, which took some time, and I never ever managed to define a sports car. The car company asked for my secretary Chris to help in their supply department, as she knew the Esprit supply situation. It was promotion for her so I had to agree. I held a monthly working lunch at the Hall for all the Chief Engineers, plus Chunky; the idea being to keep them all aware of what the others were doing, to avoid duplication and make sure they shared facilities. Chunky suggested I designed a turbocharged 2 litre, but when I gave him the costs and told him how long it would take he went off the idea. He also asked for an enlarged version of the engine. I costed this, and he told me that I had better forget that as well. I had a slight sense of being put out to grass. In Chunky's system, anybody over 50 was definitely over the hill. When he came back from his summer holiday he gave me the armchair and sherry treatment, which was always dangerous.

He handed me a 28-page folder in his neat handwriting saying: 'You have had a long enough holiday from F1, it's time you got down to some serious work.' He listed all the unknown factors — as far as he was concerned — for the design of a F1 car. 'When you have all these answers we will know how to build a good car.' Team Lotus was in a trough. The Lotus 76 had not worked, and they were launching the fully-adjustable Type 77. I had already shown him my calculation that it would take 14 months to try every possible combination. I was sent away to read the 28 pages, prepare a programme to obtain the answers, together with the names of the project team I needed. Among the questions was: which is best, a full width chisel nose or a needle nose with two big aerofoils? I asked for Peter Wright, as most of the questions involved aerodynamics, Charlie Prior to make the models and Ralph Bellamy to draw my schemes. We used the Imperial College wind tunnel, but until we had some results Ralph could not start designing the car structure, so he went along to help Peter. To preserve confidentiality we only tested between 5.00 and 10.00 p.m., running the quarter-scale tunnel ourselves. It had a rubber belt to simulate the road. We had not been testing the needle nose with wings set-up for long when Peter noticed that the rubber belt was rising under the wings. There was some delay while we improved the road retention system, then we confirmed that an inverted aerofoil close to the road had its effect magnified by the interaction with the road, particularly if used with end plates.

In these early stages we used to have an hour-long meeting with Chunky on Saturday mornings to review our results. After looking at them, Chunky asked: 'What happens if you make the whole car like an inverted wing?' Peter gave a wry smile and produced his photographs of the ill-fated 1969 BRM wing car (see p 94 of Doug Nye's *The History of the Grand Prix Car* published by Osprey). Ralph quickly drew, and Charlie Prior just as quickly made a model of what became the Type 78. We had some discussion about the radiators and I proposed that we fitted them in the leading edge of the wing rather like the Mosquito aeroplane, except that the exit ducts would be in the upper surface. Peter devised a very crafty way of simulating radiators for the wind tunnel, heat and all. I received a jubilant telex just as I was setting off for Graham Hill's funeral — 'the Mosquito flies'. I kept the stiffness and freedom-from-friction flags flying, while Ralph came up with a very stiff folded aluminium honeycomb construction. By the end of January 1976 we had the basic design complete and called upon Team Lotus, still based at Hethel, to supply people to detail and build the car.

Chunky and I had a meeting with Geoffrey Kent, of John Player. We explained the concept to him, and bravely he agreed to fund it over and above their basic JPS contribution. We built an enormous hydraulic rig to test the structure and suspension, which someone nicknamed 'Ecofisk' after one of the big North Sea oil platforms.

We saw very little of Chunky during the final phases of the Type 78, the boat companies claiming much of his time. He had produced a glass fibre hull for Versilcraft of Viareggio, for their wooden 4-berth, 13.8 metre (42 ft) Mystère, powered by Perkins 280 hp diesel V8s. Hangar 3 on the airfield at Hethel had been converted to build the big boats, Mystères and Marauders. John Pettifer from the car production line was in charge, and John Kelly was running Moonraker, as David Lane had taken up another appointment away from Lotus. The boats in Hangar 3 were built stern-on to a transverse mezzanine, a very inefficient layout and discarding all of David's teaching for unrestricted access. All the workers trooped across the stern inflicting much damage, they all queued up waiting their turn to get on, or much worse get off, getting in the way of people trying to work aboard. John Pettifer saw this clearly, but was very sensitive, being the new boy in the boat world. He hesitated to cross swords with Colin, who he revered, like most people did.

The Marauder was giving a lot of trouble. Chunky was obsessed with the idea of having a totally clean hull. He adopted the idea, from a pre-World War II motor torpedo boat, of supporting the propeller end of the shaft on the base of the rudder, avoiding the drag and turbulence of a 'P' bracket. This was not the root cause of the Marauder's troubles, but the traditional boat builders were very conservative and blamed all the problems onto the absence of a P bracket.

The boat problems provoked a repetition of one of Chunky's favourite dictums. 'Development is the last resort of an incompetent designer.' What he meant was a little extra time thinking at the design stage (what GM calls failure mode analysis) avoids a major upset once the design actually exists and goes wrong. It is much easier to rub out a few lines than it is to retool. In later years his young turks took this too literally and eliminated any development capability within the boat companies. When his dictum was quoted as the reason for the elimination of development capacity he set off into orbit with Mars as his target. Most of his young men thought the way to promotion and prosperity was to implement his every word. One of them once remarked to Chunky that he was always in trouble for following his dictums, yet I, who often challenged or ignored them never seemed to get into trouble: 'Because he uses his loaf,' snorted Chunky. 'I wish you would sometimes.'

As we moved into the summer and started to build the Type 78 with Team Lotus labour drafted to Ketteringham Hall, I became more and more involved in boat problems. There were now four complete Marauders afloat in the Moonraker basin at Brundall. There was, however, a 136-item snag list which had to be cleared before they could be delivered, and some of them were quite serious. John Kelly said they were nothing to do with him, apart from the boats getting in his way. Pettifer said he had built them to specification, he was not going to send his staff to work on them to the detriment of his production programmes unless he had a proper specification and Chunky's authority. Chunky was trying to make sense out of the F1 Type 77 which proved to be even less competitive than the 76.

In the middle of it all, Richard Morley who had been running the car company, left for a well paid job in Nigeria, taking Martin Long, Purchase Manager, with him. I knew the car company was losing money, even though many of the early warning management systems had been discarded. One day Fred Bushell and Sir Leonard, knowing I was in regular contact with Chunky concerning boat and F1 matters, persuaded me to tell him the bad news — that the car company had lost a million. I suspect this was on the basis that, as I had plenty of bad news to give him, a little more could not get the messenger killed a second time. I had quite a reasoned discussion with Chunky, but I declined his proposal to take over running the car company, arguing that I was a fireman, a troubleshooter if you like. Methodically running a business on ordered lines, and avoiding crises was not for me. I might even get bored and start a fire to have the excitement of putting it out. I thought he agreed with me rather quickly. We then discussed promoting Mike Kimberley. I said I thought he could do the job, but he lived on his nerves and would need watching in case he worked himself into a breakdown. We agreed to give him a try. No doubt Chunky obtained other people's opinions as well as mine. Mike was duly installed as Operations Director. I was told to look after him and it was agreed that as soon as I had cleared the boat problems, I would spend more time at Hethel.

The trouble was the boat problems took much longer to solve than Chunky expected. The steering problem, where after a few minutes at speed the flybridge system became ineffective, was easy to diagnose, but more difficult to cure. There was not enough head for the hydraulic fluid to recuperate, I proved this by hanging a car brake fluid reservoir from the radio aerial, much to Chunky's disgust. The fly-bridge steering position, beautifully sleek, styled by Chunky himself, did not have enough space for a separate recuperation chamber and the only system which would fit and work was a Canadian Capilano system which cost £60 more than Chunky's favoured system. Chunky would have none of it. After a convincing Sunday afternoon sea trial, performing figure eights through our own wake, proving that the Capilano system completely cured the trouble, we met on the following Monday afternoon in the Ketteringham Hall Boardroom to thrash out the solutions. I had both steering units stripped, and laid out on paper-covered felt pads on the Boardroom table. Chunky saw his £60 slipping away fast. He picked up one of the main castings weighing 3 kg (6½ lb), bristling with studs and sharp edges, and hurled it down the table (the scars are still there) shouting: 'You would argue the hind leg off a donkey. Do what you like!'

Later that afternoon, during a meeting of boat company executives on some other matter, he told them that I had made him eat humble pie as an engineer and they were to see that it did not happen again. The air-conditioning problem took a little longer to sort. The system was fine in the marina, but after about 30 minutes at sea the safety devices tripped and the system switched off. Eventually we found that when the boat had lifted up on the plane, the inlet for the cooling water for the heat-exchanger came out of the sea. It was extremely difficult to move the intake aft and Chunky would not have my scoop which defiled his beautifully clean hull. In the end we compromised by moving it as far aft as we could and fitting the smallest possible scoop.

Andretti tested the Type 78, when it was immediately clear we had a winner. It was a good two seconds a lap quicker than the 77s and there was more to come. The 'queer box' design was complete, we even had some components, and two Marauders had been delivered. I took Pam on holiday to convalesce after her operation for the removal of gallstones.

Chunky had a habit, when someone was in trouble, of seating them in a hard chair in the full light of the window. If he wanted you to do something especially difficult he gave you the armchair and sherry treatment. On my return from holiday I was offered the hard chair in the window. He opened fire saying: 'This is going to be a very disagreeable interview.' I wondered what I had done wrong, but he continued. 'The Type 78 is good enough to race now, but I have decided to save it until next season.' I said: 'I should hope so, if we race it now, people will see what we have done and they will have time to copy it.' His face cleared and he said: 'Oh, that's fine, did you have good holiday?' He gave me some sherry and told me that Chris Craft, one of the best-known American boat companies had picked up a magazine account of a North Sea crossing by a glass fibre Mystère and had expressed interest in the VARI process and buying a large number of boats.

He gave me my next project — a low-line diesel. Most of the 6-cylinder marine diesels were derived from a Ford truck engine designed, in the truck application, to be inclined at 45 degrees. The marinizers stood them upright, but Chunky's idea was to leave it inclined. We had already looked at the Ford York diesel but had decided that it would not stand turbocharging. I put together a programme with Mercraft, based near Royston, for two 180 hp prototypes with an aluminium exhaust manifold saving 30 kg (66 lb) in weight and £65 machining costs. The plan was to fit these engines into the Mamba, a new 10.5 metre (34½ ft) boat, using a two-thirds scaled down Marauder hull. I suspect this boat was intended to be the Moonraker's successor. He was always complaining that the Moonraker was not his sort of boat, too clumsy, too noisy, too much vibration, etc. He already had under construction a six-berth version of the Mystère with two 212 hp Sabre engines under the afterdeck with their fly wheels facing forward driving Borg Warner Z-drives. The engines sat above their propellers. This boat had P brackets, Capilano steering and an extra two-berth cabin, with its saloon extended forwards. It was a very clever layout. Around that time I had become the JCL representative on the SBBNF (Ship and Boat Builders National Federation), the marine equivalent of the SMMT.

A high-powered Chris Craft party duly arrived, Chairman, President and lawyers, and agreed to buy the VARI process and 50 boats. I think Chunky thought he had fallen asleep and woken up in heaven. He had an exciting new F1 car, the car company was back into profit, the Esprit was selling well and Rolls-Royce Motors were interested in taking over the sale of Lotus cars in the USA. He also had plenty of money to indulge in his boat plans, so he took a large stand for the Earls Court Boat Show, planning to display a more powerful Moonraker, a restyled Marauder, the new six-berth Mystère and the completely new Mamba. He started to sketch the 18-metre

(59 ft) three-decked Mangusta and bought himself a new aeroplane.

The Chris Craft party struck a slightly discordant note when they reminded us that there would have to be many changes in the boat for the US market and to meet their Coast Guard requirements. Chunky brushed that aside : 'No problem, talk to Tony.' He briefed me: 'Charge them for everything — tooling, redundant material — you know exactly what to do, just how our suppliers screw the car company when we want to delete something.'

JPS, sensing they had something with the new Type 78 about which Andretti was particularly enthusiastic, demanded a big Press launch with all the razzmatazz, at the Royal Garden Hotel in London. They insisted that it was known as the JPS Mark III instead of the Lotus Type 78. Chunky's father, Stan, was killed in a car crash on his way to Norfolk to spend Christmas with Chunky and his family, so I had to take Chunky's place at the launch, chairing a panel discussion with Peter Wright and Ralph Bellamy, all of us strictly enjoined not to give anything away — just say it's something for nothing.

Preparations for the Boat Show were all going terribly wrong. Upholstery and trim is very difficult to draw and specify. It began to look doubtful if we would get all the boats to the Show, despite my borrowing staff from the car company. Eventually Chunky blew his top on Christmas Eve. He thrust a purple face against mine — (although I was still just a visiting fireman) and demanded: 'What is wrong with my boat companies?' 'You!' I told him. He did his impersonation of the pantomime demon king, disappearing in a puff of smoke, leaving me to find my own way back to Ketteringham Hall. After Christmas at the Boat Show we had a gang of trimmers and upholsterers disguised as stand builders finishing off the boats — hiding the evidence that neither the Mamba nor the Mystère (called the Mirage in its US form and the Mistral in European form) would even float, far less had working engines. In the middle of all this I was handed a note appointing me Chief Executive of the boat company, still retaining all my other duties.

Before I had recovered from the shock the Chris Craft party arrived, Chairman Herbie Siegel, his wife and President Jim Rochlis. Herbie was a financial wizard but Jim knew his boats. Chunky proudly showed them over the new Mirage. I thought it was a very nice boat, and was starting to work out how I could get my hands on one, when I became aware all was not well. The Chris Craft party departed in a huff. Chunky also swept off, saying they were Philistines and did not know a good boat when they saw one — leaving a nonplussed newly-appointed Chief Executive and crestfallen working party to cope with the Press. They seemed on better terms next day, Chunky having taken them out, finishing up at Annabel's nightclub.

Eventually Jim Rochlis told me that the feature of the Mystère that had attracted them, was its Caribbean styling, cool melamine enamel and wet-look ciré plastic, now they were being offered walnut veneers and classic rough tweed, which they could do just as well themselves. It was obvious that they had wounded each other deeply. Jim kept on saying: 'We will never ever buy another boat sight unseen again.' Jim remained to work out details with me, insisting on 'riding a boat' before finalizing his changes, while Chunky took the new Type 78 to its first race where, appropriately, the fire extinguisher bottle burst. I rearranged the workshop mezzanines, to build the boats alongside to improve the workers' access.

It took until late February to complete the boat. Jim, who had returned to New York, came over. The North Sea was not very pleasant, Jim finding the boat was far too noisy and vibrated too much. The job list grew, but as it did Jim and I became good friends. Finally he returned to New York to discuss the implications and cost effect of all the changes with Chairman Siegel, while I did the same with Chairman Chapman. There was then a major delay while Jim had open heart surgery and I had treatment for a burst blood vessel at the back of my eye.

Amongst the other exciting events at this time was the discovery that scaling-down a Marauder hull to create a Mamba did not work — the boat would not even get up onto the plane. Someone also had the propeller sums wrong, although fitting Moonraker propellers improved it a little. I was accused of getting my engine sums wrong, too, but neither a Mercraft uprating to 210 hp nor a clandestine and very temporary 235 hp produced the desired performance. The boat also had a very bare looking saloon which may have created the impression that it was not value for money as it never sold well.

While Jim and I were convalescing the prototype six berth Mirage was sold with an agreement that it could be used as a demonstrator, the new owner basing it at Cogolin near St Tropez.

We quickly found the Achilles heel of the Type 78. If it was crashed, the aluminium honeycomb panels buckled and could not be straightened, so the monocoque structure had to be thrown away. This was not so bad if you had plenty of spares, which we did not. Team Lotus had now moved to Ketteringham Hall, but my ground effect project team had dispersed and Peter Wright left to become a currant farmer. Ralph Bellamy, a typically outspoken Australian who did not suffer fools gladly, did not fit into the new Team Lotus so he was sent to Lotus Cars to try to sort out the Esprit steering problem, primarily caused by the change of brakes. Here he fell foul of the Lotus Cars Norfolk mafia and resigned.

After Jim's three-months' convalescence we picked up the threads and met at Cogolin with the demonstrator, fitted with felt silencers in an air-intake extended up to the flybridge. We ran down the coast to Bandol and back again. On the way we caught up with and passed a Riva America, about our size, but costing twice as much. On our return, to let the Americans see the beaches of St Tropez, we ran close in shore at 6 knots in 1.8 metres of water. Jim said that the vibration levels were now acceptable but the boat was still too noisy. While I was convalescing, Tim Enright, Chunky's personal assistant who had always wanted to show what he was made of by running a company, took over the boat company in my place. I was told my first priority was the Chris Craft relationship.

I started work on the often postponed 4 litre 32-valve V8, but first of all I had to negotiate some help with its funding from the Department of Trade and Industry (DTI) and establish concept viability. Mike Kimberley reminded Chunky that I was supposed to be helping him at Hethel. I moved from Ketteringham Hall to Boats and then to Hethel all in five months, this time to Sir Leonard Crossland's old office, Sir Leonard having retired. I also collected responsibility for quality again, which was now a rare old problem. One of the American importers had modified some cars in America. Some of the modifications, such as an after-market air-conditioning system, caused much trouble with the cooling system. There was also a spate of product liability actions relating to eighth- and tenth-hand much-modified Europas. I had a hotch-potch of jobs with the young turks trying to carve up my responsibilities between them. I had on display in my office a notice which I had bought in America. It read: 'Old age and treachery always beats youth and enthusiasm.'

One morning at about 11 a.m. Chunky told me he was due to speak as an eminent designer at the ceremonies to dedicate the new Sainsbury Centre of Modern Art at the University of East Anglia. He could not go, would I please deputize for him. I said 'Yes, when is it?' 'Twelve noon today,' he replied. When I had recovered, I asked: 'Can I have your speech please?' He replied: 'I have not written one, you will have to improvize.' I must have managed somehow, because as a result I was invited to address the Royal Institute of British Architects Annual Meeting in London shortly afterwards.

Assisted by Gordon Sprules, one of the bright young men from the Finance Department, I made our pitch for DTI support on the V8 engine and for the VARI process. As a first step towards the 4 litre V8, I modified a production 2 litre Type 907 4-valve to prove our ideas. We used the BRM-type water flow system, with 33 per cent of the cool water from the pump passing around the aluminium cylinder liner, the remainder across the head from the exhaust side to the inlet. We used water-cooled exhaust valve guides with solid valves and eventually equalized all the exhaust valve head temperatures to 620°C (1148°F) from the hottest at 760°C (1400°F). We persuaded the engine to run at 11.5:1 compression ratio on 91 octane unleaded fuel and stoked the power up from 160 to 187 hp. All we needed now was the money to build them.

The engineering team I had built up by 1974 had been decimated by the recession, but was growing again. There was also an unfortunate tendency by some managers never to hire someone with the ability which might make the newcomer a challenge to his position, so there was an unfortunate degree of mediocrity in some areas. Graham Atkin was not amongst these. If he thought the man was good, he hired him, so there was plenty of talent in Powertrain that I expected to be able to call upon.

At the Southampton Boat Show we again 'rode a boat' with Jim Rochlis, this time with silencers in the exhaust system. With a conventional installation of midship engines the exhaust and cooling water was carried to the stern in long boxes down the side of the boat, just above the water line. This achieved an adequate degree of noise reduction. However, in the Mirage and Mistral the exhaust emerged right at the stern so we lost this effect, also the overhanging fly-bridge acted as a sounding board and magnified the noise. We put plenty of absorbent material into the fly-bridge floor and had two sizes of silencer to try. We were afraid of loss of performance from the silencer's back pressure. One of the attractions of the boat was its 14 gph cruising fuel consumption at 22 knots, together with a maximum of over 25 knots. With small silencers it was still too noisy for Jim but there was no measurable loss in performance. The big silencers were nearly acceptable and we were still on the right side of 25 knots. The boat had been fully instrumented to measure the noise levels, we were down to 78 perceived decibels (dBa) on the afterdeck from a starting point of 90 (a modern car is about 72). Jim said if we could get the noise level down to

76, by these methods, it would be acceptable and he would not need to come over again. We agreed to meet in New York to finalize the specification. From a distance the Mirage and Mistral always had a very distinctive exhaust bark. Recently, on holiday in the Mediterranean, I heard this distinctive exhaust bark. There in the marina I found a Brighton-registered Mistral adorned with the most attractive young ladies.

Tim Enright and I formed the JCL delegation to negotiate the final specification with Chris Craft at their headquarters, in Madison Avenue, New York. We could then start to build their 50 boats. Just before we were due to leave (this was in the era of standby air fares which particularly appealed to Chunky — you drew £100 in cash and queued at Heathrow for a standby seat to New York) we received a message that a Marauder on its way to Hamburg had lost a large piece of outer skin. JCL boats had a foam sandwich skinned hull; foam between two layers of glass fibre. The basic Marauder structure was designed to have the minimum number of ribs, which meant large unsupported panels, and therefore a thicker foam layer, which nevertheless gave a light hull. The Mystère inherited many more ribs, so its panels were smaller and the foam thinner. Albert Adams and I went to investigate. We were fog-bound overnight at Amsterdam airport. Eventually we found the Marauder at Cuxhaven, and discovered that the failure had originated from a sharp corner, which was less likely to affect the small panelled Mirage. After a night in Hamburg, I flew to Heathrow and joined up with Tim to queue for a standby seat. We spent four days at Chris Craft working our way down Jim's list. We cleared most of the main issues. Tim returned to England while I went to EPA in Detroit and then went back to New York to finalize the details.

During our first spell in the Chris Craft offices I was invited to meet one of their non-executive directors, a John Z. DeLorean. My first impression was of his piercing eyes and resonant voice, which reminded me of a Methodist lay preacher. I knew of his reputation as a GM whiz kid who had revitalized Pontiac and Chevrolet and was the driving force behind the GM muscle cars. He had walked out when he was head of GM's North American operations and in line for promotion to President. He showed me a *Car and Driver* description of his new ecologically moral car which had a Giugiaro-designed body. He asked me if I would like to drive it. I said I would, so he arranged with his Vice President, Product, Bill Collins, for me to do so during my forthcoming trip to Detroit.

I was rather guarded as it looked to me to be a competitor to the Esprit. He planned to make 20,000 a year, selling for somewhere between $11,000 and $12,000. The Corvette was going out of production, so his timing was ideal. He had an arrangement whereby he would build the cars in Puerto Rico, a source of good quality cheap labour and not too far from the USA. When I met Bill Collins in Detroit it was a wet slushy day. I drove the Citroen-engined prototype around Warren — GM territory. I was shown the second prototype in build. It had Ford Pinto suspension components, was well engineered and extremely well made, but it looked fearfully tail heavy as the engine was behind the rear-axle centre-line.

Bill took me out for lunch and gave me his budgets, manning levels and development programme — lethal information to give to the Chief Engineer of a rival manufacturer. On the flight back to New York I read them through. The budgets were frugal, even by Lotus standards and I was particularly struck that there was no contingency in the plan, it was all based on being right first time. I was invited to dinner with John and his wife, top model Christina Ferrare, and then it all became clear. He invited me to join his company, saying he would make me a millionaire in three years.

My job was to set up a European Research and Development (R&D) centre, probably in England, staffed equally by Europeans and Americans. I had already said I did not wish to live and work in Detroit. My salary from all sources at Lotus at that time was around £15,000 per year. Chunky exploited the idea that people looked upon Lotus as a post-graduate course and were willing to work there for less than the going-rate anywhere else. The work was stimulating and exciting. Where else, for example, would I have had the chance to mastermind the design of an F1 car, a new V8 engine, a new transmission and the Esprit, all in the same three years. DeLorean spoke of two salaries, one as a consultant, the other to run the R&D centre, with stock options. I said I was very interested, but I would need some time to think it over.

I had the final meetings with Jim — long ones — either in his apartment or his office. We hammered out a reasonable agreement. I won on plastic windows and doors rather than toughened glass, but conceded Raritan Crown porcelain toilets with 36-gallon holding-tanks, rather than our own plastic caravan porta-potties with eight-gallon holding tanks. When I told Chunky of this, on a bad telephone line, there were howls of rage at the other end. 'What, you have agreed to put a quarter of a ton of **** in the bottom of my boat!' I believed that the agreed changes gave us a better boat; also Chris Craft were going to make generous payments for the work. We needed the income that 50 boats would give us.

Herbie Siegel signed the agreement, complimented Jim and me on our work and we had a celebration dinner together. I queued all next day for my standby flight home. To my surprise Chunky said he would not sign the agreement. There was no longer any chance of making a profit from it. He made no comment when I said: 'Then I have been wasting my time for the last six months.' Extricating us from the contracts took Fred Bushell some two years and destroyed the boat companies financially.

Chunky was always saying that he would retire when he was 50 and spend his time on a beach in the Bahamas. He was approaching 50, so I wondered how his refusal of a £5m contract fitted in with these plans. With the appointment of Sir Leonard Crosland, Chunky had started to distance himself from the car company, although he still retained financial control. Did this mean he was going to do the same with the boat companies and that he felt that Chris Craft would become too powerful? Was all this in preparation for his retirement? Myself, I was a long way off being able to afford to retire, and it looked as if I would have to go the course to 65. I had no wish for my future to be left in the hands of Chunky's young men after he had retired, so I was very receptive to DeLorean's overtures.

The V8 was proceeding quite well, although on an absolute shoe-string. Chunky had told me I was to recruit my own team from outside. 'Do not interfere with Kimbo' (Mike Kimberley) was one of my instructions. 'Do not invent anything and do not do anything that has not been done before' was another. I managed to persuade Lucas to provide fuel injection development free of charge, and the ignition system came from the Rolls-Royce V8, so I did not need any development. I managed to assemble an absolutely first-class team; Brian Bayliss as Chief Draughtsman, assisted by Tom Brindley with Malcolm MacDonald from Cranfield College as the stress and crankshaft balance man. Brian kept telling me that he had no experience whatever of designing for diecasting, but his V8 crankcase was a work of art — lighter than the 4-cylinder crankcase.

I now had no involvement with F1 apart from designing a bell housing oil tank. The Type 78 had won four races but it had retired from four more with engine failure when comfortably in the lead. We found that when Andretti eased off on instructions from his pit, he reduced rpm to a speed which coincided with a camshaft resonance that overstressed the valve-springs, just as Cosworth hit a minor valve-spring problem. To overcome difficulties with the honeycomb buckling, Peter Wright (lured back from the currants) and Chunky developed a carbon composite structure, which I criticized as nothing like stiff enough from the suspension aspect. I had also been fairly outspoken about the treatment of Ralph Bellamy, so I was slightly *persona non grata* with Team Lotus, especially after my remarks when I found the stiffness test-rig had been discarded. Chunky still took me through the workshop to see new developments, and discussed them with me.

In January 1978 DeLorean sent me draft contracts which provided a salary equivalent to £40,000 per year and stock options for 20,000 shares a year in the DeLorean Corporation which I could buy at ten cents a share, they were then trading at $5. We had numerous phone conversations. I met Bill Collins several times at Heathrow during his visits to Giugiaro in Turin. I suggested setting up the R&D centre in Milton Keynes, convenient to Heathrow, Coventry, Birmingham, Luton and Basildon and even had some recruits identified. Then DeLorean went quiet for a month.

I also had to sort out the Press car situation which was attracting criticism from various journalists, the system I had originally devised having been discarded. My routine had started with random selection of a car to the required specification by the Quality Department. It was then audited, rectified as necessary by the production team — so that putting their mistakes right cost them money. The car was run in, reassessed and then passed to me for approval before being taken on the Press car fleet. This gave Quality information and ensured that the car the customer bought was exactly the same as the car road-tested by the Press. This procedure had been replaced by a system of blue-printing an engine (taking every component to the favourable end of the tolerance band), then power testing and rectifying any faults. Similarly, a selected gearbox from a run in a development car would be used. This procedure meant that the Press tested a special car which had been pulled to pieces and rebuilt several times. Even though it might have very good performance, it tended to be a bit tatty. I fought a long and unsuccessful battle to return to the old system.

I was also aware of rumbles of trouble elsewhere. The basic rear-suspension system, dating from 1970, using a fixed length half-shaft as the upper link made for simplicity and cost-effectiveness. It worked reasonably well on the front-engined cars with a stiffly mounted differential. The mid-engined cars, where cornering loads reacted on the engine-transaxle unit and thence into the engine mounting, meant a compromise in the mounting-rubber stiffness. If they were soft enough to absorb engine vibrations, they were far too soft to maintain the suspension geometry and there was excessive camber change under cornering loads. On the other hand, if they were made stiff enough for good road holding, most of the engine vibrations were transmitted into the car.

DeLorean came to life again. He had an offer from the State of Michigan to set up their plant in the old Budd railway wagon plant, north of Detroit. My R&D Centre would have to be located in the same building and I would have to overcome my objections to working in Detroit. To help me decide, a salary of $127,500 was proposed, about £70,000 at the February 1978 rate of exchange. To this salary was added an apartment, either in Troy or nearby, with amenities including electricity, heating, phone, etc. paid for, together with a car, either an Alpine or a Porsche 928. The offer of share options remained unchanged. I expressed some concern over my tax liabilities. 'No problem,' said John, 'Mark McCormack is an old friend. I will get him on to it.' Two or three days later their London office came up with the idea that I would set up a consultancy business in England, with myself as its principal employee, paid a salary of £20,000 in the UK on which I would pay normal UK income tax, the balance (some £50,000) would go into an annuity, probably in Liechtenstein, which would mature in five years. I would take up my share options, sell the shares, hopefully for $600,000, buy a Chris Craft boat (or boats) which would be fitted with British engines and found a charter business operating out of British Bermuda. There would be some justification for this as they saw my profession as that of a boat engineer. Eventually this business would close down through lack of customers and revenue, and the assets (that is the boats) would be returned to the UK and sold, without attracting much tax or duty, to supplement the annuity.

I still dithered, so DeLorean paid for Pam and me to visit Detroit over the Easter holiday, mainly for Pam to see the district and choose an apartment. Our eldest daughter Carolyn was engaged and not involved, but Lesley, the middle one, was at University and greatly attracted by the idea of a post-graduate course at Michigan State University. The youngest, Philippa, was coming up to her O-levels and should not be moved, so Pam would have to spend school terms in England and school holidays in Detroit. Nina Collins, Bill's wife, showed Pam around Troy and Bloomfield Hills which she liked very much, while I had meetings with DeLorean, Bill Collins and finance man Dewey. Pam and I exchanged positions, she became more enthusiastic, as I became slightly less so. We returned to England with only the date of my joining DeLorean to be settled. A week later, Pam and I were talking through the details, when I suddenly decided I did not want to go. We agreed to sleep on it, but next morning I was, if anything, even more certain. I rang John DeLorean that evening and told him I would not join him. He did not seem surprised, nor did he try to change my mind.

A few days later, early on a beautiful spring Saturday afternoon, I met Chunky by chance in the Directors' garage. He said: 'So you have given up the idea of DeLorean then?' I replied: 'Yes.' He asked: 'What in the world possessed you to think of it in the first place?' '$127,500,' was my reply. He whistled: 'That's more than I get, still money is not everything, there must have been something else.' I told him he was always talking of retiring when he was 50, and I did not care to entrust my declining years to his young men. He latched on to this, and said he would see I had nothing to worry about. As we got into our respective cars, he threw over his shoulder: 'If you speak to DeLorean again, tell him to bring his car here and we will finish it for him.' I soon had an opportunity to pass on Chunky's message, DeLorean rang me and asked if I would meet Bill Collins again at Heathrow. They had had an offer from the Irish government, who asked for independent assessments of the project's viability. Could I suggest some suitable people and tell Bill about them when I met him? The proposed plant had been a tyrecord factory in Limerick. I shook Bill when I told him of its notoriety following the kidnapping of its Dutch Chief Executive, Dr Herrema.

The new composite car, the Type 79, was devastating F1. Team Lotus had changed, they were now very secretive, almost furtive. Peter Warr had left. With sponsorship and Bernie's FOCA, Team Lotus had gone from a happy-go-lucky outfit working on a shoe-string, typified by the cars being carried on a Ford pick-up and trailer, to one of the best-funded, best-equipped, highly-professional outfits. Chunky gave some of the credit to Peter. One day we were boarding the aircraft to go to London, when a box of bloaters was handed to me at the last minute. 'What on earth's that?' asked Chunky. I explained that my host at Shell had confessed to a love of Yarmouth bloaters, so I was taking him some fresh ones. He said that he wished he could remember that sort of thing, it was what made Peter Warr so good at dealing with the sponsors.

The systems and Teutonic efficiency that Team Lotus developed was also down to Peter. He was an ideal complement to Chunky's mercurial ways. I had been asked to interview candidates for a Chief Engineer to work under Chunky, and had recommended a relatively unknown South African, Rory Byrne, but Chunky chose Tony Southgate, ex-BRM and Shadow, despite my warning that he was probably only coming to learn as much as he could about ground-effect before moving on! Chunky took me to the Spanish GP, via his villa in Ibiza where a new water system was being installed. I was sent to buy a new electric water pump. I returned with one, commenting that they also had an all-plastic pump, but it was four times as expensive. This led to a tirade. 'That is your trouble all over; indecision; can't make your mind up. Go and get the plastic one, it will last six times as long.' After the tongue lashings I used to get for increasing the cost of a boat, this seemed very odd.

I read that John DeLorean had signed an agreement with Labour's Northern Ireland Minister, Roy Mason, to build his car plant at Dunmurry just outside Belfast. This was completely against the advice of the DTI. Mike Kimberley told me that he and Chunky were going to Phoenix, Arizona, at DeLorean's expense to try one of the DMC12 prototype cars, and asked what they should look for? I gave him a list, but on his return he was extremely guarded. Apparently the fuel injection system failed after a few miles leaving them stranded on the freeway. Chunky had remarked that the car was an absolute dog. Now he knew why Tony had turned the job down.

In September 1978 Ronnie Peterson died from injuries received in a crash at Monza driving a Type 78. This time no one tried to blame Chunky who was nevertheless bitterly angry. He told me that Ronnie's injuries would have been nothing like as severe had he been driving a Type 79. The honeycomb panels had crumpled around his legs inflicting serious injuries. He was only in a 78 because of a shortage of spares, which was a disgrace after nearly a season with the Type 79. The Italian doctors should have foreseen the complications that ensued and caused his death. He tried to use the annual end-of-season pay review for Team Lotus to change the whole system, to ensure that he would never run out of spares through lack of labour again. Actually the problem arose through lack of planning, not lack of effort. He instructed his bright young men to impose the changes. They were good with numbers but not with human beings and it developed into a serious confrontation. The staff demanded a meeting with Chunky, which would have defused the situation, but he flatly refused to meet them.

Team Lotus had by now won the World Championship, and I realized how far I had fallen from favour because of my flirtation with DeLorean, when I found I was omitted from most of the celebration guest lists, even though I was a director of Team Lotus. I was invited to one or two events with other Lotus Cars directors. At one, given by the Norfolk County Council in their offices, Chunky told me that it looked as if we might have a deal with DeLorean, and if so I would get the money I needed to finish the V8. I had suspected something was going on. During the Motor Show at NEC Birmingham I found Colin Spooner, although he was still with Lucas Marine, on our stand. He assumed I knew all about the DeLorean project, which I did not. Then Bill Collins rang me at home. He said he had been working at Ketteringham Hall for a fortnight and was surprised he had not seen me.

Finally Mike Kimberley told me they had a contract to complete the development of the DMC12 vehicle. It would be fitted with a 2.85 litre PRV (Peugeot Renault Volvo) V6 engine, in the form Volvo used for their cars sold in America. Colin Spooner would lead the team. There was no engine work, and Lotus was specifically excluded from how the car was manufactured — any form of production engineering — or quality matter. DeLorean appointed a Managing Director, Chuck Bennington, who had been working for Chrysler in South Africa. Chuck had a tremendous reputation for setting up new, green-field plants. I assumed once Dunmurry was up and running he would move on. I was invited, at the last minute, to a ceremonial boardroom lunch with John DeLorean, who was very friendly and said in a jocular fashion, that I had cost him an awful lot of money. It was very clear to me that by a Lotus decision I was not involved in the project. Chuck Bennington would often drop into my office for a chat, assuming I knew more than I did.

The boat companies were declining badly and were desperately short of money. The Moonraker was an old out-of-date design and it needed a face-lift but everyone was concentrating on the new boats. The Marauder now had a very bad reputation for reliability, so no one bought one; the Mamba was poor value for money, very expensive and sparsely equipped, and the Mystère derivatives still needed refining, but the staff required had been axed, someone having taken 'development is the last resort of an incompetent designer' too literally. They were at the beginning of a vicious downhill spiral, cutting staff and costs, then losing sales, because they could not meet customers' needs.

The car company was wobbling on the same brink. It badly needed a new car, and the existing ones needed revitalizing and bringing up to date, but funds were short. Lucas had said they could no longer continue to fund our V8 development. If we wanted them to continue we would have to pay for it. We had achieved some very impressive results with their injection system. It was possible to drive a V8-engined Esprit to and from Birmingham a little faster than was legally permitted at an average consumption of 37 mpg from its 325 hp 185 kg (408 lb) weight engine. Emission results were also extremely good. It was very frustrating to have to put it on ice just on the brink of success. The two engineers concerned left Lucas and founded their own business, known as 'Zytek', now very successful in the competition world. Giugiaro had produced a face-lifted version of the Esprit ready for the V8. This was eventually used for the Turbo Esprit. There were no significant financial benefits from DeLorean until well into 1979. I was somewhat at a loose end, with the V8 being on ice, and there was nothing for me on the boats. Mike Kimberley had two teams working hard, one to develop a turbo version of the 2 litre for the Esprit and the other a 2.2 litre engine for the Chrysler Sunbeam and the M50 family.

I had been deeply involved in labour relations through the winter. As usual I chaired the Joint Negotiating Committee meeting between Management and the Staff Council. We had reached a critical phase. The staff had put in a claim which we could not afford, and which would breach the government guidelines (already broken by Ford). We were heavily dependent on government goodwill because of our DTI grants of over £1m for the V8 and VARI, so we dare not incur their displeasure. Events were moving towards a climax with the House of Commons due to debate the situation that day — particularly the Ford action. Mike was out of the country somewhere, Chunky was in South America F1 testing, so I was handling the pay negotiations on my own. If we did not reach agreement before the House voted, expected to be around 10 p.m. and the Ford breach of the guidelines was permitted we would be in a desperate situation. Early in the evening Chunky rang from South America to ask how I was getting on. I said I was stuck. The staff had suggested an attendance allowance as a way around the guidelines, which permitted genuine productivity agreements. Chunky exploded. 'Why should we pay them twice to come to work?' he demanded. I reminded him of the imminent House of Commons vote. If Ford got away with breaking the guidelines, we would be faced with an impossible wage demand. I had to have an agreement before the vote at 10 p.m. 'Do the best you can,' he said, and rang off. I finally managed to reach agreement on an attendance allowance, forfeit if they lost more than five minutes in a week. Morris Dowton, the Production Manager, said the men thought it was Christmas already. Chunky said it was a good deal, and we signed it 30 minutes before the House vote, which opened the floodgates.

Jingling with medals as a negotiator, I was given the job of sorting out the problems at Team Lotus. The damage had already been done. Some very good men had left, bitterness remained and Chunky permanently distanced himself from the workshops. It was all very stupid because his basic offer was quite fair and reasonable. It was so badly handled that he was never again on the same good terms with the men. John Player gave us a tremendous farewell dinner as they were pulling out of racing, to which I was invited and received a number of compliments.

I became involved in the 2 litre engine improvement programmes. The turbo engine had developed a very bad habit of burning holes in its pistons, particularly during full-throttle runs on the eight mile circuit at Nardo in

Italy. It had a dry-sump oil system to help cool the pistons, and sodium filled valves, but for some reason did not have water-cooled guides to get the heat away, as did the V8. By rearranging the water flow through the engine we cured the piston burning. We also changed to forged pistons, primarily because the sales people told all and sundry, panting for Turbo Esprits that we were waiting for forged pistons which were essential for turbo-charged engines. This led to an unnecessary and expensive piston and ring development programme. We had to use the aluminium cylinder liners from the V8 before we were completely out of trouble.

The 2.2 litre engine (the increase in capacity was achieved by a longer stroke) was in trouble in the front-engined cars. Vibration levels were unacceptable, although they seemed just tolerable in the Esprit. With the assistance of Malcolm MacDonald and Melody Stokes, the latter one of our new generation of brilliant young women engineers, both from the V8 team, we determined that, as I feared, the crankshaft web between the rear pin and journal was twisting under full power. Because of gyroscopic precession, the flywheel remained in its plane of rotation, and the front of the engine jumped up and down.

I delved back into my memory and recalled that the Mark V Bentley engine had the same problem, so I applied the same cure — a flywheel with a flexible steel disc in the centre. It solved the problem, but we needed an intensive durability programme. Car sales, with the increased torque engine, had to be suspended until these were complete. The customer would not have been amused to have received a pedicure from a hot flywheel if the flex plate failed. Another of our new bright young engineers, Ian Doble, distinguished himself by devising a very effective test in a sandbagged emplacement to prove durability in double-quick time.

I had quite a brush with Chunky when it was all over. He said: 'You told me you could not increase the size of the engine or turbocharge it, now look.' I reminded him that I did not say it could not be done, just that we could not afford it. The turbo development programme had exceeded its budget by a factor of three and the 2.2 by a factor of 1.5 and was five months late, costing us £1.5m in lost sales. Most people can do that! He was feeling a bit sore at the time as the new F1 car, the Type 80, was not even as quick as the 79. Everyone else had learned about ground effect, and produced a stiffer copy of the 79, so their cars were quicker than the 79 and 80. The star had really fallen off the Team Lotus wand. Even though Peter Warr had returned, after his year with Walter Wolf, frustration was added to furtiveness. In the old days, if Team Lotus had a problem they used to seek help from the car factory and everyone would willingly give it, without exception, now everything was kept a secret. Having me around chanting: 'I told you what would happen' did not make me very popular either.

In September 1979 I went to Le Puy in the Auvergne to represent the company at the launch of the Lotus Sunbeam (just after Peugeot bought the operation from the ailing Chrysler UK). It was a spectacular and lavish presentation lasting over two weeks. Thirty Lotus Sunbeams were involved, and 12 to 15 journalists were flown in by special plane every other day for a briefing, a non-alcoholic lunch followed by a 200 km (124 mile) drive around the Auvergne, debrief and a splendid dinner in the Chateaux Chevanac LaFayette. The intermediate day was spent by a large joint

working-party retrieving and repairing the shunted and inverted cars ready
for the next influx of journalists.

I had been told that the ecologically moral DeLorean DMC12 had
produced a CAFE number of 25 mpg in a private laboratory in Detroit. I
said it was absolutely impossible, it could not do better than 20 mpg. CAFE
(Corporate Average Fuel Economy) was a standard laid down by EPA to
regulate fuel consumption. I told Chuck Bennington that I did not believe it.
The lighter Esprit with a 2.2 litre engine only managed 22.6 mpg, and I
reminded him that EPA imposed a series of penalties and punitive fines on
cars that failed to meet their target fuel consumption. In the case of the
DMC12 it was 22 mpg. I warned him of the risks. If they did not find they
had this problem until the cars were in production they would not have time
to effect a cure, and would have to pay the fines on every car.

Chunky had found himself a new F1 sponsor — David Thieme, head of
the Monaco-based Essex Petroleum Company. Now, one of the policies on
which Chunky and I were in complete and total agreement was, never again
would we go to Le Mans. Chunky's convictions stemmed from his
experiences when a car was disqualified on a regulation technicality many
years ago, and mine through my experiences with the Rover BRMs.
However, David was very keen to run a turbine car and willing to pay for a
design study, so I was put to work. I found that a Rolls-Royce Gem 2000 hp
helicopter engine would do the job, and even though it would have to refuel
22 times, the car should win by 18 minutes. It was too late to start that year,
so the design and plans were filed away, and fortunately a regulation change
made it impossible!

I was immersed in a project turbocharging a Peugeot engine as an
engineering sub-contract, as a consequence of our good relations with
Peugeot arising from the Lotus Sunbeam. This was becoming what some
people would call 'a nice little earner', when the bomb burst. DMC12 No.
12 was found to give only 18.6 mpg on its CAFE test. It was quickly
established this was not a freak; other cars gave similar results. I soon found
what the Detroit testers had done wrong. They had not adjusted their
dynamometer for vehicle inertia correctly.

From having absolutely nothing to do with DeLorean I was now deeply
involved, in charge of a crash programme to put things right. Mike Loasby
had just been appointed their Chief Engineer. I knew him slightly from his
work on the cylinder head for the 2.6 litre 6-cylinder Rover Triumph
engine, which was generally considered by the industry to be a near perfect
example of how to design a cylinder head for die-casting. I did not know
very much about his activities at Aston Martin. In his new job he could not
do much about the emission problems until the DMC laboratory was built
and working in Dunmurry, probably more than a year away.

The problem quickly turned into a nightmare. The 2.85 litre V6 engine
was made at Douvrin by PRV. In the case of this version of the engine,
Volvo were the design parents, but sales were handled by a division of
Renault. Barry Wills, DeLorean Purchase Director recognized the potential
complications and set up a meeting in Paris of all the interested parties to
establish the rules. In addition to Renault and Volvo, Lotus and DeLorean,
there were representatives of PRV and Bosch; in all some 20 people. To
give some idea of the problems we had, just tracing one change I wanted to
make through the procedures will suffice. I found that a revised ignition

advance curve was worth 1.2 mpg. This presented no problem, the Volvo car was heavier and had to take into account the possibility that somebody might use it to tow a caravan; a contingency very unlikely on the DeLorean sports car which, in any case, had nowhere to attach a towing hook.

EPA certification procedure required that the durability of the emission control systems and devices be proved by running several representative cars to 50,000 miles with emission tests every 4000 miles, which also established what was known as the 'Deterioration Factor'. This factor was then applied to the emission levels of a new car to ensure that a car with 50,000 miles on it still met the regulations. There was also a procedure whereby a certified proven engine could be used in other vehicles providing they were similar in most respects, without the need for 50,000 miles proving. For example, neither the weight nor the gear ratios could vary by more than 10 per cent. This procedure was known as 'carry-over' and of course offered manufacturers tremendous cost and time savings.

The 50,000-mile durability test had to be carried out at an average speed of 30.3 mph, stopping every 4000 miles for an emission test — which by itself took 24 hours, with all the procedures involved — plus changing drivers, refuelling, replacing tyres etc., all of which took time. If your model range included manual and automatic gearboxes, EPA would certainly insist that you tested at least one of each. Four months and $500,000 per car was not abnormal for this work. DeLorean were planning to use carry-over based on the 2.85 litre Volvo sold in the United States.

Having therefore established what changing the ignition curve would do, and knowing the rules of the game, I went to Paris to meet with Renault to get their agreement. They saw no problems, so after adding the Renault liaison engineer to the party, we all trooped off to Gothenberg to obtain Volvo's approval. No serious problems. After some telephoning we arranged a meeting at PRV with Lotus, DeLorean, Volvo and Renault representatives. PRV said: 'Yes, but please bear in mind that it is a Bosch ignition system and distributor you are changing.' So we added the PRV man to the party and spent a day in Stuttgart convincing Bosch that everything came out of their standard parts bins.

They agreed, but after 12 hours hard talking they pointed out that the modified distributor would need a new part number to distinguish it from the standard one, whereupon PRV said fine, we will deliver the first modified engine in seven months. I nearly had a fit, but they pointed out that their production schedules were issued six months in advance. We had just missed the next issue. This was solved by Bosch delivering modified distributors to the production line at Dunmurry for DMC to fit to the engines. This was the easy part. I now had to persuade EPA that the change did not make any difference to the carry-over procedure. After sending them letters and telexes describing the change they refused us permission. They argued that if I had made a 6 per cent improvement in fuel economy, without changing capacity or compression ratio, we must have altered the combustion process and they would therefore need proof that the changes did not affect durability. This meant 50,000 miles durability proving.

Gene Cafiero, formerly President of Chrysler was appointed President of the DeLorean Motor Corporation. It was surprising how nearly all the recruits to DeLorean came from Chrysler. At a meeting with Gene and Chuck it was agreed that I should go to Detroit to try to talk EPA round.

After 30 minutes talking, EPA agreed that we had not really changed the combustion process, it was merely the way the car was driven. The whole process of getting approval to change the ignition timing took two months, two visits to France, one each to Sweden, Germany and the US. During his next visit, all this was explained to DeLorean, who directed that I mastermind the negotiations, and use Concorde. He said from his knowledge of American bureaucracy they are impressed by the top man. 'You are the top man, if you have come over on Concorde, they will recognize that it is extremely important and you will get all the attention you need. It will save time and money in the long run.'

I developed a routine of taking the evening Concorde from Paris to Washington, a North West Airlines flight from Washington to Detroit, then falling into a hotel bed in Ann Arbor opposite the gates of EPA upon which I would be knocking at 7.30 the following morning. After a one-hour meeting I would drive back to Detroit Metro airport, take the American Airlines flight to New York and the afternoon Concorde back to London. Some of the changes we came up with, which produced a significant improvement in fuel economy were rejected by EPA, such as air-stream injection, again on the grounds that it changed the combustion process, which it undoubtedly did. We finally came up with a package of measures acceptable to EPA which did the job and in the Lotus laboratory registered 22.6 mpg.

Mike Loasby had recommended that it would be cheaper to pay the penalty on the first batch of cars rather than this very expensive panic programme. This was a practical commonsense suggestion and would have saved money, but of course it got him into serious trouble with John DeLorean, who could not contemplate his ecologically moral car paying penalties for excessive fuel consumption.

The next stage in the procedure was to submit cars to EPA for them to test and determine that it met the emission laws, all of the carry-over requirements, and for EPA to determine the CAFE number. Chuck Bennington ruled that the DMC organization would handle certification. This was a complicated business, starting with a 180-page application for certification. It lists, amongst other things, all the emission control measures and how DeLorean planned to ensure conformity of production, so that every car they built would meet this standard. I repeatedly warned them that in the course of our work we had found very serious weakness in their suppliers' conformity of production systems. For instance, components that were supposed to have 2 or 5 per cent tolerance on their performance would vary by as much as 20 or 25 per cent. They needed to set up a very effective quality control and conformity of production system, to ensure that they and their suppliers met their standards. EPA were empowered to check this by taking a car at random from a dealer's showrooms, an extremely probable situation in view of the high profile of the DeLorean project.

We received their certification cars, which had to be truly representative production cars; you could not build a special car for certification, and we had to emission test them before and after 4000 miles. Not only did Lotus have an EPA-recognized laboratory, we had an approved emission test circuit as well and DMC's laboratory was still not ready. I was appalled, but not surprised, by the amount that the cars were outside the limits. I did not seem to be getting the message across to the DeLorean personnel of the problems they were going to have with conformity of production. They had assured me that all their purchase orders specified to the suppliers that standards had to be maintained. They were adopting the modern system of building-in quality, rather than the old fashioned system of trying to inspect quality in, that my approach implied. I never got across to the DMC people that, under EPA rules, responsibility for conformity of production was theirs.

After some major upheavals another batch of cars was received, which were good enough. They were tested, we did the 4000 miles and then fell into another controversy. It was Lotus policy to carry out the post-4000 mile test in a Detroit laboratory, which was permissible under the rules. On the face of it, this did not make much sense. Test — 4000 miles — then test again in the very same laboratory, avoided laboratory to laboratory variations and was quicker and cheaper. We had found, by bitter experience, that all manner of strange things happened between Lotus and the EPA laboratory at Ann Arbor. Nevertheless DeLorean were handling certification. They pooh-poohed our 'Mickey Mouse', time-wasting, expensive and illogical procedures; had us carry out the post-4000 mile test, and shipped the cars straight to Detroit. Even though the cars started life as absolutely standard vehicles off the production line, they were heavily modified for test purposes. Not only were there tappings into the manifolds and exhaust systems to measure temperatures, pressures etc., but the fuel tanks were wrapped in electric blankets to control the temperature of the fuel for the evaporative loss tests.

Time was slipping by, production had started at Dunmurry in a desultory fashion and the American dealers were clamouring for cars. We had an efficient information network in Detroit and EPA, and we learnt before Chuck Bennington that the cars had failed the emission part of the test. One not by much but another by a serious amount. Chuck tried to telephone his team in Detroit for more information, ignoring the five-hour time difference, but they had left instructions with the hotel switchboard they were not to be disturbed on any account. I can still hear Chuck shouting at the top of his voice: 'I am their boss.' The operator at the other end stood fast. Chuck was nearly incandescent with rage.

It transpired that when the cars were flown out the airline personnel smelt fuel, even though the cars had been drained absolutely dry. They followed their standard practice of purging the fuel lines with an inert gas, nitrogen. In the process they were too enthusiastic, the pressure applied damaged one of the diaphragms in the fuel injection system, which accounted for the serious failure. The near miss was probably due to an EPA tester not familiar with a mid-engined car with a 5-speed manual transmission. You were not allowed to shrug your shoulders and send them some more cars. There had been a failure, therefore there had to be an inquest, and a design change made to ensure that there could be no repetition. The shippers might purge the fuel system of more cars. It all had to be examined, discussed with and approved by EPA, then the application for certification modified and resubmitted to them.

Chuck decided that second time round Lotus should handle certification, apart from the paperwork. This also put them in the position that if anything went wrong, Lotus got the blame. Fortunately nothing went wrong and the cars passed. However, the vital certificate was temporarily withheld because

DeLorean's reproduction of the EPA logo on the proposed showroom sticker showing fuel consumption recorded was not quite correct. This wasted another ten days.

The next step was to get the cars certified by the Californian Air Resources Board (CARB) for sale in California, where tighter emission levels were required. Small volume manufacturers, such as ourselves and DeLorean, generally use a common standard of car, which although more difficult to achieve, is less trouble and expense on the production line, than building two different vehicles for the United States. In these circumstances CARB accept the EPA documentation, although it takes some time. In this case, approval was delayed, awaiting the production of the service manuals. Correct maintenance is an essential part of ensuring that emission performance is maintained. Then they reviewed the Volvo documentation, used for the carry-over procedure and found some fault with that, which took even more time to sort out.

I was in Japan with Mike Kimberley pursuing the possibility of sub-contract engineering business, when I received a panic phone call. The first batch of DMC vehicles had been delivered, as planned, to the US East Coast, where they were certified, but the DeLorean sales organization in the United States wished to have a Press ride and drive in the Los Angeles area. To do this they needed cars, and to have cars in California they needed CARB's certificate. I had to fly from Japan to Los Angeles which involves crossing the International Date Line, when you leave Tokyo at 10.30 p.m. and arrive in Los Angeles at noon on the same day. This takes a little getting used to. I managed to clear the problem at the CARB headquarters in El Monte. Confusion on these occasions nearly always arises from the differences between American and English. Winston Churchill certainly knew what he was talking about when he said England and America are separated by a common language. That is why a personal visit generally resolves problems in minutes, even though Los Angeles is some ten hours flying away. I heaved an enormous sigh of relief and thought that was the end of the DeLorean problems.

They worked up to 80 cars a day using the VARI process. In the course of their production they built something like 9000 cars, but they had dreadful quality and built conformity problems. If a car was built to specification it was fine, but their system of building-in quality depended, above everything else, on operator training, which seemed to be lacking. There was the case of the operator's lunch sandwiches moulded into the body under the driver's seat. When we carried out emission data audits for them, we often found components 20 per cent out on a 5 per cent tolerance. This issue remained a major bone of contention. I have seen in books about DeLorean, reference to the now famous meeting when I wrote the Minutes. The meeting was to resolve the specification for emission conformity. We agreed on the specification and standard, but I could not get DeLorean personnel to understand and accept their responsibility for conformity of production. I refused to sign the Minutes that I had written, as I knew they were worthless until some action was taken to enforce the standards we had just agreed.

I believe the DeLorean DMC12 vehicle, certainly the version developed and specified by Lotus, stood a chance of selling well if quality had been half way reasonable and there had not been so many avoidable delays in getting the cars to the point of sale in the USA. DeLorean might have survived at least for a few years, despite Corvette sales remaining healthy and in competition. The high selling price hurt them badly, this was partly because of currency fluctuations. I recall that DeLorean originally told me he planned to sell it for between $11,000 and $12,000. Now it was going on the market at $22,000. The cost of having the factory standing around waiting for revenue from cars they had spent money building months ago, had to be funded somehow, yet there were only two sources of money, the British government or the eventual customer. This cost was shared, which meant the selling price was increased, which in turn made them harder to sell.

It was not my kind of car really, but there are millions of cars that are not my kind of car, yet they still sell and make a profit. The gull-wing doors never troubled me. I thought Grumman did a particularly good job on the balanced hinges, but I never understood the logic of a stainless steel skin on a monolithic glass fibre body. The car that went into production was vastly different from the second prototype, 'Doris'. We could not overcome the problems of welding the stainless steel backbone and had to settle for galvanized steel. The 90 different styling versions of the steering wheel have passed into legend. The multitude of engineering problems that were overcome have been forgotten in the aftermath of the various non-engineering sensations. But I am quite sure that if the cars had reached the market nine months sooner, with reasonable quality (all of which was possible) there might not have been the drug bust, and some issues might not have surfaced for many years, if ever.

Soon after Chunky had told me there might be a deal with DeLorean, I heard that a cheque for more than £2m had arrived from a DeLorean source. It was at a time when we were more short of money than usual, but not absolutely desperate. Mike told me that he had been told by Chunky to keep his hands off it, it was a good faith deposit and had to be returned when the contract was implemented. I never saw any evidence of it in our monthly reports, which were incredibly detailed. Even £200 would have stuck out like a sore thumb. Mike told me a few months later that the deposit had been returned.

Late in 1978, Product Liability actions against us in the US, most of which I handled, were still being discussed at Board meetings. To us, accustomed to English Law, they seemed ridiculous. We had several multi-million dollar claims against us, relating to eighth- or tenth-hand 1969 and 1970 Europas, crudely and intensively modified to increase their performance, running on a mixture of bald crossply and radial tyres; having had accidents when driven at speeds in excess of 100 mph by drivers who had spent several hours in a bar. Our insurers and American lawyers told us the claims against us would succeed, even though they would be reduced by a factor of 10 or 20. We were concerned by the effects of these claims on our insurance premiums. The cost of importing into the US was becoming prohibitive. These extra costs would make our cars unsaleable.

In this atmosphere, I knew Chunky was aware of the risks we would run with this sort of exposure working for DeLorean. He said this was the reason GPD were involved. They were a fusable link in the chain. I knew Grand Prix Developments as an offshoot of the Lotus importer into Switzerland — Lotus Suisse — run by Jerry Juhan, with support from a very wealthy wife. In the early 1970s Jerry was trying to interest us in his version of the Lotus Europa fitted with a 150 hp Renault injection engine, and suitably modified. It was a good car but prohibitively expensive. I suspected that GPD was also a means of racing drivers avoiding tax, although I had no proof.

Jerry was always having bright ideas, some of which worked. In 1982 he converted one of our 2 litres to direct petrol injection through the cylinder wall, which interested me — it nearly worked! Chunky's reasoning was that — hopefully — a would-be litigant would come up against Swiss law and be deterred. A few months later he commented: 'We don't need GPD any more, anyone thinking of going for us will now see the British government as the ultimate "Deep Pocket".' (This was an American expression for an attractive target for litigation.)

The money, which the DeLorean receivers Cork Gulley said went walkabout, certainly never walked through Group Lotus. When I was seconded to Team Lotus in 1989 I was told by the British members of the Group Board to ensure the operation was whiter than white, and by the Americans 'cleaner than a hound's tooth!', and at the first sign of anything fishy to ring the bell. Needless to say I had a good look and was very wary, but I never found the slightest trace of anything untoward and I probably had a better idea of where to look than the various investigators.

Some of my American contacts expressed surprise that Lotus was prepared to work for a rival car manufacturer. Some even said they had heard that Chunky had demanded several millions as compensation for possible loss of sales because of competition from DeLorean. I never saw it as a problem, once I had seen and driven the car and heard DeLorean's plans. We were not in the same part of the marketplace. He was going for ten times our volumes, with a much more conservative car. As we developed the DMC12 and the Turbo Esprit, the two cars grew even further apart. I always believed that my 1977 meeting with John DeLorean in New York was the first step that brought Chunky and DeLorean together, but when I was questioned by the various investigating bodies, I realized they had already been in contact. Perhaps that is how Chunky knew so much of what transpired between DeLorean and me in 1978. To this day I still do not know what really happened, or why I suddenly decided not to join DeLorean — but it was a lucky decision. I sometimes wonder how different our piece of history would have been had I accepted.

While the DeLorean affair was grinding towards its conclusion, Chunky got himself into a terrible mess with the ill-fated twin-chassis Type 88 F1 car. The concept would have worked. I proved that some eight or nine years later when we adopted the principle for the Corvette Indy. Isolation from the road was complete. It felt just like a low-flying aircraft until you touched the steering wheel. Chunky refused to admit defeat at the hands of the bureaucrats and wasted a whole season in fruitless argument. He had become more or less completely isolated from the car company and to a lesser degree from Team Lotus. The boat companies had by now gone into liquidation. He would appear at a race meeting in time for first practice and depart as soon as the post-race debrief was completed. David Thieme had got into trouble and failed to make one of the major sponsorship payments, but fortunately John Player reappeared just before complete disaster.

Chunky had broken his own rules in 1978 and allowed Group Lotus to borrow £2m to keep the car company alive from American Express International Banking Company, making its first — ill-fated — foray into the venture capital business.

The changes in Chunky were most noticeable, he had become much harder and more cynical. He had learned the meaning of the rosettes in the Michelin guides; stayed at the best hotels and used the best restaurants, when before a Kit-Kat and a bag of peanuts in the aircraft sufficed. Lotus 'Airlines' now boasted four aeroplanes — a Citation executive jet, two twin-engined Cessnas and a Bell Jet Ranger helicopter. I had more of my regular arguments with him, concerning his treatment of the aircraft. If he was piloting himself, as soon as the engines fired he was off. If the wind for take-off was from the west, they did have a chance to warm up a little while taxiing to the far end of the runway, but an east wind meant take-off power before the oil temperature had even moved the needles on the gauge.

He made a cult out of his impatience and intolerance of anything that appeared to him to be wasting time. This applied to everything — not only the aircraft. Once established in the cruise he would weaken the mixture right off to save fuel. We had enormous repair bills for engines, sometimes amounting to 10 per cent of the cost of the aeroplane, which was also out of service for weeks. Time and time again I would tell him he was neither saving time nor money, but it had absolutely no effect. We had one major engine failure two hours into a five hour flight. The aircraft was still over the maximum permitted take-off weight when it had to make an emergency landing on one engine. He took no risks with the weather, though. He just had a much greater faith than I did in the ability of the engines to withstand abuse, and I had the job of sorting out all the bills, claims and arguments.

This phase developed noticeably around the time of the death of Ronnie Peterson, and what we called 'the Essex connection'. There would be whole days when he was his old cheerful self. It was just as if he devised the character that he thought the world wanted him to be, and he was playing that part.

I was often told that Chunky operated Lotus cars to fund his motor racing. He never said this to me. However, by the time of the 1978 Championship, F1 costs had exploded, Team Lotus's annual budgets far exceeded the best profits Lotus Cars — now a public company with shareholders, published accounts and Annual General Meetings — had ever made (about £1.25m). Most of Team Lotus's income came from sponsors. Group Lotus voted £100,000 a year to Team for the Publicity, but that was all. I do not know whether this contributed to Chunky's waning interest in the car company. I know that the various construction regulations infuriated him. Half the cost of developing a new car went into making it meet bureaucratic regulations, not in making it faster or more economical. EEC regulations were the last straw. He felt the same over Lloyds and US Coastguard regulations for boats, although he conceded there was some commonsense in a few of the Coastguard regulations. His lack of enchantment with the car company was completed by 'Kimbo's' (Mike Kimberley) "incessant bleating for money".

During 1981 and 1982 I was busy with the beginnings of what became Lotus Engineering. In addition to a major project with Peugeot, we had two smaller ones with Austin Rover, including turbocharging the Metro. This had a farcical interlude. Our contracts nearly always required us to conceal the existence of the project, but when the Metro Turbo was shown to the Press, Rover told them that the work was done by Lotus. However, they forgot to tell us that they had lifted the ban. We responded to requests from journalists for our version, by denying all knowledge of the project. We were also developing strong business ties with Japan. Chunky was becoming interested in microlight aircraft, and he had me chasing various engine designs all over the world, especially the Continental Tiara, an opposed engine driving the propeller from the camshaft at half engine speed.

I went with him to Renault, when he was negotiating an agreement whereby they would supply their successful turbo engine for use by Team Lotus. Unfortunately, their supply position was such that they could only provide sufficient engines to support one car for the first half of the season. They would not be in a position to supply enough engines for the second car until half way through the season, that is by the British GP at Silverstone.

In September 1982 Chunky said that he had missed the boat on surf boards, but he was not going to miss the boat on microlights. He wanted me to design an engine family — a 25 hp and a 50 hp — the 25 was to weigh 30 lb (13.6 kg) and sell for $1000 — the 50 hp should weigh 50 lb (22.7 kg) and sell for $1600.

I absorbed the low cost idea and produced a fairly crude push-rod engine design using Vauxhall Chevette valves and rockers, which would meet his cost and power targets but would probably be too heavy. He was scathing. 'Ugh, I do not like that,' he said, 'it looks like a shoe box. Can't you do better than that.' Rather stung, I came up with an aluminium monobloc with Nikasil treated bores; that is the head, cylinder block and half the crankcase were all one casting. A pair of them, opposed, with a reduction gear casing on the front, gave you the 25 hp engine and you just bolted another pair on to the back for 50 hp. There was an absolute minimum number of parts and fixings. The individual components were cheap but the initial tooling costs would be high, and we would probably have to sell 600 of the small engines and 300 of the big ones to get our money back. When he looked at the drawings, he grumbled. 'You have gone to the other extreme. I did not say I wanted a Swiss watch.' I had used Ian Doble, from the flex plate flywheel days, as the project engineer. I think he was shaken by his exposure to Chunky, and our exchanges. He said he would allow us £14,000 to build two prototypes. Nothing like enough.

A few days later he made one of his rare visits to Hethel and sat himself down at my desk, saying: 'Tell me about Nikasil.' I took him in the workshop to show him some examples. He was surprised and impressed by the amount of external work I had on the go, and said he was amazed that there was so much. He had no idea what we were doing. When I told him that there was a chance that we would reach £1m that year, he nearly fell out of the chair. He said: 'Why is Kimbo always asking me for money when you have a little gold mine going here?' I did not know the answer, but I could see what was coming. I told him we were about at our limit. We could not expand because to do so we would need facilities and capital. I realized that if I had the facilities he would monopolize them for all his special projects. I would be forever explaining to infuriated customers why I had failed to meet their deadlines because I had taken personnel and facilities for one of Chunky's ideas. I probably could have lived with that, but I would also have had his bright young men crawling all over me, making sure I ran the business according to their rules. I would be spending at least 25 per cent of my time reporting why I was behind schedule, because I was spending so much of my time explaining why I could not work their system.

From then on the chill thawed, and he would occasionally pop in and see me, but more often he invited me to Ketteringham Hall. He told me that he was pressing to make 'Engineering' a separate company, but 'Kimbo was violently opposed'. Chunky said it was 'because he is afraid of losing some of his empire.' I disagreed, and said he was probably objecting for the same reasons as I would, and stuck to my no expansion guns. I told him that if we expanded within the car company's empire we would always be fighting them for space, and we would be carrying an exorbitant share of their overheads — we went up and down that road — and discussed the question of how much of the car company overheads were already being unloaded on my customers. He was a bit mollified when he found out that the Engineering order book for 1983 already stood at over £3m. He held out all sorts of bait. I told him that his Directors' profit sharing scheme, which we called 'the vanishing carrot', had absolutely no value. It was so wrapped up in caveats, escape routes and loopholes that none of the managers or directors ever even thought about it. He then tried another tack. He was thinking of enlarging the Group Board. What if he put me on it? I told him I was quite happy being left alone, I had 28 people each generating over £60,000 a year. If he tried to expand he would fatten the goose laying the golden egg to the point where it burst.

I told him that what he should think about was a similar parallel operation working on composites — say 25 people, using the same system — no overheads, just using the surplus capacity. Maybe he could even have a third unit on vehicles or styling. He took all the arguments with remarkable good humour, frequently saying that no one had ever told him what I was up to. We discussed the Lotus V8, which was now on the shelf. It was his view that it was no good putting it in either the Esprit or the Elite as they were ten-year-old designs. It needed a new car.

We had nearly returned to the 1970s relationship — although, of course, he was nothing like the same old Chunky — when he unfortunately died. I was suddenly awakened by a phone call from Security for an imperative meeting of directors, where Mike Kimberley broke the news. I was in fact just going out of the front door, when Fred called Pam and asked her to go and stay with Hazel until her children got home. I then had the very unhappy task of breaking the news to the assembled factory.

My relationship with Chunky went through three phases. The first stage of our relationship was when we were racing rivals, but good friends. This ran from my first acquaintance with him in 1954 until 1969. I first came to know him when the scrutineers rejected his F2 car at Goodwood as it did not have a fireproof bulkhead. The next day he was back with a cardboard map from the garage wall painted with aluminium paint as his fireproof bulkhead! The scrutineers tried to persuade me, amongst others, to protest. I told them to do their own dirty work, and look at the regulations. The regulations required 'that there be some means interposed between the engine and the driving compartment, safe and sufficient in the case of an emergency to prevent the passage of flame'. Chunky's piece of cardboard might just work; all it had to do was to keep the flames away from the driver long enough for him to slow the car down to a speed where he could jump out, and this is what it might do. Somehow he heard about this and came and thanked me, saying that not all the racing fraternity would take my attitude with him.

The next phase was as an employee of Lotus from 1969 to 1977 up to my flirtation with DeLorean. I had to make a very conscious effort to change the relationship, as I was viewed with some suspicion when I first joined Lotus as a personal friend of the Old Man. From 1978 until his death the chill descended and our relationship was much more formal and at arm's length; he just could not understand why anyone should wish to leave the Lotus family. There was a thaw towards the end of 1982. He was particularly entranced when I said I thought we would have £1m turnover by the end of the year. He would probably have had a lot to say when at £973,000 we just missed.

His personality also went through three phases but they did not coincide or overlap my three phases. The first was the happy-go-lucky phase which lasted until the deaths of Jim Clark and Mike Spence. As I have already said, I always thought he took Jimmy's death remarkably well, as if he had mentally conditioned himself to the fact that it might happen one day. But the death of Mike Spence, so soon afterwards, really seemed to hurt him. He gradually hardened and grew more cynical, and there was a significant change with the death of Jochen Rindt. The final stage in the hardening phase came with the death of Ronnie Peterson.

His meeting with David Thieme of Essex completed the transition. He isolated himself from all his companies and he never in my hearing referred to the financial collapse of the boat companies, which was largely because of his spending the profits made by Moonraker before his new designs were established. His first attempt, the Marauder, was a disaster. His second attempt, the Mirage and the Mistral were very nearly world-beaters. They weighed less than eight tons compared with the 13 tons of their wooden parent the Mystère, and gave better performance with two 210 hp engines than the original with two 285 hp engines. If only he had developed one boat at a time and had controlled his spending on development, probably the third attempt would have ended up with an extremely successful boat. He was never really involved in the DeLorean project. It was all left to Colin Spooner and Mike Kimberley after the initial stages.

After the 1978 Championships there was a move to get him a knighthood. After all, Jack Brabham had been knighted for much less than Chunky had achieved. None of us begrudged Jack his honour — he richly deserved it — but so did Chunky. It was decided, as I had a less vague idea than my colleagues as to where the corridors of power were, that I should mastermind the campaign. It came to nothing because some of the people concerned died unexpectedly.

I never rowed with Chunky about Lotus Cars affairs or Team Lotus, although we had some meteoric bust-ups over the boats. He accused me of always compromising, to which I would reply, he was the compromiser, look at the rear suspension of the Lotus 25. He had the inner end of the top-rear wishbone and the top attachment of the spring-damper unit secured to the rear cross member by one big bolt. This broke his rules about off-set loads and compromised because the upper end of the rear spring was not in the ideal position, and neither was the inner end of the rear wishbone — it was all a great big compromise to obtain simplicity. The same assembly on the BRM 261 had a small bolt and ferrules and a separate mounting for the inner end of the rear spring and another bolt, ferrules, links etc. in a different plane for the inner end of the rear-top suspension link. I had not compromised, but I had 25 pieces where he had five. They were good-humoured arguments.

Several people have suggested that he was a genius, but I do not think he ever set out to be. He was a brilliant structural stress man. He was deeply hurt after the 1960 Spa crashes, when he was attacked for making unsafe racing cars. He always told me not to invent anything new and, whatever I did, do not try to break the laws of physics. I believe a genius is someone who manages to do that and get away with it. He was an absolute past master at soaking up knowledge. Albert Adams tells many tales of the early days, when Lotus went into glass fibre, because Chunky was appalled at the cost of the aluminium bodies of the Lotus 11s. He read all the books that he could find on the subject, and soaked up the knowledge. It was the same with boats and again with microlights. He would take an idea and make it work. The average motor racing enthusiast will tell you that the monocoque was Chunky's idea. Killeen had one 18 years before, and there were several more in between, including the Type 27 BRM. It was just that Chunky made one that worked. Again he is credited with the idea of using the engine as a stressed member of a racing car structure — agricultural tractors have been doing so for years. The Lancia D50 tried it in 1955 and we at BRM were doing it before Lotus, but he made it really effective and successful. He may have known about aircraft ground-effect, but it certainly was not what he was looking for when he started me off in 1976 with the 28-page folder which eventually led to the ground-effect Lotus 78. If he was not a genius by my definition, he will certainly go down in history as the British (or English) Bugatti, and certainly as great a man as Ferrari.

His talent as an engineer was matched by his understanding of what motivated people. As Fred Bushell said of him: 'He was a man who could persuade people to climb mountains, who only thought they could climb over stiles.' I would confront him breathing fire and brimstone, and flatly refusing to do something. A few minutes later I would be completely talked around and trying as hard as I could to make it work. He had everybody around him analysed, and catalogued. He knew that the way to get me to perform was to say: 'When I am in trouble I always know which of my old friends to turn to.' He used a different technique with different people. He always argued that he did not understand high finance, but it was surprising how many finance people he managed to charm into providing him with millions to fund Team Lotus and, despite the criticisms, they certainly got value for money from their investments.

He was an incredibly quick cross-country driver, yet I never felt frightened with him. We were once due to go with our wives to the British Racing Mechanics Annual Dinner in Coventry, but at the last minute we were prevented from flying by a very heavy fog. We had to drive all the way in his Mercedes, on roads he claimed not to know, but which I knew pretty well. It developed into my telling him where we were and the sort of road we were on. We covered the 150 miles, in the dark and in thick fog, in a little over two hours! The following morning, in the daylight and dry, we did the journey in one hour thirty five minutes. I think it was part of his mystique, that he imparted confidence into the people around him. You had the feeling, however bad things were, somehow or other Chunky would get you out of it. You forgot that he probably got you into the mess in the first place.

# CHAPTER TWENTY-ONE

# Lotus after 'Chunky'

THIS WAS A difficult chapter for me to write because much of it concerns the activities of Lotus Engineering (as distinct from Lotus Cars). Nearly all their contracts were endorsed with the words: 'If the existence of this project becomes public knowledge, the contract is cancelled.' Therefore, much of what happened has to remain confidential, and I can only write about those projects in which the customer has permitted us to reveal our involvement — and even in some of these cases I am not able to recount all the details. Thus there is a risk that the incomplete story gives a lop-sided picture.

I had often said that if ever anything should happen to Chunky, Lotus would not last much more than a year. Now I had to prove myself wrong. Our share price fluctuated violently because of the various rumours. Fred sold all the aeroplanes, which helped the immediate cash flow situation. It was agreed that my job was to do everything I could to increase external engineering work, drawing on the car company for staff if necessary. Fortunately we had a fairly full order book, and our Japanese customers, particularly Toyota, were extremely helpful. On the downside, American Express decided to withdraw from the venture capital business, which had not worked out as they had hoped, and they gave us notice that they would be calling in their loans. This notice went out to other people as well as Lotus. It looked as if we had some six months to find another source of capital; but without Chunky we were a less attractive proposition.

Some of our overseas contracts involved American electronics. We were also certifying the Turbo Esprit for sale in the USA by a new importer, replacing Rolls-Royce who had also suffered badly in the second oil recession. I was, therefore, spending much time in the USA, or in the air between the USA, England and Japan.

Fred Bushell then asked me if I could lend a hand at Team Lotus. Their problems were acute, they were racing with three different cars, none of them competitive. There was a Renault Turbo Type 91, designed for skirts, but — just as Chunky died — the regulations changed, and they were banned, so it was converted to a flat bottom. There was a Cosworth-engined Type 92, with the first version of full active suspension (it could not be run with the active system disconnected like some of today's cars), and the third

car was a standard Type 92. Peter Warr was acutely aware that the fortunes
of Team Lotus depended on him, and they were not on the crest of a wave.
Unfortunately he and Peter Wright did not understand one another, and
Peter Wright was dedicated to the pursuit of perfection rather than
excellence. They were both extremely talented and hard working, and they
both tried very hard to work with each other, but they just could not
communicate effectively.

My first race as temporary Chief Engineer was at Long Beach, California,
where I joined them after a trip to Silicon Valley. Nigel Mansell neither
liked nor trusted the active suspension car with which he was allocated, and
his dour and dogged approach did not endear him to Peter Warr, either. Elio
de Angelis's Renault-engined car did not suit the circuit and, along with
Benetton, we were using Pirelli tyres; so we had plenty of problems. We
were pretty desperate during practice so we discarded the front roll bar
completely on the Type 91 which moved us up about 15 places on the grid.

On my return to England I made some drastic changes. Renault could not
supply engines for a second car until the British GP at Silverstone. Active
suspension, at this early stage of its development, posed a number of
problems. The increase in weight of its components and the power required
to drive the pump just about cancelled out its performance advantage over
the standard Cosworth car. Its potential was obvious, but the car's
preparation and operation was demanding more of the Team's resources that
its race results were justifying.

Recognizing this potential, I transferred Peter Wright from Team Lotus to
the growing Lotus Engineering team, with instructions to take stock of the
situation and then make a determined onslaught to interest one of the major
passenger car manufacturers. We converted the active Type 92 back to
standard. The Renault car was far too heavy and did not handle well.

Chief Mechanic Bob Dance, noting that most teams were refuelling as
well as changing tyres, had suggested that we put the Renault engine in
place of the Cosworth in the Type 92. It would not have sufficient fuel
capacity, but if we faced up to the fact that we were going to refuel every
race when we changed tyres it would not cost us much extra time during the
stop, and we might save much more in lap times. This made sense and,
having confirmed it was feasible, the Drawing Office was put to work on
this conversion.

Peter Warr had inherited Chunky's belief that one man can make all the
difference. In Peter's case that one man was Gerard Ducarouge. I knew
Gerard, who was Chief Engineer to the Alfa Romeo team and had made a
name for himself with Ligier and Matra, and I did not disagree with Peter's
assessment of his ability. However, I was not sure that Gerard alone would
solve all the Team's problems. One was the antipathy between Peter and
Nigel. I noticed, for example, that there never seemed to be a reasoned
discussion between them on tactics. Despite his outward show of
determination, Nigel needed someone to show some confidence in him and
help him develop in the same way as Ken Tyrrell and, latterly, Eddie Jordan
did with their drivers. Nigel shone on street circuits such as Monaco and
Detroit.

Elio de Angelis was a much more complex character. He came from an
extremely wealthy family, and fundamentally he was not hungry enough.
We never quite knew how he was going to perform. There was a touch of

Pedro Rodriguez about him. These problems cannot be dealt with formally at a meeting. You have to pick your moment when you think the other party will be receptive, and it takes time — attitudes have to change. This was difficult for me as I was heavily into transatlantic commuting to try to find more business for Lotus Engineering.

I had been provided with a driver, rather to my dismay, it having been suggested that driving myself back from Heathrow after a 10-hour transatlantic flight was not very wise. The driver was an ex-Grenadier Guardsman called Wally. He soon became adept at routines such as meeting me from the 9.40 p.m. British Airways day flight; handing me a bag containing my JPS gear, taking me to Gatwick to catch the FOCA special for a race; and taking home my briefcase and the clothes I had worn in America. He then met me late Sunday night from the charter, handed me a briefcase appropriately repacked by secretary Diana, and fresh clothes prepared by Pam, and took me to a Heathrow Hotel en route for Japan or some other place!

At Monaco we did a deal with Gerard Ducarouge in Hazel's hotel room. He took over putting the Renault engine into the Type 92, making major improvements to the suspension and our build techniques in the process, while I did my best at the GPs in Detroit and Montreal.

I spent the Thursday before the GP in Detroit having meetings with Chrysler, wearing my Lotus Engineering hat, and the next three days, including a wet practice, were devoted to Team Lotus. Immediately after the race on Sunday, when Nigel showed a brief glimpse of the talent he would eventually display, I left Pam watching TV in our room at the Westin Hotel and flew back to London, via Washington, courtesy of British Airways, incidentally sitting next to former Ferrari, now Alfa Romeo, Chief Engineer Chiti. Next morning I was met at Heathrow by one of my bright project engineers, Roger Stone, and whisked off to an airport hotel for a meeting on turbocharging with our consultant Geoffrey ('Oscar') Wilde, now retired from Rolls-Royce, and some of our Japanese customers. After the meeting Roger just got me back to the airport in time to board the 1.30 p.m. British Airways flight to San Francisco, where I arrived in time to meet Pam off her flight from Detroit. There I had a business dinner with our electronic colleagues, and after two hectic days we flew to Montreal via Chicago ready for the Canadian GP. After a disappointing race we flew to New York on Sunday evening. After meetings next day it was back to England.

With a struggle, we got the new Renault-engined cars to Silverstone. Nigel's car suffered from a mysterious electrical fault, which we did not succeed in curing until race morning. Fortunately Elio's car ran well and we were able to sort it in practice and transfer the knowledge gained to Nigel's car for the race. However, the performance of the small-tank-capacity Renault-engined cars in the race was extremely encouraging, and we now had a full complement of Renault engines. Peter Warr and Gerard Ducarouge appeared to have things under control, and worked well together, so I could devote all my time to Lotus Engineering again.

At Group Lotus there were plenty of problems, such as thinly disguised take-over bids. There were also talks with David Wickens of British Car Auctions, who had been considering a one-race sponsorship programme with Team Lotus. He became interested in Group Lotus and — with our other new Group Board Member, Alan Curtis — rescued us from the consequences of the American Express withdrawal. The Lotus Engineering order book was growing, especially in Japan, but I could not make a breakthrough in Europe or the United States. Peter Wright had reviewed the active suspension programme and had come up with a package that would be attractive for a standard passenger car. This soaked up some of Engineering's profit but I felt it was a worthwhile investment.

Restructuring of Group Lotus proceeded apace, propelled by David Wickens. There was a rights issue, effective on the 7 September 1983, which gave one new share at 40 pence for each share already held. I took up my full allocation. My mother had often given me small parcels of shares, and I had often bought some, so I had to scratch around to pay for them. This also produced a dramatic change in the stockholding and power structure, and of course a £5m increase in our capital. David Wickens and British Car Auctions emerged with over 29 per cent of the restructured capital. Toyota Motor Company had 25 per cent, earth movers JCB 15 per cent and merchant bankers Schroder Wagg (representing a group) 10 per cent. The Chapman family did not take up the offer and, in fact, disposed of some of their holdings so they no longer held a significant stake. David Wickens told me he knew nothing about engineering, but as long as I kept the money coming in he would look after me. Mike Kimberley took the bit between his teeth, and fortified with the additional capital, embarked on a programme for a successor to the original Elan which had done so much for Lotus. It was to be powered by a Toyota engine and transmission unit, with as many other Toyota parts as he could lay his hands on.

It began to look to me that Lotus Engineering's 1982 £973,000 turnover might be surpassed by the 1984 profit figure. But the real breakthrough still eluded me — a major contract from one of the American car companies; although we were getting close with active suspension. Peter Wright was giving a number of demonstrations to a steady stream of visitors. I had put Peter in touch with my old friend Bill Milliken, who had his own vehicle dynamics consultancy business in the States, and was in touch with most of the people who counted in the suspension world. I was still notching up the miles on air travel and was getting very close to Chrysler, who were talking of 4-valve heads for both their turbo engine and their projected 2.4 litre balancer-shaft normally-aspirated engine. I was also still trying very hard to interest someone in the Lotus 4 litre V8 that was gathering dust on the shelf.

I recall being shown the new Chrysler plant at Trenton, south-east of Detroit Metro Airport, which compared well with the Japanese plants I had visited, all producing more than 3,000 engines a day, The Japanese plant operated in complete darkness (there would be an occasional maintenance engineer roaming a catwalk in the roof) with completed engines passing on conveyors to test carousels carrying 60 engines which rotated once an hour, driven round by the engines under test. Torque was gradually increased while slow running, ignition timing etc., was adjusted. The newer Chrysler plant was different: brightly lit, with individual engine test stands, but I suspect it contained even fewer actual operators than the 16 in the Japanese plant.

Finally we concluded the deal with Chrysler to design and develop 4-valve heads for both engines. At the same time Peter Wright secured active suspension development contracts from GM, Volvo and the Japanese. So, with the 1984 order book standing at £8m, we had to start recruiting. I had got my foot into the door at GM, but we were talking about a twin-engined Corvette, or rather GM were. For a time their rationalized engine policy specified a 4-cylinder engine with or without turbos, a V6 with or without turbos and a V8. Their manufacturing organization grouped Chevrolet, Pontiac and Canada together. This group was known as CPC, while Buick, Oldsmobile and Cadillac were in a second group known as BOC. CPC could use the four or the V6, whereas BOC could have the V6 and the V8. Under this arrangement the only hope for the new Corvette from Chevrolet was two engines, a normally aspirated V6 driving the front wheels and a turbo V6 the back! I was counselled by some of my colleagues not to touch such a stupid idea, but to me it was a source of money. What Sir Alfred would have said if he had witnessed my zeal in pursuit of engineering business I have no idea.

Then the tax authorities dumped a protective tax assessment on us for many millions of pounds, alleging that we had received much more money from DeLorean than we had. As they were not sure which company it might have been, or when, they played safe and put the assessment on all of the companies, and for several years. Knowing how strapped for cash we had been at the time it did not make much sense to me, and I resented the time it took preparing our defence. In the light of later events it became more understandable, but I still feel the refusal of Queen's Awards to Lotus Engineering for their foreign currency achievements was vindictive.

We had a visit from Russ Gee, Director, Powertrain Engineering of CPC, as part of a European tour taking in Porsche, Ricardo, Ilmor, Cosworth and others. He told us he was looking for a universal engine to replace GM's classic small-block 5.7 litre V8, code-named L98 dating back to 1957. His idea was a base engine, with high performance versions right up to an engine which could be used as the basis for a stock-block Indy unit. We must have made a good impression on each other because Lotus were asked to come up with a proposal for 4-valve heads for L98; and this eventually became a firm contract. The Indy version became a separate project, and led to the Ilmor turbo V8, part-funded by Roger Penske.

While we were pursuing these and other contracts we carried out a series of design studies for JCB, and Sir Anthony Bamford joined the Group Lotus Board. Through the Department of Trade and Industry's Aid for Industry scheme we became involved with Gloster Saro, working on their Airport Fire Engine (called a Rapid Intervention Vehicle).

I was invited to address the British Association for the Advancement of Science on the subject of the 'Car of the Future'. Sir Daermid Downes of Ricardo spoke on the engine for this car and John Coplin of Rolls-Royce on the aero-engine of the future. I gave our new Chairman, David Wickens (Fred Bushell had withdrawn to become Chairman of Team Lotus), a copy of my address, and he promptly sent it to Roger Smith at GM, Lee Iacoca at Chrysler and Henry Ford. I had realized that you cannot advertise for consultancy business, because no customer likes the world to be told that Lotus is designing something for his new car due out in two years or so. Either it is copied or no one buys the existing product, preferring to wait for the wonderful new one, much to the detriment of current sales. However, addresses to learned bodies such as the British Association do get wide publicity and it tells the world you are in this type of business. I noted how

Ricardo used this technique. There is never a conference without a contribution from Ricardo, and this certainly helped to build up their considerable reputation.

I had a near disaster. While somewhat jet-lagged ex-Japan, I confused GM data with that of Chrysler at a Chrysler meeting and nearly gave the game away! After that I made a rule — never, despite the amount of travel involved, try to combine engineering meetings with two customers on the same visit; go home and back again. I was extremely impressed by the Chrysler approach to our contract, which included a black book some 2.8 inches thick, specifying the test methods we were to use, the equipment, details of all their test circuits and procedures, etc., material specifications, drawing sizes — with nothing whatever left to chance or our discretion. Several misunderstandings were avoided as the project proceeded because everything was spelt out in the black book. GM, however, changed the pitch, the game, duration of the match and size of the ball as we went along. It took about six months for the paperwork to catch up. Much of this problem was because of the fact that a number of things we needed to know were confidential, such as their test procedures, and we could not be told.

On 3 April 1985 we had our first meeting with CPC in Detroit to report on progress for the 4-valve head for the L98. The major stumbling block was that engines for the Corvette chassis had to be bottom-loaded. That is, they were mounted on the front suspension cross-member and pushed up into the car from underneath. There was, therefore, a maximum dimension for the overall width of the engine, otherwise the engine would not pass between the frame rails which were 690 mm apart. The first real sticking point was that there is a minimum size for the rubber belt pulleys to drive the overhead camshafts, beyond which the belt supplier will not let you go, and the belt will not survive for long either. This means a very big pulley on the overhead camshafts, and with a 90 degree V8 with four overhead camshafts this defeated any chance of arriving at a narrow enough engine. We had proposed a minimum power during the initial negotiations of 400 hp, so I was not very enthusiastic about a single overhead camshaft and rockers as it makes the plug location very awkward — although Honda seem to get away with it. On my board at home I drew a cylinder-head tilted towards the inlet side, with chain drives to the camshafts, permitting the use of much smaller sprockets, which could just be squeezed in. With our GM team I was commuting once a month to Detroit reporting progress. In the case of Chrysler our team visited every other month, alternating with their visits to Norfolk.

In the course of our May 1985 meeting with GM I was invited by another GM group to a typical American breakfast meeting at my hotel, the Hyatt Regency in Dearborn. My paper on the 'Car of the Future' was held up by one corner as if it gave off a faintly offensive smell, and I was asked if I had written it. I had to confess I had, and they then said: 'Would you like to build it?' I swallowed and said: 'Yes.' It transpired that they were working on a supercar concept called the Corvette Indy, which included a de-rated Ilmor turbo Chevrolet engine. Some of the major features they planned were described in my paper and we appeared to have some knowledge of how to make them work, so it was agreed that we would participate in the project, which would be run in three phases. First, phase one, a non-running mock-up to gauge reaction from the Press and public; followed by phase two, a running car which included absolutely everything, route-finding, anti-collision-sonar, active suspension, thinking-four-wheel-drive, four-wheel-steer — in fact every advanced engineering buzz-word you could think of. The third phase would be the definitive refined prototypes.

In a mixture of confusion and exhilaration I went on to the Corvette engine meeting. Project leader Roy Midgley had considered our lopsided head, and he very politely asked: 'Had we any experience of this arrangement?' I confessed that we had not. 'Then we prefer not to do it', he said. However, the idea later appeared on Cadillac's 4-valve V8 engine 'North Star' and on the VW Golf engine. Undoubtedly Roy was wise, in view of the tight timetable, to ensure that we did not become involved in something on which neither of us had any experience. He was also hesitant over our roller-chain camshaft drive proposal. Perhaps with a little justification, as we found as the project proceeded. However, at the time, I said: 'Let's go to a used car lot; find a high mileage Jaguar and see if you can hear the chains.' This did the trick.

Without Roy the project would have collapsed about every third month. He stamped hard on any activity that might lead to friction between GM and Lotus, or the project and supporting GM companies. He was only interested in getting the best possible engine within his brief, and he made sure GM got it. He was a classic example of total integrity, and assembled a GM support team for the project which was second to none. I had to give the Lotus team a series of pep talks to keep them in line. 'Never forget that the people at GM you are working with could build a better one, if only they got down to it.' Neither Roy nor I ever had to arbitrate in a dispute between the teams and there was a completely free exchange of information.

At this meeting I explained that the length of connecting rod controlled the width of the engine. From the gudgeon pin upwards you have a fixed number of piston rings and thus a finite dimension. The valve size and length is fixed by the power required, which dictates the port size, and the rest is fixed by the size of the spring and tappet. I had found that — with bucket tappets — the dimension from the cylinder-head joint face to the camshaft centre was always more than 160 mm. Therefore, the only dimension we had to play with was the connecting rod length; which meant a completely new engine, not just a new cylinder head. Roy fully understood this and took me off to meet Russ Gee, who was adamant that whatever we did we must still meet the introduction date.

We retired to Russ's home for a barbecue. Like nearly all the GM senior engineering staff I have ever met, Russ lived on the shores of a lake and had a large powerboat. As you rose in rank, so the boat and the lake became bigger. It was agreed that they would consider the points we had made, and a party from CPC would visit us next month with their decision. The Lotus team had their hearts in their mouth for fear the project would get cancelled, while I radiated complete confidence. Dave McLellan, the Corvette Platform Manager, gave me a plastic model Corvette kit saying: 'It's very accurate. Make a model of your engine and see if you can get it in.'

Peter Wright, by then, had six customers for active suspension, and his share of the order book was well over £3m. David Wickens had heard that the Benetton F1 operation was for sale, so Mike Kimberley and I were sent to visit them and also have a look at Brian Hart. I had been to a conference in Washington on air bags (passive restraint) and had briefed the US Department of Transport on active suspension as they seemed rather suspicious, and were making noises which sounded like legislation that would have made it difficult to use it on American cars. It was the usual common language problem — easily resolved. In the year so far (June) I had made three trips to Japan, 11 to the US, hosted nine major visits from potential customers and attended seven VIP Boardroom lunches arranged by Chairman Wickens. I had also made three trips to Paris and two to Geneva. I was surprised that my dog still let me in!

Then the CPC team arrived and really laid it on the line. The order would be amended to cover a new aluminium cylinder block; the value of the contract would be increased; and we could have more money, but no more time. Instead of one team working on the cylinder-head, there would now be three teams working in parallel. The second on the block and accessories and a third on the crankshaft assembly, including connecting rods and our recommended end-to-end oil feed. The engine would be known as LT5. No waffle — just straight to the point. I had to find the nucleus of the extra staff immediately, and somewhere to put them. After some head-scratching the directors abandoned their garage; we sealed the main doors and installed the LT5 team under Ian Doble.

I put Hugh Kemp in charge of the Chrysler projects. He was a very strong personality reminiscent of Stephan Williams, with both feet firmly on the ground. I would, for the time being, stay much closer to LT5 as some of it was still in my head. GM insisted that the cylinder pitch remained at 4.4 inches — the same as all the GM small-block V8s. This changed the stroke/bore ratio and upset our performance predictions, so we compromised on 385 hp.

When I stopped to draw breath the order book was looking like £29m. The next urgent problem was to find a way of building the first Corvette Indy; that is, the non-running prototype known as the Press car. I needed space and people, and time was running short, but we were waiting for GM styling to supply the body masters from which to work. 'Chuck' Jordan, Vice President GM Design (styling) Staff, had taken me into the holy of holies (his design studio) where Jerry Palmer, Head of the Advanced Automotive Design Staff, was hard at work on the body shape. Colin Spooner by now was well into the Toyota-powered new Elan and unable to spare many people.

I had even become — through the DTI — involved in a 16-seat 15 inch (348 mm) gauge railway carriage for use in coal mines. With some of the working faces 30 minutes ride away from the lift cage, if we could produce a higher speed carriage we would increase the actual working time of the miners below ground. But by the time we succeeded, the mining industry had started to contract and there were plenty of more easily reached efficient faces. The microlight engine had been revived and we had them running, fitted with propellers, out in the open. We had now become one of Portakabin's best customers, while I was still sticking firmly to my no overhead rules and corner-shop accounting.

I had Peter Riches, ex-Team Lotus looking after resources, finding people to do the work, and advising the hours they spent on each project to Warren King, another Lotus stalwart who seemed to have been involved in all the disasters — winding up our own abortive American import venture, the boat companies and DeLorean. I also had ex-Secretary Chris Garrett from the Esprit days running our procurement system. I had a phobia about overheads and therefore had a 'no passenger' rule. Work was charged for by the hour; material purchased had a percentage added to meet the cost of three or four months bank charges between our paying for it and receiving payment from the customer. It also covered the cost of collecting, inspecting, storing, and the supply group's salaries locating the best supplier. A smaller percentage was added to travel and hotel bills, which paid for the secretary who made the arrangements. Some of the more computer-literate groups claimed they no longer needed a secretary; they could use word processors. I enquired mildly who would provide their coffee and answer the telephone. It was not long before I noticed that the most computer-orientated groups, also had the most personable and efficient secretaries, even if there was only one between 20 engineers.

I had become Managing Director of the newly re-formed Lotus Engineering. I was encouraged to keep my links with Team Lotus, remaining a director of what had otherwise become an arms-length operation. When the majority shareholders of Group Lotus were also majority shareholders in Team Lotus, there was a certain amount of overlapping, such as the use of the airfield and test track. With the new situation this had to be formalized. A major agreement between the two parties was drawn up, including the use of the logo. David Wickens believed the Lotus ACBC logo should be changed to signify the changes, but when this was done with a changed shape and colour and omitting Colin Chapman's initials there was an outcry, so when GM acquired the Group the original badge was reinstated.

I was now into a more intensive transatlantic commuting routine. I recalled my flying instructor telling me that only birds, bats and bloody fools fly, and only bats at night. I therefore avoided flying through the night, whenever possible, This virtually solved the jet lag problem. I became a permanent feature on British Airways flight 178 from New York to London, departing at 10.00 a.m. and arriving Heathrow at 9.40 p.m. This increased amount of travel was made easier by a new driver, Joe Bedford; and when GM became involved, it became more comfortable and relaxing in a stretched Cadillac.

I was surprised and very honoured to be elected a Fellow of the Society of Automotive Engineers. At the time, with over 45,000 members, there were only 250 Fellows and only 15 of them were British. The actual presentation was made in February at an Honours Convocation during the 1986 SAE congress in Detroit. Among those similarly honoured was Dr Siffert, Director of Research of Volkswagen, and Zora Arkus Duntov, formerly Chief Engineer, Corvette, of General Motors, who I knew from his days with Allard in the late 1940s. I had already been invited to speak at the Automotive News World Congress in company with Dr. Hahn, of Volkswagen and Hal Sperlich, President of Chrysler. I also addressed GM's private Product Engineering Technology Conference on 'How many valves?'

I was now well into my public speaking mode, and I was asked to speak on behalf of all the British car designers, not just Lotus, at the 36th World Design Conference in Aspen, Colorado during June 1986. The British designers also speaking included Zandra Rhodes, Bruce Oldfield, David Putnam, Jocelyn Stevens, then head of the Royal College of Art, Sir Hugh Casson, Norman Foster, David Hockney and Minister John Butcher of the DTI. I had to speak for an hour followed by 30 minutes of questions, in the Paepcke Auditorium, which was the largest of several.

Early on in the proceedings a member of the British party (do not look for his name above, I have omitted it!) told the large — predominantly American and Japanese — audience that Britain was finished as an industrial nation, but might survive on its service industries. This infuriated me, so I spent the night rewriting my address. I showed slides of the Rolls-Royce RB 211-524 jet engine, a Harrier jump-jet, the March 1986 C-type Indianapolis car that finished 1, 2, 3 and 4 at the 1986 race and said: 'You may have been told the British are finished, well don't believe it. Send for Paul Revere, the British are coming!' From Aspen I went to Detroit where Team Lotus and Ayrton Senna, at that time their No. 1 driver, helped my sales pitch by winning the Detroit GP while I had lunch with a party of top executives from Chrysler.

As part of Expo 86 at Vancouver the organizers arranged an Innovative Vehicle Design Competition, hosted by the University of British Columbia and open to any University. First prize was an award of $500,000 to the University concerned. The competition, which took nearly a week of tests and judging, was to be judged by a distinguished international panel, including the Canadian Minister of Transport; two Japanese engineers, from Honda and Toyota; Frank Walters of Chrysler, 1986 SAE President; engineers from Mercedes, GM, Ford and myself from Lotus. The competition also coincided with British week at Expo, to be opened by Mrs Thatcher, so Pam and I travelled out to Vancouver in her specially-chartered Concorde. As Pam, like Mrs Thatcher, was born in Grantham, there was some reminiscing between them.

I was invited by the High Commissioner to join Mrs Thatcher's party for the opening of British week. She found me, wearing a carnation and propping up a red Lotus Esprit with my old friend and room-mate, the Bishop of Willesden Green — John Craig, who had not yet retired, and was doing the same with a blue Rolls-Royce. The white car was a Jaguar. I was extremely impressed by the stage management that accompanied Mrs Thatcher's opening speech. When she reached her words concerning Britain's transatlantic air transport achievements she said: '. . . and Britain was first across the Atlantic with a supersonic aircraft. I came over in Concorde yesterday.' She raised her hand to the sky, and at that precise moment Concorde emerged from the clouds and flew low over the auditorium in salute.

It was a very busy week with a very interesting and impressive competition. Seven years ago Sherbrooke University of Montreal showed us a car steered with a joy stick. No steering wheel — you pushed the lever forward to go faster, pulled it back to stop, and sideways to turn a corner. Now a European manufacturer has one. Unfortunately a wire fell off Sherbrooke's car at a vital moment so we placed it second. It is a felicitous custom on these occasions to present the judges and speakers with a small souvenir. We were told that Vancouver is going to be different, and it was. We were given the use of a helicopter for one hour. The pilot is instructed to take you where you wish, providing he thinks it is safe. He took me around

Expo and then up into the mountains behind Vancouver.

At the conclusion of the contest, after the judging, the contestants were invited to ask questions of the judges. We were asked, in view of the complexity of some new vehicles — particularly a recently announced new Mercedes — whether drivers should be required to pass an operator's test before being allowed to buy one. I said I did not think it was necessary; if the purchaser had the wit to amass enough money to buy such an expensive motor car, he would be bright enough to know how to work all its systems. Possibly as a result of this, just as I was going into the Prize Giving dinner, I was asked (as a designer) to make an informal speech to the students after the formal speeches and awards. Having fortified myself with a champagne cocktail I let myself go and told them how much I envied them, at the threshold of their careers, while mine was entering its closing stages. I had several more speaking engagements before the end of that year, but these were the highlights of a memorable year.

I had become aware that the new Elan project was soaking up most of Engineering's profits. I realized that it would, in fact, cost more than we could earn. A proportion of our engineering profits were being invested in new facilities under our percentage system. We had, for example, two new computer-controlled super test cells, where we could, if we wished, run an F1 engine on open exhausts, controlled by a telephone link from a circuit on the other side of the world. It would have made Willy Southcott's eyes pop. We needed more facilities, and Lotus Cars needed more capital.

In the autumn of 1985 I came up with the idea that we should invite the principal customers of Lotus Engineering to contribute to its capitalization, which would provide us with more facilities (and funds for the Elan), by floating it as a public company. We would offer our major customers the chance to take a 10 per cent holding, still leaving Group Lotus with a controlling interest. Chrysler and Toyota expressed an interest but GM said they had already given the United States Treasury an undertaking not to enter into any more joint ventures with overseas companies. I had to abandon my first attempt at high finance.

Shortly after I floated this idea, when we were negotiating the contract for the purchase of engines and transmission units from Toyota, a dispute arose between their management and David Wickens. I was not present so cannot comment on the details, but eventually David Wickens's and BCA's shares were offered to Chrysler. This frightened me out of my wits, as I was well aware that if Chrysler held a major stake in Lotus, GM would walk out on the spot. I telephoned my GM contacts over the Christmas holidays, but they were doubtful if GM would be interested in view of their undertaking to the US Treasury. However, a few days later I received a telephone call to ask for the nearest convenient airport where GM's Gulfstream executive jet could land.

# CHAPTER TWENTY-TWO

# Lotus with General Motors

BY 22 JANUARY 1986 GM held the majority holding in Group Lotus by purchasing the shares of David Wickens and BCA, JCB and Schroder Wagg. I was very pleased. I liked the GM people; they proved they could move quickly when necessary, if you found and pressed the right button. As a shareholder I would be receiving £1.295 for each of the shares I bought in 1983 for 40p, plus my original holding. The Lotus directors were summoned to Detroit to be given a briefing on General Motors and how it operated — particularly all the new developments in the pipeline — but when Chairman Roger Smith found out he cut the visit short because, it is alleged, he wanted us to retain our 'rustic simplicity'.

The only time GM ever interfered with our Engineering activities, to my knowledge, was when they told us to close down the Microlight aero-engine programme. This was because of their concern that GM involvement with Lotus might increase the incidence of product liability claims once the engine was in common use. We were told that GM did not intend to invest any money in the business, neither did they intend to take any out. The profits, which in the case of Engineering were substantial, could be ploughed back for new models, and we could borrow up to a very substantial amount.

LT5 was thundering along. The first engine had run to schedule and when Roger Smith visited us, to see what he had actually bought, we were putting one into a car, also on schedule. We had some initial problems with the engine throwing oil out of its breathers, which I half expected. It was the outcome of sacrificing half the breather volume to accommodate the starter motor in the V of the engine. The catalysts had taken the space where the starter motor was usually mounted — alongside the crankcase. This layout improved emission performance, so it was a reasonable exchange.

There was some debate concerning our proposed ladder-frame lower half crankcase. GM preferred a deep crankcase with four or more bolts holding iron bearing caps. I argued against the weight and machining problems, and repeated that our proposal would make the engine much quieter mechanically. GM compromised after we devised a way of encapsulating a four-legged iron bearing cap within the aluminium casting, which solved my machining fears and gave GM their four bolts. Thick-wall shell bearings would have solved all the difficulties but Vandervell were not prepared to guarantee thick-wall bearings in time, and we were not prepared to use any other make of bearing. It is, however, highly significant that Cadillac's North Star engine has an all-aluminium ladder frame with thick-wall bearings and its cylinder liners are made from cast iron encapsulated within the aluminium crankcase. Once we had the engine in the car we embarked on GM's durability proving schedules, which were very impressive.

The durability programme included several engines cycling from peak torque to peak power for 200 hours at a time. I queried whether an engine in a 180 mph car would need all this full-power durability as it would take many years for it to manage 200 hours at 180 mph. I was told, very firmly, that we had to equal L98 in reliability and quality, but it would be better if we managed to surpass it. I had to admit that it was all worthwhile when, after two years, LT5 actually did produce better in-service figures.

First we had timing chain failures: a combination of factors — shock loads from the hydraulic tensioners — no one having much experience of the sort of loads that LT5 imposed. We took a sledgehammer to this problem by adopting a double-row chain, with consequent changes in main castings and a slight increase in engine length. We had some problems around the front end of the cast-iron crankshaft, and changing to steel cured these.

After we had reached an agreed level of durability on the test-bed, GM started running a fleet of cars on their proving ground at Milford in Michigan and on public roads. Later this was extended to include high-speed running at their desert proving ground near Phoenix, Arizona. It was recognized that some of the customers would eventually race their cars, and in any case there is nothing like racing conditions for bringing weaknesses to light. We started race circuit testing, looking for things like oil surge and brake fade, during which I renewed my acquaintance with Riverside, California.

GM decided not to build LT5 themselves — 8 to 10,000 engines a year was not their scene, and they proposed to sub-contract its manufacture. We hoped to get this production contract as well, and we argued that as components for the engine came from all over the world (cylinder heads and crankshafts from England, pistons and liners from Germany) it did not really matter where it was built. Finally the choice was narrowed down to Lotus or Mercury Marine, probably the largest manufacturer of outboard motors in the world, who also produced exquisite diecastings and had an unequalled reputation for quality. We were disappointed when the contract went to them, but at least we knew there would be no quality problems.

While we were in the durability phase we had a visit from Lloyd Reuss, who at the time was Executive Vice President, CPC. He stood one of our many ZR1s — the code name for LT5-engined Corvettes — on its ear at Hethel and appeared to enjoy it. We then made a formal American-style presentation to him on what had been achieved, and the work remaining. As Project Manager the presentation devolved upon Ian Doble who, in view of the eminence of Lloyd Reuss, was naturally rather nervous. I told him not to worry, and that if I felt he was not getting a point across I would ask a question. I think it is called 'leading the witness'. I must have overdone it. I heard later that Mr Reuss commented I was not the whiz kid he expected to find as I did not seem to know what was going on, and was asking

questions about nearly everything. I consoled myself that you cannot win
them all!

As part of the GM takeover I agreed to a new 5-year Service Contract,
which meant putting off my retirement for three years. It was something of
a blow but I consoled myself with the thought of the extra money and
pension. During the negotiations I assured everyone I was 100 per cent fit,
but a few days later I was whipped off to hospital in the middle of the night.
I was slightly offended when I heard the doctor say to the ambulance driver:
'Use the blue light, but you do not need the bell.' Apparently I had some
travel-induced stomach complaint and was home within a week.

In the ensuing discussion on my health it was suggested that I should take
a holiday at the end of every winter, which struck me as a very good idea.
My new contract provided me theoretically with more leisure. So, claiming
it was on medical advice, we took holidays in Maui, one of the Hawaiian
Islands, Miami, Acapulco, the Caymans and the Florida Gulf coast. Two of
my daughters were now married and the youngest had just started to earn
her living as a junior solicitor in London, so we could afford some
indulgences. Personally I like Maui best, although Pam said it was too far
away.

I began to develop preferences for hotels and airlines. I used British
Airways travelling transatlantic and to Japan, American Airlines within the
United States, and Singapore Airlines across the Pacific. I preferred the
Hyatt Regency hotel at the foot of the Bay Bridge when in San Francisco
and the same chain at Dearborn outside Detroit. My choice of Dearborn
caused raised eyebrows at GM, Dearborn being in the heart of Ford country,
but, as I pointed out, it was half way and on a straight line from the airport
to the GM Engineering Centre at Warren and not too far from their proving
ground at Milford. I used the Marriotts at La Guardia and Los Angeles
airports and in Washington when I visited the American Department of
Transport. I was rather surprised that, although I became well known in
these hotels and with the airline groundstaffs, I hardly ever met the same
cabin crew a second time around.

I fought a long battle with nearly everyone during 1986 on overheads.
Lotus Engineering was heading towards £5m-a-year profit and I was told
that I ought to have a proper finance department. Inspired by Chunky, I
argued: 'If you want to count the money you are most welcome, but don't
ask me to pay for the process.' The flood gates had been eased, though, and
finally GM insisted.

When I retired, Lotus Engineering had nearly 600 staff, but nearly 80 of
them could not be charged directly to projects — they were overheads —
compared with the three or four I had in 1987 with over 500 staff. I argued
it would mean that we would have to increase our charge-out rate to our
customers, which might make us uncompetitive. What was worrying me
even more was that our successes were going to some of our more
academically brilliant people's heads, and they were becoming arrogant.
They said: 'We do not wish to work with these people, they are stupid.' I
told them that the stupid people were the ones who needed us most. Esprit
de Corps was one thing, but arrogance was fatal.

It was a difficult enough struggle to persuade the members of a
customer's Engineering Department to accept that Lotus had been brought
in to do their job because of a management decision. They obviously

thought that they could do the job better and quicker than we could, given the chance. It required great tact and diplomacy to strike the right note. If you started to give the impression you thought you were cleverer than they were you caused resentment, and if you deprecated your abilities they went straight back to their management and said, so and so from Lotus has told me they are not up to the job. I used to take the line that we were a small group with a very short chain of command and the ability to react quickly. Between us we could do a much better job than either group separately. It generally worked, but I found myself spending more and more time smoothing down ruffled feathers and justifying increased costs.

The first Corvette Indy caused me plenty of worry and trouble in the autumn of 1985. The GM styling group took longer than anticipated before they were satisfied with their designs. The masters from which we were to make the moulds, promised by late August, did not arrive until late autumn. By this time the waiting build team had been raided so often that our only hope was to sub-contract most of the work to a firm in Turin. The crunch came around Christmas. To be in time for the Detroit Motor Show the car had to be shipped by the last day of the year, and much remained to be completed. Jack Schwartz of the GM Special Projects Team, the actual customer for the 'Press' car who was in Turin overseeing its completion, developed the most dreadful cold and refused to go home to the USA, even for Christmas Day. I went to Turin to see him in the period between Christmas and the New Year. I had my share of excitement, what with airport bomb scares and flights diverted through fog. Fortunately our project engineer, Dick Angier, was just as tough as Jack Schwartz, and he had to ferry part-finished components to and from Turin. It all worked out in the end and the car (in wood and plaster) was the star of the show, serving its purpose in drawing comments and opinions on its more revolutionary features.

No sooner had we waved the non-runner goodbye than we had to start on Phase Two. Ilmor asked to be excused from supplying a derated Indianapolis turbo engine in view of their heavy racing programme. After a number of meetings my proposed 650 hp normally aspirated LT5 was rejected in favour of a 750 hp twin turbo LT5. This engine had an insatiable appetite for gearboxes. I began to include Hydra-Matic at Ypsilanti and Willow Run, about 20 miles west of Detroit airport, in my itinerary.

I have already emphasized that, understandably, we were not allowed to reveal the existence of many of our projects, but LT5, the Corvette Indy and Chrysler are amongst those we are allowed to talk about, so it probably gives a distorted picture of our activities. I calculated in 1987 that there were 1,100,000 engines produced that year in which Lotus had been involved, and 35 different models of various cars. 97.3 per cent of our income came in foreign currency.

Colin Spooner was by now extremely busy with the next Elan and could make few contributions other than advice. Soon after GM took control, Toyota pulled out and Colin had to start all over again using GM sources of components, especially engines. Most of the money and effort we had already put into the car was thus wasted. He just had to start from scratch again. I supported the idea of a small car to replace the Elan, but as the project developed I felt the car had become sanitized. For me, much of the fun of driving a Lotus, or any car for that matter, comes through knowing the car's characteristics and idiosyncrasies and using my skill to get the best from it. They had carefully designed and developed all the idiosyncrasy out of the Elan. My feelings are perhaps the same as for my first two Astons. For me, a Lotus has to be coaxed and caressed into giving its best. The Elan tended to be a car that any fool could drive, unless you did something really stupid.

I also argued against planning that the Elan would earn nearly half its revenue from the United States. I pointed out that Lotus had never sold front-engined cars in any significant quantity in America. It would appear that the American enthusiast associates Lotus with F1 and Indianapolis, which means a mid-engined car. In the early '70s we used to sell ten or more Europas for every Elan in the United States. When Rolls-Royce took over our sales in America they said this was because we did not understand how to sell our cars, but they soon fell into the pit. They could sell the Esprits but they had two year-old Elites in their showrooms. I feared that history would repeat itself with the Elan, and I was right!

I was also worrying the more staid members of our community by the promises I made to our customers, and the hair-raising projects I got them into. How could we expect to produce a 385 hp engine with a CAFE rating of 22.5 mpg with our resources, when the much better equipped competition, with much larger staffs, was only achieving just over 300 hp and 13 mpg. When these people saw the monthly crises and panics they wrung their hands. The Corvette Indy was even worse, it needed two alternators to give a combined output of 360 amps to drive all its electrical services. Finally, when I proposed large diameter tubular driveshafts, filled with a mixture of washing-up liquid and brake fluid, they knew I had flipped. I was trying to explain what rheological fluid was. We planned to use it as a torque control device!

1986 flew by, and so did most of 1987. There was a pleasant interlude in August when I was invited to a race meeting in Michigan where they were focusing on Lotus cars. I was Grand Marshal and rode in state in the procession, made speeches, wandered about the circuit looking at the cars — it was very like a club meeting at Silverstone or Goodwood years ago. Next day I was a judge at the Meadow Brook Concourse d'Elegance. Meadow Brook was the home of the Dodge family in the grounds of the University of Michigan. The team to which I was assigned judged International Sports Cars. I was especially intrigued to see the former Rubery Owen Press Officer Rivers Fletcher's old Speed 25 Alvis, complete with BRDC badge, in the collection. It was an extremely hot but impressive and rewarding day. Fortunately there were a number of my friends and acquaintances in my team so I did not feel too much like a fish out of water. The cars were incredibly well cared for and I was surprised by the immense numbers of Duesenbergs and Packards in showroom condition. They were all driven in parade after judging.

In February 1987 I was invited to join the Board of Group Lotus, which administered the whole of the Lotus activities, except Team Lotus. There were three British members and three Americans under the chairmanship of Alan Curtis. I was also made Deputy Chairman of Lotus Engineering, and Dr Cedric Ashley from MIRA (Motor Industry Research Association) was brought in to take my place as Managing Director. The idea was to leave me free to do what I was best at, namely engineering and finding business. I started a campaign trying to generate business from Europe and Korea. This was to reduce our dependence on the United States, and the problems which the dollar rate of exchange caused us. Over 67 per cent of our business was from the United States. It was not a healthy situation. It did not need a big fluctuation in dollar rates of exchange to hurt us badly.

I was surprised to find that the Koreans were very different from the Japanese. Negotiating a contract with the Japanese involved long periods of detailed discussion, every aspect of the project being dissected. Finally they obtained a consensus from all their people involved, and once you had shaken hands on the deal they meticulously observed every detail of their part of the contract. They paid in full, literally on the minute. If there was a query they would pay first and argue later. They were a pleasure to deal with, once the contract had been struck. However, the Koreans — perhaps a younger, developing nation — often changed their minds. They did not need a consensus to start with. But as the contract worked its way up the chain for approval, it could and did get changed drastically. I did not enjoy frequent trips to Japan and Korea and wherever possible left it to the others, but I could not escape them all. One final presentation for a major Korean contract was being handled by Hugh Kemp, by now Head of Powertrain. He had been in Korea for a few days finalizing the details, when I arrived, more or less as an ornament, at the last minute.

The presentation was to be made to the company's Technical Director. Oriental protocol normally required that only people of equal rank spoke to one another, hence my presence. We were told that the presentation had been delayed as the Company President wished to attend. Then there was another delay as the Chairman had now indicated his intention to be present. I replaced my Technical Director Group Lotus visiting cards with Deputy Chairman Lotus Engineering cards to preserve protocol — very important. I noticed while all this was going on that Hugh Kemp changed from yellow to green, to a luminous white. Obviously he had a violent tummy upset. I just had time to skim through his presentation before he disappeared and I had to take his place. I performed in a large boardroom with the inscrutable Chairman never uttering a word, sitting wreathed in cigarette smoke. There was a pitched battle in Korean between the Technical and Production Directors as I proceeded with the presentation. Fortunately Hugh recovered in time to field some of the more difficult questions. After all the alarms I was surprised when we landed that contract, which as usual was modified a few times as the work proceeded.

I had another major public engagement in January 1987 when I was invited to chair a session at the joint Society of Automotive Engineers and Fédération International des Sociétés d'Ingénieurs des Techniques de l'Automobile, Auto Technology Conference at Monte Carlo. I persuaded some of our bright young men to present papers at this conference. They did extremely well and were in the running for the Charles Deutsch award for the idea judged to be of the greatest potential value to the automotive industry. I thoroughly enjoyed meeting the senior engineers from European industry. They were much more relaxed and urbane than their American counterparts, but far less flexible in changing their opinions — positively stubborn in fact. After the event I was invited to join the panel of judges (jury in French) for the Charles Deutsch Award. Monaco in January is very different from the Monaco of the GP week. I also gave the keynote address at Bath University based on my 1984 Car of the Future paper, but brought up to date with the work on the Corvette Indy, as by then the running Phase Two version was nearing completion.

This car consisted of a large aluminium casting containing the front differential, upon which the steering and active front suspension reacted. It was joined to the rear-mounted transverse engine and gearbox unit by a large carbon fibre tube. The rear steering and active rear suspension reacted on the engine gearbox mass which also included the torque-splitting unit controlled by the active suspension computer. The complete body was softly mounted on this mass — a Lotus 88 all over again. I was thus able to show the graduates at Bath how the theory was developing. I was very impressed by the quality of their graduates, and we gave them a small contract to devise a method of setting the valve timing on the LT5 engine. I had reasoned that with hydraulic tappets there was no need ever to remove the camshaft covers, and we could therefore include the upper camshaft bearings in the cover. This made it a tricky business to time the camshafts. Bath University graduates solved it and were rewarded with a trip to the US to see their ideas being put into practice.

In Detroit I made a presentation to all the GM purchasing officers on 'Who and What is Lotus', followed by another one to GM engineers at their annual Project Engineering and Technology Conference, this time on 'the passenger car engine of the year 2000'. I argued that there must be an optimum cylinder and combustion chamber size and configuration for a given fuel and duty. I suggested, on what we knew, that it would be a 4-valve monobloc somewhere between 500 and 625 cc in capacity, developing around 50 hp. If the designer needed 200 hp, he threaded four such cylinders on to a stick; if he wanted 400 hp, he used eight. I also participated in some technology trend conferences for a National Economic Development Office and DTI workshop on future engine technology. I had written a paper for the Institute of International Research on 'Contract R & D and how to make Technology Pay', but I was called to Detroit, so Chris Kerns, General Manager Vehicle Engineering at Lotus, delivered it in my place.

Team Lotus set out on an active suspension season for 1987. I felt rather uneasy about this. The 1987 flat-bottomed cars were, in effect, Go-Karts. The tyres constituted most of the suspension; wheel movement was less than 10 mm, so active suspension would do very little for them. I fully understood that with a new sponsor, Camel, Team Lotus needed to put something in the shop window. The then current version of Lotus Active Suspension was being overtaken by what Chrysler called the 70 per cent solution, where they could get 70 per cent of the benefits for 30 per cent of the cost just by controlling damping and roll without the expensive pump and shuttle valves. I was also jealously guarding Lotus Engineering's profits, as I suspected that on the planned expenditure there would be a serious overrun.

It is, of course, always easy to be wise after the event; but it all happened as I feared. There was a 100 per cent budget overrun. Active worked best on the slow circuits, helping them to win at Monaco and Detroit. There were some development problems; the sensitive electronic systems did not like the vibrations of an F1 engine, and it took some time to persuade the accelerometers to distinguish between movement due to deflection of the vibration insulators and cornering loads. We learned much, and I am sure that if we had been able to afford a second season they would have won several more races. It was clear to me that Lotus Active was being developed to have tremendous capacity — much more than was needed by the cars of the 1990s. In fact, the pace of active development outstripped car development. In addition to running the active suspension systems, it could easily control four-wheel-drive torque-split, four-wheel-steer, even active control of the steering — that is drive by wire. The car industry was not ready for this degree of sophistication, and preferred the simpler less powerful systems of damper control and levelling as is typified by Peugeot, Citroen and Nissan. It was another example of the pursuit of perfection rather than excellence. I made a prophesy in 1984 that you would be able to buy a passenger car with active suspension in the early 90s. I have had to advance my prophesy by 10 years.

LT5 moved into the pre-production phase. Mercury decided, rather to my surprise, not to build the engine in Wisconsin where they had a wealth of experienced operators, but in their Mercruiser transmission plant at Stillwater, Oklahoma. They would be starting with green labour. However, they made a clever blend of experience and enthusiasm; Vice President—Manufacturing, Bud Agner, typifying experience, and newly-graduated Terry Stimpson providing the enthusiasm.

There were a number of problems in the certification programme. The weight of the additional features of ZR1 moved the car up an inertia weight class, after we had hit the original target. The new targets were even harder to achieve, and then the bigger tyres increased the rolling resistance which changed the laboratory dynamometer inertia settings. We had to achieve the CAFE target three times from three different starting points. But, unlike DeLorean ten years before, there was an abundance of skill and talent to help us. Another problem was that the various American suppliers of emission control devices, sensors and the like, had not really believed that the engine would reach production, so they were literally caught with their pants down and came up with all sorts of wild excuses.

Roy Midgley, with the might of GM behind him, nailed them methodically one by one. ZR1 and a sectioned engine was shown to the Press and GM dealers at a typical American-style convention at Riverside, California, which made everyone sit up and realize that ZR1 was really going into production. All manner of rumours circulated about non-existent problems, such as extreme overheating turning the plastic bonnet yellow. After initial problems, compromising between the rate of flow we specified and the rate of flow the radiator manufacturers could provide, the cooling system was, to the best of my knowledge, trouble free.

I was disappointed to find that our old haunt, the Mission Inn at Riverside, had been closed for renovation. I took Ian Doble to see the Queen Mary and the Spruce Goose at Long Beach. At this convention and in the light of the growing number of supply problems, Roy and I agreed on a weekly meeting to get everybody together and resolve the innumerable detail problems. It was convenient to have these meetings on Fridays at the GM Proving Ground at Milford, Michigan, wheeling the various protagonists in and out as the day progressed. The session started with coffee and doughnuts at 7.30 a.m. and continued until late in the evening. At first the agenda grew, then as the worst problems were eliminated we were able to go over to a fortnightly meeting and, after several months, to meeting once a month.

The Elan was in the same state back at Lotus, so I agreed to release Ian Doble to take charge and ramrod the Elan through, as his work on LT5 was nearly complete. His deputy, Dave Whitehead, took over. Dave was large and calm. The GM team held him in high esteem and he exerted the right kind of steadying influence. Lloyd Reuss had insisted that I had remained in control of the project, so I had to put my transatlantic commuting into overdrive. I generally flew out on Thursdays, meeting Dave and the leaders of our 20-strong LT5 team based in the USA at the Hyatt for a briefing at 6.30 p.m. I would be up at 6 a.m. on Friday morning ready to drive to Milford for the meeting. Some of the party might leave at 4.15 p.m. to catch the overnight flight direct to England and other destinations. But I stayed on and caught the 7.20 p.m. flight to New York getting into the hotel just before the dining room closed at 10 p.m. I took the British Airways day flight home on Saturday morning and was sometimes lucky enough to be upgraded to the 9.30 a.m. Concorde. As a variation I would go out a day earlier (on Wednesday), fly American Airlines from Gatwick via Dallas to Tulsa and then drive some 60 miles down the Cimarron trail, past Pawnee Bill's Museum to spend Thursday with Mercury at Stillwater, and then going on to Detroit late that evening. A further variation on this theme was Dallas to Phoenix to the high-speed proving ground. Sometimes I reversed the process and went to Phoenix after the Milford meeting. I was somewhat daunted by the number of problems, but inexorably the GM machine ground them all away.

I was extremely flattered to be asked to present the keynote address on 'Imagination and Innovation' at the 1988 SAE Congress. Walking back with Honda's first F1 Engineer, Yoshio Nakamura, he suggested it was the first time that a non-American had ever been so honoured. I found it a bit daunting to face such a large international audience at 9 a.m. on a dull, cold Detroit Monday morning. Bob Stempel, soon to become GM chairman, gave his address at the Banquet, spending about an hour on a revolving platform in the floodlights, so he could not see his audience of 5,500. When I was speaking I used to watch the audience to see if they nodded off, or failed to laugh, then I would change my tactics, but he could not see when this happened.

I was also invited to join 100 Guests of Honour at the Banquet, selected from the leaders of the world automotive industry. We sat at raised tables across the corners of the room and had to stand in the glare of spotlights while we were introduced one by one. I enjoyed meeting them at the cocktail party before the dinner, and marvelled at the organization that served 5,500 steaks simultaneously. The Guests of Honour were invited to an 'afterglow' reception where we could really let our hair down. Until I retired, the Congress became part of the February scene for me.

I opened up a contact with Cadillac which lead to a batch of Lotus 4 litre 32-valve engines being adapted for the Allante and a 48-valve V12 engine for another prototype vehicle, which was designed and built quickly on a limited budget. The V12 was not very inspiring, but as it happened the car for which it was intended was abandoned. This led to involvement in the Cadillac North Star engine programme, another 32-valve V8. The Cadillac team under Tom Stevens was small and very efficient. Tom is now Director of Engineering of the GM Engine Division, a new organization. I was intrigued that whereas Chevrolet and CPC appeared to be wedded to toothed rubber-belts to drive the camshaft, this was complete anathema to the BOC group. Only heathens used rubber belts. Students of engine design may care to take this book and compare the BRM engine activities, the Lotus 2 and 4 litre engines, the Corvette LT5 and North Star, where they may be able to trace a development pattern. One eminent journalist asked me if Lotus had been involved in a certain engine, as it had 'Lotus written all over it'. We are still bound by the confidentiality clause.

At the 1989 Monaco Auto Technologies Conference I again served as a member of the Charles Deutsch jury. The jury consisted of Yoshio Nakamura (Honda); Michel Alige (Technical Director, Peugeot [PSA]); Hans Mezger (Technical Director, Porsche); Mauro Forghieri (formerly Ferrari, now Lamborghini); George Muller (President, AIR Foundation, USA); Jan Crister Persson (Vice President, Engineering, Volvo). I had to disqualify myself from voting because the front runner was the paper from Peter Wright and Dave Williams on the development of Lotus Active Suspension, which won. On my way to Monte Carlo I stopped overnight with my old friend Alain Nogier at his home in the Ardèche to have dinner with Maurice Trintignant, who had not changed a scrap in 30 years.

GM sent Mike Kimberley for a three-month course at Harvard Business College, which he assumed indicated he was in line for early promotion.

After the SAE Congress in Detroit, I had to get back quickly for the Geneva Motor Show and the real launch of the Chevrolet Corvette ZR1 which took place in a separate auditorium below the Main Hall. I was placed on Bob Stempel's table for the Launch Dinner. The follow-up was for the 12 most senior American newspaper and magazine publishers to drive ZR1s from Geneva to Valence, via Grenoble; next day westwards through the Gorges du Tarn to Rodez, for lunch, and then through Albi to the second night stop at Carcassonne. The run was to finish at the Goodyear Proving Ground at Mireval, where they could really put the car through its paces. The navigator of each car was a senior GM official or personality, including Don Runkle, VP Advanced Engineering, Arv Mueller, VP Engineering, CPC, and down the social scale to me. Drivers switched vehicles at meal and fuel stops so they were able to talk to a different person. During dinner at Valence, the party discovered it was my birthday, so it was rather a late night.

The organization was superb. You just left your bag in your room, and when you arrived at your next hotel, there was your bag. Because of a combination of inexperience on minor French roads and a certain amount of jet-lag, one of the cars was damaged just before a lunch stop. After lunch there was an identical replacement Corvette, complete with autoroute toll and fuel credit cards. I managed to switch to driving on the Rodez to Carcassonne leg and looked out for the roads around Albi where I had driven that V16 BRM at over 200 mph some 40 years before, but everything had changed so much I could not recognize anything.

There had also been changes within Lotus Engineering. Cedric Ashley had left, and Peter Wright and Martin Long were now Joint Managing Directors. Bill Larson, an old friend from his days as Chief Engineer at Vauxhall in the early 70s, was now with GM Truck and Bus in Detroit but still responsible for the former Vauxhall Millbrook proving ground near

Ampthill in Bedfordshire. An English proving ground was something of an anachronism for a Detroit operation, so Bill contacted me and offered to transfer Millbrook to us. After GM approved the deal, the proving ground and some 200 staff were transferred to Group Lotus. I became a director and I spent some time persuading Lotus Engineering staff and Millbrook to work together in harmony. We were nearly there when I retired. It made sense for Lotus Engineering to have its own proving ground and, after some false starts, Malcolm MacDonald got his anechoic chamber, costing nearly £1m, which completed our planned facilities.

Negotiations for the next phase of LT5, where the dollar rate of exchange worked against us, plus our higher costs because of increased overheads, was my next task. This was made even more difficult by GM changing their own internal costing system, and removing some overheads from their R & D operations. This was punctuated by a very pleasant trip to Michigan for the SAE presentation on LT5 by my GM colleagues. I seemed to be having a steady round of Board meetings — Group Lotus, Cars, Engineering, Millbrook and Team Lotus punctuated by trips to the United States to visit system suppliers such as AC Delco, Delco Remy, Delco Electronics, AC Rochester, Paris for Delco Moraine, Dieppe for the Renault Alpine anniversary celebrations. My annual jaunt to the Shell Mileage Marathon at Silverstone with my fellow judges, Keith Duckworth, Dean Delamont, and Bob Eden made a pleasant change.

I was very surprised to receive a phone call from Camel, who were the Team Lotus main sponsors, inviting me to join them in London for dinner. I had no idea what their interest was, and half hoped they were going to commission us to design an F1 engine for Team Lotus. I was completely wrong. They came straight to the point — they were extremely dissatisfied with the performance of Team Lotus. Gerard Ducarouge had been replaced by Frank Dernie, and Camel had put up a substantial sum of money to attract Nelson Piquet. Then Nakajima had failed to qualify at Monte Carlo, which took me back to some of my arguments with Chunky in the 1960s. 'Team' had slipped from the situation they were in with Senna in 1986 and 1987, and Honda had transferred their engine to McLaren. I knew money was short but I was not prepared for such a blockbuster. 'Why tell me?' I asked them, 'I am only a non-executive director.' They asked me if I was not familiar with the role of a non-executive director.

At the end of the evening I undertook to see what I could do, and first talked to Fred Bushell, Chairman of Team Lotus, who was as concerned as I was, but found it equally difficult to find a solution. I was invited to another meeting with Camel, this time at a higher level, when they spelt out their conditions. Peter Warr had to go; probably Fred as well. Also, we had to improve our organization and find a more powerful engine than the Judd V8 we were using. It sounded rather as if there had been some pressure from Piquet. Fred and I started a dialogue with Eddie Jordan and two other parties. Eddie was more inclined to a partnership leading to purchase of the team, which was not really on offer. Camel steadily increased the pressure. I made a presentation to their top management on the future of Team Lotus, without dealing with the immediate present. They were all very polite but made no comment. Team Lotus put up a rather better performance at Silverstone, but Camel inexorably increased the pressure. I arranged for them to meet Hazel Chapman, Colin's widow and the Team's principal shareholder, where there was some very straight talking.

Then, a few days later, while at a dinner at the Savoy to mark Walter Hayes's retirement from the Ford Motor Company, we heard that Fred Bushell had been charged concerning the DeLorean affair, which brought the whole matter to a head. None of the solutions we considered were very good. However, the one which appeared least unpalatable was for me to become Executive Chairman of Team Lotus for a limited period. I spoke to Mike Kimberley and Alan Curtis and obtained their agreement to my secondment to Team Lotus on a part-time basis for a year.

In retrospect, it was not a very sensible solution. A part-time 66-year-old is not the best choice to take on the full-time 40-year-old tigers running the opposition teams. I operated through an Executive Committee consisting of Rupert Manwaring, Team manager; Frank Dernie, Chief Engineer; Noel Stanbury, Commercial Manager; and Manning Buckle, Company Secretary, with Clive Chapman, Colin's son, as my assistant. I explained the situation to Peter Warr who, quite understandably, did not care for it one little bit.

I then took myself off to my first race at Hockenheim. Nelson Piquet seemed pleased to see me, and was most helpful. Saturo Nakajima did not speak much English, so I had to talk to him through his manager, but he seemed quite friendly.

After some negotiations with Honda, who offered their V10 engine at a price we could not afford, I struck a deal with Lamborghini for their V12. I had a high regard for Forghieri, who had designed it and was now their Chief Engineer, and thought that any engine he produced would be a good one. However, I regretted that I could not afford Nelson Piquet, who struck me as a more knowledgeable and tigerish version of Pedro Rodriguez. Rupert was very keen on Derek Warwick. Derek was a very good choice — tough and a very loyal team member. Unfortunately, as we could not afford the Honda engine we had to part with Saturo and our Japanese sponsors. We took up our option with Martin Donnelly, who was then our test driver. It looked like the best possible package for the funds available and a good driving team, and of course they were British.

One of my first problems was the Team's finances, which were not in particularly good shape. Being rather naive about such things, and having read the book on how directors should conduct their company's affairs, I took our Bank Manager into our confidence, which turned out to be a very fortunate decision. He supported us through the difficult negotiating phase, and fortunately for me and our Bank Manager's trust, we came out of it in the black.

I had told my family early in 1989: 'Things are getting quieter for me. We should be able to take a long leisurely holiday this summer.' As things turned out I spent two days with them before flying off to fail to qualify for the Belgian GP. I had to return to Group Lotus for a few days; then another three days holiday, back to Monza for practice and a Press Conference to announce our plans for next season, leaving before the race for a Group Lotus Board meeting in Frankfurt. Back to Lotus for a meeting with senior people from CPC concerning LT5's future on the Tuesday.

The gentle rundown I had planned prior to retiring actually became one of the most hectic periods of my career! After the Group Board meeting I spent three days in London meeting lawyers; chairing an Institution of Mechanical Engineers session; and having a pleasant dinner in the Royal

Engineers' Mess at Chatham, as the guest of Alan Curtis. Then I flew to Detroit for meetings with Cadillac, then back to Europe for the Portuguese GP, back home on Monday, complicated by an airline strike, New York on Tuesday morning for meetings with Roger Penske in the afternoon, and dinner with Peter Kirwan Taylor, a merchant banker, to seek his advice. Peter played a large part in the earlier days of Lotus, including the original Elite and the public flotation. He now lived and worked in New York. I went on to Detroit to meet Chrysler's new Chief Engineer, François Castaing, and to talk to Goodyear about tyres for Team Lotus next year. Then I had a meeting with Don Runkle, GM Vice President Advanced Engineering, followed by a very pleasant evening aboard his Chrysler-engined vintage Chris Craft powerboat on Orchard Lake.

On my return, so much work had piled up that I gave the Spanish GP a miss and spent a few days clearing the papers from my desk. I was becoming worried about the shrinking Lotus Engineering order book which had dropped badly from the £30m of the good old days. The Elan was also soaking up our declining profits, and Peter Wright was very unhappy with repeated cuts in his R & D budget. We were losing customers because of our increasing charges which made us less competitive. Moreover, our arrogance was antagonizing some of our would-be and existing customers. The continuing pursuit of perfection rather than the acceptance of excellence was irritating customers and costing us friends. But, as we were still making substantial profits, I was rather a lone voice crying in the wilderness.

I then had a very punishing trip to Japan. I travelled first to Dallas on an American Airlines DC10, and after an afternoon of meetings, I travelled on to Tokyo next day spending over 13 hours in a Long Range 747, to be met at the airport by our old friend Kichinosuke Nohara, our Japanese importer and a World War II pilot. He had been a good friend over many years, and had introduced us to Japanese standards of hospitality and courtesy. Mr Nohara always looked after us from the minute we set foot in Japan until he put us aboard the plane to depart. Nothing was ever too much trouble for him. I travelled by bullet train to Nagoya with Naomichi Fukuda, Satoru's manager, changing onto a local train for Susuka, where we stayed in an enormous hotel on the circuit. Mr Honda had accommodation in the same wing as I had. We met by chance. He was very friendly and claimed to remember our talks at Watkins Glen some 25 years before. He seemed to know a great deal about our relationship with Toyota.

The place was incredibly crowded. It was impossible to find a table at any of the European style restaurants, so we virtually existed on pot noodles prepared by Rupert Manwaring at the circuit. Satoru and his manager took us out for dinner one night. Don Runkle came to Japan early en route for the Tokyo Motor Show. He and I spent a pleasant evening with Mr Kawamoto, head of Honda R & D, and later with Mr Kimbara, now Senior Managing Director—Engineering at Toyota, an old friend from the early days. I noticed the Japanese talked freely to the Americans and to us, but not to one another. We were fortunate to pick up extra points following Senna's disqualification. On the Monday after the race, the Japanese Camel people drove us to Nagoya and handed me over to another old friend from our Toyota relationship, Tsutomu Tomita (now in charge of their competition engine programme) when I met Mr Kimbara again. They took me to dinner that evening and remembered my liking for shabu shabu, when you cook your own meat and vegetables at the table in boiling water, rather like a fondue.

With typical courtesy, Toyota provided an escort to look after me on the bullet train to Tokyo next morning. I had a set of cards, written in Japanese, which I hoped said, for example, 'Please give him a ticket to Tokyo' which I used to present at the ticket office. I don't know what else it said, but it produced a ticket and a wry smile, I had similar cards for hotels. I had contracted a fearful cold and missed the welcome dinner Mr Nohara gave that evening for my Lotus colleagues, who had arrived for the Toyko Motor Show. I spent a full day at the Show, after which Mr Nohara's son took me to the airport for Singapore Airlines to deliver me in Los Angeles at about the same time as I had reached the Motor Show that morning! After a quick shower I drove to Garratt at Torrance and persuaded them to provide ceramic rotor turbos for the Lotus Carlton engine. (Unfortunately the engine preferred the standard machine.) I had a very good relationship with Garratt dating back from our attempts to turbocharge the DeLorean V6.

Next morning (Thursday) I caught American Airlines first flight of the day to San Francisco (which was a British-built BAe 146) to discuss electronic controls for a proposed valve lift and timing reducing scheme — which is a step beyond variable valve timing — arriving in San Francisco only eight days after the earthquake, to find a remarkable mixture of chaos and recovery. The restaurant in the basement of the hotel was closed — fears of earthquake damage. However, the rotating bar and restaurant on the roof was still open, and revolving, but I was about their only customer! 8 a.m. the following morning saw me aboard an American Airlines 767 on my way to New York for another meeting over dinner in the Russian Tea Rooms. Then the British Airways day flight home. I decided not to go to the Australian GP, as my presence would not make much difference. I had far too much to do, including visits to Lamborghini and my old friend Forghieri, to finalize the details of our engine and gearbox. I also had several speaking engagements and two more trips to the United States to fit in before Christmas.

I began to worry as the new F1 car was slipping behind its programme, and the one month of testing we had planned before the first race at Phoenix was being eroded. Most of the delays were with the new transverse gearbox where we were putting Lamborghini gears in our own casing. Its manufacture took much longer than anticipated and I was not quick enough to spot the slippage. We arrived at Phoenix, untested and in a state of complete chaos from which we never recovered. The only bright spot of the trip was a message that the ZR1's attempt on the 24-hour record had succeeded, with an average speed of over 175 mph. The car was what the Americans call showroom stock, although it had a much bigger fuel tank and a transmission oil cooler. It went on to take the 5,000 mile record, after which I suspect the drivers got bored.

I saw this as an ideal opportunity for Lotus Engineering to get some valuable publicity. So I drafted a proposed advertisement for the European Press along the lines that Lotus Engineering congratulated their friends at Chevrolet on the records and were proud to have made a contribution. Mike Kimberley agreed it was a good idea, but it never appeared. When I tried to find out why, I was told that it was not news in Europe. There seemed to be a definite policy at Lotus to play down Engineering's achievements. Whether they felt it detracted from the prestige and sales of the cars I never quite knew. I believe that many people reading this book will be quite surprised, both by the achievements of Lotus Engineering and the fact that no effort was made to bring them to public notice, which can only have helped their sales. I cannot imagine our rivals passing up these opportunities. I never found out who was behind this policy.

I was invited to become a governor of a local Grant Maintained School — Wymondham College — which had an extremely good reputation. I was particularly pleased as I had always felt that engineers did not do enough to reproduce themselves, and here was a chance for me to do something about it.

In practice at Phoenix we had a multitude of problems leading to a fiasco in the race. First of all we could not start the engine! The starter motor drive, now very complicated through having to reach through the rear suspension to the transverse bottom shaft, was not up to the job. Several alternators failed, and Derek Warwick had a rear suspension bracket pull out of the gearbox fortunately without causing an accident. There were teething troubles using the Lamborghini Bosch computerized data recovery system, complicated by its operation by English-, French-, Italian- and American-speaking people. We could have sorted out most of this in the planned month's testing. I blamed myself. If I had not been a part-time Chief Executive I would have sensed the developing situation and done something about it.

The bright spot was the behaviour and performance of the drivers. In particular, after Derek Warwick's suspension failure, I told Martin Donnelly that he should not go out again, even though he was at some risk in qualifying, as we were not sure that he would not have a similar failure. He said he needed more time on the circuit and he needed to protect his qualifying position. He knew the problem existed and he would watch for it. In any case his car had done far fewer miles than Derek's. He did manage to improve his grid position, but the starter motor failed on the grid on race day. In the evenings Camel and Lotus Cars gave big parties — again it was my birthday, so I had to make more speeches than I anticipated. When I got back to Ketteringham Hall I did my best to sort things out. Everyone knew what they had to do, so my role was reduced to hand-wringing in the background. I persuaded Chairman Alan Curtis to release me from my Group Lotus duties for a short time, so that I could work full time at Team Lotus to resolve the worst of the troubles.

I went out to Brazil at the last possible moment, via Miami, arriving just as a wet practice began. At least we could start the car and keep it on the road, but we lost much practice time due to electrical problems, which was especially hard on Martin. We still had a long way to go, but after a lot of hard work and several test sessions, both cars finished well at Imola, which cheered us all up.

Monaco looked even better in practice. Derek was well placed, but it all went wrong on race day. Martin's car needed two engine changes between the morning warm-up and the race — the first did not work — which, although it reflected great credit on the mechanics, did not do much for Martin's confidence, racing on a difficult circuit knowing that he was on his third engine of the day. The carbon fibre brake discs wore out on Derek's car towards the end of the race, when he was well in the money. I was particularly disappointed by this, as he had gone so well in practice. He tried extremely hard, and there was a touch of Graham Hill in his determination. I felt he deserved to finish in the first three.

To make it even worse there was a high-level party at Monaco from Camel USA, who were not impressed. While we were desperately trying to catch up, the other teams were improving and getting further away. The French GP was the ultimate low point, leaving us scratching about to qualify. I had given Camel an assessment that they should not expect us to beat McLaren or Williams or even Ferrari, but they could expect us to be ahead of the other teams and we would occasionally pick up points when one of the top three teams dropped out. This began to look pretty stupid.

I tried to persuade GM Europe to fund an F1 engine. The policy of GM in the USA was that F1 was a European affair; CART and Indy were for the USA and they were on top with the Ilmor-Chevrolet engine. They had no need to worry about Europe where they could sell every car they could make, so why waste money on F1? (this was in early 1990). However, within the top management of GM Europe there was a glimmer of interest. We presented our ideas for an extremely compact 120-degree V12 taking the drive out of the centre, which aroused their interest, but our dismal performance in the early races enabled the doubters to kill off the project.

I had a long standing commitment to chair a session at SITEV (the International Exhibition of Suppliers to the Vehicle Industry) in Geneva during May 1990. My secretary, Diana, had been congratulating herself that she no longer had to go through several drafts of my speeches (chairing a session involved no speeches) when I was invited to present the bi-annual Sir Henry Royce Memorial lecture, an honour I could not refuse — but at least it was not until November. I realized that Camel was slipping away from us, and we had failed to attract additional sponsors, so our finances were getting difficult again. I worked out that it cost $1m to earn a World Championship point. If one takes into account how much the engine suppliers and sponsors put into a team, it was correct for McLaren and Williams. However, Ferrari were even higher at about $1.6m a point. In 1989 Team Lotus spent $780,000 for a point. However, these were only excuses.

I was also aware that there were various moves to transfer part of the ownership of the team. I therefore had to keep fighting while the would-be purchasers raised the necessary money. This was extremely difficult, as there was much speculation in the Press which affected our staff, did nothing for the confidence of our creditors and made my job of keeping the team in the fight incredibly difficult. In July I was reminded that my year was up and of the parlous state of Lotus Engineering's order book, but I still went to the German GP, where I was conscious of a growing sense of fatigue and a nagging doubt that it was not the right way for an old age pensioner to spend his weekends — even if 'Chopper' Tyrrell did!

I missed Hungary but felt I must go to the Belgian GP to lay the ghost of non-qualifying the previous year. I was slightly cheered that the Lotus Engineering order book was beginning to revive, although it was still a shadow of its former self, and 'active' was noticeably inactive. This was mainly because of some unfortunate supplier agreement which had added to their problems. Powertrain, the largest group, was still marching doggedly on. They had done an extremely good job on the intercooled Esprit with GM injection, which attracted considerable attention from potential external customers. I had tried to sell LT5 to other car manufacturers, in one case I was very nearly there when GM said 'no'. By the time the potential buyer had made alternative plans GM changed their mind and said 'yes', but it was too late. It would have been of considerable benefit to all parties had the deal been clinched, and the ownership of some well-known names might have been different.

I was fully into my much reduced part-time mode with Team Lotus by September and was not at Monza for Derek's spectacular crash on the first lap, neither was I in Spain for Martin Donnelly's dreadful accident. I received the news mid-afternoon and thereafter had hourly bulletins. At first it was feared that a front suspension pull-rod had failed, but after doing some quick sums it looked very unlikely, and further investigation confirmed that it had broken in the crash. The pull-rod was made of a unique aircraft steel which had an unusually fine grain failure characteristic, which led people on the spot to jump, at first, to the wrong conclusions. The wreckage of the car filled four plastic bin liners. Fortunately, despite his dreadful injuries, Martin survived after a number of complications. I am still not clear as to what actually happened. The FOCA medical system got him to the best care with the minimum delay, I hope he gets back into F1 where I believe he has the ability and determination to be an asset to any team.

Team Lotus completed a very unhappy season, with my part-time involvement — not the way I would have chosen to end over 50 years in motor racing, and I did not play a significant part in making the arrangements with Peter Collins and Peter Wright for them to take over running the Team.

I made my usual trip to America for the Department of Energy Fuel Economy Co-ordination meetings, and for a tour of LT5 activities, now in full production. I found myself chairing Group Lotus Executive Committee meetings, in addition to my normal round, because of Mike Kimberley's absence on sick leave. So, instead of the fading-away process, I became more and more involved in the day-to-day affairs of running the business. I presented the Henry Royce Memorial Lecture at the Institution of Mechanical Engineers headquarters in Birdcage Walk, and was delighted to receive a suitably mounted and inscribed Silver Lady as a memento.

I had a pleasant lunch as a guest of the Honourable Company of Carriage and Harness Makers in support of Alan Curtis, to receive their award for the Elan. I had to make the speech of thanks, and told them that some of the Lotus staff came from long-established high performance carriage-making families — Boadicea's chariot must have been made in our part of Norfolk.

My duties in the factory curtailed my travels, and all too soon it was over. A party in the Lotus clubhouse with all my friends, with presentations and speeches. I had guessed that they would do something, but I was not prepared for the scale of the effort. There was a cake with a green BRM 'Old Faithful' depicting its stack pipes, and bearing its Zandvoort numbers — the work of Jenny, reserve driver of our stretched Cadillac, who spent many hours waiting for me from delayed flights at various airports. There were letters from my fellow GM Group Board directors, large photographs bearing many signatures from my friends in the US and at Millbrook, a Colin Spooner model, sun loungers, engraved fruit bowls, and many others. I was so overwhelmed by it all that I was very ungracious and unusually tongue-tied. However, during the ensuing months I was very surprised how easily I slipped into the role of a retired old fogey.

# Index